Spain and the Loss of America

Timothy E. Anna

Spain &
the Loss of
America

University of Nebraska Press
Lincoln & London

The paper in this book meets the guidelines for permanence
and durability of the Committee on Production Guidelines
for Book Longevity of the Council on Library Resources.

Library of Congress Cataloging in Publication Data

Anna, Timothy E., 1944-
Spain and the loss of America.

Bibliography: p.
Includes index.
1. Latin America – History – Wars of Independence,
1806-1830. 2. Spain – Politics and government – 1808-1814.
3. Spain – Politics and government – 1813-1833. I. Title.
F1412.A6 1983   980'.02   82-11118
ISBN 0-8032-1014-0

For my daughter Elizabeth Eugenia

Contents

Preface

Between 1810 and 1825 the crown of Spain lost control of one of the largest and richest empires in world history. Thirteen immense territories were lost—Argentina, Chile, Peru, Ecuador, Bolivia, Venezuela, Colombia, Mexico, Central America, Paraguay, Uruguay, Santo Domingo, and Florida. Four gigantic viceroyalties (New Spain, Peru, New Granada, and Río de la Plata) ceased to exist, along with nine great kingdoms or so-called presidencies and captaincies general (Chile, Charcas, Quito, Venezuela, Santo Domingo, Guatemala, Yucatán, New Galicia, and the Provincias Internas). Over sixteen million people, more than half the total population of the empire, wrested political control of their homelands from the European metropolis and launched themselves upon the great adventure of national self-determination. Sixteen individual republics would eventually come into existence in those Spanish lands, joining the two independent republics—the one English, the other French—that already existed in the hemisphere and adding massive weight to one of the most significant shifts that occurred in history—the development of liberal republics and the erection in the New World of a counterweight to the power of the Old. By 1825 the map of the world was radically changed, and the crown of Spain possessed but three of its former overseas colonies—the Philippines, Cuba, and Puerto Rico.

One is inclined to imagine, in view of this massive debacle, that every waking moment of every Spaniard of the day, from the king down to the commonest subject, must have been absorbed in thought, worry, and hard work in an effort to resist the destruction of their nation's great heritage. As a matter of fact, the entire Spanish nation was not preoccupied with the loss of America, for the American wars of independence, like the discovery of America itself in the first instance, were not the chief object of every Spaniard's attention. Just as in 1492 and subsequent years the "discovery" and settlement of America took second place to the conquest of Granada and the consolidation of a united kingdom, so in the decade of the 1810s the "pacification" of America (as it was called) took second place to the domestic peninsular struggle to throw off the yoke of the "Tyrant of Europe," Napoleon, and to the initiation of a struggle between conservatism and liberalism that would tear the Spanish state apart for decades to come. Spain was engaged in its own "war of independence" from 1808 to 1814, and then its own "revolution" from 1820 to 1823. As a result, in the eyes of Spanish policy-makers the long wars of independence in America were "insurrections" or "rebellions" of less direct consequence than the events then transpiring at home. The attitude of Spain was only partly the result of ethnocentrism. The events of the 1810s in the peninsula really were of great significance, for Spain's resistance against the French helped defeat the imperial plans of Napoleon, brought into being a new "modern" form of warfare, and restored Spain to her own dynasty and her own sons. Meanwhile, the beginning of the bourgeois revolution in Spain would ultimately launch it on the path of liberal constitutional monarchy. The political transformation of the nineteenth century was at least as important to Spain as her unification under a central monarchy in the fifteenth and sixteenth centuries. Fundamentally, Spain never came up with any unified policy for meeting the challenge of American independence.

So, although the modern observer might at first be somewhat startled by Spain's inability to arrive at a unified policy, it is essential to keep affairs in context, to remember that what to a Spanish American might be the single most important event in his national history was, to a Spaniard, if not unimportant, at least not as important as events that American historians sometimes overlook. The Spanish kingdoms in America were never really viewed by Spain as "equal," despite its declaration to that effect in 1810. Spain had created a vast colonial empire, and even as late as the nineteenth century this imperialism affected, perhaps unconsciously, the thinking of all Spanish policy-makers. When Spain became involved in a life-or-death struggle against Napoleon, the peninsula viewed the colonies as a source of wealth with which to rescue the metropolis. And when the empire was gone, when it was all lost, many Spaniards viewed it as deeply regrettable, even distressing, but not the end of the world. This is not to argue that the loss of America was unimportant to Spain. The commercial and economic consequences were immense, and Spain plunged suddenly to the second or third rank of European powers. But the fuller effects, what might be called the psychological consequences, were not perceived because, on the one hand, there were still Cuba, Puerto Rico, and the Philippines (and these loomed ever larger in the thought of policy-makers in the decades to come), and because, on the other hand, some Spaniards assumed that America's independence was but a "momentary reverse," as one newspaper described the defeat of Ayacucho, and that the American lands would gratefully restore themselves to Spain once they had recognized their inability to function alone. A few Spaniards viewed American questions as an interference in the main task of reforming and modernizing Spain. It was certainly easier for Spain to rid herself of her sixteenth-century institutions without the massive burden of so many colonies to administer. A few even viewed American independence as the inevitable result of the children's having grown to maturity and having decided to depart from their parental house.

Unavoidably, the figure of Ferdinand VII looms over all. He is probably the most difficult sovereign in Spanish history to assess. The overwhelming view of him adopted by historians and writers is that of a glowering, vicious, paranoid individual. He came to the throne in 1808 by overthrowing his father, Charles IV—no king in the history of the united Spain had ever done that. He fell almost immediately to the infinitely superior cunning of Napoleon. For six long years he was a captive in France, and a symbol in Spain. He was "the desired one," *el deseado*. No Spanish monarch ever bore such a brilliant title so filled with the longing of his nation. In 1814 the symbol returned to rule, and he restored a form of government that was actually the overwhelming choice of his people. Yet his reign, begun with such glory, was an unparalleled disaster. Battered by revolution and foreign invasion, unable to produce a male heir by no fewer than four wives, variously humane and vicious in policy, unable even to control his own disputatious family, he died in 1833, an old man at the age of forty-eight, after a reign that technically covered twenty-five years and that was effective for nineteen of them. At his death the pent-up furies were unleashed, his brother Carlos and his daughter Isabel became the symbols of opposing camps, and Spain hurled itself into the first of its great modern civil wars. Yet it is worth emphasizing that Ferdinand actually triumphed over his domestic and foreign enemies. For much of his lifetime he was a victor, although the victories were perhaps Pyrhhic. Modern historians such as Luis Comellas and Miguel Artola view his reign as one of the most significant in all of Spanish history. It is worth emphasizing, too, that Ferdinand's historical reputation, like that of many major figures, varies over the generations and with the shifts of public opinion in Spain.

As some explanation of the motivation for this study I could do no better than to cite the thoughts of Juan Friede in explaining the motivation for a work of his entitled *La otra verdad, la independencia americana vista por los Españoles*. Though he concentrates exclusively on questions affecting Colombia, Friede makes the important point that almost all the existing historiography on the American independence concentrates on "the sum of individual actions, mainly military and political, of a generation that seems to have acted in a vacuum, without the concurrence of those conditions that engendered their actions . . . and that decided the final outcome."[1] He points out that historians who depend for their studies of American independence exclusively on American sources are led to a false view of Spain, and that it was, indeed, the massive weakening of the old principles of society and government in the peninsula that made American independence possible. Even in the relatively specific realm of military action, the reader will discover that there was a party or group of Spaniards who strongly opposed the military clique that exercised influence over the king in the years from 1816 to 1819. More important, there were advisors who advocated a negotiated settlement of the American rebellions and who sometimes held the highest positions of power in peninsular councils and ministries. Over all is the fact that Spain, in the reign of Ferdinand VII, was a nation first awakening to the structural and institutional changes of the age of revolution. Although some attention has been paid to the Spanish background to American independence in the era of the Bourbon reforms, equal attention has not been given to peninsular policy in the very period of the wars for American independence. Besides Friede's, the only works that focus on the peninsula as the other side of the American wars of independence study the rebellions' effects on Spain rather than Spain's policy toward the rebellions.[2] There are also a number of works on the role of England, France, the United States, and Russia in Latin American independence. Yet, strangely enough, there is little on the role of Spain in Latin American independence.

Spain must be the focus of our attention because, as Claudio Véliz has reminded us, the major political transformations in Latin American history must be addressed in the perspective of the centralist tradition, without which they make inadequate sense. Jorge Domínguez, in another very recent work, has emphasized the extent to which the response to dissent of the royal governments in America helped forestall or provoke rebellion, a principle that obviously extends to the metropolis as well.[3] The empire had to disintegrate at its core. What were the policy decisions of king and council, Cortes and Regency, relating to American insurrection? What motivated and changed policy? Did the king and his councilors even have accurate information on the state of the American rebellions? Did they understand their causes and did they ever attempt to solve them? Despite the vast bibliography on Latin American independence from the perspective of individual liberated countries, these questions relating to the core need much more attention. The focus throughout this book is thus on the highest levels of power in Spain—the king, the Cortes, the councils—because they were the core. It was at that level that the ultimate power to establish and change policy lay.

Concentrating on the highest levels of power in the empire leads one to realize that, contrary to the implication of much of the historiography, the real failure of empire occurred after 1814 rather than before. From 1808 to 1814, when the state was disrupted by foreign conquest and warfare, the overseas empire began its slow and massive awakening. It stirred but it did not escape. With the exception of the Río de la Plata, local viceregal governments were able to overcome or to contain the powers of the rebels. It was after the king's restoration in 1814, rather, that the genuine failures on the peninsula's part occurred. It was during the period of the first restoration (1814–20) and the constitutional triennium (1820–23) that the state was whole again, that is to say, no longer kingless, and a political solution for the American crisis could be considered. This is why, though it may at first be surprising to hear, most of the real debate over American policy took place in this later period.

We will discover that the policy the Spaniards adopted for America made sense to them within the context of the limitations that prevailed. There were institutional limitations in the form in which both the absolutist regime and the constitutional regime had to work. The constitutional regime required unity of purpose between the king (or Regency) and Cortes, as well as unity of purpose between the American and the European deputies, to come up with a workable American policy; such unity was usually absent. The absolutist regime, on the other hand, though not impeded by formal blocks to action, was weakened by the existence of a camarilla that often made policy without the knowledge of ministers, by sycophancy, by ministerial timidity, and by the personality of Ferdinand VII himself. For a variety of reasons, the absolutist regime was no system of government at all. Both regimes were weakened by the dispersion of advisory powers on American policy among competing agencies or administrators and by the resulting failure to deal with American questions specifically and efficiently. There were also resource limitations caused by Spain's European wars and by the American wars, by the destruction of the fleet, and by the simple lack of funds to rebuild navies and to man armies. Above all, there were human limitations—in ministers who could not take action from fear of losing their offices, in councils that could advise but could not enact policy, in a camarilla that fought for pride of place with sycophancy and mindless reaction, and in a king who had too few options and too much contradictory advice, who lacked the strength to choose boldly, and for whom the peninsula itself was already enough responsibility. There was no lack of imaginative suggestions, but there was usually a lack of consensus. Spain's failure can be explained. Indeed, this study might be subtitled "Lessons in How to Lose an Empire."

The failure to reach consensus is, in fact, the element that ties together and runs through all three of the major changes of government in Spain during the era of American independence. The liberal regime of 1808 to 1814 could not have differed more radically from the restored absolutism of 1814 to 1820. And the restored liberal regime of 1820 to 1823 differed from both of them, for it was not an exact duplicate of the earlier constitutional era in that the state was now headed by a king and the Constitution was, for the first time, fully enacted. Yet in each of these widely differing systems there existed complex structural impediments—the product of the institutional and human limitations that prevailed—that served to make impossible not only continuity of policy but even the reaching of consensus. What we witness is constant vacillation—between promise and performance under the Constitution, between moderate and militarist under the absolutist regime. In these circumstances, a universal policy for America, logically conceived and consistently applied, became an impossibility.

Over and above the story of Spain's institutional, economic, and human limitations, one can also trace a consistent thread of what might be called systemic dysfunction. This is an explanation that, though it has been sensed by many historians involved with the independence era, needs to be sketched as a whole. Under the first constitutional regime, under the first restoration regime, under the second constitutional regime, and under the second restoration regime, the governmental, policy-making, information-transmitting, and consensus-generating mechanisms of the Spanish state failed to work. In each of these starkly different regimes, stumbling over each other in wild abandon, there remained a bewildering confusion of voices and a failure to come to grips with the American crisis. The

governmental systems that appear on their surfaces to be so cohesive—from the idealist reformism of the Cortes to the hard-headed
reaction of Ferdinand VII—were each characterized by frequent institutional failure.

Since the story of the fall of vast empires lends itself naturally to a
certain patina of romanticism, a word of warning is in order. There is
no room for nostalgia in the story of Spain's loss of empire; the facts do
not warrant it. But this is not a tragic story for Spain either, for the
collapse of the center released the hitherto tethered powers of more
than a score of former colonies that were now free to make their unique
contributions to the world. "And from the Spanish lion a thousand
whelps have sprung" is how Rubén Darío expressed the relation
between mother Spain and her liberated offspring. This has always
been, and properly so, a pride-giving and hope-renewing fact for
Spain.

Chronology (1808–25)

Year	Date	Spain	America
1808	17–19 March	Uprising of Aranjuez against Godoy, Charles IV abdicates	
	23 March	French forces enter Madrid	
	2 May	Uprising of Madrid	
	5–8 May	Abdications in Bayonne	
	25 May	Junta of Oviedo rises, followed by others	
	6 June	José, king of Spain	
	19–20 July	Battle of Bailén, entry of José in Madrid	Overthrow of Iturrigaray of Mexico (16 September)
	25 Sepember	Opening of Junta Central at Aranjuez	
	4 December	Surrender of Madrid to Napoleon, Junta Central flees to Seville	
1809	9 January	Spanish-English treaty of alliance	Failed attempt to overthrow Liniers in Buenos Aires (1 January)

Year	Date	Spain	America
1809 cont'd.			Junta Central declares American lands are not colonies (January)
	20 February	Surrender of Zaragoza	Cisneros named viceroy of Buenos Aires (March)
			Junta formed in La Paz (16 July)
	27–28 July	Battle of Talavera	Junta formed in Quito (9 August)
	19 November	Battle of Ocaña	Junta formed in Colombia (10 August)
	9 December	Surrender of Gerona	
1810	January	Collapse of Junta Central	
	February	Creation of Regency in Cádiz	Revolution of Caracas (19 April)
			Revolution of Buenos Aires (22 May)
			Revolution of Bogotá (20 July)
			Grito de Dolores of Hidalgo in Mexico (16 September)
	24 September	Opening of Cortes of Cádiz	Revolution in Santiago, Chile (18 September)
	15 October	Cortes decrees equality of Americans	
	10 November	Decree of Free Press	

Year	Date	Spain	America
1810 cont'd.	16 December	American deputies present eleven demands to Cortes	
1811	13 March	Cortes abolishes tribute	
	May	British propose mediation in America	
			Colombia declares independence (5 July)
	1 August	American deputies propose provincial juntas for America	Hidalgo captured (30 July)
	6 August	Cortes abolishes jurisdictional privileges	
	17 August	Decree abolishes proof of pure blood for entry in the army	Meeting of congresses in Caracas, Santiago, etc.
1812	19 March	Constitution approved by Cortes and Regency	
			Insurrection of Morelos in Mexico
	16 July	Cortes rejects British bases for mediation	
			Royal army of Monteverde defeats Miranda in Venezuela
	22–23 July	Wellington wins in Salamanca and José retires from Madrid	
1813	18 February	Cortes limits religious communities	
	22 February	Cortes suppresses Inquisition	

Year	Date	Spain	America
1813 cont'd.	19 May	Council of State urges British mediation	
	21 June	Battle of Vitoria	Congress of Chilpancingo proclaims Mexican independence (6 November)
	10–11 December	Treaty of Valencay, liberation of Ferdinand VII	
1814	15 January	Cortes reopens in Madrid	
	22 March	Ferdinand VII enters Spain	
	12 April	Manifesto of Persas presented to king	
	4 May	Royal decree abolishes Constitution, imprisonment of deputies	
	13 May	Ferdinand VII enters Madrid	
	27 May– 2 October	Royal decrees restore institutions to the condition of 1808	Cuzco uprising of Pumacahua (2 August)
	2 July	Council of the Indies restored	Osorio pacifies Chile (October)
1815	10 January	King restores tribute	
	17 February	Departure of Morillo expedition	Expedition of Morillo in Venezuela and New Granada
	15 April	Prohibition on press except for *Gaceta de Madrid*	

Year	Date	Spain	America
1815 cont'd.	14 May	Spain reopens British mediation question	Capture of Morelos in Mexico (5 November)
1816	30 January	Papal encyclical "Etsi longissimo"	Portuguese invasion of Banda Oriental (June)
			Congress of Tucumán declares Argentine independence (9 July)
	17 October	Spain requests Allied mediation in Banda Oriental	
	30 October	José Pizarro, minister of state	
1817	February	Junta of Pacification and Pizarro support free trade	Bolívar begins the recovery of New Granada and Venezuela
	1 June	Garay's finance plan	
	10 June	Spain adheres to the Vienna accord	San Martín's Army of the Andes enters Chile, O'Higgins supreme chief of Chile
	29 November	King turns American pacification over to Pizarro	
1818			Battle of Maipú (5 April)
	9 June	Pizarro pacification plan	
	14 August	Junta of Pacification disbanded	
	15 September	Fall of Pizarro	Contract for entry of English goods in Lima (November)

Year	Date	Spain	America
1818 *cont'd.*	26 December	Death of Queen María Isabel	
1819	22 February	Spain cedes the Floridas to United States	Congress of Angostura forms Gran Colombia
	September	Expedition to Buenos Aires nearly ready	Bolívar wins at Boyacá (7 August)
1820	1 January	Riego revolt	
	6–9 March	Ferdinand VII promises a Cortes, swears to Constitution, creation of Provisional Junta	
	11 April	Spain announces it will send commissioners to America	
	19–29 April	Royal decrees abolish Old Regime	
	9 July	Opening of Cortes	
	September	Radical decrees relating to clergy and fueros	San Martín expedition lands in Peru (10 September)
	9–21 November	Frustrated effort of Ferdinand VII to restore his rights and appoint political officers	
			Morillo departs from Venezuela (December)
1821			Overthrow of Viceroy Pezuela in Peru (29 January)

Year	Date	Spain	America
1821 cont'd.			Iturbide's Plan of Iguala (24 February)
	25 June	American Cortes deputies propose federative empire	Triumph of Bolívar in Carabobo (24 June)
			Overthrow of Viceroy Apodoca in Mexico (5 July)
			San Martín enters Lima (12 July)
			O'Donojú recognizes independence of Mexico (24 August)
			Entry of Iturbide in Mexico City (27 September)
			Central America declares independence (September)
	7 November	Council of State urges free trade and suspension of radical decrees	Santo Domingo declares independence (1 December)
1822	17 January	Ministry urges free trade, suspension of radical decrees, two-year armistice	
	13 February	Cortes rejects ministry's proposals, decides to send new commissioners	Monroe proposes recognition of new American nations (8 March)
	1–7 July	Rising of Royal Guard against liberal government	Victory of Sucre at Pichincha (24 May), independence of Ecuador

Year	Date	Spain	America
1822 cont'd.	15 August	Installation of Regency at Urgel	
	October–December	Congress of Verona	
1823	7 April to 1 October	Intervention of French army	Overthrow of Iturbide in Mexico (April)
			Guatemala separates from Mexico (1 July)
	1 October	Ferdinand leaves Cádiz	
	7 November	Riego executed in Madrid	Monroe Doctrine (2 December)
1824	26 January	Ferdinand VII withdraws American commissioners	
	30 January	Canning announces Britain's intention to recognize American states	
		Political purges in Spain	
	3 December	Britain begins recognition	Battle of Ayacucho (9 December)
1825			Defeat of Olañeta, independence of Bolivia (April)

I

Imperial Structures and Royal Squabbles

It may be that the most important fact about the fall of the Spanish empire is that it did not occur when it logically should have, for this fact makes it very clear that American independence was not inevitable. Spanish America should have become independent in 1808, or at least by 1814. The French conquest of Spain in 1808 and the collapse of its government meant that the vast empire suddenly had no ruler at all. The imperial power was devastated and paralyzed. Yet, in that moment of stupendous opportunity, the colonies, though some of them stirred, did not achieve their independence. The explanation, of course, is that too many Americans—creoles, mestizos, even Indians—remained loyal to the traditions and symbols of the motherland to permit those few who already aspired to separation from Spain to achieve success. The armies that defeated Hidalgo and Morelos in Mexico and Bolívar and Miranda in New Granada, that turned back Belgrano in Upper Peru, and that crushed the incipient rebel regime in Quito were composed chiefly of creoles, mestizos, pardos, and Indians, though they were often under the command of peninsulars. The myths and loyalties that knit the empire together did not die automatically in 1808.

The Spanish idea of empire consisted of two parts, the philosophical and the practical. Both were equally real, and they mingled, sometimes inextricably, to form a body of ideas that made for an ethos, a view of society and politics, that possessed great coherence and strength. On the philosophical level the empire consisted of an extended family of peoples subject to the authority of the father and lord, the king. On the practical level, in the Bourbon period, the empire was also a conglomeration of colonies whose mineral and

commercial wealth was destined for the glorification and enhance-
ment of Spain. The two ideals, when expressed so baldly, were
actually contradictory, yet they existed side by side until the time
when Americans came to recognize the contradictions. When Spain's
Cortes set about writing the monarchy's first constitution, the contradictions appeared in all their glaring reality and proved impossible to
resolve.

Recent research has considerably clarified the political philosophy of the Spanish colonial empire.[1] There were many occasions in the
period after 1808 when colonial loyalties to Spain reasserted themselves even in the face of the most massive assaults from the mother
country itself against the residue of good will possessed by the colonial
subjects. To a very great extent indeed, the Spanish empire was as
much an idea as it was anything else. Historically, Spain was viewed,
especially by conservative Latin Americans, as much more than the
Conqueror. Spain was the Founder. In that incomparable sixteenth
century of discovery and conquest in America, Spain had created
civilization. It was a civilization that encompassed the moral, ethical,
religious, intellectual, and political precepts of its adherents. This
concept, obviously, largely ignored the separate cultures and civiliza-
tions of the advanced Indian populations that had been absorbed in
Mexico, Central America, and the Andes. To the creole and peninsular populations who ruled America and set its cultural norms, Spain
was the mother.

The cultural loyalty to the mother country was enhanced by
centuries of transoceanic immigration, by the educational system of
the elite, and by the teaching of the church, and had led to the
existence of a powerful concept, even among the most outspoken
creoles, of the "ties that bind." This idea was stated explicitly by such
widely differing spokesmen as Simón Bolívar, the Liberator of South
America, and the Spanish Junta Central. In his "Letter from
Jamaica," Bolívar pointed out that Spain's authority over America was
founded on "ties that bind." In his words these were "the habit of
obedience; a community of interest, of understanding, of religion;
mutual good will; a tender regard for the birthplace and good name of
our forefathers." These had created what Bolívar called "a principle of

affinity."[2] The Junta Central of Spain, in a letter to the city council of Bogotá in 1809, expressed an identical thought: "[There exists] a union between the two hemispheres, between the Spaniards of Europe and of America, a union that can never be destroyed either by intrigue or the force of tyrants because it is grounded upon the most solid bases that tie men together: a common origin, the same language, the same laws, the same customs, the same religion, the same honor to principles and sentiments, and the same relations and interests. These are the ties that unite us."[3] A peninsular publicist, Juan López Cancelada, reemphasized the matriarchal role of Spain in this relationship in his Cádiz periodical *El Telégrafo Americano*: "Generous Spain, wise and enlightened mother; America will be yours eternally; the impotent forces of the rebels will never be enough to break a union of three centuries."[4]

Uniting and solidifying the personal ties was the concept of the empire as a single family under the father king, the Rey Padre as he was frequently called in loyalist propaganda. It does not seem possible to overemphasize this idea, at once both subtle and naive. It echoed across the vast distances of the empire, and had its refrains in everything from the sermons of archbishops to the simple representations of Indian villages. It originated in the Hapsburg era, when the empire was founded, and it continued in the popular mind to be the important element of political organization during the Bourbon era. Richard Graham has pointed out that the more enlightened, more "modern" Bourbons resisted this traditional role but that Americans "clung to the Hapsburg image of the patriarchal state and resisted the Bourbons' political philosophy."[5] Even so, the concept of the patrimonial empire was the foundation of Bourbon policy as it had been of Hapsburg, and definite echoes of the concept can be found in the pronouncements and decrees of the early nineteenth century. It was the backbone of the Spanish resistance to the French conquest as well as of the loyalist resistance to American rebellion. In the period after the defeat of Napoleon it was one of the fundamental premises of the Holy Alliance, a concept to which the Spanish king Ferdinand VII was personally devoted, if not officially. So important is the concept that it has led one writer to assert, perhaps exaggeratedly, in reference to the Spanish American independence movement:

> In the years 1808 to 1824, the creoles led the way in overthrow-
> ing the royal father-figure. This was the central and "traumatic"
> event in all Spanish American history. It represented the acting
> out of Oedipal desires to slay the father, creating a collective
> guilt which Spanish America has never overcome. Much of the
> rebelliousness in modern Spanish American history represents a
> search for a paternal replacement for the Kings of Spain.[6]

The American territories were the patrimonial property of the
king; he was Señor, or Lord. They did not belong to the Spanish
nation but to the crown of Castile. Traditionally, therefore, and
certainly in the Hapsburg era, the American territories were not
colonies. They were kingdoms, vicekingdoms, dominions (these
terms were used interchangeably and without precise definition), and
their only ruler was the sovereign or his properly delegated representative. But softening and adding efficiency to this essentially absolutist
patrimonial system was the fact that Spanish political philosophy, particularly as represented by the sixteenth-century Thomis-
tic philosopher Francisco Suárez, also believed in the principle of
consent. Suárez taught that sovereignty originates with the collectiv-
ity of men. The people had formed a contract with the monarch, by
which they vested power in him, unconditional power. That is, the
people did not merely delegate authority to their prince, they alien-
ated it to him utterly. By contract, then, the prince was superior to
the people. But the prince must, according to all precepts of Thom-
ism, rule justly and in the best interest of the people. Not to do so
constitutes, of course, tyranny, for Suárez also taught that the law of
the prince loses its force if it is unjust (for an unjust law is not a law), if
it is too harsh, or if the majority of the people have already ceased to
obey it.[7] Ferdinand VII, on his return to Spain in 1814, could
unashamedly assert, in the act overthrowing the Constitution of
1812, that Spanish kings had never been tyrants. In other words,
Spanish kings depended for their authority on the right to rule, but
they were not bound by a law, even so sweeping a law as the first
written constitution of the monarchy, if, in their role as interpreter of

the nations' wishes, they felt the call of a higher ethic. This was not simple reaction, for man-made laws, even folkways and custom, were of lesser moral and spiritual—and therefore legal—value than the edicts of the king.[8]

Yet there was in this system a vague but nonetheless operative guarantee against excess. The king both made the law and interpreted or changed the law in response to perceived needs in society. Throughout the entire history of the Spanish empire the tradition was widely maintained that everyone, whether viceroy or peasant, whether corporate power or private individual, possessed the right to appeal to the king, to express grievances, and to plead for reform. The king could and did hear petitions from his subjects to overthrow or change the very law he had himself decreed. Indeed, one of the most startling aspects of the reign of Ferdinand VII, as for that matter of previous Spanish kings, is the number and volume of private, unsolicited petitions and letters of advice the king received and frequently read. It was the king's (or his council's) moral duty to hear the petitions of his people. In 1814 Ferdinand exercised this duty quite literally and declared that he perceived that the nation did not desire the Constitution.

It need hardly be asserted, of course, that a necessary concomitant of the sovereign's authority was that he had also a duty to hear his American subjects, and this, it will become clear, he failed to do with the same degree of attention as when listening to his European subjects. In a sense, of course, he was faced with the literally insoluble dilemma of balancing imperial objectives, even the survival of Spain itself, against the countless grievances of his American subjects. The fact remains that Ferdinand VII must bear some degree of personal responsibility for the loss of his empire—assuming, that is, that he was in full possession of the facts about the condition and wishes of America. It will be seen that he was.

The king, of course, did not rule alone, for he had, of necessity, to delegate functional powers to his Council of State, Council of the Indies, and Council of the Treasury, his ministers and departments, his commanders, viceroys, and captains general. Extensive special privileges had been delegated to various corporate groups—nobles, clergy, cities, guilds—which made the state function on the basis of corporatism. The king himself was surrounded by a variety of councils on which he called for advice, giving the system, when it worked smoothly, a certain degree of collegiality that was a source of considerable strength. In addition, the longstanding tradition that colonial, or peninsular, officials refused to obey or implement laws or decrees of the crown that were perceived as being inappropriate to local conditions served to lessen the danger of unlimited absolutism. In return for ultimate loyalty to his sovereignty, the king had, so to speak, given royal sanction to the disobeying of individual laws. This was the principle of "Obedezco pero no cumplo" (I obey but do not comply). This principle permitted the state to function, for it enabled Spain to govern a gigantic empire of widely differing ethnic and cultural groups without the use of force. It also explains how, despite the apparent illogic of it, many Americans in 1810 could simultaneously proclaim "Long live the King" and "Death to Bad Government," how they could raise rebellions against Spain while protesting loyalty to Spain's king.[9]

Almost every historian who has approached the imperial structure from this viewpoint has concluded by saying that the regimen of Father King and moderator sovereign was disrupted and, for America, destroyed by the Napoleonic conquest of Spain in 1808. Yet it is equally true to say that the events of 1808 demonstrated the essential continuity of the imperial structures. Although 1808 was certainly a catastrophe the likes of which few European nations had ever before faced, and although the capture of Ferdinand VII certainly created a massive constitutional crisis by confusing the traditionally agreed-on locus of authority, and although the events of 1808 certainly prompted Americans to create their own provisional governments, which later could become independent governments, the fact remains that six years later, in 1814, the king was restored to the plenitude of his powers and that the American empire was still largely intact. Only the Río de la Plata "got away" in the first round of rebellions. To conservative Spaniards the years from 1808 to 1814 were something unreal, a moment of time that had frozen. Indeed, the king decreed in

1814 that all institutions, political personnel, and other adjuncts of the state were to return to the exact conditions that had prevailed in March 1808 at the time of his accession to the throne, as if turning the clock back would wipe the slate clean. There occurred, at any rate, a restoration of his authority, and the leaders of the empire fervently expected that there would be a restoration of the empire as well. Consequently, once we work our way through the confusion and turmoil of the period 1808 to 1814, it will become clear that the real failure, the actual loss of empire, occurred in the so-called first restoration, from 1814 to 1820, and in the so-called constitutional triennium from 1820 to 1823.

The patrimonial authoritarian regime sketched here was not, however, static and changeless. The Bourbon dynasty, particularly Charles III, grandfather of Ferdinand VII, had set about consciously to increase the element of authoritarianism within the system, particularly to strengthen the political centrality of Madrid. Yet the traditional modes of expression and thought remained dominant throughout the empire, even in the period from 1808 to 1814 when the recognized king was a captive in France. The object of the Bourbon reforms initiated by Charles III and continued under Charles IV was the establishment of a "new imperialism" or the fulfillment of a "second Conquest of America."[10] The Bourbons had built the restoration of Spain's international power and prestige on a policy of more conscious, more planned, exploitation of the riches of America. Through a series of administrative and economic changes they had set about to make America pay for Spain's European wars, to reap more of the bullion and commercial wealth of the empire. They had attempted to adopt a sort of mercantilist policy. So great was their success that returns from America to Spain had increased from 74.5 million reales in 1778 to 1.2 billion in 1784. New Spain and Peru particularly were the treasure houses of the empire. But all the empire, including not only the two newer viceroyalties of Río de la Plata and New Granada but also such peripheral seats of empire as Central America and Cuba, were expected to churn out profits in proportion to their state of advancement or their natural resources.

Only the vast frontier territories, such as Chile, the north of Mexico, or the Floridas, continued as a net drain on imperial revenues.

In the course of exploiting the overseas territories more efficiently, some planners got into the habit of calling them "colonies." This was really the first time that the term had been used, and it constituted essentially a foreign import. Spaniards had traditionally denigrated Americans and American plant and animal life as being somehow less vigorous, less mature, than the human beings and plant and animal life of the Old World. Yet the concept of the overseas lands as "colonies" had never been widespread in Spain. Even at the beginning of the nineteenth century, the term "colony" was employed mainly in private or in internal state papers, rarely publicly, to refer to those lands previously called "the Indies," "the American dominions," or "the overseas provinces." Even so, it is of the greatest importance to remember, as Lynch put it, that "in the twilight of empire Spain became not less but more imperialist."[11] The reforms affected almost every field of endeavor, including commercial, economic, political, military, and even cultural life.

The Bourbon reforms regarding commerce and trade were apparently the most important, to judge at least from the complaints against them by Americans, complaints that continued and reached new heights in the middle years of the wars of independence. Between 1765 and 1776 Spain did away with many of the centuries-old barriers to inter-colonial trade, abolishing the monopoly of Cádiz and Seville, lowering tariffs, authorizing inter-colonial trade, and permitting free communication between the peninsular ports and America. In 1778 the so-called *comercio libre* was extended to include Buenos Aires, Chile, and Peru, and in 1789 Venezuela and Mexico. "Free trade" meant simply that the various ports of peninsular Spain were now able to trade directly with the American territories rather than having to ship all goods through designated Spanish or American ports. America remained prohibited, with minor exceptions, from trading with non-Spanish merchants, with North America, or with Britain. Cádiz, formerly the only designated entrepôt for European trade with America, continued to dominate the overseas trade (to the tune of approximately 90 percent) because of its excellent location and because of the experience of many decades, but it ceased to have an absolute legal monopoly.

The net effect of the loosening of trade restrictions was to throw America open to massive commercial exploitation from Europe while simultaneously wrecking some of the basic American industries, such as textile manufacture, that could not compete with imported goods. To an extent never previously experienced, America became a consumer of European manufactured goods and an exporter of bullion and other raw materials. Americans thus became more dependent on Spain, while a new wave of Spanish immigrants flocked to the colonies to take advantage of the many trading opportunities newly opened to them. Spain was at last exercising "classical" commercial imperialism. Colonial industries were unprotected and unable to resist the increased influx of European manufactured goods, while Americans themselves could pay for those goods only by increasing their bullion production and export. Spanish imperial planners clearly perceived the political importance of maintaining the European monopoly, as the viceroy of Peru, José de Abascal, made clear when he pointed out that free trade "would be tantamount to decreeing the separation of these dominions from the Mother Country, since, once direct trade with foreigners was established on the wide basis which they demand, the fate of European Spain would matter little to them."[12] Even so, the exigencies of warfare in the last decade of the eighteenth century and the first decade of the nineteenth forced Spain to permit the entry of neutral foreign trading vessels in America in 1797–99, 1801–02, and 1804–08.[13] By 1805 neutral shipping dominated the trade in some American ports, such as Havana and Veracruz, as Spanish commercial shipping disappeared in the wars in Europe. In the mid-1810s the Spanish Junta of Pacification and the Council of the Indies recognized the widely destructive nature of the peninsular monopoly for American economies, but for many Spaniards it had become "a matter of principle," and genuine free foreign trade was never permitted.

As in trade and commerce, the Bourbon reforms in politics and administration were designed to renew the policy ties that knit America to the peninsula. New viceroyalties were at first created in

Río de la Plata (Buenos Aires) and New Granada (Bogotá). The importation and establishment of the French system of local government, the intendants, was the major structural reform. Adopted in Río de la Plata in 1782, in Peru in 1784, in Mexico in 1786, this reform replaced the former local administrators—corregidores and alcaldes mayores—with intendants and subdelegates, royal officials charged with all aspects of government and social control in the local regions of America. Its object was to abolish the corruption of the corregidores and their abuse of the lower classes and, simultaneously, to strengthen Madrid's direct political control over the farthest reaches of the empire. The first object was only temporarily achieved (the intendants sometimes became as corrupt as the corregidores and alcaldes mayores had been), but the second objective was accomplished, at least for strictly administrative purposes. As far as physical conditions and the imperative of distance permitted, Madrid did control every local district in the empire. This sytem of "government by remote control," as Juan Friede has dubbed it, made for political cohesion and also for the most extraordinary delays and frustrations in policy planning. Functionaries of the royal court in Spain continued to make, or try to make, day-to-day decisions for places as farflung as Florida, Yucatán, Panama, La Paz, and Chiloé. Whether the supreme governing body for America was the Council of the Indies, the Ministry of the Indies, the Council of State, the Junta of Pacification, or some other agency, imperial Spain held the reins of political power in a tight grip.

Another aspect of the administrative reorganization of the empire in the Bourbon reforms was the gradual replacement of American-born or creole royal appointees with peninsulars. This was a particular grievance of the creole elites, because in all the more advanced parts of America, particularly in regions where large and established universities existed, young creoles tended to aim for careers in the law, in government, in the church, or, toward the end of the imperial era, in American militias. There were, indeed, few other honorable careers open to creoles who did not inherit land, and, with the prevailing institution of entail of property, only the eldest son of a wealthy family would inherit land. In the case of late colonial Lima, for example, 62.6 percent of the Lima male elite were employed in the church, in royal service, or in the practice of law. [14] Yet, in the decades after the 1770s, the Spanish imperial regime, following the tenets of renewed centralism, pursued a conscious program of replacing retiring bureaucrats, as frequently as not creoles, with peninsulars. Nowhere was this policy as acute or as clear as in the make-up of the royal high courts, the audiencias, which shared power in America with viceroys or captains general. The problem with the audiencias was not only that creoles had come to hold what was considered a disproportionate number of positions but that native sons, men born in the city of their magistracy, did too. The study of audiencia personnel by Mark A. Burkholder and D. S. Chandler has shown that in 1750 creoles and native sons held 55 percent of all audiencia positions in America. By 1785, however, the tables had been radically reversed, and only 23 percent of all audiencia members were Americans, whereas 77 percent were peninsulars. [15] Spain had reasserted control over the high courts, as it did in the same period over military commands, prelacies, local government in the intendancies, and other levels of power. Viceroys, captains general, and presidents of audiencias continued, as before, to be peninsulars.

Along with tightening control over the civil bureaucracy, the Bourbons also strengthened imperial control over the church and the army. In 1767 Charles III ordered the expulsion of the Jesuits from America. There were some 2,500 in all, many of them creoles who had possessed a type of semi-independence from Madrid in their control of the Jesuit order, considered by planners to be a virtual state within the state. [16] Over the years the Bourbons also launched a considerable assault on the corporate privileges of ecclesiastics, particularly on the fuero, their privilege of immunity from civil prosecution. [17] Toward the military, Spain's policy consisted essentially of two largely contradictory objectives. First, it expanded the system of military defense through the creation of many local creole militias, to the point, indeed, that militias became the fundamental military power in America. This was essential, since Spain lacked the money or manpower to establish expeditionary forces throughout America. To attract American recruits, the military fuero, or exemption from civil prosecution, was extended to creoles in the militia.[18] The militia thus became a source of considerable social advancement for both creoles and non-white Americans. However, when the danger that excessive power might devolve to creoles was perceived in individual locations—as in the mountainous intendancies of Peru after the suppression of the Túpac Amaru rebellion of 1780—the Bourbons would demobilize the militias and replace them with small garrisons of disciplined and trained regular soldiers.[19] Supervision of the militias would thus require constant vigilance and forethought on Spain's part, and although there is no doubt that the American militias eventually became a focus of creole dissent, it should still be emphasized that even in a country like Mexico, where the militia by 1816 numbered 44,000 men (as compared to 39,000 men in the regular army), the militia did much of the fighting that preserved Spain's control after the rebellions broke out.

A further element of the Bourbon reconquest of empire was its revived cultural imperialism. Under this vague term could be classified a number of developments, including the new emphasis on missionary conquest on the frontiers of California and Chile, the constant effort of imperial administrators to check and control the curriculum of the more advanced teaching institutions such as the Colegio de San Carlos in Lima, the creation of new cultural or technical institutions such as the Mexican Mining College and the Academy of Art, and the frequently-repeated imperial directive to bring young creoles to Spain for education and indoctrination. Spanish planners remained aware of the importance of cultural influences and, well into the wars of independence, were still suggesting that one way to settle the rebellions would be to bring creoles to Spain for education and to send missionaries, teachers, and propaganda to America. An important element in Spain's increased cultural imperialism was the influx of new peninsular settlers in the American territories. Attracted by the opportunity that the colonies held out to immigrants from the metropolis, Spaniards, particularly men from northern Spain, came to Mexico, Venezuela, New Granada, Buenos

Aires, and Peru in large numbers. They established themselves, as D. A. Brading has sketched it, as junior employees in the businesses founded by earlier peninsular immigrants—often relatives—and worked their way, by diligence and frugality, up to wealth and social influence, literally inheriting the accumulated wealth of great creole families through marriage.[20] Peninsulars still remained a tiny minority of the total American population (only 150,000 of the total of 3.2 million whites in America, according to Humboldt; only about 15,000 of the total population of Mexico), yet they exerted disproportionate power through their control of the state, the church, and the import-export trade.[21]

In general, then, the reigns of Charles III and Charles IV saw the widespread application of enlightened techniques that strengthened the commercial and political control of Spain over its empire, even if the reforms also chipped away at the ideal of the community of kingdoms united under the benevolent person of the sovereign. The question of whether the Bourbon reforms actually made Spain's empire more secure is one that is often avoided by saying that the catastrophe of 1808 disrupted all normal imperial development in such a way as to make a final judgment on the value of the reforms impossible. Yet, when viewed in its widest perspective, it seems the reforms were successful, since the empire continued to function, almost by inertia, for two long years after the captivity of the king in 1808. After restoration of peace to the peninsula in 1814, the empire was still not lost. That constitutes, perhaps, adequate proof of performance for any political institution, or so, at least, the king and his councils believed in the first restoration, for they refused to alter any of the inherited system of the Old Regime.

A more critical historiographical question about the Bourbon reforms is whether they served to disrupt the time-honored flexibility of the empire, thereby provoking dissent from Americans who were used to the more easy-going policies, the virtual local autonomy, of the Hapsburg regime. Since our purpose in this book is to consider the fall of the empire from the Spanish viewpoint, it is not possible to reach a final determination of the question. It can be said, however, that recent studies have shown that much of the old Hapsburg way of doing things continued unchanged even amid the rationalizing and modernizing Bourbons. Jacques Barbier, for example, has studied the admittedly narrow but perhaps still representative case of late colonial Chile, and has concluded that "the reestablishment of certain traditional patterns demonstrates that the impact of the reforms on the administration was less revolutionary than is often alleged." In the administration of Captain General Ambrosio O'Higgins (1788–96), during the "salad days" of the Bourbon reforms, he found that the old-fashioned, traditional forms of interaction between royal governor and colonial institutions and bureaucrats were constantly reasserting themselves. O'Higgins wisely adopted the same patterns of the patrimonial empire—he overlooked royal directives that were considered inappropriate for local conditions or temperament, he worked unceasingly to accommodate the increased revenue demands of the crown to local sensibilities, he ruled almost autonomously. The Bourbons, though unprepared to let America go its own way as the late Hapsburgs had been, nonetheless continued to depend on flexibility and feasibility, permitting the colonial population its traditional means of influencing policy formation.[22] They could not alter the social reality. Brian R. Hamnett has emphasized much the same transition in Mexico, pointing out that although Bourbon administrative reforms brought new tensions between peninsular mercantile and bureaucratic groups and the creole elite, by 1808 little remained of the attempted absolutist centralism of the reforms. "Instead, an uneasy patchwork of balances and compromises ensured the coexistence of the deeply-rooted with such elements of innovation that had managed against the odds to survive in barren soil."[23]

It is important to note that the same Spain that was so active in trying to increase the dependence of its colonies was, at the beginning of the nineteenth century, a very weak and undeveloped metropolis. It was still predominantly agricultural, with vast tracts of land remaining in the hands of great nobles, especially in the south. Although peripheral provinces had developed some modern industry—cotton and woolen production in Catalonia, trade and some shipbuilding in the Basque ports—the internal infrastructure was outmoded and weak, and Spain could not fill the needs of the American colonies. The transportation system between the eastern and northern productive provinces and the interior of the peninsula, unable to meet the demands placed on it, prevented the development of internal markets and slowed internal exchange. The commercial system was so retarded that coastal regions imported foodstuffs even while the interior produced a sufficient supply of grain. Catalonia traded with overseas markets more efficiently than it traded with Castile. The largest manufacturing establishments in the country were the state tobacco factories, which provided one of the major sources of state revenue throughout the nineteenth century. Even the Catalan and Valencian textile industry began its major period of growth only in the 1820s. The limited commercial and industrial class was divided over whether to support protectionism for industrial development or free trade for the encouragement of commerce. In Spain as a whole there was as yet no stock exchange, few joint-stock companies, and only one bank (the government-sponsored Banco de San Carlos, which collapsed in the Napoleonic invasion). In the very period in which Britain was experiencing the revolutionary effect of industrialization on a wide scale, from 1780 to about 1800, Spain languished in economic stagnation and backwardness. By 1808 Spain could not supply its own overseas colonies with manufactured goods, thereby forcing the Americans to look to the British merchants who increasingly entered the New World market. After 1808, and throughout the entire reign of Ferdinand VII, the mother country faced the danger of bankruptcy and got in the habit of foreign borrowing to survive. The entire national economic structure was in need of drastic reform, which would occur only after the death of Ferdinand VII.[24]

Along with metropolitan economic stagnation, the reign of Charles IV had also seen some depreciation in the prestige of the king, for, although he himself was a man of nearly puritan morals, he presided over a court that by the first decade of the nineteenth century was internationally notorious for its scandals and favoritism. The great scandal of Charles IV's reign, in the eyes of all royalists in Europe and America, was the ascendancy of Manuel de Godoy, the king's chief minister and reputed lover of the queen, María Luisa. The overweening power and authority of a court favorite was not new in Spanish history, but the peculiar relationship of the "earthly trinity," as María Luisa herself called the three of them, was. Godoy, a young member of the royal guard, first attracted the queen's attention in about 1785. His rise to power was meteoric, and by all accounts not the result of any particular talent as a statesman. By 1792 he was a grandee, a duke, and, at the age of twenty-five, the chief minister. Following the settlement of the war with the French Republic in 1795 he was given the unprecedented title Prince of the Peace. The title of prince in Spain was normally reserved for only the heir to the throne, the Prince of Asturias. Forced out of office in 1798 at the behest of Gaspar Melchor de Jovellanos, one of the great enlightened ministers, Godoy never lost royal favor and continued to live in the palace. By 1799 he had reasserted his control of the government and remained in command until the catastrophe of 1808, administering a government that became hated by Spaniards as a regime of "ministerial despotism."

Throughout the years, Godoy was first and foremost the queen's intimate and, through her, the power that controlled the king. Every foreign ambassador at the court followed the favorite's daily routine with the attention they would normally have lavished on the sovereign. The king himself, as he actually confessed to Napoleon, hunted from morning to lunch, then from lunch until dusk. Godoy would attend the king and queen at lunch, then retire to his apartments, where the queen, once Charles had returned to his sport, would join him. In the evening Godoy and the queen reported to the monarch, bringing to his attention those matters they thought it best for him to know. Through it all the king remained utterly dependent on Godoy and, to the scandal of every court in Europe, either unaware of the relationship of his wife and chief minister or else unwilling to order it stopped. The scandal continued long after the overthrow of Charles IV, for Godoy joined the royal couple in exile in France and Italy after 1808 and remained with them until shortly before their deaths in 1819. The relationship of the "earthly trinity" spanned thirty-four years, and as the king and queen aged they came to view Godoy as a beloved son.[25] The king's actual son, Ferdinand, the Prince of Asturias, was catapulted into the position of being the chief symbol of opposition to Godoy. This was of the most extraordinary consequence, for it made Ferdinand "the desired one," the hope of the empire, even before anyone knew anything about him. As a young man in his twenties he became the source of salvation to his millions of subjects, and they lavished on him an affection and a degree of support and enthusiasm that he had done nothing to deserve.

Ferdinand's childhood had been a terrible trial that deeply affected, and certainly damaged, his personality. He was born in 1785, the very year his mother brought Godoy into the palace, and for the first twenty-three years of his life he stood in the shadow of, and in fear of, Godoy. He suffered countless abuses from the tyranny of his mother, the threats of disinheritance by his father, and the plottings of Godoy. One of Ferdinand's tutors and few friends, the conservative churchman Juan de Escoiquiz, left a touching picture of a young man whose bright prospects for intellectual and personal development were blighted by his surroundings. Escoiquiz said that Ferdinand was permitted but one hour a day for his studies; the remainder of the day he was forced to live in "monastic retirement" because of his parents' refusal to grant him the usual income to form his own court as Prince of Asturias. Thus denied a chance for normal growth in a separate residence, a privilege his own father had enjoyed when he was Prince of Asturias, Ferdinand grew to adulthood amid the pettiness of his parents and the gossip of the court.[26] In 1802 Ferdinand married María Antonia de Borbón-Sicilia, daughter of the king of Naples, and his sister María Isabel married Francis, heir to the throne of the Two Sicilies. It was the first of the famous double marriages, and its real object was to guarantee the third daughter of the Spanish rulers a throne of her own, as had already been done for their two elder daughters, married to the heir of Portugal and the king of Etruria. Since Ferdinand's young wife immediately took his side against Godoy, further signs of domestic discord and outright hatred titillated the courts of Europe. The mother of the new Princess of Asturias, Queen Carolina of Naples, referred to the Madrid Bourbons as "that family of cretins," while Queen María Luisa complained to Godoy about "this slut who fans the flames, my daughter-in-law."[27] The young princess, frail and consumptive, died in March 1806, having left no children.

The young secretary of the Council of State, José García de León y Pizarro, left a series of assessments of the personalities who ruled Spain in the period before 1808. Though he never let slip a harsh word for the sovereigns, Pizarro, who was an early devotee of the cause of Ferdinand, made it clear that this was a regime in the grip of incompetents. Pedro Cevallos served during these years as minister of state, technically the premier rank. But Godoy ruled. Besides, Cevallos was married to Godoy's cousin. Pizarro described Cevallos as torpid, listless, cold, interested only in his personal advancement, opposed to work, dogmatic, and liable to embarrassment or compromise in his conferences with foreign diplomats. "In the office he slept hours on end in order to go out late without detriment to his health."[28] Pizarro described how 10,000 members of the court made the great journey to Barcelona for the royal weddings in 1802. While there, the king and court frequently went to sea to review the fleet, everyone, that is, except Godoy, who was supreme admiral of the fleet. He stayed on dry land because he was afraid of water "and pretended that in order to command the navy it is not even necessary to know sea water."[29]

In the era of Napoleon, Godoy's hollow pretenses to grandeur led Spain to national disaster. In 1796 Spain and France became allies, as the peninsula hastened to put itself on what appeared the stronger side in the European balance. War with Britain followed, and Spain lost its fleet to Nelson at Cape St. Vincent. In 1801 Spain attacked Portugal, under French pressure, in what was called the "war of the Oranges." Spain took the Portuguese city of Olivenza.[30] By 1803 France and Britain were again at war, and Spain, twice burnt, desperately tried to keep itself from becoming militarily involved. Although France demanded that Spain join, in October 1803 it was content to sign a new treaty that permitted Spain to remain neutral in return for a tribute of six million gold francs a month. It was clear to Spaniards everywhere that Godoy was prepared to sacrifice even the nation's honor to maintain Napoleon's friendship, as for over a year the nation and empire were bled dry to pay tribute to France. In order to end the Spanish subsidies to Napoleon, the British attacked Spanish ships carrying bullion from America, forcing Spain to declare war on 12 December 1804. Within a year Spain witnessed the annihilation of its fleet at Trafalgar, losing eleven of its fifteen battleships involved, including the *Santísima Trinidad*, the largest warship in the world.

As Napoleon expanded his empire through the creation of tributary thrones possessed by members of his family, the dynastic interests of the Spanish Bourbons were seriously threatened. In December 1805 Napoleon made his brother Joseph king of the Two Sicilies, overthrowing Charles IV's brother to do so. In 1807 and 1808 Charles's daughter María Luisa, Queen Regent of Etruria, was evicted from her Italian kingdom, and another daughter, Carlota Joaquina, princess regent and future queen of Portugal, was driven from Lisbon to what she considered a hellish exile of thirteen years in Brazil. This was a very peculiar alliance indeed, deeply damaging to Spain's national and dynastic interests alike.

All Spaniards, already hating Godoy, were now convinced that he was at fault for their nation's desperate decline. Indeed, Godoy was ruled more by his personal interests than by those of the nation, and he clung to the French alliance in the hope that it would make possible some splendid achievements for Spain and for himself personally. In October 1807 the fatal die was cast when Spain signed with France the Treaty of Fontainebleau, by which France would be permitted to send troops across Spain to attack Portugal, and in which it was agreed to divide Portugal in three parts, with Godoy being granted the southern territories of the Algarve, the central regions being retained by Napoleon, and the northern provinces going to the dispossessed Queen of Etruria and her young son.[31] A French army of 28,000 men under General Andoche Junot had already crossed into Spain before the treaty was signed. It entered and occupied Portugal in a month; the Portuguese royal family fled across the Atlantic to Brazil.

As French forces began to flood into Spain, the personal and political breach that had long divided the royal family widened into an unbridgeable abyss. Ferdinand, his legitimate ambitions thwarted for years by the overbearing Godoy, now made his first move to free himself from what all Spain viewed as the despotism of the favorite. In an attempt to gain pride of place for himself in the eyes of the French emperor, already the undoubted arbiter of Spain's future, the Prince of Asturias wrote on 11 October 1807 a letter of groveling submission to the emperor, requesting him to provide a princess of the imperial family for him to marry and expressing deep malice for Godoy and the queen. Godoy's agents informed Charles IV that his son was plotting against him and the queen, seeking Napoleon's aid in the overthrow of the favorite. Since the court was then residing at the Escorial, the ensuing crisis became known as the "affair of the Escorial." The king, infuriated by his son's independence, ordered Ferdinand arrested and had his papers seized. These papers included Ferdinand's secret correspondence in cipher with his old tutor Escoiquiz, in which they discussed means of removing Godoy. Ferdinand begged his father's forgiveness, which was granted on 5 November and publicized by royal decree. The heir's most intimate friends, including the Duke of Infantado and the Marqués de Ayerbe, remained under arrest, and plans were made for their trials on a charge of treason. All were subsequently acquitted, more because of the popular outcry in their favor than anything else, but they were ordered banished from Madrid.[32] According to Escoiquiz, Ferdinand was convinced that Napoleon wanted to see him on the throne, replacing Charles IV and Godoy, and that the French ambassador Beauharnais indicated as much to the heir.[33]

Madrid's furious hatred of Godoy was now unrestrained, and Ferdinand now enjoyed the overwhelming popularity of the nation. Antonio Alcalá Galiano described in his memoirs the tensions that prevailed in Madrid. The court, he said, did not even come to Madrid in 1807 because the king and queen feared they might be overthrown by the mob. From the outlying royal palaces of the Escorial, Aranjuez, or La Granja the government and court looked on Madrid as the enemy:

> The Government was generally abhorred and scorned. This it deserved without doubt, but perhaps it exceeded what was merited. The hatred did not reach up to the king, but the scorn did. . . . The hatred of the queen reached an incredible height, only equalled by that for the Prince of the Peace. . . . The Prince

of Asturias, afterward Ferdinand VII, was not one myth only, but many, with people of diverse and contrary opinions imagining him to possess all the endowments they desired of a future monarch.[34]

Thus Ferdinand continued his ascent as the symbol of unity and freedom from oppression. In the depths of his despair, he did not recognize as yet the extraordinary potential his mere name possessed in the eyes of his people; he would not recognize it until 1814. In the short run, however, the final acknowledgment of the dynastic squabble between the Reyes Padres and their son opened the door for Napoleon to control Spain, for both the royal family and the people of Spain in general turned to Napoleon to determine whether Charles IV would continue as king or be replaced by his son.

Throughout the last months of 1807, Napoleon turned over in his mind several options in regard to Spain. He contemplated sending one of his nieces, perhaps a daughter of his brother Lucien, as a wife for Ferdinand. He considered the possibility of forcing the resignation of Godoy and of seizing the Spanish provinces that bordered France. And, of course, he weighed the odds of a total French takeover of Spain, replacing the Bourbons with a new sovereign chosen from his own family. As he had not yet determined which course to follow, he contented himself for the time being with sending huge numbers of French troops into northern Spain, ostensibly to serve as reinforcements for the army in Portugal. Between December 1807 and March 1808 Napoleon dispatched several armies, a total of more than 100,000 men, into Spain. Though it was in fact an invasion—the French troops began to seize northern towns—the Spanish people were not at first alarmed. There were many Spaniards who saw the French troops as support for their idol, Ferdinand, in his struggle to be free of Godoy, and there were others who believed that the French would bring with them to Spain desirable modernization and reform. The attitude of most Spaniards began to change, of course, when the French began to seize major northern fortresses, including the citadel of Pamplona, the citadel and castle of Montjuich in Barcelona, the town and fortress of San Sebastián, the castle of Pancorbo, and others.

Although some Spaniards began to resist the haughty behavior and confiscations of the French, the nation as a whole did not awaken to the fact that the foreign troops were not allies but conquerors until it was too late.[35] In March 1808 Napoleon sent a private envoy to the court at Aranjuez with the ultimatum that Spain cede its northern provinces between the Pyrenees and the Ebro River in exchange for central Portugal, that France be granted open trading privileges in Spanish America, and that Prince Ferdinand submit himself to the control of his father in return for marriage to a French princess. The response of the Godoy government was to order the transfer of Spanish troops to Aranjuez, where the royal family was residing, in preparation for a planned evacuation of the king and family to Andalusia. Meanwhile, Napoleon's brother-in-law, Joachim Murat, the grand duke of Berg, entered Spain as commander of the French forces and Napoleon's lieutenant.

In this general crisis, Prince Ferdinand was moved to action. His agents spread the rumor that the royal family was about to flee to the south, taking the people's beloved prince with them. Thousands of peasants flocked to the royal palace of Aranjuez, joining the thousands of troops ordered there by Godoy. On the night of 17 March they began the "insurrection of Aranjuez," which Gabriel H. Lovett calls "the first revolution of modern Spain."[36] Mobs of people attacked the residence of Godoy, where the favorite hid in the attic for thirty-six hours until found and carried off to the barracks of the Royal Guard. The king, having dismissed Godoy on the initiation of the riot, asked Prince Ferdinand, who possessed the support of the mob, to spare the favorite's life. Ferdinand did so. The mob now rioted through the royal precinct, demanding the abdication of Charles IV and María Luisa. Charles abdicated on 19 March and that same evening Ferdinand was acclaimed king. In Madrid, the people went wild with joy, sacking the houses of Godoy and his relatives and acclaiming the new king. On 23 March the French forces entered Madrid under the command of Murat. On 24 March King Ferdinand VII made his triumphal entry, cheered by the multitude with enthusiasm in what is described by observers as the most joyful reception ever accorded a

Spanish sovereign. Ferdinand commenced his reign, content in the erroneous assumption that Napoleon would recognize him as king.

In the first moments of his reign, Ferdinand VII gave indications of the kind of personal and political failures that would torment his whole regime and ultimately lead some historians to consider him Spain's worst king. His position, of course, was immensely dangerous; he was, after all, the first king in the history of the united Spain to overthrow his father, and the northern provinces from the Pyrenees to Madrid were occupied by French troops who were becoming openly hostile. Still, Ferdinand possessed the most extraordinary support from his people. There existed a vast well of national support and love for him as a symbol, and in only a few months it would be clear that Spaniards were prepared to fight with ultimate devotion in his name. Yet Ferdinand made two fatal errors. He was so unsure of his own position that he determined to await the official recognition of Napoleon to guarantee him his throne. In the next weeks he fawned on and flattered Murat, assuring him of his undiminished love for Napoleon. This was an incredible weakness, for it alerted Napoleon to the fact that Ferdinand would not stand up against him.

In addition, Ferdinand called to his side in the first days of his reign those friends and flatterers who had supported him or helped him in his long years of frustration. He ordered Escoiquiz released from confinement in his monastery and brought him to Madrid as a chief advisor and member of the Council of State. The Duke of Infantado was made president of the Council of Castile. The Dukes of Medinaceli and Frías and Count Fernán Núñes were dispatched to Paris to negotiate with Napoleon. The king's inner circle in Madrid and later at Bayonne also included Pedro Cevallos, the minister of state; the American-born Duke of San Carlos; Pedro Gómez Labrador; Pascual Vallejo; and Eusebio Bardají—all described by Pizarro as self-seeking sycophants or weaklings. These are the men who would surround Ferdinand and make up his closest advisors and colleagues throughout most of the rest of his reign. They possessed an almost uncanny ability to offer bad advice, and would continue to do so for many years to come.

Ferdinand, catapulted to the throne without warning and deficient in his prior training, was unprepared for power. The combination of two chief ingredients—personal weakness on the part of the new king and uncommonly bad advice from his trusted cohorts—played into Napoleon's hands and made his task of removing the Spanish Bourbons—an objective he had determined to pursue the moment he heard of the insurrection of Aranjuez—absurdly easy. Having determined to remove the Spanish Bourbons from the throne, Napoleon invited both Ferdinand and the royal parents to confer with him at the French border town of Bayonne. Charles and María Luisa quickly consented to meet Napoleon, for they had decided on 22 March to revoke their abdication and they assumed the French emperor would reinstate them on the throne.

But why did Ferdinand make the disastrous mistake of going to Bayonne, thereby placing himself in Napoleon's control? This is where the influence of bad advisors and unclear thinking played a vital part. Escoiquiz explained that the Council of State discussed the question in detail and decided that Ferdinand should go to Bayonne. Napoleon's demand for cession of the northern Spanish provinces actually led the council to believe that France's intentions were not to remove the Spanish dynasty from the throne. In the past, Escoiquiz explained, France's object had not been to replace dynasties but simply to add territory to France from neighboring countries and to bind them to France. Napoleon could have dethroned the Austrian emperor and the Prussian king after the battles of Austerlitz and Jena, but he had contented himself with removing some of their territories, adding them to the kingdoms of Bavaria and the newly created Westphalia. Thus Napoleon's policy, the council believed, had been to aggrandize his allies at the cost of his enemies and to establish buffers around France. Thus he had made the rulers of Bavaria and Wurtemburg kings, and had added to those countries possessions taken from Austria; he had added to other principalities in the Rhine confederation; he had formed two kingdoms in Holland and Westphalia for two of his brothers; he had formed the kingdom of Italy to be inherited by his son; he had given the principality of Lucca to a sister, the grand duchy of Berg to another sister, and Naples to another brother, all at the cost of his enemies. Of course, he had dethroned the Bourbon king of Naples, but this was an isolated exception. Escoiquiz continued: "In view, then, of these events, which proved that the constant system of Napoleon was not to remove even his enemies from their thrones, was there cause to suspect that he would vary it and follow a diametrically opposite system with a king who was his ally, with a friendly nation that had sacrificed for him, with a young monarch whose only wish was to marry a princess of his blood?"

Furthermore, the council assumed that the cost of trying to conquer Spain would be too great for Napoleon, for it would leave him a ruined and hostile country in place of a friendly ally bound by marriage. Spain would lose its colonies, opening them to English aggrandizement. The transfer of American trade to England from Spain would ruin Napoleon's European embargo, allowing England to seize control of America's bullion. Escoiquiz concluded: "Such were the convincing arguments concerning the Emperor's and France's self-interest, which persuaded me it was impossible [that Napoleon could be planning] to dethrone the Bourbon dynasty of Spain."[37] It is clear that Escoiquiz and the other advisors should have thought more of Spain's self-interest instead of trying to anticipate France's.

Thus assured that he was on his way to a grand party at which his noble ally would bestow on him his official blessing, and perhaps even a wife, Ferdinand departed Madrid for Bayonne on 10 April, leaving behind a junta headed by his uncle Don Antonio to govern in Spain. At Vitoria, Ferdinand hesitated, having received ominous warnings from Napoleon. But his fears were allayed by Napoleon's agent, General A. J. M. R. Savary, who is reported to have assured Ferdinand: "I will let myself be beheaded if the Emperor has not recognized Your Majesty as King of Spain and the Indies a quarter of an hour after your arrival at Bayonne."[38] On 20 April Ferdinand arrived at Bayonne. That night he was informed that Napoleon's object was determined: Ferdinand must renounce the throne of Spain and the Indies in favor of the Bonaparte dynasty. Ferdinand and his advisors vainly resisted Napoleon's ultimatum for several days, but since they had made the error of placing themselves in Napoleon's control there

was nothing they could do. Furthermore, the former king and queen, Charles and María Luisa, were expected soon in Bayonne, and Napoleon determined to overlook Ferdinand and work through the parents. He wrote Talleyrand: "This tragedy, if I am not mistaken, is in its fifth act."[39] The play was soon complete. After the arrival of the old king and queen, Ferdinand formally returned the throne to them on 6 May. Charles had already yielded his rights to the throne to Napoleon on the day before. Napoleon then called on his brother Joseph, king of Naples, to come and assume the Spanish throne. Ferdinand was held a prisoner for the next six years at Talleyrand's comfortable country estate, Valencay, in the south of France. Charles, María Luisa, and Godoy lived for some years in France before moving to Italy.

And what of America? Escoiquiz recorded a series of conversations he had with Napoleon during those decisive days at Bayonne. In one of them, held on 21 May, he broached the topic of America. What good would it do France, he asked, to conquer a ruined and devastated Spain bereft of its colonies? He had no doubt that the forced change of dynasty would spell the separation of America. Even if Ferdinand remained on the throne, he said, the slightest discontent "would be enough to break a union that nowadays depends on nothing but the weakest ties of habit." Napoleon had his own ambitions for America and countered Escoiquiz's arguments imperiously: "You go too fast, Canon; you assume it is certain that Spain will lose its colonies; and I, on the contrary, have well-founded hopes of conserving them. Do not believe that I have been sleeping. I have intelligence from Spanish America."[40] Escoiquiz responded by saying simply that the French conquest of Spain would serve merely to direct America's bullion into English coffers.

For once in this tragic episode the vision of the Spaniards was clearer than that of the French. Undoubtedly Napoleon's unbridled pride and ambition, to say nothing of his delight at realizing how inept the Spanish crown really was, led him to overestimate his own powers. He was soon disabused of his ill-conceived dreams of taking over the Spanish empire in America, as he was also gradually led to regret the day he had ever made the decision to overthrow the Bourbon dynasty in Spain itself.[41] What is equally significant, however, is the extent to which defeatism and weakness underscored all the actions of the Spanish crown in the gloomy days of Bayonne. No wonder Napoleon threw caution to the winds. He repeated over and over at Bayonne that the conquest of Spain would be simplicity itself. Who would not make such an error after watching the royal dynasty fight out its petty quarrels while the fate of the nation hung in the balance? Ferdinand and his intimate advisors put up no resistance; they followed the easy path; they showed themselves lacking not only in courage but even in wits. They did not perceive that the great source of Ferdinand's future strength and power was as a symbol, not only to the millions of Spaniards who would soon resist Napoleon, but also to the millions of Americans.

What both Napoleon and Ferdinand had not counted on was the massive and virtually spontaneous uprising of the Spanish people against the French conquerors that began in late May 1808 and that quickly engulfed all the provinces not under French military control. The famous riot of the citizens of Madrid on 2 May was the first, and symbolically most important, of the uprisings, but the French forces occupying the capital brutally suppressed it with wide-scale executions. It was only toward the end of May, after news of the abdications of the royal family reached Spain and after the French ordered the remaining members of the dynasty to come to Bayonne, that the various provinces began to mobilize themselves, organizing governing juntas to direct political and military activities.

The first of the provincial juntas was organized in Oviedo, capital of Asturias, and on 25 May the "Supreme Junta of Government" proclaimed itself the possessor of sovereign powers in the name of the captive Ferdinand VII. The Junta of Oviedo immediately sent representatives to England to request, and receive, military and financial aid from Napoleon's chief enemy. In a breathless moment that few Spaniards had ever dreamed possible, England became Spain's chief ally. Other juntas quickly rose in Santander (Burgos), La Coruña (Galicia), Segovia, Logroño (Castile), León and Zamora, Ciudad Rodrigo (Salamanca), Zaragoza (Aragon), Valencia, Murcia, and Seville. In all the nation the insurrection against the intruders spread like fire. The junta that came into existence in Seville and that styled itself the "Supreme Junta of Spain and the Indies" spoke for the nation when it stated in its declaration of war against France: "We shall not put aside our weapons until Emperor Napoleon restores to Spain her king and Lord, Ferdinand VII, and the other members of the Royal Family and respects the sacred rights of the Nation, which he has violated, as well as its liberty, integrity, and independence."[42] The entire nation rose of its own accord, rejecting the constituted authorities who had cowered and temporized in the face of Napoleon's demands. The single person of Ferdinand became the national symbol of independence, freedom from conquest, and reestablishment of political, social, and religious institutions. It was the first spontaneous war of national resistance in modern history.

II

"A Kingless People for a Nerveless State"

All of Spain and its empire was swept into a maelstrom of war and revolution in response to the events of March-May 1808 at Aranjuez, Madrid, and Bayonne. But in America the uprisings, which were eventually to become wars of independence, were slow in coming. The initial response of the overseas kingdoms was not unlike that of the various peninsular provinces. There was at first widespread enthusiasm for the news of the overthrow of Godoy, who was as widely hated in America among peninsulars living there and among loyal Americans as he was in Spain itself. Some of the viceroys and audiencia members governing in America in 1808 were protégés or appointees of Godoy, which led to an initial wave of discontent against the favorite's friends, who, like the viceroy of Mexico, were quickly either overthrown by local response among loyalist peninsulars or else replaced by new appointees from the government that came into existence in free Spain. At any rate, we cannot trace in any detail here the story of the gradual coalescing of creolism and the eventual rising of American dissent against imperial rule, for what we are concerned with is Spain's response to the American insurrections.

The various provincial juntas of government that came into existence in Spain to fill the vacuum left by the king's capture led the national resistance to Napoleon for about four months. The most powerful of the juntas came to be the one at Seville. In July 1808 the armies fielded by Seville and other parts of Andalusia won a brilliant victory in the battle of Bailén, north of Jaén, temporarily clearing all of Andalusia of the previously victorious French armies. It was the first time since the creation of the French Empire of Napoleon in 1804 that a French army had signed a treaty of capitulation. The Spanish commander, General Francisco Xavier Castaños, became the first of the great heroes of the national resistance. Napoleon was stunned, and by the end of July his brother, the usurping King Joseph, was forced to evacuate Madrid after a residence there of but ten days. The victory, however, was only temporary and its effects incomplete, for Napoleon had many armies on Spanish soil and was able to divert further forces to the peninsula. In November the French emperor himself entered Spain to command his armies, and by 4 December Madrid had capitulated and the French were once again in the ascendant.

To provide a greater degree of efficiency in the conduct of the national resistance, the various provincial juntas eventually agreed to join together in a Supreme Central Governing Junta of Spain and the Indies, usually called the Junta Central. It was composed of two deputies from each of the provincial juntas, and eventually it invited the American territories to send deputies as well (although few Americans arrived in time to take their place on the junta). Under the presidency of eighty-year-old Count Floridablanca, a long-time minister of Charles III and Charles IV and a leader of the conservative patriots who looked for a restoration of the Old Regime, the Junta Central began meeting on 25 September 1808 at the royal palace of Aranjuez. The dominant personality in the Junta Central was Gaspar Melchor de Jovellanos, a moderate reformist who had been the chief victim of Godoy's despotism and had been jailed for seven years by the former despot. The celebrated poet Manuel José Quintana, foremost literary figure of the day in Spain, was the chief propagandist for the junta; Martín de Garay, a reformer and past and future finance minister, was its secretary-general. Giving itself the title of Majesty, the Junta Central created five ministries: State, Justice, War, Navy, and Finance. The Junta Central was wracked by political disagreement between conservatives and reformers, and the authority to create such a national government was openly doubted by the Council of Castile, to say nothing of many American creoles. Yet for a year and a half the Junta Central provided Spain and the empire with its only recognized government in opposition to the regime of Joseph Bonaparte. Many Spaniards advocated the creation of a regency of one, three, or five members to represent the captive king, and the all-important British allies, through their ministers to the Junta Central, John H. Frere (1808–09), Richard Wellesley (summer of 1809), and his brother Henry Wellesley (1809–22), strongly advocated both the creation of a regency and the calling of a parliament, or Cortes.

Even before the Junta Central came into existence, however, the two chief Spanish provincial juntas hastened to send word of their existence to the American territories and to dispatch commissioners to go in person to persuade the Americans to declare their adhesion to Ferdinand VII and to the particular junta in question. Although the Junta of Oviedo sent representatives to Mexico, the Junta Suprema of Seville (as it called itself) sent commissioners to all the major American territories. The Junta of Seville, indeed, considered itself the natural heir to the deposed monarch's mantle of authority in America and at first appears to have given little thought to whether the Americans would have a similar view of the situation or whether the other peninsular juntas would question Seville's authority. For a few brief months, from June to about August 1808, some of the American territories thus received highly contradictory statements from Spain concerning the vital question of who was ruling them. The extent of the confusion depended largely on ease of communication, so that the American kingdoms most quickly reached from Spain were subjected to intense, and dangerous, confusion in the summer of 1808, while those territories more distant from the homeland avoided much of the confusion.

New Spain, or Mexico, was the richest Spanish American colony, and it was the target of the most confusing directives from Spain. For example, Mexico City was informed of the overthrow of Charles IV by Ferdinand VII on 9 June 1808, less than three months after the event. It heard of Ferdinand VII's overthrow by Napoleon on 16 July, slightly over two months after the event. It was thus sufficiently abreast of the latest sensational news that local dissidents in the city council of Mexico City had adequate time to launch a campaign to induce the viceroy, José de Iturrigaray, a protégé of Godoy and a man hated by the Spanish peninsulars living in Mexico, to take the lead in establishing an autonomous Mexican junta. Throughout late July and early August, Mexico continued to receive word of the dramatic events in Spain—the rising of Madrid on 2 May and the creation of provincial juntas of government in Valencia, Seville, and Oviedo. The extreme confusion of the moment, and the viceroy's image as a tool of the hated Godoy, provoked a struggle in the capital between a handful of creoles who believed that the creation of provincial juntas in Spain was the signal for the establishment of local autonomy in America, and the peninsulars, powerful and entrenched, who decided to resist any change in the Old Regime even in the midst of the unparalleled constitutional crisis caused by the removal of the only legitimate sovereign.

Thus Viceroy Iturrigaray called a series of meetings of the capital city's leading citizens on 9 and 31 August, and on 1 and 9 September, to discuss Mexico's response. After the first of the convocations occurred, two commissioners from the Junta of Seville arrived, calling on Mexico to give its loyalty to Seville. This question divided the ruling elite further, since forty-nine members of the convocation voted to recognize Seville's authority and twenty-nine voted against. The very same day, representatives arrived from the Junta of Oviedo, provoking nearly everyone to confusion. As Viceroy Iturrigaray declared in the third meeting, on 1 September, "Spain is now in a state of anarchy, there are Supreme Juntas everywhere, and we should therefore not obey any of them." Fifty-four of the members of the convocation then voted to recognize none of the contending juntas in Spain. This stalemate forced Iturrigaray into a position that could be interpreted by his opponents as treasonous, and on 16 September 1808 the viceroy was overthrown by a cabal of conservative peninsular landowners and merchants in Mexico City, who replaced him with an octogenarian retired military officer who they thought would do their bidding.[1] Recognizing that a government created by act of the resident peninsulars was the most inclined to continue loyal to Spain, the representative of Seville, Juan Jabat, a vigorous and outspoken Spanish loyalist, assured the leaders of the coup in Mexico that their action would be perfectly acceptable in Seville.

At the other extreme is the example of Spain's second-greatest American viceroyalty, Peru. Because of the much greater difficulty of communication, Peru was months behind other parts of America in learning of the disaster in Spain. And its response, paradoxical though it may seem, was peaceful and tranquil in direct proportion to the lateness of the news. For example, it was never fully aware of the brief contest for leadership among the various Spanish juntas, because by the time news arrived in Peru various struggles in Spain had already been settled. Peru did not hear of the overthrow of Charles IV by Ferdinand VII until 9 August, nearly five months after the event. It did not hear of the abdications at Bayonne until 4 October, also five months after the event. And it took Peru over six months to hear of the creation of the Junta Central in Spain. Furthermore, because of Peru's geographical isolation the news that arrived there usually came at second or third hand. It heard of the dramatic events in Spain from the governors of Panama or Chile. When news did finally arrive, it was already laundered by other loyalist officials in other territories to remove the uncertainty or anxiety of the situation.

Naturally, other factors played a role in Peru's relative tranquility in the face of the undreamed-of disaster of 1808. Its viceroy, José de Abascal, was widely respected by the peninsulars living in Peru; he was not a protégé of Godoy, and his utter loyalty to the principles of Spanish colonialism and to the crown was never doubted.[2] Abascal, on hearing of Ferdinand's accession to the throne, declared that Peru would recognize him and, on hearing of Ferdinand's capture, simply moved up the date for the proclamation of the new king's accession. No one questioned whether Ferdinand should be recognized; no one agonized about which agency or junta should be recognized as speaking for Ferdinand. The new king was formally proclaimed on 13 October.

In the third great viceregal capital, Bogotá in New Granada, confusion was kept to a minimum by the apparent tact and diplomacy of the commissioner sent out by the Junta of Seville, Juan José de Sanllorente. He left Cádiz on 26 June as the Seville junta's delegate to the viceroy of New Granada; he arrived at Cartagena on 9 August and finally made it to the capital of Bogotá on 2 September. Though that was the very moment when the Junta Central was consolidating power from the regional juntas, little difficulty seems to have been encountered in Bogotá, because Sanllorente was chiefly concerned to have the authorities there recognize Ferdinand VII. The viceroy, Antonio Amar, reported that Sanllorente delivered all the news at once—of Ferdinand's accession, of his capture, and of the existence of a government of national resistance, whatever it might be called. Amar complimented the commissioner highly.[3] Meantime, naval officer Antonio Vacaro had also been sent by Seville as commissioner to Cartagena to bring the news of the capture of the king and royal family.[4] The viceroy of New Granada proclaimed the new king on 11 September.

Other commissioners carried the news to other major centers. The Marqués del Real Tesoro was sent by the Junta of Seville to inform Puerto Rico and Havana. The captain general of Cuba then officially informed the governor of Panama and the captain general of Guatemala in August, sending similar statements to the governments in Buenos Aires, Peru, and Chile.[5] The governor of Maracaibo in Venezuela was informed by the English governor of Curaçao, James Cockburn. He hesitated, however, to proclaim the news until he heard officially from the captain general of Caracas. Spain had sent the naval captain Joseph Meléndez, apparently representing Seville but like Sanllorente more concerned with the general question of recognizing Ferdinand VII, as its official commissioner to Caracas.[6] In Caracas the news of the French conquest had, however, provoked a struggle for power between the acting captain general and the acting regent of the audiencia, which was resolved in favor of the captain general.[7] Even in Buenos Aires, capital of the fourth viceroyalty, that of the Río de la Plata, the new king was loyally proclaimed, although in that territory the creoles, already conscious of their own power after ousting a British invasion in 1806 and again in 1807, were locked in a struggle for power with the peninsulars, who in turn were convinced that the acting viceroy, Santiago Liniers, a French-born officer, was in league with either the creoles or the French. On 1 January 1809 the prominent peninsulars in Buenos Aires failed in an attempt to overthrow the viceroy in the same way that prominent peninsulars in Mexico had overthrown the viceroy there, and the struggle for creole dominance was considerably advanced.[8]

The situation in Buenos Aires immediately commanded the special attention of the Junta of Seville, as it would command the special attention of all of the successive Spanish regimes throughout the next decade and a half. Buenos Aires was the only major center where it could be said that the struggle for independence had already begun even before the abdications of the Bourbons. The irregular manner in which Santiago Liniers had become acting viceroy, virtually as the self-proclaimed choice of the city's creoles, was so troubling that the Junta of Seville on 9 August 1808 appointed a second special commissioner, Joaquín de Molina, to go to Buenos Aires to investigate the charges that Liniers was about to go over to the French. In a series of reports written in January 1809, Molina reported that after conferring with the royalist governor of Montevideo, Francisco Javier Elío (Liniers's chief opponent), and after visiting Buenos Aires, he was convinced that Liniers was not guilty of pro-French aspirations.

But he also reported that his heart was still not at rest, "because I know that if there is no proof of his adhesion to France and to the plans of the Tyrant Bonaparte, nothing can deny that there is sufficient evidence to inspire a well-founded lack of confidence in his loyalty." He cited particularly the fact that Liniers had been in correspondence with a "foreign prince," that is, with the Prince Regent of Brazil and his wife, the Spanish infanta and sister of Ferdinand VII, Carlota Joaquina. This redoubtable lady had already launched a campaign to have herself recognized in Buenos Aires as the regent for her brother, since she was the only Spanish Bourbon not captive in France. Any movement to recognize her authority would, of course, have constituted the virtual transfer of Buenos Aires to the sovereignty of Portugal, as the porteños themselves recognized. The attempt came to nothing, but as of January 1809 Molina still feared that Brazil might make some move to take over Montevideo or that Carlota Joaquina herself might come in person to claim the sovereignty of Buenos Aires.

About the governor of Montevideo, Elío, who had created his own governing junta out of suspicion of the objectives of Viceroy Liniers, Molina declared that he was a hot-headed and intemperate leader but a man of loyalty and military talent. The attempted coup of

1 January, when the peninsulars who controlled the city council of
Buenos Aires attempted to force Liniers's resignation but were defeated by the creole troops of the viceroy, further convinced Molina
that both Liniers and Elío should be called to Spain to answer for their
conduct and that an effective new viceroy should be sent out from the
peninsula. He also urged Seville to distribute rewards to the creoles in
Buenos Aires for their defeat of the English invaders in 1806 and
1807.[9]

Another of the Seville commissioners to America, and in some
ways the most significant, was the Peruvian-born officer José Manuel
de Goyeneche. He was the man who actually brought Buenos Aires its
first official news of the calamity at Bayonne. He was the first man to
report to Seville on the suspicious conduct of both Liniers and Elío. As
a creole himself, Goyeneche's attitude toward the two leaders in the
Río de la Plata was markedly different from Molina's. For example, he
reported that Liniers was "generous and full of honor. He does not
know fear." But Elío he found "insubordinate and scandalous."
Goyeneche's real object, after bringing news of the establishment of
the Junta of Seville to both Buenos Aires and Montevideo, was to cross
the continent and obtain the support of Córdoba, Tucumán, Chuquisaca, Cuzco, Arequipa (his birthplace), and Lima. In Buenos Aires
on 27 August 1808 he wrote by hand the following message to the
viceroy of Peru and the presidents of Chuquisaca and Cuzco: "The
Emperor of the French and his government is our open enemy and any
of his subjects who appear by land or sea in these territories is to be
taken prisoner. We are at peace with England and Portugal."[10]

The reports sent back by the Seville commissioners were generally characterized by their comprehension of affairs in the various
American territories and in some cases by notable foresight. To a
government entirely dependent on written and oral reports for the
formulation of policy, this was of great importance, for the powers
that made decisions in Spain could not experience American events at
first hand as they could in the peninsula. The problem of conflicting,
unclear, or prejudiced information was inherent in a system of "government by remote control." And "remote control" it was, too. It
took from two to six months for information to reach the American

capitals from Spain, then it took the same time for responses to return to Spain, and again the same time for replies and orders to come back to America. In the case of Peru, for example, a year and a half might elapse between the initiation of a question in Spain, a response in Lima, and the return of a decision to the colony.

José Manuel de Goyeneche, for example, finally completed his arduous overland passage from Buenos Aires to Lima, which he had begun on 20 September 1808, in April 1809. En route he had sent back first-hand information about many cities and governments. Peru was his major objective, and he was able to report on 22 April 1809 that all of Cuzco and Lima were loyal to Ferdinand VII; indeed, he defined their loyalty as "electric." Of Lima he said: "This capital can glory with justice in the fact that nobody has vacillated for one minute." He sounded a prophetic note, however, when he reported that although he had not been to Chile he was aware that its government was weak and undefended, and declared: "It is the throat of South America, and once lost, Peru is lost."[11] Unlike the other commissioners, Goyeneche remained in America. In June he was appointed interim president of the audiencia of Cuzco, and would subsequently become a royalist commander in Upper Peru.

Juan Jabat, the commissioner of Seville to Mexico City, also played a major role in the country to which he was sent. He took an active part in the overthrow of Viceroy Iturrigaray and in the appointment of his successor by Spanish officials and merchants living in Mexico City. He wrote extensive reports to Seville, explicitly accusing Iturrigaray of having plotted to make himself ruler of an independent Mexico. He openly congratulated and encouraged the leaders of the coup, requesting that Spain ennoble and reward the chief peninsulars. He wrote the strongest accusations against the creoles on the city council, accusations that tend to receive credit in the traditional historiography and to lead some historians to believe that Iturrigaray and the cabildo were plotting independence. He urged Spain to throw the existing city councilors out of office and replace them with a cabildo made up half of Spaniards and half of creoles. He advocated a widespread program to bring young creoles to Spain for education and career service and young Spaniards to Mexico in order to overcome the rivalry he saw between peninsulars and Americans. He urged the appointment of a military officer as viceroy of Mexico and the establishment of a high-ranking officer as sub-inspector general of the army to take the place of the viceroy in case of death or disability. He demanded, in order to avoid the graft for which not only Viceroy Iturrigaray but also his wife and children were notorious, that any new viceroy be required to leave his family at home in Spain. To assure against the false politics of any future viceroy, he suggested that the audiencias at Mexico City and Guadalajara be made entirely separate from the viceroys, free of their influence, and that the salaries of the audiencia members be raised so high that they would never be tempted to give in to local pressures. He urged the establishment of urban militias of peninsulars and wealthy creoles in all of America to provide armed force for the maintenance of Spanish power. Finally, he urged the sending of a visitor general to conduct a high-powered investigation and reform of the entire political and military structure in New Spain.

In separate reports, Jabat also called the peninsula's attention to the threat of territorial aggression by the United States against the far north of Mexico, the Internal Provinces of the East and West. In this he was repeating the ideas of the Spanish Colonel Félix Calleja, who in 1813 would become the viceroy of Mexico and victor in the struggles against the great rebellions of Hidalgo and Morelos. It was Calleja's firm belief, as he wrote to Seville in a special report invited by Jabat, that "the United States, by their proximity, interest, and relations, must always be our natural and permanent enemies." Calleja believed an Anglo-American invasion of northern Mexico would occur in the spring of 1809, and he and Jabat proposed a series of military steps that could be taken to increase the defenses of the Internal Provinces. Fundamentally, Calleja believed that the only permanent solution to the danger was to populate the vast expanses of the north, and he proposed the establishment of colonies of soldiers who would be given land to plant and would be sent to the north with their families to create a series of twenty settlements along the Texas border to provide a permanent barrier against North American expansion. Jabat merely echoed Calleja's belief that North America was Mexico's natural enemy, suggesting that Anglo-American control of the Mississippi, Colorado, Arkansas, and Missouri rivers provided them easy access into the three frontier provinces of Nuevo México, Nevo León, and Téjas. He urged that Viceroy Iturrigaray's defunct plan to invite Catholic Louisianians to settle in the north be reactivated and that German allies of Spain be invited to settle there too.[12]

While the initial reports and suggestions of the commissioners sent to America by the Junta of Seville were being received and noted, the Junta Central, formed out of the various regional Juntas in September 1808, began to turn its attention toward clarifying its authority in the American territories. It was clear to the Junta Central's leadership that compromise was necessary in order to increase the chances of Seville's joining the central body. For example, three American advisors presented the Junta Central a memorial in September 1808 pointing out the extent to which the loyalty of the American subjects had vacillated since May according to whether their news of events in the peninsula came from France or from the juntas at Seville or Oviedo. They recommended dispatching new officials from the Junta Central to counteract the confusion, and they suggested a series of administrative reforms for Peru, Buenos Aires, and Montevideo.[13]

An equally serious difficulty was the long delay in the Junta of Seville's recognition of the full authority of the Junta Central. In August 1808, during the weeks that the Junta Central was coalescing in Madrid as the self-proclaimed chief authority in the empire, the Junta Suprema of Seville struggled to retain the prestige and power it had garnered for itself through its early organization of armies, its victory at Bailén, its early communication with American kingdoms, and its dispatch of commissioners to America. One section of the instructions of the Junta Suprema of Seville to its deputies to the Junta Central was entitled "Of the Indies and Its Navigation." Seville insisted that the central body recognize its right to exert authority over those American and Asian territories that recognized it, as well as over the kingdoms of Córdoba and Jaén and the Canary Islands, which had also joined the Seville junta. Overseas provinces that refused to recognize Seville were to be permitted to organize their own juntas supremas "and will have the government of their own provinces in the same manner enjoyed by the Juntas Supremas of Spain." These American juntas would propose candidates to be selected by the Junta Central as their viceroy, captain general, or commandant. Matters of trade and navigation would be decided by the juntas supremas in the American ports and in the Spanish ports engaged in American trade.

In other words, the Junta of Seville argued for autonomy for the existing peninsular juntas supremas and for any that might exist in America (there were none as yet). It insisted that "this power [regional autonomy] is inviolably sacred, since it comes from the people, and neither the Junta Central nor any other authority, with the exception of our king Ferdinand VII, upon his restitution to the throne, can curtail or diminish it." In addition to being the major impediment to the formulation of a central authority for all Spain, the Junta of Seville's startling support for the principle of regional autonomy, if it had become known in America, might have hastened the creation of the American provincial juntas that were finally organized in 1809 (in Quito and elsewhere) and in 1810 (in much of the rest of the empire).

The attitude of the Junta of Seville toward regional autonomy, and its insistence that American territories that already had regional juntas should also possess autonomy, is the first in a series of steps by which an embattled Spain came to proclaim the equality of the overseas territories with the peninsula. The real object of Seville was to assure its own continued dominance over American trade and American government, or, more precisely, to restore the monopoly of power that it had lost a century earlier when the old monopoly of American commerce had been transferred to Cádiz. Yet Seville proposed, as the means of maintaining its influence, the one idea— regional autonomy—that was most attractive to the colonial elites. As events turned out, it is uncertain whether Seville or any other peninsular power center would seriously have fulfilled a promise to extend full autonomy to American territories. The idea, however, would resurface over and over again, often initiated by the peninsula. Two years later the Cortes of Cádiz would proclaim in terms of crystal clarity that all overseas territories were equal to peninsular territories but, as will be seen, the principle would remain for Americans an unfulfilled aspiration.

At any rate, the Junta Central in Madrid did not accept Seville's pretense of possessing a prior right over American affairs, and through several months of intense political struggle it fought for primacy over Seville. With the help of the British, who preferred any central authority over regional authorities in the war effort, and as a result of the later failure of Seville's military endeavors, by January 1809 the Junta Central had emerged as clearly the dominant power. On 1 January the Junta Central decreed a series of regulations limiting the powers of the provincial juntas in Spain, theoretically to assure their equality with each other. They were no longer permitted to call themselves "Juntas Supremas," and became instead "Juntas Superiores Provinciales," subject to the Junta Central. Seville protested throughout January in three long statements. By this time, incidentally, the success of French arms in northern and central Spain had forced the Junta Central to flee to Seville itself, so that both of the contending juntas were now located in the same city. By February the Central issued a long and reasoned reply to Seville, apparently trying to sooth ruffled feelings in the name of war unity. In March the Central agreed to allow the Seville junta members to be called "Your Excellency," and Seville agreed to give in to the Central.[14]

Compromise was also the keynote of the Junta Central's choice of ministers and other individuals to head its government. As of October 1808 the government consisted of a noted liberal, Martín de Garay, as secretary general of the Junta, with a noted carry-over from the Old Regime of Charles IV, Pedro Cevallos, as minister of state. Benito Hermida was minister of grace and justice, and two war heroes, Antonio Cornel and Antonio Escaño, were ministers of war and navy respectively. Francisco Saavedra, a former finance minister under Charles IV, held that portfolio for the first ministry of the Junta Central.[15] Such was the state of confusion in political affairs, however, that incumbent ministers were constantly changing. Indeed, within a matter of a few days two of the five ministers appointed on 13–15 October 1808 had been shifted to different portfolios. Administrative confusion, which would be a notorious element of the reign of Ferdinand VII after his restoration in May 1814, was just as prevalent under the wartime governments. Between March 1808 (the overthrow of Charles IV) and May 1814 (the restoration of Ferdinand VII) the Ministry of State was held by thirteen men, Grace and Justice by nine, War by eleven, Navy by six, and Finance by fifteen.[16]

As the victorious French forces swept into Madrid in December 1808, the Junta Central and its followers fled in great confusion to Andalusia. José García de León y Pizarro described in his memoirs the confusion and sacrifice of those days. He fled Madrid on foot on 1 December, together with many prominent persons, but they were forced by the mob to return to the city. A few days later Madrid fell to the French and everyone underwent a harrowing flight through countryside occupied by the enemy. Many government leaders were without food or horses. The Duke and Duchess of Medinaceli fled Madrid on foot. Mobs in the outlying vicinity murdered some fleeing officers too closely associated with Godoy. After settling in Seville, according to Pizarro, at least, the Junta Central implemented rigid tests of the loyalty of those emigrants who had come from Madrid, often condemning good men as French supporters on the grounds of political partisanship. More than six thousand emigrants had fled to Córdoba, where the Junta Central ordered those people whose loyalty was not yet proven to remain. Pizarro insisted that the junta was interested only in creating vacancies in the bureaucracy to be filled by favorites, creating what he called "a monstrous government." It is worth noting, of course, that Pizarro condemned nearly every government in power in Spain between 1808 and 1833, with the obvious exception of his own when he was minister of state in 1812 and again in 1816–18.[17] In Seville, the president and chief figure of the Junta Central, Floridablanca, died. Even the venerable Council of State, the king's closest body of advisors and normally the most prestigious and powerful collegiate organ in the regime, was so disrupted by the flight from Madrid and the collapse of all of Spain except the south that it failed to meet. Indeed, from May 1808 until the meeting of the Cortes in September 1810, almost nothing was heard from the council at all, although some of its members did escape to Seville and others were newly appointed. After the Cortes began to meet, occasional references to the council appear in documents, but it was not an active agency again until the creation of a constitutional Council of State in January 1812.[18] Spain had become, as Lord Byron phrased it, "a nerveless state" that would ultimately be liberated only by the work of its own "kingless people." Pizarro put it similarly, saying that in all the crises that threatened the Spanish state "the Spanish people have saved it themselves, in spite of the frequent treason and continuous stupidity of their rulers."[19]

The Junta Central, then, was a highly disrupted government. Even so, it was all there was. Gripped by confusion and fear, loyal Spaniards everywhere turned their eyes to the Junta Central in the fervent hope that it would provide the government of salvation needed to rescue Spain. Between August 1808 and February 1809 duly-constituted authorities of the American territories—viceroys, city councils, prelates, corporations and institutions—recognized the Junta Central.[20] There was frequently a tone of desperation in the letters, but all recognized that it was a marked improvement for Spain to possess a single government that could have some pretense of speaking legitimately for the nation. The Mexico City Mining Tribunal touched on the theme of legitimacy when it declared that the Junta Central "constituted a single indivisible moral power which, legitimately representing the nation in its measures and resolutions, can provide uniformity, entirely extirpating even the slightest motive of division, discord, or partisanship."[21] The American dependencies, however, would never be the same again. The disaster of 1808 had brought down the political arm of the Old Regime and had served to release the heretofore pent-up aspirations of new social and political forces in both the peninsula and America. The Mexico City Mining Tribunal was wrong: the Junta Central not only could not stamp out the motives of division, discord, or partisanship that lay beneath the previously placid surface of the empire, it could but assist in releasing them.

According to Vicente Palacio Atard, the Old Regime in Spain had come to an end in social terms by the beginning of the nineteenth century. One cause was the rise of a new class of bourgeoisie—

centered on urban merchants and manufacturers—and a corresponding decline in the size and power of the privileged estates—the clergy and nobility—in the peninsula. The old society of estates (estamentos) was thus gradually disappearing, although the political structure before 1808 did not reflect the fact. Between 1768 and 1797, for example, the proportion of the national population of Spain who were of the noble estate (a privileged category including but not exclusive to holders of titles of nobility, since certain segments of the population, particularly in the north, also possessed this status) declined from 7.2 percent to 3.8 percent (or from 722,794 to 402,059 persons). Similarly, the estamento eclesiástico, the ecclesiastical estate, declined in the same years from 2.2 percent of the population to 1.6 percent (from 226,187 to 172,231 religious). The bourgeoisie, on the other hand, increased from 310,739 in 1787 to 533,769 in 1797.

Meantime, juridical privileges and guarantees for the two estates were being gradually worn away. The fueros and entail privileges, critical to the support of vested classes, were whittled away by various acts of Bourbon legislation. In the middle of the eighteenth century, for example, 80 percent of all land in Spain belonged to the crown, the nobility, and the church. This had been a force of great social stability in the Old Regime. The attack of the absolute monarchy against the privileges of the estates was directed chiefly against the practice of the sale and family alienation of public office, the institution of mayorazgo, or property entail, and the noble and ecclesiastical jurisdiction over rural land and rural administration of justice, the señorío or seigniory. From the time of Ferdinand VI the crown had begun to decrease the number of salable and inheritable offices. The campaign against the mayorazgo was initiated in 1764, the result of the Council of Castile's opinion that mayorazgos were generally harmful and should be permitted only in order to preserve titled noble families. Restrictions were placed on the kinds of properties that could be entailed; a new tax was legislated in 1795 requiring a 15 percent contribution to the state before establishing a new entail; and in 1789 and 1798 the crown authorized the withdrawal or alienation of certain types of property in mayorazgo. Palacio Atard says that from the end of the eighteenth century the mayorazgo was mortally wounded, and Doris Ladd has reaffirmed this for early nineteenth-century Mexico.

Meanwhile, Charles III initiated the attack against señoríos, and Charles IV continued it. Palacio Atard estimates that up to 25 percent of the national population, and up to 65 percent of the cultivated surface of Spain, were under señorío. Various royal orders—in 1787, 1802, and 1803—restricted the faculties of the lords by naming justices and authorities in their territories, eliminating their exclusive jurisdiction. In 1805, ecclesiastical señoríos were declared incorporated in the crown. The Cortes of Cádiz finally suppressed señoríos entirely, and though Ferdinand VII restored them in 1814 he did not return to the señores their privilege to name justices in all their jurisdictions. Add to these developments the long-term encouragement the Bourbon monarchs gave to the development of technology and enterprise capital in Spain, the policy of weakening the old artisanal craft guilds (gremios) under Campomanes, the coming of Enlightenment ideas in Spain, the Bourbon policy of industrial protectionism combined with limited commercial reformism, the encouragement provided even to foreigners and women to enter the work force, and the royal policy of appointing non-titled nobles to the highest positions in the bureaucracy, and it is clear that by 1808 the Old Regime was rapidly deteriorating.

Palacio Atard concluded his essay on this theme, however, by pointing out that the catastrophe of 1808 actually hastened the rise to power of the liberal bourgeoisie in Spain before that class was ready to possess power. The bourgeoisie was too weak, too undeveloped, to supplant the society of estates entirely. He cites two items to suggest the weakness of the bourgeoisie: despite the growth in economic power of this class, incomes obtained from commerce and industry still came to only 25 percent of the income of the nation in general, and, despite the rapid growth of the urban population throughout the eighteenth century, only forty cities in the 1797 census had more than 10,000 inhabitants in a total peninsular population of 10.5 million. Thus the bourgeoisie, who took power in the wartime emergency of 1808, were thrust prematurely into office and were organically weak as a class, not yet having achieved total social or cultural dominance.

The Old Regime was mortally wounded; the new regime was not yet mature; and the generation of 1808 would lead Spain into an era of massive turmoil.[22]

The effective paralysis of the Junta Central was largely owing to the fact that it symbolized and indeed incorporated the incipient power struggle between the old order and the bourgeoisie. It was composed of both and satisfied neither. It could not conduct the war at home, and rapidly lost credibility. It could not command the undivided loyalty of Americans, either. After all, in Mexico a coup to overthrow the incumbent viceroy and install a successor hand-picked by resident peninsulars was required before that territory even recognized the Junta Central. Richard Wellesley, during the five months in 1809 when he was British plenipotentiary to the Junta Central in Seville, complained frequently and bitterly of its ineffectiveness, claiming especially that it was jealous of the British armies fighting in Spain and reluctant to make special efforts to aid them. He insisted that the junta's chief weakness was that "its strange and anomalous constitution unites the contradictory inconveniences of every known form of government, without possessing the advantages of any. It is not an instrument of sufficient power to accomplish the purposes for which it was formed."

Of greater long-term consequence was the danger posed by the precedent of a self-mandated government speaking for the absent king. In a letter from Seville shortly before he returned to England to become foreign secretary, Wellesley insisted that "the duration of the present system of government in Spain cannot fail to prove highly dangerous to the genuine principles of her hereditary monarchy, by gradually establishing habits, interests, and views inconsistent with the lawful form and order of the government." Wellesley was a chief advocate of the idea that the Junta Central should dissolve itself and be supplanted by a regency of five persons representing the sovereign and a Cortes acting as parliament.[23] When Richard Wellesley left Spain at the end of 1809 he was replaced as British ambassador by his brother, Henry, who would serve in that capacity until 1822. Of course, yet another Wellesley brother, Arthur, future Duke of Wellington, was commander of the British expeditionary forces in the peninsula and soon to become commander in chief of all the Allies in Spain.

It is not surprising that the Junta Central's responses toward the grumblings it detected in America were disjointed, reflecting a government in crisis. The conservative and liberal elements within the junta contradicted each other. Throughout 1809, for example, the junta went to great lengths to keep American officials informed of the condition of Spain and the state of the peninsular war, apparently on the assumption that only forthrightness could defeat the alarmist propaganda of French agents. It was vital to show the Americans that Spain was still afloat in order to allay American fears of metropolitan defeat. In May the junta issued a general circular filled with optimism, pointing out that although the war was going badly the critical element to keep in mind was that Spain's resistance had forced Napoleon to commit so many troops to Spain that Austria was allowed to rearm. The intendant of the army in Havana wrote back to say how much the junta's circular had helped, for Cuba had been, "if not in ignorance, at least in uncertainty" about the condition of Spain. This was a common response. In July the junta's public circular could report French defeats in battles at Santiago, Lugo, and Puerto de San Payo and announce that Asturias had been cleared of French arms. However, the circular also detailed the defeat of General Joaquín Blake's attempt to reconquer Zaragoza when his conscript troops fled in panic. Most cheering was the news of the Anglo-Spanish victory at Talavera. By this point the junta was also promising reforms, speaking in terms of a "revolution in the Metropolis."

By the end of the year, the junta's circulars spoke of repeated military setbacks, counterbalanced, it hoped, by the junta's hastening of its plans to call the Cortes. Major reforms in tax collection had been adopted, and commissions had been appointed to draft reforms in law, in treasury, in ecclesiastical affairs, and in education.[24] Yet, in other circulars, intended for a more limited audience, the tone of the junta's communications was quite different. For example, it informed the Inquisition of Mexico in early 1809 that the French conquerors were bent on the destruction of religion, having already decreed the abolition of the Inquisition in localities they controlled and having taken the members of the Supreme Tribunal of the Inquisition as captives to France. They had also ordered the reduction of the population of convents by one third. These were the very same kinds of reforms the Cortes would advocate only a year later.[25]

Similarly, in the critical task of appointing new viceroys the Junta Central demonstrated its weakness. In early February 1809 the junta members discussed the qualities of the men who were to be chosen for the two viceroyalties in need of new appointments, New Spain and Río de la Plata. One advisor insisted that, in addition to the appointment of very strong viceroys, the junta should also select a capable individual from military ranks to head viceregal secretariats, apparently to supervise the viceroys. An indication of the level of personage the advisor had in mind is that he advocated choosing Pedro Agar, director of the royal naval academies and future member of the Regency, as viceregal secretary in Mexico.[26] He also advocated the removal from the various audiencias of all American-born members and the appointment of a new audiencia regent in Mexico. The proposal was firmly resisted by another advisor, who pointed out that the establishment of any office that would divide the viceroy's power or appear to demean his authority would seriously weaken Spanish control. He insisted that "the slightest alteration in the system of government observed [in America] since the Conquest is very dangerous." Furthermore, the junta debated but eventually rejected the idea that the new viceroy of Mexico should be chosen from among a member of the junta itself, so as to guarantee his absolute loyalty to that government. When the voting for the two viceroys occurred, the men chosen were of such extraordinary prestige as to make it clear that the junta wished to upgrade significantly the stature of the viceroys. Chosen as viceroy of Mexico was Antonio Cornel, and as viceroy of Río de la Plata, Antonio Escaño. Both were military heroes and then held or had recently held ministries—Cornel was briefly minister of war, Escaño was minister of navy and would be in 1810 a member of the first Regency.[27] Both men, active in the war effort, immediately refused the appointments. Escaño lamented that he had to refuse the viceroyalty, a position "that has always been the object of the emulation and hopes of so many, that has been viewed as the most brilliant and flattering termination of ambition," in order to retain his position as minister of the navy.

The outcome of the attempt to appoint two well-known military leaders to the two viceroyalties provides an example of the scatter-shot approach of the Junta Central. In Río de la Plata it appointed, instead of Escaño, a relatively qualified but little-known naval officer and veteran of Trafalgar, Baltasar Hidalgo de Cisneros. For Mexico, the richest of all overseas possessions and the one whose revenues were most vital to the peninsular war effort, the junta fumbled badly, appointing instead of a vigorous war hero and officer the elderly and virtually incompetent Archbishop of Mexico City, Francisco Javier Lizana y Beaumont. Both of the new viceroys took office in July 1809; both were removed from office less than a year later in May 1810— Cisneros was deposed by the creoles of Buenos Aires, Lizana was removed by decree of Spain on the urging of peninsulars living in Mexico who attested to his ineptness. Neither man ever gained the total support of even the peninsulars they were supposed to govern, much less the creoles. It was not until August 1810 that Mexico finally had a viceroy who was a vigorous and respected military officer as originally advocated, in the person of Lieutenant General Francisco Javier Venegas, but two days after his arrival in Mexico City open rebellion broke out in New Spain as well.

One of the examples of the difficulties of Spain's remote-control government of America, and an illustration of the complexities the Junta Central was unable to cope with, is the instructions Viceroy Cisneros carried with him to Buenos Aires in 1809. To be more precise, there were four sets of instructions. His initial instructions on 24 March ordered him to dissolve the pro-Spanish junta that Governor Francisco Javier Elío had created in Montevideo to resist the suspected pro-French leanings of the incumbent viceroy, Santiago Liniers. Cisneros was told in the most sweeping terms to apply liberal and just methods, avoiding force, and to do everything possible to protect and increase Platine commerce. On 9 April, however, a set of additional instructions for the new viceroy, who was about to sail from Cádiz, set a very different tone. He was informed that Viceroy Liniers had been corrupted by the political meddling of the Portuguese Princess Regent of Brazil, Carlota Joaquina. Suspicious of the pretenses of the princess to speak for her captive brother, Ferdinand VII, in claiming the loyalties of the Río de la Plata, the junta now told Cisneros to do everything possible to strengthen the pro-Spanish party of Governor Elío by naming him second in command of all the viceroyalty's forces. The new viceroy was to fix his residence in Montevideo and to send secret letters to commanders ordering them to obey no orders but his. He was to publish a proclamation promising reform in trade, agriculture, commerce, and taxation. As there was now to be a Spanish minister at the court of Brazil, the new viceroy was not to answer any letters from the princess or to have direct relations with the Portuguese court.

After Cisneros's departure from Cádiz the junta received new and disquieting news about the Río de la Plata with the receipt of English newspapers. Cisneros was informed that, according to the English, Viceroy Liniers had led a revolt in Buenos Aires and had been triumphant. In addition, Liniers was further connected to the French by the recent marriage of his daughter to a Frenchman. The junta concluded that although the English newspaper was not totally accurate, it contained enough news to provoke suspicion. It is notable that the junta had already received the initial reports of its commissioner to Buenos Aires, Joaquín de Molina, containing similar evidence, evidence that Molina himself shortly contradicted. At any rate, Cisneros was now ordered to take Liniers into custody at any cost and to bring charges against him and all the civilian and military leaders of the attempted revolt of 1 January. Imprisonment or death of the leaders was to be the new viceroy's chief duty. He was to win back the support of those troops loyal to Liniers by using force, by depriving them of support and funds, or by playing up the belief that Liniers had sold out to the French. He was to extend a general amnesty to those who had been led to revolt, removing their leaders from the country and promising reforms to all and sundry. The junta concluded, pointedly using the rarely-heard word "colony": "Their Majesties [the junta] know how harmful is the example of a revolution in America that aims at independence, how interested many European powers are in fomenting it, and how terrible this blow would be for the Metropolis in a time in which the extraordinary expenses of the war cannot be sustained without the revenues of the colonies, and it wants you at all costs to conserve Buenos Aires."

Finally, on 22 May, after Cisneros had long since departed, the junta sent him yet a fourth instruction, to the effect that they had now received commissioner Molina's later reports, that they knew the 1 January tumult in Buenos Aires was not a revolution as the English papers had said, and that Liniers had recognized Ferdinand VII and the Junta Central. Thus, the junta was still suspicious of Liniers but advised Cisneros to ignore their previous crisis instructions and to respond as conditions in Buenos Aires warranted.[28] So, in the span of less than three months, Cisneros was ordered to oppose Elío and support Liniers, to oppose Liniers and support Elío, to arrest Liniers, to do nothing about Liniers, to employ military force to subdue Buenos Aires, to issue promises of liberal reforms while avoiding the use of force, and finally, to do as he saw fit. As it happened, on his arrival in the Río de la Plata he removed Elío from office and sent him back to Spain where Elío would then be appointed by the Regency as the new viceroy and returned again to Montevideo.

Much the same confusion could be cited in instructions to other viceroys and commanders throughout the empire. It is not surprising, either, for the war in Spain was going so badly that the junta was in total crisis. Even as it announced its intention of receiving American delegates to sit as members of the junta, even as it proclaimed its intention shortly to call the Cortes, it let its real feelings show in private correspondence by calling the overseas territories colonies. It was because Buenos Aires was a colony, after all, that it was permitted no direct communication with Princess Carlota, the only member of the Spanish dynasty free of French captivity. Yet, three months before the instructions to Cisneros, the Junta Central had issued the first of several ringing promises of reform that Spain would issue. In January 1809 the Junta Central called on American territories to send delegates to join the junta, declaring: "The King . . . and in his royal name the Supreme Junta Central . . . considering that the vast and precious dominions that Spain possesses in the Indies are not properly colonies or factories as are those of other nations, but an essential and integral part of the Spanish Monarchy, [orders] that the kingdoms, provinces, and islands that make up said Dominions should have national representation . . . and should constitute part of the Junta Central." There would be one deputy from each of the four viceroyalties and from Cuba, Puerto Rico, Guatemala, Chile, Venezuela, and the Philippines.[29] This decree, which effectively proclaimed the overseas dominions equal to the peninsular ones, was a major step toward the declaration of outright equality for Spanish Americans.

Yet the number of representatives allowed to the Americans was so grossly disproportional as to make it clear that full political equality was not yet contemplated. Each viceroyalty and captaincy general was to send a delegate to the junta—chosen from a list of three candidates proposed by the city council of the capital. This, of course, was disproportionate even among the overseas territories, for Mexico, with six million people, was to have no more representation than Puerto Rico. In addition, however, there was a great disproportion between peninsular membership of the junta and American membership, for each of the peninsular provinces that had founded its own junta in 1808 was permitted two members on the Junta Central. In early 1809 there were two members each from Aragon, Asturias, Old Castile, Catalonia, Córdoba, Extremadura, Granada, Jaén, the Baleares, Murcia, Seville, Toledo, and Valencia, for a total of twenty-six, whereas the new decree allowed for only ten overseas members.[30]

Even when deputies to the junta were duly chosen by the American capital cities, usually amid great enthusiasm, they rarely got to Spain. The Peruvian delegate had traveled only as far as Mexico when he heard of the dissolution of the Junta Central and turned back to Peru. The rare example of the Mexican delegate illustrates the essential meaninglessness of the invitation. Mexico City nominated three candidates, two of whom, the brothers Manuel and Miguel de Lardizábal y Uribe, had lived nearly all their adult lives in Spain. The name of Miguel de Lardizábal y Uribe was chosen by lots and he became one of the few American members of the Junta Central actually to take his seat. Only a year later he became the token American member of the Council of Regency. But except for place of birth it is hard to see how Lardizábal would be considered an American. He had studied at Valladolid in Spain, had been appointed by Floridablanca to the Ministry of State (where he became official mayor), and had associated himself early with the party of the Prince of Asturias. After the French invasion he supported the resistance loyally and was duly rewarded. His election as Mexican deputy to the Junta Central was celebrated in Mexico City with public illuminations and an absurdly grandiloquent ode, written by the city treasurer, that concluded with the words: "Mexico chooses him whom God has chosen; Mexico boasts of him whom God inspires."[31] Yet, all through his career, as Regency member, councilor of state, and finally minister of the Indies, Lardizábal spoke for the peninsula, not for America. He was also a reactionary who, as a regent, would strongly oppose calling the Cortes.

It is clear that the Junta Central did not, indeed could not, provide a skilled government for the overseas empire. Its own internal weaknesses, the peoples' perception of it as a stop-gap emergency government, and the essential anomaly of a junta functioning as sovereign in the name of a captive monarch—all would have guaranteed its failure even if it had not also faced a victorious foreign enemy in possession of most of the peninsula. When it came to legislating for America, the Junta Central could do nothing but recognize faits accompli, as when it recognized the overthrow of Viceroy Iturrigaray in Mexico; recommend, as when it urged Governor Elío to maintain vigilance over Viceroy Liniers in Buenos Aires; or issue contradictory orders that no one could be certain would be fulfilled, as when it instructed Viceroy Cisneros to support different parties in Buenos Aires.

One of its few substantial acts in American affairs, and one of its last acts altogether, indicates its paralysis. In January 1810, less than a month before its collapse, the Junta Central decreed a series of substantial reforms for the benighted colony of Santo Domingo, including, notably, free trade, cancellation of various debts, and restoration of the archbishopric of Santo Domingo. The object was to grant rewards to the Dominicans who had struggled under Juan Sánchez to maintain a Spanish foothold against both the French and,

more seriously, the Haitians, who controlled the greater part of the
island. Santo Domingo's lamentable condition was summarized by
one advisor of the Junta Central: "Called by nature to be the first
colony of the universe, it only awaits the protection of an enlightened
government." And the Junta Central officially recognized that it had
been "unjustly ceded to the French Republic" by Spain.[32] Although
the grant of free trade without taxes on imported goods and without
payment of the sales tax on domestic goods was an extraordinary
concession—one that would have excited the aspirations of every
major territory in the empire—it was largely useless for a territory so
underpopulated and devastated as Santo Domingo. The cancellation
of official debts was motivated by the realization that the Dominicans
simply could not pay them under even the best of circumstances.
Santo Domingo was all but lost anyhow, and it counted for so little in
colonial affairs that there is no indication that any major American
territory was even aware of its having been granted absolute free trade,
nor is there any indication that local affairs in the colony permitted
such trade. For the rest of the empire, however, free trade would
become an issue of immense importance.

In the reign of Charles IV, as Spain became involved in wars
against France (1793–95) and against Britain (1796–1802) and
1804–8), the crown had surrendered its dedication to mercantilist
trade on three separate occasions and had legalized neutral trade in the
American territories. This occurred in 1797–99, in 1801–2, and in
1804–8, and was induced by war and the weakness of the Spanish
fleet.[33] It fell far short, of course, of being free trade, but it did
constitute the granting of licenses by both the metropolitan and the
colonial governments to foreign neutrals to trade in the Indies. It also
constituted, naturally, a serious blow to the interests of Spanish
merchants dependent on the maintenance of monopolies of trade,
particularly to the interests of the consulados in America and Cádiz,
the trade guilds. Not all merchants favored trade with foreign
powers—which especially meant with Britain—but some merchants, particularly the larger entrepreneurs with wide contacts in
British, French, and Dutch colonies in the Indies, did favor it
enthusiastically. The argument would continue until the outright

independence of the American countries. Despite whatever resistance might exist among consulado members in America, the strongest opposition to opening American ports to direct British or other non-Spanish trade came from peninsular agricultural and manufacturing interests and from the Consulado of Cádiz, the powerful trade guild that controlled about 90 percent of the trade between Spain and its empire. A Spanish government located in Madrid was relatively free to balance the demands of the Cádiz merchants against the overall interests, particularly the revenue interests, of Spain. But after 1808, as the government of military resistance moved first to Seville and then finally, in early 1810, to Cádiz, peninsular policies toward questions of American trade necessarily became dominated by the interests and wishes of Cádiz. This would, in effect, guarantee that Spain, even in the thick of the greatest crisis ever to face it, would not and could not lend a favorable hearing to American pleas for the loosening of trade restrictions.

Outside the control of official peninsular volition, an active and flourishing contraband trade in foreign, particularly British, goods in the American territories continued at all times. Whether in peace or war, British free ports in the West Indies, notably Jamaica and Trinidad, were the scenes of increasing trade with Spanish America, usually contraband but sometimes, as during the periods when Spain permitted neutral trade, legal. As early as 1792, the total value of British manufactures exported from the West Indies to Spanish territories reached 500,000 pounds sterling a year. By 1808 the value of such exports from Jamaica alone was over one million pounds sterling a year. British goods penetrated via Panama to Peru and Chile, via Jamaica and Trinidad to New Granada and Venezuela, via the British expeditions to Buenos Aires in 1806–7 and subsequently via Portuguese Brazil to Buenos Aires, and via Jamaica to Mexico, to such an extent that it partially made up for Britain's devastating trade losses following the creation of Napoleon's Continental System in Europe. Indeed, John Lynch argues that the compensatory effect of British trade to the Spanish colonies before 1808 accounts for Britain's official refusal to license any of the many proposals for military expeditions to conquer or emancipate various portions of Spanish

America. Britain's only false step in this process of subtle expansion of trade was the unauthorized expedition of Sir Home Popham to Buenos Aires in 1806 and the subsequent authorized expedition in 1807, which led to a British military fiasco. Even so, Buenos Aires could provide a constantly expanding market for British goods not only for consumption in the Argentine littoral but also in the vastnesses of Upper Peru. British commercial penetration of the supposedly closed Spanish American empire was well advanced before the outbreak of rebellions, and every shipment of the superior British cottons, woolens, and hardware whetted consumer appetites for more.[34]

In the realm of finance, a direct consequence of the declaration of the second war with Britain in 1804 was the extension to the American territories of the Consolidación de Vales Reales. This extraordinary and complex act was designed to disamortize or sequester the funds of pious endowments (*capellanías*), the empire's major source of mortgage capital, to pay for the European war. It ordered, in effect, the payment in full of all outstanding mortgages owed to the church funds. In some parts of America, Mexico for example, it has been estimated that full compliance with the Decree of Consolidation would have siphoned off perhaps two-thirds of all the capital in the colony, for the Mexican elite, like the elites of other American countries, traditionally borrowed heavily under very lenient terms from the pious funds (many of which had been established by their own families' bequests in earlier generations). Michael Costeloe has shown, again for Mexico, that these church funds were the closest things to banks in colonial Spanish America and performed a socially valuable function. Doris Ladd has argued that the Decree of Consolidation constituted a major political grievance against Spain among the Mexican nobility and elite. Most of the rich would have been ruined, for nearly everything they owned was mortgaged. Although no similar research has been done on the effect of the Consolidation in other American kingdoms, it may be inferred from the Mexican case that the same elite grievances would have occurred elsewhere. It is estimated that in the four years it remained in effect the Consolidation collected twelve million pesos in Mexico alone.[35] America actually

contributed very little to the disamortization program; far greater
revenues were collected in Spain, considerable amounts of which went
to Paris in the payments of Spain's tribute to France before 1804.

At any rate, the Consolidation Decree had been a bitter pill for
the Americans to swallow. Resistance to it is apparent in various pleas
of major city councils or acts of viceregal governments. In the panic
that swept America following the fall of the Bourbons in Spain it was
necessary to suspend collection of Consolidation funds. Viceroy Iturrigaray of Mexico did so, for example, on 22 July 1808, two months
before his overthrow. Much later, in October, when news of the
abdications reached Lima, the city council of that city requested
Viceroy Abascal to suspend Consolidation collections.[36] Since the
homeland itself was occupied by French forces, the Junta Central, as
one of its first acts, suspended Consolidation throughout the empire.

As the suspension of Consolidation suggests, in the wake of the
1808 crisis all normal revenue transfers between America and the
mother country were disrupted, as, indeed, was internal peninsular
taxation and collection. The Junta Central called on the American
kingdoms to contribute not only existing taxes but special collections
and donations. The response in the colonies was substantial in 1808
and 1809, that is, before the beginning of the colonial rebellions that
drained off revenues that might otherwise have been transferred
directly or indirectly to Spain. In 1809 and 1810 New Spain, for
example, collected an additional 6 million pesos from private sources
above its usual revenues for Spain. Peru sent Spain a special contribution in 1809 of 1.3 million pesos, and in 1810 it sent a contribution of
2.7 million pesos.[37] Indeed, Antonio García-Baquero shows that for
1809 the remission of funds from America to Spain at the port of
Cádiz (presumably the only effective reception center during the
peninsular war) was 43 million pesos. Of that sum, 48 percent came
from Mexico and 31.8 percent from Peru. These figures would
plummet by nearly 80 percent in 1811, and by 93 percent in 1812, as
the American wars began to have their effect. Still, the 1809 collections from America constituted a total of over a third more than the
largest revenues from America at any time during the two previous
decades.[38] Obviously, until the American rebellions broke out, the

New World could assist the mother country directly and in a way that counted.

Undeniably, the two greatest contributions of the Junta Central toward maintaining the empire intact was its effort to acquire the rapid recognition of its legality by the American territories, thus denying recognition to the French usurper who actively called on America to acknowledge his new dynasty, and its ability to collect both existing revenues (such as Consolidation money built up at Veracruz before 1808 but not yet dispatched to Spain) and new revenues (such as special donations and loans). Its two major negative effects were the initial confusion with which its foundation was accompanied—unavoidable, perhaps, under the circumstances, but clearly implying to American dissidents the weakness of Spain and the possibility of its proximate collapse—and the very precedent of the Junta Central itself.

Nearly every American territory that launched itself toward revolution in 1810 duplicated the peninsula's process of 1808—official refusal to recognize the Bonapartist usurpation, official recognition of the captivity of the legitimate monarch, official creation of a junta (in America usually called a provisional junta) to play the role the provincial juntas and Junta Central played in Spain, that of speaking for the absent monarch. In America as in Spain, the question of whether the new juntas should be based on estates, on municipalities, or on provinces remained unresolved in the general rush of crisis; in America as in Spain, the juntas shortly proved themselves unworkable; in America as in Spain, the juntas essentially represented the bourgeoisie (understood here as creoles, capitalists, landowners) rather than the bureaucratic, clerical, or noble elite; in America as in Spain, that change in representation was revolutionary in its implications. By the first months of 1810, in all parts of America, the thesis that, in the absence of the monarch, power devolved to "the people" (which in America meant white creoles and gentlemen, not Indians, mestizos, or castes of African heritage) was brought out, dusted off, and tried on for size. This was the lesson of the Dos de Mayo, of the peninsular juntas, of the rising of the Spanish people to resist imposition of a king they did not choose and did not acknowledge. What better proof was there of the continued existence of the "ties that bind" than the fact that the American Spaniards responded in the crisis of 1808 in the same way as the peninsular Spaniards? In a sense, the movement toward the creation of juntas in America was a reflection of the continuation of the transoceanic Spanish ethos, a reflection of the same constitutional weakness and of the same popular strength.

Even as the Junta Central struggled with the war in the peninsula it moved decisively toward convoking the Cortes, which would turn out to be its most important political decision. Despite disagreement between conservatives and liberals on the junta, the junta announced its intention of calling the Cortes in a decree issued on 22 May 1809. In the ensuing months a committee of five members debated the method of selecting deputies. By September the date for the opening of the Cortes was set at 1 March 1810. On 1 January 1810 the letters of convocation were dispatched, calling for one deputy to be elected for each peninsular city that had participated in the last Cortes, that of 1789,[39] plus one deputy for each peninsular provincial junta and one deputy for each 50,000 peninsular inhabitants, plus one deputy for each 100,000 *white* inhabitants overseas. The American representation was purposely kept disproportionately small, and, furthermore, since there was not enough time for American delegates to come from overseas, the colonies were to be represented initially by substitute deputies drawn from among Spanish Americans residing in the unoccupied parts of Spain. In the initial plans there were also to be representatives from the grandees, archbishops, and bishops, to represent the ecclesiastical and noble estates, but the letters of summons were never issued. Lovett explains that this was because of a lack of time and because "a full list of members of the upper classes could not be compiled in time."[40] The omission of direct representation from the nobility and clergy would profoundly alter the character of the Cortes when it eventually met, converting it from the model of the ancient Castilian Cortes, which had been based on the estates, into a modern bourgeois parliament with very different ultimate ambitions.

Then in November 1809 the fortunes of war took a very unfavorable turn. On 19 November the Spanish offensive toward Madrid was routed by a massive defeat at Ocaña. It was the worst defeat thus far in the war, with Spain suffering 10,000 dead and wounded, and losing 26,000 prisoners. Spanish morale in Andalusia, which had resisted the French and driven them out, was shattered. On 20 January 1810 the intrusive king, Joseph, personally led the French forces into the south, bursting through the defense of the Sierra Morena and within a month capturing Jaén, Córdoba, and Granada and threatening Seville itself. In the wake of the French assault on Andalusia the Junta Central collapsed. Toward the end of January 1810 its members fled south to the Isle of León and the city of Cádiz. The French armies, finding the way clear, took Seville on 1 February. They then raced to the Bay of Cádiz, where on 5 February they discovered the recently reinforced defenses of Cádiz were too strong to storm and established a siege across the bay facing the city. Here the future of Spain and its empire hung in the balance.

The Junta Central collapsed as a result of popular discontent provoked by military defeat and the French conquest of Andalusia. As its members fled south toward Cádiz, they were insulted and threatened on the road by the common people, who had lost all confidence in them. In early February, a five-man Regency replaced the defunct junta. Consisting initially of Francisco de Saavedra, Pedro de Quevedo y Quintana (bishop of Orense), Antonio Escaño, Francisco Castaños, and the Mexican Miguel de Lardizábal, the Regency now ruled free Spain. Although it was far more conservative than the Junta Central had been, it was located in the homeland of a thriving middle-class entrepreneurial population and the heartland of Spanish liberalism. At first, for example, the Regency hesitated to carry out the announced plans of the former junta to convoke the Cortes on 1 March. After many months of delay, however, the Regency was effectively forced by the organized pressure of Cádiz to convoke the Cortes, though it did not finally meet until September.

The Regency would be for the next four years a kind of hostage to the business and political interests of Cádiz. With the fall of the Junta Central, leading citizens of Cádiz had elected a new local organ of government, called the Junta Superior de Cádiz, which asserted its authority over the Regency. Since the Regency depended for funds on taxes raised in Cádiz and on the money sent to the port by Spanish America, it depended on the good will of the Cádiz junta. Lovett points out that, "in view of this, the Regency abdicated the direction of the national treasury to the local governing body."[41] This Cádiz junta consisted of about twenty leading merchants or officers and was chaired by Francisco Venegas, an officer and governor of Cádiz who would become viceroy of Mexico later that year. As long as the survival of the empire depended on the city of Cádiz, American demands for some loosening of the tight trade restrictions that encompassed them would receive no sympathy. Although the Regency and later the Cortes governed the empire, the Cádiz merchants dictated the terms of trade and commerce.

And the merchant elite felt no constraint about speaking directly to America. For example, shortly after the Regency issued a statement to America on 14 February explaining, in remarkably frank terms, the failures of the Junta Central and the reason for the creation of the Regency, the Cádiz Junta on 28 February issued its own statement to America. The Regency's decree, calling for the meeting of the Cortes, included the famous statement that would reverberate about the empire: "From this moment, Spanish Americans, you are elevated to the dignity of free men; your destinies no longer depend on ministers, or viceroys, or governors: they are in your hands." The Cádiz junta's decree, on the other hand, told of how the population of Cádiz had elected it to provide local government and proposed that this action should be a model to the empire: "This is a Junta whose formation should serve as a model to the people who wish to elect a representative government worthy of their confidence." It is true that the Cádiz Junta urged Americans to recognize the Regency as the sovereign, but it left no doubts that Cádiz was now the heart of the empire. Explaining what significance this had for the empire, Cádiz continued: "In what city, in what port, in what remote corner . . . does Cádiz not have a correspondent, a relative, or a friend? Our relations of commerce, of friendship, or of kinship extend throughout the world."[42] Cádiz was calling in its debts. The small but powerful network of merchants and monopolists who controlled intercolonial trade and influenced viceroys and governors in every American territory was thus informed of its increased importance and stature. The merchants' interests coincided with those of imperial Spain, for Spain herself needed them for survival. The two decrees were thus contradictory. The Regency, in effect, took yet another step toward declaring the equality of the overseas territories, whereas the Junta of Cádiz gave earnest of the increased strength of the monopoly merchants.

This was also, of course, a kind of imperial revolution. And thus the Regency actually called it in its decree. The bourgeoisie and liberal elements were now either in power or close to it. The crisis of war and conquest had temporarily obscured the multitude of differences that separated them from the Old Regime and the established elites; the liberals would never quite recognize that, but Ferdinand VII would when he returned in glory to his patrimony.

The fall of Andalusia convinced many Americans that Spain was now definitely lost. The rise of Cádiz convinced other Americans that the imperial trade yoke was permanent and that the monopoly merchants so hated by many creoles were now in power. And the fact that those same merchants called on Americans to elect their own local governments of confidence was a kind of signal to proceed to the selection of American juntas even in places that had attempted unsuccessfully to do so in 1808 or 1809. The rise to power of the liberals, the shift of the center of authority from Madrid or Seville to commercial Cádiz, was in itself an element in the initiation of the American rebellions. Spain was still a "kingless people," but with the rise of Cádiz it ceased to be a "nerveless state." The problem that faced both Spain and America was, of course, that the nerve center represented something very different from the traditional authority of king and council. All the signal flags were flying now to alert Americans that a new era was upon them, the empire was doomed, Spain was breathing its last and resorting to obviously desperate measures to provide the semblance of a government, anyone who did not act now would drown in the wake.

The Americans acted. Believing the loss of Spain to be near, Americans acted on their pent-up grievances by proclaiming their right to select juntas of government in the name of the absent king, just as the peninsular provinces had done and continued to do. But because these were imperial possessions rather than provinces of the homeland, their actions were deemed, both by Spanish authorities in America and by Spain itself, as revolts. During the months of shock following the fall of Andalusia the American insurrections began. Quito had already created a junta in 1809; it did so again in 1810. Other insurrections commenced, in Venezuela on 19 April, in Buenos Aires and Upper Peru on 22–25 May, in New Granada on 20 July, in Mexico on 16 September, and in Chile on 18 September. By the time of the first meeting of the Cortes, all of Spanish America except Peru, Central America, and the Caribbean islands was in revolt.

III

Promise versus Performance

The primary effect of Spain's first experiment in parliamentary and constitutional reform in the years from 1810 to 1814 under the Cortes and Constitution was that it revealed to Americans the essence of their status as colonial subjects. It was the hypocrisy of reform that was most salient. When the reforms of the Cortes, significant as they are, are applied against a yardstick of American implementation, when all the sound and fury of the first major clash between liberalism and conservatism in Spain is separated from performance, it becomes clear that the Cortes and Constitution of Cádiz did nothing to solve the American crisis.

Most histories of the era, largely written from a liberal point of view, laud the efforts of the liberals in the Cortes to reform Spain's political structure, an effort that reached its culmination in March 1812 with the promulgation of the Constitution of the Spanish Monarchy, Spain's first written constitution and the precedent for several Latin American constitutions. Of course the effort was laudable, and the men who made up the Cortes and wrote the Constitution included some of the most attractive figures in Spanish history. Nor was the liberal impulse an artificial or meaningless tradition in Spanish political culture, for the gradual decline of the Old Regime was, as we have seen, well advanced and the gaping void had to be filled. The fundamental problem is that the Cortes and Constitution were the work of one small portion of Spain and Spaniards, thrown into power by the exigencies of the peninsular war against the French conqueror. The war, the very thing that made the liberals' accession to power possible, also made the genuine implementation of their reforms impossible. Whether they consciously recognized it or not, almost every act of the Cortes was the act of a wartime government fighting for the liberation of the nation. The deputies might dream of a bright world to come, but in the meantime they had to win the war. And they were Spaniards, and the object of having an empire in the first place was so that it might produce revenues and goods for the well-being of the mother country. It is no surprise that the Cortes's promises turned out to be empty. It was, nonetheless, a surprise to many Americans. The overriding paradox is that this liberal and reformist government did nothing to satisfy the grievances of Americans, did nothing, indeed, to unite the two hemispheres of the empire. The Englishman William Walton, a noted opponent of the Cortes and Constitution, declared: "How a party of politicians and philosophers, circumscribed to a small spot of ground and protected only by the naval force of an ally, could during eighteen months sit quietly down and frame a constitution for the acceptance of nearly thirty millions of people, situated in three quarters of the globe, and opposed in interests as well as in habits, on a plan so defective in all its parts, is the most extraordinary of the many singularities which marked the Spanish contest."[1]

Although Walton's population figures erred on the side of generosity (the generally accepted population figures of 1810 were 10.5 million for peninsular Spain, and between 15 and 16.9 million for America and the Philippines) his essential point is worth emphasizing. In a number of ways they did not themselves recognize, the deputies who answered the Regency's summons and convened in the general and extraordinary Cortes on the Isle of León on 24 September 1810 represented only a small portion of peninsular Spanish thought, to say nothing, indeed, of overseas opinion. Even by the time of the promulgation of the Constitution a year and a half later, that weakness had not really been corrected. In addition to the major problem of inequality of representation among the various parts of the empire, later events would suggest that the liberal impulse itself did not represent the general objectives of peninsular Spain. The full depth of the failure of the Cortes in American questions can best be measured in three broad categories: its failure to accede to the two fundamental demands of the Americans who were prepared to give Spain the chance to respond—the demand for equality of representation and for freedom of trade—as well as to a multitude of local or regional requests for reform; its failure to arrive at a general policy for the pacification of the American territories; and its failure to command complete implementation of the acts it did legislate, most notably the Constitution. Perhaps at no other point in Spanish history did so much promise produce so little performance.

The matter of equal representation and the failure of Americans to achieve it was fundamental. The initial convocation of the Cortes issued on 1 January 1810 by the Junta Central called for one American deputy for each 100,000 *white* inhabitants overseas, who would make up a disproportionately small delegation compared to peninsular deputies, who were to be elected on the basis of one for each city with a vote in the previous Cortes, one for each provincial junta, and one for each 50,000 inhabitants. The American territories, furthermore, were to be represented at first by substitute deputies (as were the occupied provinces of Spain) consisting of natives of those provinces resident in Spain. After the fall of the Junta Central, the creation of the Regency, and the flight to Cádiz, the scope for selection of substitute deputies was considerably narrowed. In August 1810 it was decided that the substitute deputies representing both America and the occupied peninsular provinces should be chosen from persons native to those provinces resident in Cádiz. There would be fifty-three substitutes in all, of whom thirty would be from America. The selection process was thus simplified, and the politics of candidates was pre-determined by the fact that only those Mexicans or Peruvians, Castilians or Catalans resident in Cádiz were eligible and they were selected by their own countrymen. Consequently, the first members of the extraordinary Cortes were largely liberals, patriots, and surprisingly young, because the people who had fled to Cádiz were largely liberals, patriots, and young enough to have undertaken the arduous journey to what was thought of as a last enclave of free Spain. When the Cortes first met in the church of San Pedro on the Isle of León on 24 September 1810, there were 104 deputies, 47 of them were substitutes, and 30 of those represented overseas territories.[2] Of course elections for proprietary deputies from overseas were being conducted in America, and those Cortes members would be arriving in the months ahead. At its highest, the total number of deputies in the Cortes was over 300. Artola says that at no time did more than 223 deputies ever sign an official act of the Cortes.[3]

The first act of the Cortes on 24 September was to declare the Cortes the possessor of national sovereignty, an act of extraordinary significance in what had heretofore been an absolute monarchy in which all power rested with the king as sovereign. Henceforth the king was head of state, and in his absence the Regency. The act of 24 September also recognized Ferdinand VII as legitimate king, declared the abdications of Bayonne null and void, and divided the government into the three branches of legislative, executive, and judiciary. Two of the five regents—the chairman the bishop of Orense and the American Miguel de Lardizábal—were actively hostile to this new body that now declared itself to be the seat of sovereignty, thereby relegating the Regency to the position of executive. On the night of 24 September the bishop of Orense refused to appear to take the oath of loyalty to the Cortes. By the end of the next month the Cortes accepted the resignation of all the first Council of Regency and appointed a new Regency consisting of three members: Joaquín Blake, a general; Gabriel Císcar, a naval commander; and Pedro Agar, a frigate commander who represented America. Henceforth the Regency was subservient to the Cortes.

The American deputies, under the able leadership of the young liberal representing New Granada, José Mejía Lequerica, immediately launched their struggle to obtain equal representation for America. Since the peninsular population was then 10.5 million and the overseas population, for which no single valid census existed, numbered between 15 and 16.9 million, control of the Cortes rested in the balance. Indeed, even before the Cortes opening the Americans in Cádiz had presented a protest saying that they expected parity in the matter of representation. On 25 September, the day after the opening of the Cortes, a party of the American substitute deputies submitted a draft decree providing that immediate steps be taken to raise the American representation to the same basis as the peninsular, that is, one for each 50,000 inhabitants, and that the count should be based on all free subjects, that is, including all Indians, mestizos, and castes of African heritage in America. The peninsular deputies strongly opposed the proposal and rejected the draft decree. The key to the problem is that, although there were far more Americans than peninsulars, there were far fewer American whites (2.5 to 3.2 million) than peninsular whites (10.5 million). Thus, as Rodríguez phrased it: "Spaniards adamantly resisted any attempt to give two and a half to three million whites overseas the opportunity to control Spain's parliamentary system because of their dominant position in the societies of America and the Philippines. This would mean that an overseas white would have three times the political power of a Peninsular."[4]

On 1 October, Mejía, who is generally reputed to have been the finest orator of the entire Cortes, the only real rival of the leader of the peninsular liberals, Agustín Argüelles, and whose brilliant career was cut short by his death from yellow fever in 1813 at the age of thirty-four, returned to the fray with a proposal that the overseas territories be granted a decree proclaiming the equality of "their natives and free inhabitants" with the peninsular population. Arguing in moving terms for recognition of the equality of the vast American populations of mixed blood, Mejía pointed out that the American rebellions owed much of their force to their ability to attract the support of that population. Impressed by the potentially inflammatory nature of the matter, the Cortes deferred further debate on American equality to future closed sessions. According to James F. King, the question quickly came to rest on whether the castes (mixed persons of African heritage) should be counted in apportionment of representation. There was general agreement that the creoles, Indians, and mestizos should be counted, although the equality of the Indians and mestizos would remain purely nominal. Once the debate was centered on the status of the free black population—which formed a large portion of the population in many American territories and whose social threat many white Americans fully recognized—a compromise became possible. On 15 October the Cortes accepted a compromise decree proposed by Ramón Power of Puerto Rico that declared that Spain recognized the "indisputable concept that the Spanish dominions of both hemispheres form a single monarchy, a single nation, and a single family," and that "natives derived from the said European and overseas dominions are equal in rights to those of this peninsula." This, in other words, excluded from equality those persons not "derived" from America or Europe, that is, the blacks and mulattoes who were deemed to have "derived" from Africa. The Cortes decree also announced that those countries where "commotions" existed would be granted a general amnesty if they recognized the "legitimate sovereign authority" of the Cortes.[5]

The decree of 15 October constituted the formal declaration of the equality of all white, Indian, and mestizo Americans with peninsulars and of the overseas territories with metropolitan Spain. The process begun in 1809 with the recognition of the overseas territories as integral parts of the monarchy was thus completed with the declaration of their equality. This was the most momentous promise Spain ever made to its empire. Spain thus added the principle of equality to the other leading concepts on which the imperial ethos was based. Indeed, the concept of the empire as "a single monarchy, a single nation, and a single family" incorporated the ideals of "Father King" and "the ties that bind." But in bringing these concepts to their logical conclusion Spain also stumbled into a political and ideological trap from which it could not extricate itself. The issue of equality became the cutting edge that would demonstrate to moderate Americans the inherent contradiction of empire, for neither the Constitution and Cortes nor the restored absolutist regime of Ferdinand VII after 1814 would prove able to deal satisfactorily with the problem of equality. Once it was officially declared, the ideal of imperial equality could not be withdrawn without doing irreparable harm to the political relations of America with the peninsula. At no point, not even after 1814, was the official principle specifically nullified.

But if it was impossible to withdraw, it was also impossible to implement, for to do so would deprive Spain of the benefits of empire. These benefits were not merely, or even primarily, financial; they were also psychological. Just as the Spain of 1810 needed the support of the dominions to save itself from foreign conquest, so the Spain of post-1814 would define its national greatness in its role as the founder of a New World empire. How could the father of this single family permit the separation of his children? How could the single monarchy and the single nation be divided? The Americans, for their part, threw themselves into the attempt to win implementation of the decree of equality. It would form the fundamental basis of debate over American policy throughout the remaining years of Spanish control. The debate, in the Cortes and after its demise, would revolve around the two key questions of political equality and equality of trade and commerce. These were the issues that defined America's complaint. In an effort to win the support of the overseas territories for its struggle against the French, Spain in 1810 had declared America to be equal; yet it could not and would not treat it as equal.

Leadership of the American caucus on the representation question now passed to the Peruvian substitute deputy Vicente Morales Duárez, less radical than Mejía but a liberal nonetheless, another young deputy who would also die in his early thirties in Cádiz, in this case in 1812 just a few days after being elected president of the Cortes (the first American so honored). It was Morales Duárez who led the fight and apparently wrote the eleven propositions presented by all the American deputies to the Cortes on 16 December 1810. The eleven propositions, about which more will be said later, constituted the basic program of the American caucus in the extraordinary Cortes, and included a demand for free cultivation of all crops, free trade within the empire and with other nations, the abolition of monopolies, free mining and sale of mercury (which was the essential ingredient used in the refining of silver), equality of creole appointment to public office, and a number of major items. The first proposition, however, was for equality of representation between Spain and the colonies for "natives derived from both hemispheres, Spaniards as well as Indians." In other words, it asked for implementation of the 15 October decree, but excluded free black men, a proposition of which Morales Duárez, at least, approved. Thus, by the end of 1810 even the Americans themselves defined the term "equal representation" as equality of representation for Indian, mestizo, and creole inhabitants only, already excluding the large black populations. King believes some American deputies adopted the formula merely as a minimum demand, intending to return to the question of African representation at a future time. Debate on the question continued from 8 January 1811 intermittently until 7 February. The Americans demanded that further deputies be summoned from overseas; the peninsulars countered by arguing that the matter should not be dealt with until the writing of the forthcoming constitution. The proposition was effectively nullified when on 7 February the Cortes voted in favor of recognizing the general principal of equality of representation for whites, Indians, and mestizos but voted against applying the principle to the existing Cortes, which was even then beginning debate on the constitution.[6]

The question of "equality" had now narrowed down to a debate over how to exclude the vast population of African descent without appearing to nullify all the high-sounding pronouncements of the last three years. In the draft constitution presented for Cortes debate on 18 August 1811 the matter was settled by giving an affirmative sound to an essentially negative enactment. Article 1 of the constitutional draft declared that "the Spanish Nation is the union of all Spaniards of both hemispheres," and Article 5 defined "Spaniards" as "free men born and domiciled in the domains of the Spains," foreigners who had acquired letters of naturalization from the Cortes, foreigners who had resided ten years in the monarchy, and freedmen from the moment of their emancipation. By this article, then, all American Indians, mestizos, and castes of African heritage were proclaimed "Spaniards." But being a "Spaniard" was not the same as being a "citizen." Article 18 proclaimed that citizens—that is, persons able to exercise the vote and on whose numbers apportionment would be based—were "Spaniards who on both sides trace their ancestry to the Spanish dominions of both hemispheres." In short the compromise of the 15 October decree was continued in the Constitution. Article 22 dealt with persons of African origin as a separate element in the population, proclaiming for them the creation of "a door of virtue and merit." The Cortes would grant citizenship to such persons who had given "meritorious services" to the nation and who were of good conduct, so long as they were legitimately born, were married, exercised some "useful" profession or occupation, and possessed capital. Finally, Article 29 declared that the basis for apportioning representation in Spain and the Indies was "the population composed of those native-born who from both lines are derived from the Spanish domains."[7] These principles having been accepted, although Article 29 was over the strong objections of Americans, there was no danger in Article 28, which declared that "the base for national representation is the same in both hemispheres," or in Article 31, which declared that there would be a deputy for every 70,000 population in both America and the peninsula. Thus on paper the apportionment was equal, one deputy for each 70,000, and the blacks were granted an "open door" to citizenship through merit and virtue. But in fact the black population in America was excluded from being counted and from participation. This would guarantee a peninsular majority in the Cortes.[8]

It is a startling feature, indeed, of this most liberal, even revolutionary, constitution that it built in gross discrimination against America. It thus set the tone for all Cortes actions toward America. Although many American creoles would find themselves deeply compromised in their own attitudes toward the mulattoes and blacks who lived among them, the fact remains that America was denied its just representation, a representation that would have given Americans a majority in the Cortes. This would naturally haunt all further dealings between the overseas territories and the supreme parliament that now declared itself the possessor of sovereign power. King says that "the denial of an equal basis of representation, more than any other act of the Cortes, encouraged and justified incipient revolt in America." It provided fuel for anti-Spanish propaganda, agitated and angered even the most pro-Spanish elements among the creoles, and reaffirmed the peninsulars' smug possession of power. Even some of the American deputies to the Cortes favored excluding the blacks and mulattoes from active participation in politics, but only one favored overlooking them in apportionment. Five of the twelve men who drafted the Constitution in special committee were American. Of these, three supported Article 22—the Peruvian Morales Duárez, who felt the blacks were a social threat; the future bishop of Puebla, in Mexico, Antonio Joaquín Pérez, who actively courted Spanish peninsular favor and was conciliatory on American matters; and the Cuban Andrés Jáuregui, who feared suppression of the slave trade. Only the Mexican Mariano Mendiola and the Chilean Joaquín Fernández de Leyva, reflecting the fact that their countries had few blacks, strongly favored citizenship for them. In discussions of the apportionment article, Article 29, only Pérez voted with the peninsular majority.

More ominous, perhaps, was the fact that the committee to draft the constitution also included Spain's foremost liberals, the very men who were promoting reform in so many other questions such as possession of sovereignty, free press, abolition of señoríos, and abolition of the Inquisition. Agustín Argüelles, the leader of the liberals, and Diego Muñoz Torrero, president of the constitutional commission and the leader of the liberal clergymen, the man who proposed the decree of 24 September that transferred national sovereignty to the Cortes, both supported and argued for Articles 22 and 29. Even at its best, then, Spanish liberalism did not extend to the point of risking Spain's dominance over its colonies. Even to the liberals, under the screen of decrees proclaiming the equality and integral nature of the overseas territories, America remained a group of colonies. This was the fundamental failure of vision of the Cortes as it affected American questions. Argüelles admitted that he found "an insuperable obstacle" in "a population which exceeds that of the mother country."[9]

It was not simply the failure of the Cortes to implement the full equality of Americans that offended, it was also the terms employed by peninsulars to describe Americans in this and other debates. Three years later, the Peruvian José de Baquíjano, Conde de Vistaflorida and a former councilor of state, wrote a scathing indictment of what he called the "antipolitical conduct" of the Cortes and of the peninsulars. He remembered the debate over Article 29, in which, he said, "the leader of the liberals (Argüelles) reproduced the most contemptible sophisms to argue that the Indians were slaves by nature." He continued: "One ecclesiastical deputy said, 'If [the Indians] are equal in rights it will be necessary to suppress the tributes, and that is not convenient'; another asked if Americans were white and professed the

Catholic religion; and ultimately one deputy who had extracted his wealth from South America concluded 'that it had never been known to what genus of animal the Indians belong.'"[10] Although Baquíjano might not have been quoting the deputies accurately, he was interpreting what he perceived as their view of Americans.

The most emotional point in the debate over Article 29 occurred on 16 September 1811 when a memorial from the Consulado of Mexico was read from the floor. The memorial was phrased in such violently scurrilous wording as to make it seem almost apocryphal. It was not, however, for nearly every American deputy later referred to it in various writings, Baquíjano discussed it in his memorial, the *Diario de Cortes* carried a full coverage of the American deputies' reaction to it, and Mexican rebels used it for anti-Spanish propaganda. After it was read, the entire American deputation attempted to withdraw from the Cortes but was blocked at the door by the guards on orders from the president. For the next four days discussion of Article 29 was suspended while American deputies vainly sought redress against the authors of the memorial, but the Cortes eventually voted to seal the memorial and file it in the archive. To the American deputies the Consulado of Mexico was perhaps the foremost symbol of peninsular power in American commercial and social affairs, for, in league with the Consulado of Cádiz, it dominated trade between the motherland and its richest colony. The memorial condemned all Americans of all racial categories as unfit for equal representation in the Cortes. Among other intensely insulting things, the consulado declared the Indians to be "stupid by constitution, without innovative talent nor intellectual force, abhorring the arts and occupations, drunk by instinct, . . . carnal in habit, . . . devoid of ideas about continence, honor, or incest." The mixed-blood people, it said, were "incontinent drunkards, laggards without honor, gratitude, nor loyalty, without notions of religion, nor about morals, without luxury, cleanliness, nor decency, they seem more mechanical and intemperate than even the Indians." The creoles were only more refined in their vices, "the native-born whites [waste] in a few days through gambling, lovemaking, drinking, and [extravagant] clothing the inheritances, dowries and acquisitions that should have kept them all their lives," and having done so "console themselves . . . with dreams and schemes of independence which will make them dominant over the Americas." Concluding that Mexico was Spanish by right of conquest, the consulado advocated that the country be represented in the Cortes by designated Spaniards only, and expressed the thought that the only appropriate parallel between the Indian and the Spaniard was that between "a flock of gibbon monkeys" and an advanced culture of urbanites. [11] Baquíjano later paraphrased this by saying the consulado had called the Indians orangutans, but the sentiment was the same and Americans bristled with fury. Even so, on 29 September Ignacio de la Pezuela, head of the secretariat of the Cortes, wrote the Mexican viceroy a letter of praise for the consulado, though admonishing it for its lack of discretion in the memorial. [12]

When compared to the full sweep of their reform enactments, the failure of the peninsular Cortes deputies to consider the just grievances of Americans becomes clearer. The total reform program was undoubtedly impressive, but, though it theoretically applied to the peninsula and to overseas, it was conceived of in terms of peninsular needs and reflected the interests of peninsular liberals. Americans, generally counted among the liberal camp, usually supported the reforms even though they remained disenchanted with the myopic vision of peninsular deputies. Perhaps the most significant reform, at least symbolically, was the decree of 24 September 1810 vesting sovereignty in the Cortes, later repeated in the Constitution of 1812. There were many other significant enactments, however. They included the decree of freedom of the press to publish political ideas without prior censorship (10 November 1810); the abolition of the Indian tribute in America and of the mita, or Indian forced labor (13 March 1811); the abolition of the seignorial regime in the peninsula and of all jurisdictional and feudal privileges throughout the empire (6 August 1811); the abolition of restrictions for entry into the military and naval academies to nobles (17 August 1811); the order for the sale of uncultivated or unclaimed land to private individuals (January 1813); the restriction on the numbers of religious communities destroyed or damaged in the war that could be reestablished in free Spain (18 February 1813); the abolition of the Inquisition (22 Febru-

ary 1813); the abolition of the guild system in the peninsula (June 1813); and the institution of a new peninsular system of proportional taxation (September 1813). The two acts relating to the Church—abolition of the Inquisition and restriction on the reestablishment of religious communities—had the most massive effect on domestic peninsular politics by increasing the gap that separated liberals from conservatives, or *serviles*, in the Cortes. [13] It is noteworthy that only one of these major enactments of the Cortes referred to an exclusively American question, abolition of the Indian tribute and mita, and its confused enforcement will be discussed further on.

The crowning achievement of the Cortes, of course, was the Constitution of 1812. Drafted by a commission of fifteen deputies, it was presented to the Cortes for debate in August 1811 and finally promulgated on 19 March 1812. The constitutional commission, in its preliminary discourse, written by Agustín Argüelles, argued that the new written constitution was but a restatement of traditional Spanish laws and customs drawn from the Visigothic and Medieval eras. The object, in theory, was to reestablish ancient privileges and freedoms that had been superseded by centralized absolutism and ministerial despotism since the unification of Spain. In fact, however, the Constitution of 1812 was more innovative than renovative, replete with the influence of Locke, Rousseau, and other Enlightenment thinkers. Consisting of 10 titles and 384 articles, the Constitution swept away the absolute monarchy, decreeing that "sovereignty resides essentially in the Nation" and that the Cortes was the lawmaking body whose decisions the king could veto but that could in turn override a royal veto after passing an act three separate times. It limited the king's powers in regard to legislation to those, essentially, of sanctioning and promulgating laws. It established sixteen basic powers of the king over the executive branch in the realms of appointment, treasury, the military, and diplomacy; but it provided a list of twelve restrictions on the king's authority, including the provisions that he could not leave the country, marry, enter into alliances or commercial treaties, or abdicate without the consent of the Cortes. It placed the royal family on a financial allottment determined by the Cortes. It created seven ministries and a single Council of State that took the place of all former councils. It decreed a new, separate judicial structure, specified the process for the election of Cortes deputies, created elected provincial deputations and city councils, and reduced the viceroys and governors to the status of superior political chief. The Constitution continued the practice, or myth, already established by the Cortes, Regency, and Junta Central, of viewing all parts of the empire as indivisible and one. Article 1 declared, "The Spanish Nation is the union of all Spaniards of both hemispheres," and throughout the document the political unit was called either "the Spanish Nation" or "the Spains." At no point was specific reference made to America as being in any way different from the metropolis. A fundamental error of the liberals, indeed, was that, like the conservatives, they scarcely seemed to recognize America's separate existence. The success of the Constitution might have been enhanced if it had recognized some of the complex differences in society, economics, customs, even geography that so distinguished the American Spain. It was a European constitution for a European Spain.

The Constitution's greatest weakness was thus the way in which it treated the vast empire as a monolith. No doubt the liberals intended the document to exercise a leveling influence, for their ideology required them to think in terms of one state composed of one people. Furthermore, the intent of the Constitution, like the earlier Bourbon reforms, was to continue and extend Enlightenment principles of centralization. The provincial deputations, for example, were not designed to encourage devolution of power to the provinces overseas but, rather, to serve as an agency for the implementation of central government policies. [14] It is obvious that many conservatives would despise the Constitution for its refusal to recognize fully the vast panoply of existing special privileges, the society of estates, and the royal prerogatives. The first and most famous conservatives to protest the Constitution and the actions of the Cortes were Pedro de Quevedo y Quintana, bishop of Orense and chairman of the first Regency, who was declared by the Cortes unworthy of the name of Spaniard, stripped of all honors and civil income, and expelled from Spain; and Miguel de Lardizábal, the American member of the first Regency, who was condemned to exile by a special tribunal of the

Cortes for protesting the validity of the doctrine of national sovereignty.[15] Both men would be rewarded by Ferdinand on his restoration for their defense of the royal prerogatives.

But many Americans would also come to despise the Constitution for its refusal to recognize the special status of the Indian or for its notorious discrimination against the blacks. It could be, and was, used in America to discriminate against the Indians, for it declared them to be "Spaniards," and in Article 339 it declared that taxes were to be distributed proportionally among all Spaniards without exception or special privileges. In Peru, Viceroy Abascal took this to mean, following abolition of the Indian tribute and mita, that the Indians were subject to the same taxes and customs duties as all other people, whereas traditionally the Indians were excluded from any contribution but the tribute and mita, and a previous decree of the Regency had specifically exempted the Indians from personal tax.[16] Such inherent confusion was bound to skew the application of the Constitution in America, and overseas governors and viceroys were quick to point out the inapplicability of the Constitution under the unique circumstances of their territories, to say nothing of conditions of domestic rebellion.

The Conde de Toreno reflects very briefly on this problem of trying to govern an empire with one Constitution:

> It might appear at first glance a great delirium to have adopted for the remote countries of Ultramar the same rules and Constitution as for the peninsula; but from the moment that the Junta Central declared the inhabitants of both hemispheres equal in rights, and from the moment that the American deputies were seated in the Cortes, [the Cortes] could either not approve reforms for Europe or, of necessity, extend them to those countries. There were already too many indications and proofs of disunion for the Cortes to add encouragement to the fire; and where compulsory means do not exist to check hidden or open rebellions, it becomes necessary to charm the spirits in such a way that although independence may not be impeded in

the future, the instant of a total and hostile break is at least put off.[17]

A startling confession indeed! It makes it clear that Spain had already manuevered itself into a hopeless dialectical bind. Either the overseas territories were colonies or they were not; Spain, however, had decided to have it both ways, "to charm the spirits" by telling Americans they were now equal while treating them the same as before.

Once the question of equality of representation and apportionment was concluded in a manner prejudicial to the Americans, all other questions in which the perceived interests of Spain differed from those of America would follow suit. The two most important expressions of American demands were those presented by the overseas deputies on 16 December 1810 and on 1 August 1811. They are merely the most significant of a multitude of memorials submitted individually or jointly by overseas deputies over the four years of Cortes government. Neither of them is recorded in the *Diario de Cortes*, sure indication that American demands were perceived as too dangerous for public distribution. The presentation of 16 December 1810 did, however, provoke the Cortes to agree to devote two days a week, Wednesday and Friday, to the consideration of specifically American questions.

The presentation of 16 December 1810 consisted of eleven fundamental reforms that the overseas territories demanded; it was submitted by the entire American caucus and constitutes the clearest expression of the American demand for implementation of the decreed equality. The eleven demands were: (1) equal proportionate Cortes representation; (2) freedom to plant and manufacture all previously restricted commodities; (3) freedom to import and export all goods from any part of Spain and from allied and neutral powers at all American ports in national or foreign vessels; (4) free trade between the Americas and the Asiatic possessions, and abolition of existing exclusive trade privileges; (5) free trade from any American or Philippine port with other parts of Asia; (6) suppression of all state and private monopolies; (7) free mining of mercury in America; (8) equal rights of Americans whether Spaniards or Indians to any political, ecclesiastical, or military appointment; (9) distribution of half of the positions in each American kingdom to natives of that kingdom; (10) creation of advisory committees in America for the selection of the local residents to be given those public offices; and (11) restoration of the Jesuit order in America. [18]

Three of the items revolved around the Americans' second major demand—free trade on both oceans between the American colonies and from them to Spain as well as to foreign powers and to the colonies of foreign powers. Three dealt with the demand for freedom of internal trade within the colonies—abolition of monopolies, including the mercury monopoly, and of planting and manufacturing restrictions. And three dealt with the demand for equal American employment in state and church. This was, therefore, the American legislative program in its clearest expression. All of the demands were eventually debated in the Cortes in one form or another, on the repeated insistence of American deputies. Only three were ever acted upon favorably, and even then they were modified or rendered otherwise meaningless. Item number 1, as we have seen, was approved, although it did not apply to the extraordinary Cortes then sitting and it excluded blacks. Item number 2, suppression of all existing restrictions on the planting and manufacturing of particular products in America—grapes, olives, steel blades, and other items that were thought to compete with peninsular exports—was granted. It had little effect, however, for, as previously noted by Gabriel de Yermo, one of the most powerful peninsular merchants and hacendados resident in Mexico, the major American territories such as Mexico and Peru could not hope to produce enough grapes or olives to compete with Spain, and, besides, they were already planting such crops illegally to meet local needs. [19] On Item number 7, the request for free mining of mercury in America, the Cortes agreed to partial acceptance, granting on 26 January 1811, instead of free mining, the privilege of free trade in mercury (that is, the right of anyone who had the capital to import as much mercury as he could from peninsular sources). This was chimerical, since the mines at Almadén were occupied by the French and shipment of mercury reserves from Cádiz was sporadic. For example, in 1811 and 1812 there were no mercury shipments to Peru; in 1813 and 1814 large shipments were sent as a result of allied military forces capturing reserves held by the French; but after 1814 there is no firm evidence that any further shipments reached Peru.[20] All of the other demands, however, were rejected outright in Cortes votes (Item 11); delayed pending the collection of further opinion (Items 3, 4, and 5, except that Cuba already possessed effective free trade and continued to do so); reserved for action at a later date and then not acted upon (Items 8, 9, and 10); or postponed (Item 6). The only item rejected in a clear vote was the demand for restoration of the Jesuits; the other items relating to the economic rights and condition of Spanish Americans in conflict with those of Spaniards, and representing the unanimous objectives of creole elites, were brushed aside. After the fall of the Constitution in 1814 these same demands would be brought in various forms to the king's attention, whereupon they would face the same fate.

José Baquíjano, who was not a radical by any means, was quite clear in placing the blame for the Cortes's refusal to allow free trade in America. The Consulado of Cádiz, which he termed "the absolute dictator of the resolutions of the Regency and the Cortes," was most to blame. It had informed the Cortes that in its view even the theoretical granting of full equal rights to America did not constitute granting Americans the same rights as peninsulars. Indeed, Baquíjano testified that in 1810 the Consulado of Cádiz had singlehandedly forced the Regency to withdraw a grant of free trade that it had issued.[21] This extraordinary incident constitutes a shocking example of the confusion that prevailed in American matters. The Conde de Toreno, whose chronicle presents one of the clearest pictures of the Regency and Cortes at work, explains what happened. On 17 May 1810 a decree from the Regency appeared in Cádiz granting complete freedom of trade to all American ports with all foreign colonies and European nations. Toreno says that "it stunned everyone and surprised the merchants of Cádiz, who were interested more than anyone in the overseas monopoly."[22]

The Regency received the merchants' protest and immediately

investigated, whereupon it was discovered that the secretary of the treasury department in charge of the Indies, Manuel Albuerne, had taken a Regency decree granting free trade in flour to Havana and, on his own and under the influence of two agents of the Havana merchants, had issued the decree extending free trade to all products and to all American territories. Similar limited permission for free trade would also be granted in 1811 to Panama for trade with the English colonies and to Santa Marta in New Granada to undertake commerce with the English colonies and to export bullion to them, but these fell far short of general grants of free trade.[23] In the scandal that followed, the minister of hacienda, the Marqués de las Hormazas, was arrested, along with Albuerne. After a drawn-out hearing the case was concluded and all persons involved were excused. It seems that Hormazas had simply signed the order without reading it and without being aware of its contents. On 27 June the Regency declared the decree apocryphal, null, and of no value. Authorities were ordered to collect and destroy any copies of the spurious decree, although it had already circulated throughout Cádiz.

The Regency's statement continued with special candor, saying that it had not yet been able to decide so delicate a question as granting free trade to America because, "in spite of the great desire the Council of the Regency has always had and still has to conciliate the well-being of the Americas with that of the metropolis, it has abstained from treating such a delicate and transcendent point, in which, even to make the slightest innovation, it would be necessary to overthrow existing prohibitive laws in the Indies, which act would produce the most grave consequences for the State."[24] Baquíjano did not doubt the transcendence of the subject, for, he said, America had sent the peninsula 90 million pesos of direct and indirect aid between 1808 and 1811. To alter the existing trade restrictions, argued the merchants of Cádiz, would destroy the commerce of Spain, and even the most liberal peninsular Cortes deputies agreed. "As a result . . . ," said Baquíjano, "permission to trade freely was denied, . . . verifying what the Consulado of Cádiz had said, that the rights of the Americans were not really equal but were to the contrary."

Toreno's evidence suggests that throughout most of 1810, at least, free Spain's survival literally depended on American revenue. From 28 January to 31 October 1810 the Junta Superior de Cádiz operated the Regency's treasury and during that time revenues amounted to 351 million reales de vellón, of which 195 million, or 55.5 percent, came from America. After 31 October the government rescinded the contract with Cádiz and collected revenues itself. In the last two months of 1810 total revenues were 56.7 million reales, of which 30.5 million, or 54 percent, came from America.[25] Under such circumstances no change in Spain's traditional trade exclusion was possible. In 1811 total revenues were 201.6 million, of which 70.9 million came from overseas. The American contribution had declined to 35 percent, but Toreno thought the sum was still noteworthy, given the revolts then raging overseas. Toreno, like Baquíjano, testified to the immense influence of the Cádiz merchants over the Cortes. He ascribed one of the most famous incidents of the Cortes's history — the flight in October 1812 of the conservative deputy José Pablo Valiente to a ship in the harbor and later to voluntary exile in Tangier in order to escape the anger of the mob — to the fact that Valiente was a proponent of free trade in America, especially in Cuba, where he had private interests.[26] Despite the trade monopoly, however, the rebellions in America and the war in Spain soon took their inevitable toll, for in 1812 total revenues in the central treasury amounted to no more than 138 million reales, of which only 15 million (10.8 percent) came from all sources overseas. Yet in 1814 the Cortes's first budget called for expenditures of 950 million reales a year,[27] the vast majority of it for the expenses of an armed force of 150,000 infantry and 12,000 cavalry in the peninsula. Economic necessity would determine American policy.

Having run up against the immovable obstacle of state and private peninsular interests, some of the American delegates attempted a flanking action as a means by which to acquire expanded liberty of commerce for their countries. In April 1811 the newly-arrived deputy representing Mexico City, José Ignacio Beye de Cisneros, proposed to the Cortes that the metropolis call on the great wealth of New Spain to finance the peninsular struggle against Napoleon. His scheme was that a system of provincial juntas should be established in America (like those already functioning in rebellion in Caracas, Buenos Aires, and elsewhere), authorized to declare the independence of the Americas should the motherland itself fall under complete French domination. In this eventuality, the American countries would be free to rescue themselves from the general chaos of metropolitan disaster and would move to bail Spain out with their great resources. Mexico, for example, would make massive loans to Spain by mortgaging its mines to the British. Both Servando Teresa de Mier and José Baquíjano testify that the overseas committee of the Cortes approved the plan for presentation to the body as a whole but that Europeans prevented its reading on the grounds that it was revolutionary. Baquíjano says it died after eight months on the table without ever being read.[28]

The American deputies, representing as they did the creole elite of the colonies, were so taken with Beye's plan that on 1 August 1811 all thirty-three of the overseas deputies then present made a report, in a secret session of the Cortes, that duplicated the proposal for provincial juntas. This was the second of the two major statements of what America wanted. Over a third of the deputies signing the report were Mexicans, and it appears to be an example of the more radical politics of the Mexicans, who by late 1811 were leaders of the American caucus. The report declared that the cause of the American rebellions was the perception of Americans that the governments of the Junta Central and the Cortes were illegitimate, for they did not possess the authority to speak in the name of the absent king. Only regional juntas of government, like those still functioning in Spain, possessed that power, for in the king's absence sovereignty devolved upon the people. These regional juntas would then govern America until the return of the king and would open trade with all friendly nations and thereby restore the devastated wealth of the empire. Each colony wanted to be self-governing, but under the king's suzerainty. What Americans really wanted was not independence but the right to form their own governments and to make their own decisions. It was, in short, a proposal for the establishment of an empire of autonomous states, a commonwealth of Hispanic nations.[29] The proposal was strongly supported by the influential Spanish exile José Blanco White, who, since it was not published in the *Diario* of the Cortes, published it in March 1812 in his London-based periodical *El Español*.[30] The Cortes, however, took no action on the proposal.

By mid-1811 the Cortes had been presented a clear statement of the political solution American loyalists sought in order to end the rebellions now raging overseas. All of them advocated free foreign trade, abolition of internal hindrances to production, and parity of career opportunity in army, state, and church, and most of them supported provincial autonomy. This was the American political solution. It would be restated in forum after forum, before 1814 to the Cortes, after 1814 to the king, after 1820 to the Cortes again. It expressed the aspirations of a still-loyalist creole elite continuously engaged in a contest for influence against the peninsular elites who administered America but who could not bring themselves to support the home-grown radicalism of lower-class revolt under a Morelos or Hidalgo in Mexico or a Pumacahua in Peru. They represented a middle position between absolutism and separatism.

Many of the deputies who arrived from the overseas provinces brought with them lists of demands drafted by the city councils in the capitals of their home provinces, thus adding regional demands to those general ones already drawn up by the American caucus as a group. It is impossible to piece together an overall picture of these individual demands from the *Diario de Cortes* and the testimony left by such leading memoirists as Toreno or Villanueva. Fortunately, however, an unlikely source provides an opportunity to recapture some of the scope of the Americans' particular shopping lists. On 17 June 1814, after the restoration of the king and the overthrow of the Cortes, the minister of the Indies, the reactionary Miguel de Lardizá-bal, wrote to those American deputies still on hand in Spain requesting them to submit ideas of what their regions wanted to quell the rebellions. Lardizábal had suggested this to the king "as a sign of His Majesty's interest in them."[31] At least fifty-eight former deputies were invited to send in their suggestions, of which thirty-two replies have been found, thirty of which are substantive.[32] Many of the former deputies were no longer available, and one, the Mexican

Table 1: Synopsis of Former American Deputies' Requests to Cortes, 1814

Deputy	Items: 1	2	3	4	5	6	7	8	9	10	11	12	13	14	15	16	17	18	19
Mexico																			
Angel Alonso y Pantiga, Yucatán	1		3		5					10				14	15	16			
José Miguel Gordoa y Barrios, Zacatecas			3					8											
José María Hernández y Almansa, Puebla	1	2			5			8		10							17		
Mariano Mendiola, Querétaro	1	2	3	4	5	6	7	8	9	10	11	12	13	14					
José Martínez de la Pedrera, Yucatán															15				
Antonio Joaquín Pérez, Puebla	1	2		4	5	6				10		12	13		15				
Miguel Ramos Arizpe, Coahuila				4	5								13	14	15	16	17		
José Domingo Sánchez, New Galicia		2	3		5	6		8	9		11	12	13	14	15	16	17	18	
José Vivero, San Luis Potosí						6	7	8				12				16			
Guatemala																			
José Ignacio Avila, San Salvador				4		6													
Juan José Cabarcas, Panama		2	3	4	5				9		11		13	14	15	16	17		19
Florencio Castillo, Costa Rica			3	4		6			9							16	17		
Fernando Antonio Dávila, Chiapas	1	2		4									13						
Manuel de Micheo, Guatemala																16	17		
José Santiago Milla, Honduras									9						15	16			

Table 1, *continued*

Deputy	Items:	1	2	3	4	5	6	7	8	9	10	11	12	13	14	15	16	17	18	19
José Cleto Montiel, Guatemala		1	2				6	7			10		12			15				
Mariano Robles, Chiapas		1									10						16			
Peru																				
Tadeo Gárate, Puno		1		3						9									18	
Pedro García Coronel, Trujillo				3						9					14				18	
Pablo González, Tarma		1											12	13					18	
Gregorio de Guinea, Trujillo										9				13	14	15	16		18	
Martín José de Múxica, Huamanga		1				5									14				18	
José Antonio Navarrete, Piura				3												15		17	18	19
Mariano de Rivero, Arequipa			2	3	4			7				11				15			18	
Francisco Salazar, Lima		1	2	3				7	8	9									18	

continued

KEY TO ITEMS:

1. Relating to Indians.
2. Local agricultural improvements.
3. Reduce taxes or interest rates.
4. Establish a university or seminary.
5. Establish a new creole-dominated power or agency.
6. Create a diocese or archdiocese.

7. Suppress monopolies / estancos.
8. Permit prohibited manufactures.
9. Mining reforms.
10. Suppress an existing royal office.
11. Free Asian trade.
12. Limit land speculation or alienation.
13. Improve public education.

14. City or provincial distinctions.
15. Establish a new royal agency or office.
16. Open or improve port / navigation.
17. Other major public works.
18. Reform the bureaucracy or government / church personnel.
19. Personal honors or títulos de Castilla.

Table 1, *continued*

Deputy	Items:	1	2	3	4	5	6	7	8	9	10	11	12	13	14	15	16	17	18	19
Other																				
Pedro Alcántara de Acosta, Cuba																15				
Gonzalo de Herrera, Floridas																15	16	17		
Ventura de los Reyes, Philippines												11								
Francisco López Lisperguer, B. Aires		1	2				6		8		10		12			15			18	
Mariano Rodríguez Olmedo, Charcas		1		3	4	5				9					14	15		17		19
Items:		1	2	3	4	5	6	7	8	9	10	11	12	13	14	15	16	17	18	19
Totals:		13	10	12	9	9	8	5	7	10	7	5	7	8	9	15	11	9	10	3

KEY TO ITEMS:

1. Relating to Indians.
2. Local agricultural improvements.
3. Reduce taxes or interest rates.
4. Establish a university or seminary.
5. Establish a new creole-dominated power or agency.
6. Create a diocese or archdiocese.

7. Suppress monopolies / estancos.
8. Permit prohibited manufactures.
9. Mining reforms.
10. Suppress an existing royal office.
11. Free Asian trade.
12. Limit land speculation or alienation.
13. Improve public education.

14. City or provincial distinctions.
15. Establish a new royal agency or office.
16. Open or improve port / navigation.
17. Other major public works.
18. Reform the bureaucracy or government / church personnel.
19. Personal honors or títulos de Castilla.

SOURCE:

"Nota de los Diputados de las Américas a quienes se les ha comunicado la circular de 17 de junio de 1814," and responses, AGI, Indiferente 1354 and 1355.

Miguel Ramos Arizpe, was already in jail, one of those liberals rounded up on 10 May 1814 in the first wave of repression directed by the king; he answered through a proxy. There were already few deputies left from the two viceroyalties that were most advanced in the struggle for independence—New Granada and Río de la Plata (many of whose deputies had voluntarily withdrawn during the sessions of the Cortes)—so invitations and answers reflected chiefly the objectives of New Spain, Peru, and the kingdom of Guatemala, including all of Central America, Panama, and Chiapas. It is also worthy of mention that six of the substantive responses found were from six of the ten American deputies who signed the "Manifesto of the Persians" in 1814—men thus considered to be royalists. These were Pérez of Puebla, Alonso y Pantiga of Yucatán, Gárate of Puno, García Coronel of Trujillo, Olmedo of Charcas, and Lisperguer of Buenos Aires. Table 1 shows nonetheless, that there was a notable similarity in the types of demands the American deputies were instructed to present to the Cortes. All were quite practical, quite specific, and appropriate to the authority of an imperial government. None were extravagant or impossible to accomplish; they only wanted Cortes decree. Yet very few were ever acted upon by either the Cortes or the restored absolutist regime. The moderation of these demands is their most impressive characteristic. They have been itemized here under appropriate general headings.

The request that appeared most often in the former deputies' letters was for the creation of various agencies or offices of the royal government in their local jurisdictions in order to increase direct royal judicial or administrative presence—hardly a revolutionary objective and certainly not impossible of implementation. The deputy for New Galicia asked for a viceroyalty, junta of hacienda, and acordada tribunal in Guadalajara; the deputy for Charcas requested a new viceroyalty to be established at La Plata, together with a commandancy general for Santa Cruz de la Sierra and a presidio for Charcas; the deputy for Quezaltenango, Guatemala, requested an intendancy for Quezaltenango; three deputies—for Cuba, Zacatecas, and Honduras—asked for royal mints in their home regions; both deputies for Yucatán requested an audiencia for Mérida; the deputies for Trujillo and Arequipa in Peru asked for audiencias in their capital cities; and Lisperguer of Buenos Aires requested more audiencias in general. The deputies for Puebla and for Panama asked for more lower courts, and the deputy for the Floridas asked for new military forces.

The next most frequently cited item involved matters relating to the Indians, mostly either to maintain the suppression of the tribute or, conversely, to reinstate it. A number of deputies also requested financial and administrative reorganization of Indian parishes and curacies, new hospitals for the Indians, or special efforts to improve their education. The Peruvian Martín José de Múxica asked that the cabildo of Huamanga be allowed to elect at least one Indian regidor and that Indians be allowed to be alcaldes de barrio in the same city. He specifically exempted the mixed castes from these proposed privileges. Deputy Hernández of Puebla urged that military academies and public offices be opened to the Indians and that forced repartimiento of supplies be suppressed; but his more conservative colleague from Puebla, Antonio Joaquín Pérez, urged reestablishment of the tribute, as did Olmedo of Charcas and González of Tarma. Deputy Alonso of Yucatán wanted restoration of the cacicazgos that were abolished by the Cortes decree abolishing special jurisdictions and señoríos.

Next in number of requests was the lowering of various taxes, customs duties, interest rates, or, in the case of Peru particularly, the property tax imposed by Viceroy Abascal. The next most frequently cited item was for the fitting out, improvement, or opening of ports and river navigational systems. José Domingo Sánchez of New Galicia asked for the upgrading of the port of San Blas and also for the construction of the long-discussed canal at the isthmus of Tehuantepec to be paid for by the consulados of Guadalajara, Mexico, Veracruz, and Guatemala. Manuel de Micheo suggested the opening of a river system in Guatemala and submitted two reports on it and a set of proposed regulations. Many other ports were mentioned.

No less than ten individual deputies requested local agricultural improvements, mining reforms, and a variety of changes in the civil and clerical bureaucracies. It is particularly noteworthy that every one of the Peruvian deputies requested some reform in government and church personnel, ranging from mild requests for alterations in the election in various convents to Mariano de Rivero's and Francisco Salazar's more liberal (but by now standard) request that there be equal distribution of government positions between Americans and Spaniards. Francisco Lisperguer also asked for job equality. Sánchez of New Galicia urged many reforms, most notably that promotions be based on merit rather than seniority and that the civil service be reduced in size. Seven deputies made similar requests to suppress some existing royal office, usually of the most local nature, such as Angel Alonso's request to suppress the office of teniente del resguardo created by the Junta Central, or José María Hernández's request to abolish the office of tenientes de justicia. But Lisperguer of Buenos Aires advocated doing away with the viceroyalties, creating instead captaincies general as in the peninsula.

Nine deputies brought up three other items: the establishment of a new university or seminary in their home districts (for Puebla, Saltillo, Costa Rica, Panama, Arequipa, Querétaro, Chiapas, and San Salvador, and new endowments for La Plata); the establishment of new creole-dominated powers or agencies such as a sociedad patrió-tico-económico, new city councils, mining tribunals, and professional agencies; or the granting of special distinctions, coats of arms, titles, and so forth to their home city or province. Closely allied with these were the requests made by seven deputies for the creation of a new diocese or archdiocese in their homes (Puebla, Costa Rica, San Luis Potosí, Guadalajara, San Salvador, Quezaltenango, and Río de la Plata). Many deputies wanted major public works—roads, bridges, military highways, fortifications—and the deputy for Panama re-quested special tax benefits and other assistance to rebuild the many houses destroyed in that city by three recent fires. Ramos Arizpe wanted colonization programs to develop Texas to secure it from Anglo-Saxon absorption. Trailing the field, but still mentioned by many deputies, were requests to suppress existing monopolies, to permit prohibited manufactures, to open free trade to Asia, to limit land speculation or excessive alienation, to improve public education, and to grant honors and noble titles to individual persons.

The homogeneity of the deputies' requests is impressive. The categories in table 1 express all the areas of request with the exception of only two. Deputies Sánchez of New Galicia and Salazar of Lima requested the abolition of internal customs duties within their kingdoms; Sánchez (who made more requests than any other deputy in these letters) also asked for the abolition of the slave trade. Other than those two, all the individual requests of the deputies who responded to the royal invitation can be categorized under the nineteen items listed. How many were granted by the Cortes? Effectively none. Except for the abolition of the tribute and the mita (the mita existed only in Peru), except for the declaration of the freedom to plant and manufacture (which was ineffective, as the many subsequent requests for the same attest), except for an occasional grant of a title or coat of arms to a city, except for a constitutional provision calling for the creation of city councils in small villas that did not yet possess one, except for a constitutional title encouraging increased public education, except for occasional Cortes decrees of trade exemptions for peripheral or strategic locations like Cartagena, Havana, and Santo Domingo, and except for the occasional decree (never subsequently acted upon) granting a university or an audiencia to certain locations (Querétaro was to get a university, Saltillo an audiencia), none of these requests was ever granted.

It can never be known, of course, whether the granting of some or all of these requests—both the individual ones and the empire-wide ones—would have held the empire together. But the Cortes scarcely made any pretense even of taking the American demands in good faith. Some items were perhaps financially impossible for a war-torn empire—this was no time to contemplate an isthmian canal or territorial colonization—but most of the overseas demands required no major expenditure of funds. The Americans basically asked for central government permission to pursue their own initiative in trade, production, domestic improvements, bureaucratic reforms, and rationalization. José Baquíjano summarized the Americans' complaints more eloquently than perhaps anyone else. Referring to the

Cortes and its many failures, he declared:

> This anti-political conduct has been the true origin of the desperation of those people: never have you wanted to listen to their complaints nor hear their proposals; and while you spent whole days in series of discussions over whether you should say *barra* or *barandilla*, whether you should name someone to collect the mail for the deputies or have each deputy take care of his own, you have not employed even a few moments to reflect upon means of quieting spirits and restoring peace and unity.

He concluded by warning that all Americans would remember the unkept promises and broken guarantees of the Cortes and Constitution.[33]

It is clear, then, what the Cortes and Constitution did not do for America. This raises the question, what did they do? To what extent were both the spirit and the letter of the reforms of Cortes and Constitution implemented in America? The best approach in considering the question is first to consider the effect of the implementation that did occur and then to consider elements of the reform that were blocked from full or early implementation by action of royal authorities.

There was an extraordinary degree to which the reforms that were implemented backfired or had an effect contrary to what was expected by the peninsular liberals. The effect is natural enough, given the fact that the Constitution was written with no particular attention to the circumstances of America. Many examples could be cited, according to the American territory in question. But consider, for example, the effect of the Cortes decree abolishing special jurisdictional privileges and señoríos. This was legislation designed for Spain, and clearly indicates the extent to which the peninsular liberals' ethnocentrism, or, at least, their overriding interest in Spanish problems caused them to ignore the effect of their actions in America. The problem, as the deputy from Yucatán pointed out, was that abolition of jurisdictional privileges also abolished the inherited position of chief, or cacique, in those American territories where the cacicazgo was still a basic tool of royal administration of Indians. Yet it did not alter what the Americans most objected to—the special privilege of rank and appointment of peninsulars living in America.

Another prime example was the attempt of the Constitution to rationalize the plethora of magistracies that existed throughout the empire by abolishing all existing courts of first instance and replacing them with the magistrates called jueces de letras. To begin with, this was not fully implemented, as the requests of several deputies in 1814 show. But even where it was implemented it led to the virtual destruction of local court systems. In Peru, for example, the Constitution abolished all existing courts, and ordered one juez de letras to be appointed for every 5,000 inhabitants. The problem was, the Cortes never got around to appointing the jueces. Before the reform, Lima had fourteen courts of first instance; after the reform it had only three, two of the magistrates having been appointed by Viceroy Abascal as soon as he read the Constitution but before he declared it in effect. The audiencia, the Lima city council, and the viceroy all testified that Lima and Peru in general (a country not yet engaged in domestic warfare) promptly suffered a crime wave.[34]

Yet another example of the "back-fire effect" was the abolition of the tribute decreed on 13 March 1811. Throughout the empire, as already suggested, this removed the Indians' traditional immunity from personal taxation and submitted them instead to the full panoply of exactions of any other Spaniard. In America, as in Cádiz, this led to a revived debate, often acrimonious, concerning the proper condition and status of the Indian. But its effect on those American royal regimes dependent on Indian tribute was so massive as to be virtually suicidal. In Peru, where three-quarters of the population were tributaries, abolition of the tribute cost the viceregal government one-third of its annual revenues, a crippling blow that could only be mitigated by Viceroy Abascal's decreeing a "special contribution" to take the tribute's place.[35] In Mexico, Viceroy Venegas abolished the tribute temporarily in October 1810 as a response to the outbreak of Hidalgo's insurrection, but the Cortes decree of 1811 superseded the viceregal action and it was estimated that abolition of the tribute cost the regime one million pesos a year.[36] In Central America some Indian villages themselves urged restoration of the old tribute, as it was a cheaper tax than the general levies to which they were now submitted.[37]

Then there was the more simple problem of outright non-implementation of the reforms. Many of the decrees of the Cortes that might be cited as proof of reform can also be cited as proof of non-implementation. As already discussed, this would include the decree of American and European equality, the decree of freedom to plant and manufacture, and the decrees of equal proportional representation. These important reforms remained dead letters in America because they lacked enforcing legislation, were patently hypocritical to begin with, or were amended or otherwise hedged about with so many restrictions as to invalidate them. Besides, as already seen, the core of American equality was equal representation and free trade, and these were never granted. In the Río de la Plata, of course, these reforms were not enforceable because that viceroyalty was virtually independent from 1810 onwards, and the extent and ferocity of the warfare in New Granada and Venezuela prevented the Constitution from having much effect there.

The heart of the matter, however, is that even in the viceroyalties of New Spain and Peru and the kingdom of Guatemala—where the Constitution and the Cortes decrees were promulgated—the viceroys and other royal officials went about attempting systematically to block implementation of the key freedoms of the new system. In Mexico the first popular elections ever held were annulled by Viceroy Venegas, and for four years both viceroys, Venegas and Calleja, refused to permit the decree of freedom of the press to be implemented. After the Constitution sanctioned both the free press and elections as ultimate law, Viceroy Venegas acted to influence elections, but he never implemented the free press. Calleja refused to permit two Cortes deputies elected in Mexico to proceed to Spain. Both Venegas and Calleja simply exercised selective obedience to the Constitution, permitting those political innovations that could be controlled or rendered harmless, failing to implement those they considered dangerous to royal authority. No amount of complaint from the American deputies to the Cortes could alter this viceregal despotism.[38] Direct Cortes orders were to no avail—some were openly disobeyed, others simply ignored.

Viceroy Abascal, the Peruvian autocrat, pursued a similar policy, though entirely without consultation with his Mexican colleagues. Technically Abascal adhered to the free press decree, but he intervened personally whenever he found a publication to be dangerous and made the writing of dissident literature so risky that few persons in Peru attempted it. He persecuted and arrested leading editors, sending them to Spain for trials in which they were always found not guilty. He secretly sponsored a pro-government periodical. He intervened in every constitutional election in Lima, and attempted to intervene in those in other cities and provinces. He refused to recognize the credentials of electors, he accused some of Peru's Cortes deputies of treason, he persecuted their families left behind in Peru; he manipulated, cajoled, and influenced, at all times maintaining his political dominance.[39] And in Guatemala, Captain General José de Bustamante suppressed freedom of the press, intervened in elections, and attempted to stifle the political initiative of elected city councils and provincial deputations.

In all three countries the Constitution was put into effect, but key elements of it were never implemented, and direct Cortes or Regency orders for full implementation were freely ignored. The difficulty of getting royal orders obeyed was an inherent problem in the imperial structure, but at no time since the New Laws of 1542 had so important a body of Spanish legislation been so blatantly disobeyed or ignored by royal authorities in America. The Cortes found its hands tied anyhow, for the Mexican and Peruvian viceroys and the Guatemalan captain general assured Spain that their disobedience was in the name of maintaining Spain's dominions intact and, truth to tell, the Cortes had no better means to propose.

Of all the failings of the Cortes and Regency in 1810–14, the greatest was indeed the failure, amid such talent and fervor for reform, to propose a policy for the settlement of the rebellions in America. The fatal flaw, of course, was that two-thirds of the Cortes members were peninsulars who could always overrule the American minority. Outside of the multitude of proposals of the American deputies themselves, there was actually little discussion of a broad formulation for "pacification," a term that came into increasing favor under the Cortes and that Ferdinand VII would continue to use after his return. Toreno says that initially, in 1810, the Regency, on hearing of the first outbreak of rebellion in Caracas and Buenos Aires, assumed that the disturbances would end as soon as the Americans heard that Spain had not fallen to the French. The Council of State then proposed that a high-level commissioner be sent to America with a few warships and with orders to organize the troops in Puerto Rico, Cuba, and Cartagena in order to coordinate efforts against the rebels in Venezuela. The Regency agreed, appointing Antonio Cortavarría, a distinguished magistrate and member of high royal councils, but with no American experience. He attempted with little success to secure the Caribbean and Venezuela from his vantage point at Puerto Rico. "The Spanish government," said Toreno, "wrongly figured that the days of the Mendozas and Gascas were not past, and that upon seeing the peninsular envoy all obstacles would be overcome and the popular tumults would cease."[40] The Regency later appointed Francisco Javier de Elío as viceroy of Río de la Plata and ordered him to sail to Montevideo with 500 men to take control of the situation there. This was the extent of the Regency's actions until the Cortes met.

Toreno proceeds in his brief discussion of the American rebellions to make the fundamental error that characterized all the thinking of the liberals in 1811 and 1812. He assumed that once the decree of equal rights of 15 October 1810 was passed by the Cortes, together with the other reforms, Spain had exhausted the possibility of accommodating the Americans. "After this decree (of 15 October) there came, by way of sequel, other declarations and concessions very favorable to America. . . . Through them it will be seen how hard the Cortes worked to gain the spirit of those inhabitants and to quiet the motives they had for just complaint, which should have brought an end to the turbulences, if the fire of a vast volcano could be extinguished by the hand of man."[41] Yet, as we have seen, in the absence of military force Spain had barely scraped the surface of the Americans' political and administrative complaints. Finally with the promulgation of the Constitution in March 1812, many Spanish leaders assumed the Americans' demands were answered. The Cortes in general sensed that the more extreme demands of the creoles could not be met short of full independence.

Adding considerably to the widespread paralysis was the effective dissolution of the two chief imperial agencies previously charged with American government, the Ministry of the Indies and the Council of the Indies. The Ministry of the Indies had earlier fallen victim to the constant tinkering that so plagued the Spanish system. The ministry had existed throughout most of the reign of Charles IV, but on 8 July 1787 it was abolished and replaced in function by the Secretariat of the Government of Overseas, which was a branch of the Ministry of Government, and by the American branch of the Ministry of Grace and Justice. At the time of dissolution the Ministry of the Indies had consisted of thirty-nine officials, who had been distributed more or less equally into the two offices now existing under two separate ministries. Subsequently the two branches of American affairs were again united into the Secretariat of the Government of Overseas. In the deluge of 1808 some of the officials of the secretariat fled to Cádiz to continue their work, while others remained in Madrid, and, as with all other government offices, the secretariat scarcely functioned for the next two years. Not until promulgation of the Constitution was a Ministry of the Indies again established. Even so, since the Cortes was supreme in its legislative powers, the ministry seems to have been little in evidence in the formulation of American business; it lacked the authority and freedom of action of the old ministry responsible only to the king. In June 1814, after the king's restoration and triumphal return to Madrid, the Ministry of the Indies was retained, with Miguel de Lardizábal, the former regent and defender of the royal prerogatives, as minister.[42] (It should be clear that the terms "secretariat" and "ministry," as well as "secretary" and "minister," were used interchangeably by the Spanish government).

The ancient Council of the Indies, meanwhile, underwent an equally turbulent period of disruption. When the government flfled Madrid in 1808, the council—an advisory body that, because of its prestige and the stature of its members, usually had the king's ear—disintegrated along with all the other government agencies and great councils. Some of its members fled south, others joined the French. Like the Council of Castile, the supreme advisory body for domestic peninsular questions, the Council of the Indies was scarcely heard from between 1808 and 1812. Because of the shortage of the former members, the Junta Central on 18 July 1809 joined the four major state councils—Castile, Indies, Finance, and Military Orders—into one body called the Supreme Council and Tribunal of Spain and the Indies, or simply the Consejo Reunido, which functioned as a voice of opposition to many of the decisions of the Junta Central. Then, on 16 September 1810, the first Regency in Cádiz reestablished all the old councils.[43]

Finally, in January 1812 the Cortes decreed the suppression of the individual councils again and the creation of a new supreme council, called the Council of State, and this was codified in Chapter VII of the Constitution. The Council of State was ultimately to be composed of forty persons appointed by the king on presentation of the Cortes; of this number four had to be ecclesiastics, four had to be grandees, and at least twelve had to be born overseas. The initial Council of State, however, was set up before promulgation of the Constitution, so according to the 21 January decree it consisted of only twenty members. Of these, six represented the interests of America in theory, although not all six would have been absorbed with American questions. Pedro Agar, for example, technically was a "councilor for America," but he was also a naval officer and a former regent chosen for the council because of his previous position on the second Regency. He subsequently was a member of the fourth Regency as well. The other councilors named for America were Melchor de Foncerrada (born in Mexico); José Baquíjano, Conde de Vistaflorida (born in Lima); José Mariano de Almansa (born in Veracruz); the Marqués de Piedrablanca (born in Chile); and José Aycinena (born in Guatemala).[44] The council was proclaimed "the only Council of the King" in all matters of high state policy. Although it would make major policy statements in the period of the second constitutional regime, 1820–23, during the first constitutional period it rendered only one major policy proposal concerning the American rebellions. Undoubtedly the continuing preoccupation of

Table 2: Who Advises on American Issues, by Period

	Junta Central	Regency and Cortes	Cortes and Constitution	Absolutist		Restoration		Cortes and Constitution	Second Restoration
	1808 to 1809	1810 to 1812	1812 to 1814	1814 to 1815	1815 to 1816	1816 to 1818	1818 to 1820	1820 to 1823	1823
Council of State			C	A	A	A	A	C	A
Council of the Indies		P		A	A	A	A		A
Ministry of State						A			
Ministry of War	P	P			A	A	A		A
Ministry of the Indies or Ultramar			C	A				C	A
Ministry of Hacienda	P	P							
Ministry of Grace and Justice	P	P							
Junta of Pacification				A	A				
Junta Militar de Indias					A	A	A		

KEY:

P = Pre-Constitutional (Ultimate decision belongs to Junta Central, or Regency and Cortes)

C = Constitutional (Ultimate decision belongs to Cortes or, in the later period, to king and Cortes)

A = Absolutist (Ultimate decision belongs to king)

all governmental agencies with the war in Spain accounted for this dearth of policy leadership on American questions. So confusing and contradictory was the shifting responsibility for advising on American issues that it provided a major impediment to the formulation of a policy, not only in this period but even after the king's restoration. These shifts are illustrated in table 2.

Given this confusion of authority, there was considerable room for the influence of private interests in American policy questions under the Cortes and afterward. As already seen, the Consulado of Cádiz was the most significant private interest group, and in 1811 the merchants moved to strengthen their influence by proposing that they finance military expeditions to America. The dispatch of military reinforcements was, indeed, the almost unanimous nostrum of the press throughout the liberal period, particularly of Juan López Cancelada, editor of *El Telégrafo Americano* and advocate of the consulado.[45] The Consulado of Cádiz members thus proposed the creation of a Comisión de Reemplazos by which merchants would establish a fund to be spent on the purchase of uniforms, outfitting of ships, and recruitment of troops for action in America. The Regency and Cortes accepted the plan in September 1811. The consulado moved immediately to implement its program, and with startling speed was able to send the first military expedition, consisting of 37 officers and 720 men, carried in one warship and three frigates, to Havana and Veracruz on 12 November 1811. Two weeks later a further expedition, of 7 officers and 80 men, left for Montevideo, and in December another expedition, of 10 officers and 214 men, went to Puerto Rico. In 1812 seven more expeditions were sent, consisting of almost 6,000 men. The object of the merchants was to illustrate to the Cortes that military resistance to the American rebellions was possible, thereby applying further pressure to oppose a grant of free trade as a means of pacification. The Comisión de Reemplazos remained in existence after the fall of the Constitution and between 1811 and 1820 spent 350 million reales, by its official tally, sending thirty-two expeditions involving more than 47,000 men.[46] The actions of the consulado served to scuttle the pressure of American Cortes deputies for free trade as a reform to settle the rebellions.

The intervention of the consulado to send military forces to America provoked widespread discussion and opposition among Americans who participated in Cortes affairs. José Baquíjano denounced the Cortes for punishing the overseas vassals instead of trying to correct their grievances. He proceeded to argue that this show of force had provoked angry reaction in America, while it had also wasted valuable troops, and concluded with the warning that "to make war on vassals is not a triumph nor an advantage." He said that nearly 10,000 men were sent to New Spain under the Cortes (mostly from the Caribbean rather than from Spain), of whom only 2,000 survived through 1814, the remainder dying in battle or from disease. He testified that 84 artillerymen who were landed in Veracruz died within four months of yellow fever. Five hundred and fifty-five men of the Battalion of Asturias died in a single rebel attack on a convoy.[47] From other sources it appears that an expedition of 700 men, the Talavera Battalion, went to Peru in 1812.[48] The most tragic incident in the Cortes era, however, involved the first reinforcement sent to Buenos Aires in early 1812 aboard the giant warship *Salvador*. The ship sank at sea with nearly all hands on board, a loss of 700 officers and men. In December 1812 the minister of war informed Captain General Gaspar Vigodet of Buenos Aires that new forces would be sent "and in ships under the command of officers of proven skill." In April 1813 the *Prueba* left Cádiz with about 1,000 troops in convoy destined for use in Montevideo. The minister of the navy promised that twelve days after the departure of the first expedition another one of equal size would depart under escort of the *San Pablo*.[49] Although these forces were enough to outrage the proponents of a negotiated political settlement in America, they were minimal compared to the expeditions that would be sent after the restoration. At no time was there complete agreement on the advisability of using force, and even under the king the debate would continue.

Under the Cortes, as during the restoration, there were also occasional suggestions of methods by which Spain might win back the hearts and minds of its overseas subjects without concessions or warfare. These usually revolved around the idea of rotating American youths for advanced studies in Spain and Spanish youths for America—Juan Jabat, the commissioner to Mexico, made such a proposal—or around religious or lay propaganda. Diego Clemencín suggested the publication of a gazette especially for schools, parishes, and convents throughout the empire, but the idea was abandoned because too many objections and difficulties were raised, the chief one being that the schools and monasteries would have to be required to subscribe. Many observers continued to put their faith in the magical role of religious missionaries who would serve as forces of indoctrination for church and king. Many liberal deputies even proposed this as a valid technique, no doubt making the connection between social utility for the large numbers of religious in Spain and the church's role as the flagbearer of Spanish imperialism. The problem, however, was the expense. In 1813 it was reported that the last 158 missionaries sent overseas at the expense of the royal treasury had cost over one million reales for transportation alone.[50]

In fact, the overall impression given by many sources, as well as the impression given by the sometimes surprising lack of discussion or consideration of burning American issues, is that members of the Cortes were absorbed by the "revolution" at home and by the struggle for Spain. It was the American viceregal governments that fought the rebellions initially, often with little or no advice or aid from the motherland. In addition, there was a very small group of leaders who believed that America was already lost. José García de León y Pizarro, who served briefly in 1812 as minister of state, was one of those. In his memoirs he explained his feelings in 1812:

America should follow the fortune that nature has destined for all those distant possessions separated by difficult geographical intervals from their centers; it should emancipate itself; thus it is true that the loss of our American provinces is simply the product of the nature of things; but the moment, and principally the mode, of the separation is what must fall upon those who have directed the metropolis's politics. Whatever might have been the complaints that the Americans had with our government, and whatever might have been the weaknesses of our government, still the union would have continued for many years if the Monarchy had not been disturbed in its foundations. . . . But inexperience, slovenliness, and blindness united in the rulers to anticipate the moment [of separation] and to make the catastrophe more dishonorable and damaging.

He went on to say that the proclamations of the Junta Central irritated and provoked Americans to rebellion. The Central sent obscure and imbecile commissioners like Jabat to America. "The appointments of leaders were, as in times of tranquility, given to favorites; an archbishop (Lizana y Beaumont) in Mexico, senile; a Venegas, indecisive; a Cisneros, insensible and without enterprise; a furious Elío, a stupid Vigodet." The Junta of Cádiz added further outrage by trying to maintain "an unjust monopoly" over commerce. The Cortes added to it, one moment proclaiming equality, the next infringing on it, exciting and legitimizing rebellion. On top of that, Pizarro argued, the audiencias that ruled in America at the time of the rebellions were made up of inexpert, immoral, and weak magistrates who could not land a decent job in the peninsula.[51] And yet, for all his outspoken anger over the inability and ineptness of the Spanish government, Pizarro himself in 1812 had few ideas to offer. Although in 1817 and 1818, during a second period as minister of state, he would propose one of the most interesting plans for American pacification, and perhaps the most practical, still in 1812 he not only had no suggestions to make but even attempted to impede the British mediation offer.

Of all of Spain's confessions of weakness, the British mediation question is the most definitive, for it suggests that this was a country forced by necessity to depend on its stronger ally to intervene in a colonial empire jealously guarded from all outsiders for nearly three centuries. By 1811 the possibility of British mediation had become a leading policy of the Cortes government in regard to the American pacification. Discussion of a possible mediation continued long after the end of the Cortes era. Yet there was an unavoidable impediment to a successful conclusion of the matter, which lay in the very intensity of Spain's exclusivism; it wanted the British to mediate, but it was suspicious of their motives and of the concessions they requested.

According to an abstract drawn up by the Spanish government, recounting its recollections of the matter, the British minister of foreign affairs, the Marquess Wellesley (who had briefly been ambassador to Seville) approached the Regency of Spain in August 1810 with the suggestion that the British cabinet serve as mediator with the rebellious American colonies. In May 1811 the proposal was formalized by the minister's brother, Henry Wellesley, ambassador to the Cortes.[52] The British proposed that in return for their efforts they be permitted free trade with the American territories for at least as long as the mediation effort was underway. On 1 June 1811 Eusebio Bardají, Spanish minister of state, presented the plan to the Cortes on behalf of the Regency, reporting that the Regency "for its part, quite the contrary of finding it inconvenient to permit the mediation, thought it was the most expeditious and perhaps the only way to put an end to the incalculable evils" of the American insurrections. The Regency urged acceptance of the British mediation, requiring the American territories then in rebellion to recognize the Cortes and Regency. In regard to the quid pro quo—British direct trade—the Regency pointed out that to permit it would automatically obviate any motivation the British had for illegal contact with the rebels, that it could be duly regulated, and that "it would not be just to prohibit to the Spaniards in America the advantages that those in Europe could enjoy" of direct trade with Britain. By mid-June both the Regency and the Cortes had accepted the idea and had drawn up a list of bases for the mediation, the most notable of which were: that Britain would be granted trading privileges with the rebellious colonies during the negotiations; that the negotiations should be limited to fifteen months (the Cortes had asked for a limit of ten months, but the Regency had agreed to fifteen); and (this, the most important, was in a secret clause) that, should the reconciliation not be accomplished within the time limit specified, Great Britain would suspend all communications with the rebellious territories and grant military aid to reduce them to obedience to the mother country.[53] The Regency concluded, after complaining of the pro-rebel attitude of British merchants and naval personnel in American waters, by agreeing to the appointment by both governments of commissioners of mediation who would proceed to Buenos Aires, Bogotá, Venezuela, and Cartagena.[54]

The Spanish conditions presented the British with two fundamental obstacles: the Spanish demand that British arms be employed in military reconquest, something that would convert the British into effective agents of Spain; and the Spanish insistence on limiting the mediation only to those countries where rebel governments actually existed, which excluded Mexico, the one country the British were most anxious to trade with. The Spaniards insisted the rebels were not in control of Mexico and therefore it was not subject to mediation. Both parties felt they had serious grievances against the other. The British proposed an extraordinary service to an ally but needed guaranteed recompense; in many ways they were voluntarily agreeing to control their own merchants, who were already working to penetrate the vast Latin American market. The Spanish, for their part, were seriously considering for the first time in their history abandoning their commercial exclusion in America, which, as the liberal Toreno pointed out, was a system "that had been followed in its principal bases by all nations that had colonies," and especially by Spain, "whose backward manufactures imperiously demanded, at least for a long time, the conservation of an exclusive market."[55] Negotiations stalled until early 1812, when the appointment of José García de León y Pizarro as Spanish minister of state and of Lord Castlereagh as British minister of foreign affairs permitted the reopening of discussions. In the interim, however, the British selected the three men who would make up their commissioners to the rebellious colonies, while making it clear they could never accept the secret article requiring British military aid. The Cádiz merchants also remained unalterably opposed to the granting of British free trade in America.

In May 1812 a tentative step forward occurred with regard to the secret article requiring British military force when Spain agreed to withdraw the first part of the article if the English would not put any obstacles in the way of Spanish military efforts in case the mediation failed, but it would not withdraw the second part of the article, which required Britain to break off all commercial relations with the rebellious countries in case the mediation failed. Since Minister of State Pizarro could not accede even to this limited concession, being extremely suspicious of the English motivations, he submitted his resignation after serving as minister only ninety-five days,[56] and was succeeded by the previous secretary of the Cortes, Ignacio de la Pezuela. The British responded by turning to the second point in contention, the exclusion of Mexico. Wellesley informed the Spanish government "that Mexico is not only the first object in the scale of importance, but its settlement seems indispensable to success elsewhere."[57] Thus it was the exclusion of Mexico that had become the greatest obstacle. On the question of free trade the English were quite explicit, pointing out that unless the Americans were permitted commercial advantages equal to those of Spaniards their separation from the mother country was inevitable but that, on the contrary, the pacification of America was as simple a matter as removing the restrictions on colonial commerce, "besides which the Americans could not be treated as colonies after having been recognized by the Cortes as integral parts of the Monarchy."[58]

Although it seemed there was now little hope of a successful agreement on terms, Ambassador Wellesley on 12 June 1812 presented the Spanish government with a list of ten propositions to serve as bases for renewed negotiations. Most of them repeated the earlier bases, but there were several notable changes. Item 4 called for free commerce in America but modified in such a way as to provide clear preference to Spain. Item 5 called for "admission of the native-born Americans, equally with European Spaniards, to the offices of viceroy, governors, etc., in the Americas." And, most important, item 6 called for the "concession of interim or provincial governments under the viceroys or governors to the cabildos or ayuntamientos, and admission to these bodies of native-born Americans equally with European Spaniards." These new governments were to recognize Ferdinand VII and the Cortes, were to promise to aid the allied war effort in Spain, and were to contribute funds to the mother country.[59] These were notable changes indeed, for, while they downplayed

Britain's reward for its services, they virtually called, as Toreno and the Cortes recognized, for the creation "of a new federative government" in which America would merely be called on to cooperate with Spain in the provision of revenues.[60] The establishment of provisional governments in the hands of the cabildos was, after all, the chief objective of the more moderate American rebels. Ambassador Wellesley also made threatening suggestions about terminating the negotiations, and concluded with a pointed and very intemperate reminder that Spain received the equivalent of seventeen million pounds of aid from Britain annually in the support of the British expeditionary forces, on both land and sea, then engaged in the peninsular campaign. Toreno rejected this by asking how Britain could compute the cost of its own forces as aid to Spain. Pezuela responded by reminding Britain that Spain's own immense sacrifices in the war against Napoleon had made the continued security of Britain itself possible, an early statement of a point that Spain would repeat many times over during the next few years as it watched the European allies systematically ignoring it in the post-war division of spoils. Wellesley's ten propositions, at any rate, were submitted to the Cortes for discussion, and on 16 July 1812 the Cortes rejected the British proposals by a vote of more than two to one, a vote that saw the American deputies strongly endorse the proposals while the European deputies strongly opposed them.[61]

The Cortes rejection of the British proposals did not end the negotiations entirely; they continued in a desultory fashion for yet another year. Lord Castlereagh came forward with a compromise proposal—Britain would not insist on a mediation for Mexico, rather, a Spanish commission would be sent to Mexico for mediation, but with a British observer. This would allow Spain the face-saving device of appearing not to recognize Mexico as being in full revolt, while the British would still have some influence in Mexico without insisting that British mediation efforts alone be undertaken there. By the end of 1812 the Spanish minister of state, who was now Pedro Gómez Labrador, replied to the British that the publication of the Constitution had completely altered Spain's relations with America; for the first time, a European nation had given its colonies complete equality, and no more special favors could be considered. Labrador submitted the new British proposal to the Cortes in November, but the Spaniards were in no mood to pursue the matter, replying to the British that it was only the interference of British merchants in America that had caused the rebellions in the first place. Recognizing that Spain was determined never to grant special trade privileges to Britain, Wellesley let the matter drop too. Spain had, of course, permitted itself an extraordinary admission when it failed to come to direct terms with the British suggestions for the creation of autonomous governments in America, for equal appointment of Americans to high office, and for equal trade, while all the time proclaiming that America was fully equal. Spain had told England that the two governments seemed to have different conceptions of the causes of the American rebellions—the Spanish insisting they were the work of Napoleonic agents and of British traders, the British insisting they were the work of Spanish oppression.

One final phase of the mediation question occurred before the fall of the constitutional regime. On 19 May 1813 the Council of State rendered its first comprehensive consultation on the question, and in a statement that summarized Spain's weakness of resources concluded: "The mediation offered by England should be accepted because there remain no other means that Spain can employ." The council was not prepared, however, to offer concessions. It urged that America be permitted free trade, but only in Spanish vessels. Free trade with foreigners would be considered later. But as a mark of good will to the British ally, Spain should offer a treaty of commerce with Britain, "in which it would be conceded certain and limited liberties of trade in American ports . . . in return for certain and limited aid to be received by the Spanish government during this treaty." The British ambassador would also be required to issue a joint manifesto with the Regency in which both urged Americans to lay down their arms and pointed out the fallacy of their rebellions. This manifesto would be carried to Buenos Aires, Bogotá, and Chile by joint Spanish-British commissions, and in Mexico it would be circulated by royal authorities or by a Spanish commission sent for that purpose without English membership.[62]

These proposals, of course, were entirely contrary to the British intentions, and Britain would never have consented to co-signing a manifesto to rebels pointing out the illegitimacy of their rebellions, nor to joint Spanish-British commissions in place of British commissions, nor to exclusion from Mexico. It goes without saying that Britain would not have considered granting indemnities to Spain in return for legal American trade when that trade was already flourishing illegally. Three councilors of State—Andres García, Pedro Cevallos, and Justo María Ibarnavarro—handed down individual statements (votos particulares) in which they urged that British mediation and the granting of free trade be accepted but that Spain prepare a powerful expeditionary force to be sent to America when the conciliation attempt failed. At the moment, however, this proposal not only produced no result but, as Toreno put it, "served only to add to the number of documents in the archives that time casts into oblivion."[63] The question of British mediation would be resurrected in 1815.

In the absence of adequate military resources to reconquer the dissident American provinces, and in the absence of a firm commitment to a military solution on the part of the liberals, Spain under the Cortes had effectively admitted its inability to solve the overseas rebellions and had lent an interested ear to the British offer of mediation. Yet, though the British had clearly specified the three principal objectives of the dissidents as part of their proposal—free foreign trade, equality of appointment, and domestic autonomy—the Cortes and Regency had refused to concede the bedrock issues. To have done so would have dismantled the empire, and that was the fundamental dilemma that all Spanish regimes faced when it came to granting reforms to America. While insisting that special concessions were not necessary because the Americans could send their own deputies to the Cortes, where all of the complaints and grievances could be fully heard, the liberals in the Cortes had not responded to those complaints when they were clearly and precisely specified by the American deputies. As late as 1813 the Spanish government was still insisting that it was French propaganda that provoked American rebellions, after having heard the frequent testimonials of American deputies that the rebellions resulted from Spain's colonial policies.

Symbolically, one of the last acts of the constitutional government regarding America was the annual report to the Cortes presented by the minister of ultramar in Madrid on 1 March 1814. The Constitution required such reports from the ministers on an annual basis. The report talked vaguely about the desire of the government to reform America but admitted that no one could predict when that would occur, since reform had to wait on the establishment of order in the revolted territories; in the meantime it was necessary "to restrain our excessive impatience in this regard." In a discussion of the plight of the Indians—"the miserable victims" of American discord, as they were called—the minister got distracted and ended up complimenting the Guatemalan Sociedad Económico for its efforts to expand weaving. Mining remained the chief source of wealth in America, and the government had requested reports from all America on the condition of the mines while it tried to reform abuses in the distribution of mercury and to lower its prices. The ministry had urged that mining tribunals plant trees to provide wood for the mines, had called for the establishment of new distribution networks and new roads in the mining areas, and had urged "whatever undertakings are needed." "With such assertive means the Regency does not doubt that the decadent exercise of mining in all America will be reestablished with speed." Yet the minister had taken no substantive steps toward that end, having merely ordered mining tribunals to do whatever they could. Similarly, in regard to the epidemic diseases that frequently devastated parts of America—one had just swept Mexico in 1813—the ministry had ordered precautions to be taken in Veracruz against the spread of the epidemic and had called on the political chief of Mexico to investigate the causes of the disease and means to cure and prevent it. He had also ordered the political chiefs of Cuba, Puerto Rico, and Santo Domingo to do the same with yellow fever, which had just swept those islands. The report concluded with references to the Cortes decree to distribute lands in freehold to Indians and castes in America (not yet undertaken because of lack of time) and to the hope America placed in the Cortes's decisions on the projected general plan of public instruction (not yet undertaken).[64] As with so much else over the past four years, the Cortes's final plenary presentation regarding American affairs was filled with vague generalities and promises for a brighter future at some unspecified date. The complaints of American audiencias and political chiefs that the Constitution and Cortes were destroying Spanish dominion in America by indecisiveness, political confusion, and helpless drift were correct, even though those American authorities were motivated by belief in absolutism and deep distrust of liberalism.

Two final acts of the constitutional government provide provocative indication of the direction the liberals might have moved in American affairs if they had been allotted a few more years in power. In mid-March 1814, after the king's departure from Valencay but before his entry into Spain, the Cortes seemed anxious to exert its authority in ways that might win it influence or at least a continuation of its existence. Yet the deputies were so clearly distracted by the great events sweeping the nation that their actions were not always well thought out. On 15 March 1814, for example, the Cortes decreed, in honor of the coming of Ferdinand to his native soil, that each deputy would contribute one day's salary as a dowry to be given to the first Indian woman who married a European Spaniard in one of the dissident American territories. It was not directly stated what the object of this peculiar decree might be, but presumably it was an earnest of the liberal social attitude the deputies wished to exhibit. Yet in the context of many other token acts in regard to the welfare of the empire's millions of desperate and depressed Indians, the act has a pathetic look about it.[65]

Of much greater significance—except that it was never implemented—was the Cortes decree of 19 March, issued only three days before the king's return to Spain, that ordered the suppression and dismantling of the state tobacco monopoly throughout the empire. The cultivation, fabrication, and sale of tobacco products was declared free; commerce in tobacco was declared free, with no other taxes but the usual national customs; the customs revenues were to be applied to paying off the huge national debt; and the state tobacco factories in Havana and other parts of America, and in Seville, Cádiz, and Alicante in the peninsula, were suppressed, the American ones to be sold.[66] Here was an act of genuine importance, the first example of the outright abolition by the Cortes of one of the great state monopolies against which American deputies so frequently protested. It is not clear, however, what the intention of the deputies was, though apparently their object was to divert these very significant revenues to the national debt while encouraging greater consumption of a product that was always in demand. The king's nullification of all acts of the Cortes in only two weeks' time prevented its implementation. And the fact that the Cortes decreed the sale of the American factories but not the giant peninsular ones (the tobacco factory in Seville, today the university, was one of the largest buildings in the world) indicates that the act was not undertaken solely in response to American demands but was at least as European in its orientation. In essence, it would take revenues previously applied by the colonial governments toward operating expenses in the colonies and divert them instead toward the national debt. It may not have been a concession toward the American demand for laissez-faire economics at all. Consequently, this act, like others passed in the last days of the Cortes, was not a part of a specific American policy.

The failure of the Cortes to come to grips with the American crisis provides a useful antidote to the excess admiration of the liberal regime sometimes expressed in the historiography. Despite their undoubted merits, it is clear that the Spanish liberals were no less imperialists than the absolutists who made up the Old Regime, and they did little to answer America's needs. Baquíjano testified that they did not want to meet American demands; but a fairer judgment would be that they could not, for, as Toreno and Argüelles and others hinted, to have given in to American demands would have been to dismantle the empire. Nor was it possible to ignore the powerful Cádiz merchants. This dilemma was not unique to the constitutionalists; it is just that they promised so much to America—everything from a genuine revolution in government to full equality. In 1810 Spain needed the empire to survive; by 1812 the overseas territories had their own revolutions to face and no longer supplied the metropolis with significant revenues, but by that time the unspoken guiding principle was that the glory of Spain still required possession of the empire. This would motivate Spanish intransigence even when the empire no longer served any useful purpose.

A more significant lesson, however, is that the structure of the regime of the Cortes itself militated against the solution of the American problem. The Americans had to be represented, but were not permitted parity. Once American Cortes deputies took their seats, concessions had to be made, but they were all tokens. The American deputies lacked the numbers to induce action on critical reforms. The absorption of more than purely legislative powers by the Cortes— which effectively emasculated both the Regency and the ministries in this first Cortes period—made independent action from the government impossible without Cortes consent. There could be no Cortes consent, so there was no action. The system itself was inappropriate to the solution of the American crisis. Indeed, the very momentousness of the social, political, and economic experiment they were engaged in served to obscure the importance of American complaints in most legislators' minds. In the end, they also lacked the time. The six-year experiment in liberal government from 1808 to 1814 serves to reenforce the thesis that there were political and institutional impediments at each stage of this complex story to explain how Spain failed to retain control of America.

IV

El Deseado

And then, almost as fast as it had risen, the liberal government fell. It was the king's restoration and his decree of 4 May 1814 that destroyed the Cortes and Constitution, but the liberal regime itself had begun to falter with the election of the new ordinary Cortes of 1813–14. The first Cortes, the extraordinary Cortes, had met from September 1810 until the conclusion of its term in September 1813. Having created a government, promulgated the Constitution, and instituted sweeping legislative reforms, it passed out of existence according to the terms of the Constitution with the elections through-out the empire of a new Cortes for the first regular two-year term of 1813–14. According to the Constitution, no incumbent member of parliament could stand for immediate reelection.

In the last months of the extraordinary Cortes, Spain's first two political parties had begun to emerge in the so-called liberals (an as yet ill-defined term applying principally to the more radical parliamen-tarians who had predominated in the extraordinary Cortes and had been the chief authors of the Constitution and of the new limited monarchical system), and the so-called *serviles* (an equally ill-defined term suggesting individuals servile to the throne, or royalists). The followers of the conservative modern historian Federico Suárez argue that both liberals and *serviles* were in favor of reformism, only the extent of their radicalism differed. Suárez says, for example, that in 1814 there were three defined political positions: the Old Regime, which liberals called "absolutism" and royalists called "ministerial despotism"; the liberals, reformers who had dominated in 1812 and who were often therefore referred to as *doceañistas;* and the "royalist

reformers," called by the liberals *serviles*. The first movement represented nothing but "pure inertia" he says, whereas the other two were
new political forces, awakened by the catastrophe of 1808 but profoundly opposed to each other regarding the extent to which reform
should go, especially the extent to which the royal prerogatives should
be curtailed. The Old Regime was already dead, killed by 1808,
leaving the two other forces to struggle among themselves. Even
today, Suárez says, it is not possible to say which of the reformist
currents actually won.[1] This scheme of political currents, which has
been assiduously presented by Suárez and others, including José Luis
Comellas, María del Carmen Pintos Vieites, and María Cristina
Diz-Lois, does appear to be a sensible definition of political forces at
work as of 1814, except that it may underestimate the continued life
that the Old Regime, whether it be called absolutism or ministerial
despotism, had left in it, for the person of Ferdinand VII alone was
such a powerful symbol that it temporarily put the other two political
forces to flight in the period of the first restoration.

The extraordinary crisis of 1808, the fact that Spain was swept
by what Lovett calls "the first total war" in modern history, had
temporarily obscured political differences among the political leaders
of Spain and between them and the mass of the Spanish people. The
crisis brought to power the reformers of Cádiz, whose political
objectives actually differed little from those of the French and their
Spanish collaborators, the *afrancesados*. The two liberal forces advocated similar reforms, but they broke over the question of the French
usurpation of the throne. Suárez argues that the decrees of Cádiz were
often the same as those of the usurper king Joseph as represented in the
Congress of Bayonne and subsequent royal decrees, only the Cádiz
reformers modified the liberal decrees to suit the conditions of Spain.
Thus liberalism and its relation with French thought was clear. The
mass of the Spanish people were not believers in these ideas of reform
and rationalization, and they and the patriots of Cádiz were
accidentally or temporarily on the same side in their struggle against
France. The Constitution of 1812, the ultimate expression of Spanish
liberalism, did not express the wishes of the mass of the nation. Hence
the reaction of 1814 was very popular, and it is logical that it should

be, for the people viewed the liberal ideas as the same as the French ideas they had just fought a long and bloody war to reject.[2]

This thesis seems to be substantiated by the results of the elections for the new ordinary Cortes. The more conservative vote greatly predominated, and a majority of the *serviles*, or royalists—or what Suárez calls renovators as opposed to innovators—were chosen, exceeding the liberals by a sizable margin. Toreno, a leading liberal, admitted that the new elections had chosen a majority of persons "disaffected with changes and novelties." Consequently, the liberals who controlled the extraordinary Cortes determined that they would remain in office until all the newly-elected deputies, most of whom were unable to reach Cádiz in time, could arrive. In this way the ordinary Cortes opened its sessions on 26 September 1813 with a majority of members (three-quarters of them) left over from the former Cortes. The newly-elected American deputies had not yet had time to arrive in Cádiz, and those newly elected from the peninsula chose not to travel to the city because it was then the scene of a raging yellow fever epidemic. Hence the old deputies remained as substitutes for those not yet arrived, in order that no province should be without representation.[3] The yellow fever epidemic was so extensive that it largely prevented the Cortes from taking any major action for the next two months anyhow. Of the deputies, now reduced in numbers, who participated at the sessions of the new Cortes, no less than sixty fell ill, and over twenty of those died in a few days. Among them was the leading American liberal, José Mejía, who had maintained in Cortes debates that there was no yellow fever epidemic.

The Cortes, of course, had the option of moving its site to some mainland city not affected by the disease, but it chose not to do so in order not to open its doors to the majority of *serviles* waiting on the mainland to claim their seats. In October the Cortes did remove itself to Isla de León, still avoiding the mainland in order to maintain a liberal majority. By this time the French had evacuated Madrid and the newly-elected but as yet unseated Cortes deputies clamored for the government to transfer to the capital. The new Cortes did contain some new leaders among the liberal party, men whose names would loom large in the years to come, including José Canga Argüelles and

Francisco Martínez de la Rosa. Ultimately, unable to withstand the legitimate demands of the newly-chosen proprietary deputies that they be permitted to take their seats, and no longer able to ignore the fact that Madrid was now restored to Spanish control, the ordinary Cortes suspended its sessions in Isla de León on 29 November 1813 and announced it would reopen in Madrid on 15 January 1814.[4] Thus the liberal majority came to an end, amid mourning for those lost in the epidemic and amid fears that on the reopening of sessions in Madrid the *serviles* would predominate.[5]

Beginning in the spring of 1813 the French had been gradually driven out of Spain. In March the usurper king Joseph abandoned his erstwhile capital of Madrid, and in May the French forces left behind to hold the city evacuated it. At the end of May, Wellington's combined allied forces captured Salamanca and Zamora. On 21 June, Wellington caught up with the retreating French forces at Vitoria, in the Basque province of Alava, and there the French were finally routed. Joseph fled back to France, and the vestiges of the French armies met defeat after defeat. San Sebastián was retaken in August and Pamplona in October, leaving the French in possession only of Barcelona and a few strongpoints in the northeast, from which they would shortly withdraw. In December Napoleon formally returned to the captive king Ferdinand the throne of Spain in the Treaty of Valencay, which was signed by both men. Napoleon had lost Spain, and shortly his entire empire would crumble about him.[6]

In Spain there now began a long period of tension, which lasted from January to May 1814, concerning what the response of the Desired One, El Deseado, Ferdinand VII, would be to the Constitution and Cortes. After six years of governing the nation in the name of the captive king, would the new liberal system recognize him—and would he recognize it? According to the Constitution, the king was required to take an oath of allegiance to the Constitution before the Cortes would recognize his authority. According to the Treaty of Valencay, which Ferdinand signed with Napoleon, peace was declared between France and Spain, and Napoleon recognized Ferdinand as king of Spain. Would the Old Regime be restored or would the new system prevail?

The Cortes, even though it had an increasingly large number of *serviles* arriving to assume their seats, was clear in its response. In January 1811 it had passed a decree declaring that any act of the king while still held captive would not be recognized. It so informed the king's two representatives—the Duke of San Carlos and General José de Palafox—who arrived in Madrid in January 1814 to investigate the Regency's reaction to the Treaty of Valencay. And on 2 February the Cortes decreed that the king would not be considered free and therefore would not be obeyed until he took the oath to the Constitution, that the king's itinerary from the border to Madrid would be planned by the Regency, and that the president of the Regency would hand Ferdinand a copy of the Constitution at the border and would accompany him all the way to Madrid. The king at first seemed inclined to accept these rather stringent restrictions on his freedom of action, and wrote the Regency on 10 March that "the reestablishment of the Cortes, of which the Regency has appraised me, as well as anything done during my absence that is beneficial to the kingdom, will receive my approval."[7] With this the king departed the country estate of Valencay where he had spent his long captivity and on 22 March 1814 entered Spanish territory under protection of the retreating Marshal Suchet. On 24 March the commander of the Spanish first army, Francisco de Copons, met the king at the border and handed him the Cortes decree of 2 February.

The king immediately began to illustrate his independence from the Regency by accepting the petition of the city of Zaragoza to stop there, a city that had not been on the Regency's itinerary for the royal tour. By the time his visit in Zaragoza was over he had begun to recognize that the nation responded to him personally rather than to the Cortes and Regency, and he had begun to receive the advice of intimate friends who rushed north to greet him that he not acknowledge the Constitution. Toreno says that by 11 April, after the king had left Zaragoza, he had already been talked by his intimates into waiting to see whether the nation seemed more responsive to him or to the Cortes. By this early point in his return to Spain—while he was still reorienting himself to the nation he had not seen for six years—the king was already surrounded by a group of advisors, many of them his intimate friends from 1808, some of whom had accompanied him to Valencay, whose opinion he depended upon. They included the Dukes of Frías, Osuna, and San Carlos and the Conde de Montijo, and Toreno says that by 11 April they were already discussing some coup against the Constitution. In the next few days other members of the camarilla that would continue to dominate Ferdinand's politics for the rest of his life were in attendance upon his person. By 13 April, at Teruel on his way to Valencia, General Copons having departed the official party, Toreno says there was no longer any advisor who favored the Constitution and "there was scarcely anybody at His Majesty's side of influence and weight who could balance out the unwise advice of those who imprisoned his will or gave it a deplorable bias."[8]

At Segorbe the camarilla was joined by the king's uncle Don Antonio, by Pedro de Macanaz and Pedro Gómez Labrador, and by the king's former tutor, the reactionary cleric Juan de Escoiquiz. In a meeting that night the camarilla heard Labrador angrily argue that the king should never swear to the Constitution and should "get the liberals in his grasp." By 16 April the king arrived in Valencia, where the camarilla was joined by Juan Pérez Villamil and Miguel de Lardizábal, both noted opponents of the Cortes. Here too the weak-willed president of the Regency, Cardinal Luis de Borbón, archbishop of Toledo, joined the king to represent the government. In Valencia the captain general, Francisco Javier Elío, now returned from his American adventures, drew up his army before the king, and asked his soldiers, "Do you swear to sustain the King in the plenitude of his powers?" to which they responded with shouts of enthusiasm. "And with that," says Toreno, "Ferdinand began to exercise in Valencia his sovereignty, without any consideration of what the Cortes had resolved."[9]

It seems clear that the king's decision was practically made by 16 April, but adding further support to this course of action and, according to María Cristina Diz-Lois, providing him with an actual master plan on which to model his coup d'etat was his receipt of the famous Manifesto of the Persians, or "Manifiesto de las Persas." So called because its first line referred to the practice among the ancient Persians of engaging in five days of murder and plunder on the death of a king so that they would be more grateful for the order restored by his successor, the manifesto was signed by sixty-nine Cortes deputies, the leading *serviles* or royalists. This number included ten Americans: Blas Ostolaza, the king's former chaplain and conservative deputy for Peru; Antonio Joaquín Pérez deputy for Puebla; Angel Alonso y Pantiga, Yucatán; José Cayetano de Foncerrada, Michoacán; Tadeo Gárate, Puno; Pedro García Coronel and José Gavino de Ortega y Salmón, Trujillo; Mariano Rodríguez de Olmedo, Charcas; Salvador San Martín, New Spain; and Francisco López Lisperguer, Buenos Aires. There were, at its highest point, 184 deputies in the Cortes in 1814. Of these 134 were Spanish and 59 of them signed the manifesto; and 50 were Americans, of whom 10 signed the manifesto.[10] It was thus the work of one-third of the deputies, the most conservative portion, who favored the restoration of royalist absolutism.

The fundamental argument of the Persas was that, although Ferdinand had called for the creation of the Cortes before he went into captivity, the Cortes that finally met, on invitation of the Junta Central and the Regency, was illegitimate because it was constituted by popular election, without the preservation of the estates, and because it far exceeded its power by legislating a new system of government rather than merely calling together the national armies, equipping them, and finding ways to finance them. The majority of the deputies of the provinces were labeled unrepresentative, and the practice of choosing substitute deputies from among individuals resident in Cádiz was pointed out as being particularly illegitimate. Consequently, the work of the extraordinary Cortes, including the Constitution and other legislation, was deemed illegitimate. The American deputies particularly were non-representative, as they actually represented revolted provinces no longer in obedience to the king, and the decrees of the Cortes further exacerbated aspirations to independence overseas. Paragraph 35 of the manifesto appeared to suggest that the principle of popular sovereignty had actually awakened the independence struggle in America. All the other hallmarks of the Cortes era were criticized, including freedom of the press, abolition of the señoríos, opening of the universities to castes, and abolition of the Inquisition. "All of these decrees manifested hatred for the rights and prerogatives of Your Majesty," insisted the Persas.

Indeed, it becomes difficult to accept the argument of Suárez and Diz-Lois that the Persas were actually renovators, royalist reformers, when the manifesto itself attacked every substantive reform for America, even the most symbolic, such as the abolition of the ceremony of the Royal Standard. Arguing that "absolute monarchy . . . is a work of reason and intelligence; it is subordinate to the divine law, to justice, and to the fundamental laws of the State; it was established by right of conquest or by the voluntary submission of the first men who elected their kings," the Persas went on to request full restoration of royal prerogatives, the reestablishment of the original Spanish "constitution" as it existed in the body of law and precedent, and the creation of a new Cortes called by the monarch and based on estates. The manifesto argued that "those who declaim against monarchical government confuse absolute power with arbitrary power," for in an absolute monarchy the people are more free than in a republic, in which no control over the state's authority exists. This was a basic philosophical principle Ferdinand would repeat with pleasure.

The request of the Persas was that the king should call a legitimate Cortes in the form in which it was celebrated in the medieval era and that he should declare null and void the Constitution and the Cortes of Cádiz. The Persas urged the king to reward the patriotic armies that had saved Spain, but also to bring to trial the politicians of Cádiz who had, they insisted, actually retarded the war effort. The Persas were opposed to the "ministerial despotism" that had existed before the war—a reference to the reign of Charles IV's favorite, Godoy—and asked that the new Cortes, constituted according to Spain's body of traditional law, should guarantee fair administration of justice, equitable taxation, and security for the individual. But these "renovating" requests were limited to but two of the manifesto's 143 paragraphs. It is true, as Suárez says, that "the manifesto of the Persas is for the royalists what the Constitution of 1812 was for the liberals"—for it provided the fundamental guide to the king's actions over the next few weeks and would be reflected in his 4 May decree annulling the Cortes and Constitution—but there is little evidence otherwise that it formed anything but a political pronouncement of totally negative effect, since the king never called the traditional Cortes. Suárez argues that the royalists had confidence in the word of the king to call the Cortes and therefore were not impatient over the long years from 1814 to 1820 when he continued to refuse to do so. At any rate, as Lovett points out, the Persas, who were the party of the king and were victorious in the political struggle, "did nothing after Ferdinand's reassumption of absolute power to convince the monarch to bring about these improvements."[11]

There was now nothing to stand in the way of the coup that Ferdinand had been considering for several days. Everywhere he went—in Zaragoza and in Valencia particularly—he was received by the people with great enthusiasm. His camarilla had begun to organize itself and advised him to refuse to swear to the Constitution. Escoiquiz was actively plotting against the Constitution in Valencia before the king's arrival there. General Elío had shown—in what is often called Spain's first pronunciamiento in the nineteenth century—that the army supported the restoration of absolutism. The Manifesto of the Persas showed that support existed even within the elected Cortes itself. The Cortes and Regency had made the fatal error of waiting in Madrid to see what the king's disposition would be, and Cardinal Borbón, president of the Regency, on first meeting Ferdinand on the outskirts of Valencia, had kissed the king's hand in the ancient symbol of obeisance to the sovereign.[12] Absolutist periodicals began appearing in Valencia supporting overthrow of the reforms. The king had even refused to reply to the two latest messages from the Cortes. With the support of the army, the church, the masses, there was little doubt that Ferdinand was more powerful than his erstwhile government. While an attack of gout temporarily delayed the coup, Toreno says that the king and General Elío ordered a body of troops to Madrid whose commander, when asked by the constitutional government why he had come, responded it was by order of the king. On 4 May 1814 the king sat down in Valencia with Pedro Gómez Labrador, Spain's future delegate at the Congress of Vienna, and with Juan Pérez Villamil, a former regent, and drew up the decree—which was not published until 11 May after the king's arrival near Madrid—in which he abolished the constitution and declared all the acts of the Cortes null and void. The next day Ferdinand began his trip to Madrid, escorted by the troops of General Elío. On the road the king refused to receive the six commissioners the Cortes had appointed to receive him; instead, he ordered them to wait upon him at Aranjuez.

Meanwhile, actions that Toreno said were "unheard of in the annals of Spain" were put into effect in Madrid. On the night of 10–11 May, on royal orders, the two remaining regents, Pedro Agar and Gabriel Císcar, were arrested, together with minister of government Juan Alvarez Guerra and minister of grace and justice Manuel García Herreros (the two ministers chiefly in charge of domestic police and administration), and the liberal leaders of the Cortes Diego Muñoz Torrero, Agustín Argüelles, Francisco Martínez de la Rosa, Antonio Oliveros, Manuel López Cepero, José Canga Argüelles, Antonio Larrazábal, Joaquín Lorenzo Villanueva, Miguel Ramos Arizpe, José Calatrava, Francisco Gutiérrez de Terán, and Dionisio Capaz; also the poet and leading propagandist of the Cortes Manuel José Quintana and others. The arrests were conducted by the newly-appointed captain general of New Castile, Francisco Eguía, who would also be a major figure in the king's camarilla. The arrests continued for several days and extended into the provinces. Those leading liberals not arrested, including the Conde de Toreno, fled into foreign exile. On the same night of 10–11 May, General Elío presented himself to Antonio Joaquín Pérez, the deputy from Puebla, serving then as president of the Cortes, and announced that on the orders of the king the Cortes were dissolved. The next morning the decree of 4 May, written in Valencia but kept a closely guarded secret, was promulgated.[13]

The decree of 4 May constituted, in effect, the king's reply to the requests of the Persas. In long and rambling sentences Ferdinand reviewed his accession to the throne, his captivity by Napoleon, and the rise of the Junta Central, Regency, and Cortes (the latter described in the same terms as those employed by the Persas). He declared that the Cortes, unrepresentative and self-mandated, had constituted tyranny, for the Cortes had appointed itself sovereign and its members had appropriated the powers of ultimate authority to themselves. This was usurpation, and it had led to the creation of the "yoke" of a new Constitution that did not represent the authority of any province, town, or junta. Following this initial attack on the prerogatives of the throne, the Cortes had continued to pass legislation under the influence of the Cádiz radicals in the galleries. The ancient constitution was thus replaced by "the revolutionary and democratic principles of the French Constitution of 1791." The free press then brought under attack the very honor of the royal power, "giving to all the rights of majesty the name of despotism, making synonomous the words king and despot and calling the kings tyrants." He continued, "I swear and promise to you, true and loyal Spaniards, that at the same time that I sympathize with you for the evils you have suffered, you will not be defrauded in your noble aspirations. . . . I abhor and detest despotism. . . . In Spain her kings were never despots." As a result, "I will treat with your representatives from Spain and the Indies, in Cortes legitimately congregated, composed of one and the other, just as soon as order is reestablished." This new Cortes, constituted under the traditional laws and composed of representatives of the estates, would proceed to legislate what might be necessary for the reestablishment of peace and prosperity throughout the empire. The press would also be free to communicate ideas "under the limits that sane reason . . . prescribes." The royal treasury would be separated from the expenses of the dynasty, in order to assure public confidence in the nation's credit. Having heard the voice of many representations from all over the kingdom, "I declare that my royal will is, not only not to swear nor accede to the said Constitution [of 1812], nor to any decree of the general and extraordinary Cortes and of the ordinary Cortes presently open . . . but to declare that Constitution and those decrees null and of no value nor effect, now and for all time, as if those acts had never been passed."[14] With this unpleasant business concluded, the king entered his capital of Madrid on 13 May 1814 under heavy guard of 8,500 troops.

It was Toreno's opinion that the 4 May decree was proof that the king had been converted into "a blind instrument of an implacable and self-interested faction" and that through his lack of knowledge about the state of affairs in Spain the king was inclined "to listen to erroneous advice, which had been noticed since the beginning of his reign."[15] This was not merely the raving of a displaced liberal politician, for the hallmark of Ferdinand's reign had already been and would continue to be his dependence on his camarilla and their frequently bad advice. In 1820, under pressure from the liberal regime that was restored in the revolution of that year, he was forced to admit to this charge.

Although the frequency of the appearance of the names of Ferdinand's chief advisors, whether they possessed ministerial portfolios or simply had free access to the king's presence, makes the argument of Pintos Vieites that there was no camarilla highly unlikely, it is nonetheless true that one cannot tell at any given moment precisely which of the members of the camarilla were exercising influence over him. Yet, Pintos Vieites also admits "that each of these personages exercised influence on the spirit of the Monarch seems undoubted."[16] She cites the most prominent members of the group: the Peruvian ultraroyalist Blas Ostolaza; Antonio Ugarte, a merchant who would hold no portfolio but would be constantly in attendance upon the king; the Duke of San Carlos, a Peruvian-born grandee who headed the first government of the restoration; the king's mentor Escoiquiz; the Duke of Infantado; Pedro Macanaz; Francisco Eguía; Juan Esteban Lozano de Torres. This was the camarilla; it variously included at other times, whether early in the restoration or later, Miguel de Lardizábal, Pedro Gómez Labrador, the Dukes of Frías, Osuna, and Alagón, Juan Pérez Villamil, the Conde de Montijo, Pedro Collado (a former water carrier), Guillermo Hualde (the king's confessor), the king's brother and heir Don Carlos, and the Russian ambassador Dmitri Pavlovich Tatishchev.[17] The fact that some of these men would travel abroad on diplomatic missions or would otherwise not be in attendance on the king at any given moment hardly disproves the existence of the camarilla. Pintos Vieites insists that instead of a camarilla, the policies of Ferdinand were the king's work alone, and that he made all final decisions. This is not inconsistent with the existence of a powerful group of advisors. The testimony of such highly placed ministers as Pedro Cevallos, José García de León y Pizarro, José Vázquez Figueroa, Martín Garay, and various foreign diplomats shows that the camarilla indeed existed and that it often functioned as a government within a government, as a group of advisors who influenced the king's decisions often without regard to or in direct contradiction to the advice of his duly appointed ministers. Thus there were often two governments—the ministry named by the king, and the camarilla. This would be the government's major structural weakness in the era of the restoration.

Equally doubtful is Pintos Vieites's argument that Ferdinand did not impose a reign of terror with the arrest of a number of Cortes deputies in May 1814. Her point is that the arrests were limited in number, that each individual was processed according to law, and that the sentences handed down were mild. There is no denying the truth of those statements, but the fundamental fact is that the arrest of the deputies, whether one or one hundred, constituted a type of action that, although it might well have been within the king's legal right after his restoration, was nonetheless despotic. It was the leading liberals who were arrested; the king obviously was not going to arrest every deputy, since probably a majority in 1814 were conservative royalists. Nor does Pintos Vieites take into account the fact that the formal hearings took over a year and a half to complete, with final judgments being handed down by the king on 15 December 1815, adding considerably to the time of detention of the arrested deputies, kept under house arrest in the interim. The first step in the process was the appointment of a number of minor judges charged with collecting the papers and documents of the deputies. Then the king received a résumé of the role each deputy had played in the Cortes in the process of "discrediting the king and denying his rights." After that, Minister of Grace and Justice Pedro Macanaz submitted the evidence to the alcaldes de casa y corte, the magistrates of the city of Madrid, who rendered an opinion that the cases should not be pursued. The documents then passed to the Council of Castile, which on 14 September 1814 passed them on to a second commission appointed by the king, after whose deliberations the king handed down final judgments.

The king was no doubt very scrupulous in his investigation, as

Pintos Vieites argues, but the core of his evidence rested on a request that he sent to a number of informants asking them to tell him in detail "which deputies, in either the extraordinary or ordinary Cortes, had been the prime movers of the activities of these Cortes against the sovereignty of His Majesty." The informants were twenty in number, and included such well-known conservatives as Pedro Inguanzo, then bishop of Pamplona, the Conde de Montijo, Bernardo Mozo Rosales, reputedly the author of the Manifesto of the Persas, and four of the ten American deputies who signed the manifesto—Blas Ostolaza, Antonio Joaquín Pérez, José Cayetano Foncerrada, and Tadeo Gárate; a majority were former deputies of the ordinary Cortes. The final list of accusations included having plotted against the king's sovereignty; having advocated Article 3 of the Constitution, which declared that sovereignty resided in the nation; having required the nation to swear to the Constitution; having upheld "fallacious" principles; having exercised violence against royalist deputies—and there were twenty-six others. Ultimately a total of twenty-two former deputies, along with thirty other leading liberals (including regents Císcar and Agar), were given sentences. The deputies included: Agustín Argüelles, sentenced to eight years in the presidio of Ceuta; Diego Muñoz Torrero, six years in a monastery; Antonio Larrazábal (Guatemala), six years in a convent in Guatemala; Joaquín Lorenzo Villanueva, six years in the convent of Salceda; Francisco Fernández Golfín, ten years in the castle of Alicante; Ramón Felíu (Peru), eight years in the castle of Benasque; Miguel Ramos Arizpe (Mexico), four years in the Cartuja of Valencia; Manuel García Herreros, eight years in the presidio of Alhucemas; Joaquín Maniau (Mexico), confinement to Córdoba and a fine of 20,000 reales; Francisco Martínez de la Rosa, eight years in the presidio of Peñón and banishment from Madrid and all royal residences; José Canga Argüelles, four years of exile from court and eight years in the castle of Peñíscola.[18] This may not have been oppression on the same vast scale as that after 1823, but it was oppression nonetheless. The liberals who were confined would be freed by the revolution of 1820 and take their places among the leadership of the second liberal regime.

During 1814 and 1815 there would be many more investigations into the political conduct of government officials during the French occupation. So-called "juntas of purification" were established for each ministry, council, or other governmental agency. They called for and collected mounds of personal testimony concerning individuals and their response to the intrusive king Joseph and the French invaders and to the liberal regime, and on "purifying" an individual, permitted his restoration to office. Many collaborators and liberals, and under Ferdinand it was easy to confuse the two, lost their positions, so many in fact that by 1816 the possibility of issuing a general amnesty to all political offenders was actively discussed, with the current minister of state, Pizarro, testifying that only a general amnesty could rid the nation of the civil discord and hatreds that the harrassment of liberals and supposed *afrancesados* had provoked. Pizarro believed the purifications and the mistreatment of supposed French collaborators tarnished the heroic struggle of liberation that the previous administrations had waged, but he testified that during discussions of a possible amnesty by the ministers the camarilla members Francisco Eguía and Juan Esteban Lozano de Torres scuttled the proposal, with Eguía proclaiming that amnesty was treason. [19]

The king's restoration to his throne brought with it a restoration of everything else as well. The Cortes he promised was never called. Meantime, a succession of royal decrees throughout the latter half of 1814 ordered abolition of all constitutional and elected bodies, such as the city councils, provincial deputations, and juntas of censorship (watchdog of the free press); restoration to office of all individuals who had held office as of the day of Ferdinand's accession to the throne in March 1808; reestablishment of the old councils; abolition of freedom of the press; restoration of feudal privileges and señoríos; restoration of monasteries and other properties to the regular clergy; and even reestablishment of the Inquisition. The latter brought a special protest from the king of Prussia, who complained that Ferdinand owed his restoration not a little to the effort of allied Protestant forces in Spain. [20]

The evidence, at any rate, is that the reaction was overwhelmingly popular in Spain. Liberalism had been the creed of a minority of the population, of the professional and educated classes, of the Cádiz

Table 3: Mesas in the Restored Ministry of the Indies, 1814.

Official	Ramo	Responsibilities or Mesa
Sr. Calomarde		Review of all expedientes to be signed, interior management of ministry, distribution of papers, normal expenditures
Sr. Tejada	Hacienda	Peru and Buenos Aires
Sr. Romero	Hacienda	Commerce, consulados, juzgados de arribadas, Company of the Philippines.
Sr. Morán	Hacienda	Bogotá, tobacco for all dominions
Sr. Hore	Hacienda	New Spain, business relating to Almadén, mercury, mining in all dominions
Sr. Salcedo	Hacienda	Provincias Internas and casas de moneda
Sr. Pedroso	Hacienda	Floridas, Louisiana, Santo Domingo, Council of Indies, and Contaduría General
Sr. Cubello	Hacienda	Guatemala, Yucatán, Philippines
Sr. Michelena	Hacienda	Cuba, P. Rico, Company of Havana, Medical Society of Seville, theaters and public diversions
Sr. Rios	Hacienda	Venezuela, Chile, botanical expeditions, mails, and everything not assigned to other mesas
Sr. Ocerín	Hacienda	Quito, protomedicato, juntas of health, projects for agriculture, arts, industry
Sr. Antelo	Grace, Justice, Government	Guatemala, Santo Domingo, Cuba, P. Rico, Louisiana, Honduras, ecclesiastical and secular
Sr. Larrañaga	G, J, G	Philippines, Chile, hospitals, jails, cemeteries, ecclesiastical and secular
Sr. Collar	G, J, G	Bogotá, Panama, Portobelo, Cartagena, Santa Marta, Quito, Popayán, ecclesiastical and secular

Table 3 *continued*

Official	Ramo	Responsibilities or Mesa
Sr. Urquinaona	G, J, G	Venezuela, passports, general
Sr. Tordero	G, J, G	Peru, ecclesiastical and secular, dispatch of works of former American deputies
Sr. Agüero	G, J, G	New Spain, Provincias Internas, ecclesiastical and secular, Archivo General de Indias
Sr. Herreros	G, J, G	Buenos Aires, ecclesiastical and secular
Sr. Cidón	G, J, G	Science and arts, public press, foreign press, correspondence with minister to United States, audiencias of Charcas and Cuzco, Montepío of the ministry
Sr. Domínguez	War	Militias in America
Sr. Sevilla	War	Troops of the line
Sr. Göosen	War	Artillery, engineers, fortifications

SOURCE:
Reglamento, Secretaria Universal de Indias, Madrid,
August 15, 1814, AGI, Indiferente 1355.

merchants, of the bourgeoisie. The vast majority of the artisans, the peasants, and other elements of the lower classes had found little concrete meaning in the Constitution, especially in view of the clergy's resistance. Ferdinand was their idol, for he was the symbol that had been held out to them of what they were fighting for during all those years. The Duke of Wellington wrote Charles Stuart on 25 May 1814: "You will have heard of the extraordinary occurrences here, though not probably with surprise. Nothing can be more popular than the King and his measures, as far as they have gone to the overthrow of the Constitution. The imprisonment of the *Liberales* is thought by some, I believe with justice, unnecessary, and it is certainly highly impolitic; but it is liked by the people at large."[21] It may, indeed, have been the one moment in Ferdinand's life in which he clearly read the popular sentiment and acted on it, though response to public opinion was hardly his motive.

In America the response of royal authorities to the restoration of the desired one was universal enthusiasm and relief. At last there would be a central decision-making power of undoubted authority. In Mexico, Viceroy Calleja received news of the king's return and annullment of the Constitution on 5 August 1814 and reacted, as he wrote, with "unspeakable joy." He informed the various constitutional bodies of their dissolution with considerable glee, conducting his own mini-coup. In Peru, the steadfast Viceroy Abascal, who had been aiding the resistance of royalist governments all over the continent, published the king's nullification decree on 6 October 1814 and responded also with scarcely restrained joy. Both men's enthusiasm was naturally heightened by the realization that the overthrow of the Constitution restored them to their positions as viceroy rather than the downgraded status of superior political chief. In Guatemala the restoration saved Captain General José de Bustamante, whose removal from office and replacement by a Guatemalan creole had been decreed by the Cortes in its last months.[22]

In Spain the old Ministry of the Indies was immediately reestablished, with Miguel de Lardizábal being appointed by the king as minister, and within a month he presented to his own department the regulations for its internal governance. Lardizábal restored the old technique of dividing the ministry into a number of *mesas*, or tables, charged with particular duties in the three realms of treasury, grace and justice and government, and war. It was a logical, if slightly makeshift, division of duties that had the advantage of making it clear to royal authorities in America to whom they should correspond in regard to a particular question. This degree of clarity had not existed under the Cortes, when the secretariat had complained, on moving back to Madrid, that it was allotted only four rooms in the residence of the Infante Don Antonio in which to conduct its business. Lardizábal's scheme of duties and responsibilities in the Ministry of the Indies is shown in table 3. Each official was to make up the extracts of papers in his field for presentation to the minister; all paperwork was to be done in duplicate or triplicate, with a sufficient number of copyists assigned to each official. Officials were to attend the office with sword when the king was in Madrid.[23]

Meanwhile, the Council of the Indies was restored by a decree of 2 July 1814 and was to consist, as before, of three salas or chambers — two of government and one of justice — with five ministers *de capa y espada* (a term used to distinguish non-lawyers from university-trained lawyers or *letrados* on high state councils) and fourteen *ministros togados* (or professional lawyers, judges), with two fiscales (crown attorneys or advocates), two secretaries, and a treasurer. The Duke of Montemar was president of the council, and a number of former deputies were included as members, among them the conservative José Pablo Valiente.[24] In the initial announcement of members José de Baquíjano was listed as a member. He had been appointed because of his friendship with the new minister of state, the Peruvian-born Duke of San Carlos, his family relationship with the minister of the Indies, Miguel de Lardizábal, and his friendship with the new minister of government, Pedro de Macanaz; but he refused the appointment. Shortly after, he lost favor, suffering the same fate as many of the Spanish liberals. He was confined to house arrest in Seville, where he died in 1817.[25]

Other changes in the membership of the council apparently occurred in the first months after restoration, for by 5 September 1814, when the council formally advised the king of its support for the restoration of government in America to what it was before the Cortes, only fifteen members took part in the discussion. The king, by the way, naturally accepted the council's advice and formally decreed in November the restoration of all government and economic affairs in America to the conditions that prevailed before the Cortes. The members of the council at that time were the Duke of Montemar as president, Pedro Aparici, Francisco Requena, the Conde de Torremuzquiz, Ignacio Omulrrían, José Pablo Valiente, Antonio de Gamiz, Francisco de la Vega, Cayetano Urbina, Joaquín Mosquera, Francisco Ibáñez de Leyva, Antonio Martínez Salcedo, Francisco Xavier Caro, Jose Navia Bolaños, and Manuel María Junco.[26] Eight of those had been on the council as reconstituted in September 1810 by the Cortes,[27] suggesting that the determining factor was to have successfully undergone the process of "purification"—and thus being shown not to have participated in the attempt to denigrate the king's majesty—rather than having participated in the Cortes regime.

Subalterns of the Council of the Indies also underwent the purification process. Most were restored to office if they had followed the free Spanish government to the south, had stayed in Madrid but had not participated in the French government, or had stayed in Madrid and participated in the French government merely in order to provide a living for their families. From the testimony of the city council of Madrid and individual parish priests, a profile was put together for each employee, note was taken of any particular heroism or any particular show of support for the French, and only those who were absolutely "pure" in regard to both the French intrusion and the constitutional attempt to denigrate the throne were restored to office.[28] Although this did not constitute the type of witch-hunt that Ferdinand would launch in 1823 upon his second restoration to full authority, the 1814 purification process must have disrupted the careful consideration of massive policy questions that the great councils were supposed to engage in.

In the first three months of the restoration there was every indication that the king wanted to know what America had to say. On Lardizábal's advice he called for and received summaries of the recommendations of the ex-deputies from America who were still in Spain or, with one or two exceptions, politically centrist and still loyal to the motherland. These were discussed in the previous chapter because the replies reflected as much on American wishes under the Cortes as on American wishes after the restoration. Three things are important to add here, however. First, the fact that almost all the requests of the American deputies had not been acted on by the Cortes shows the extent to which reform, real and practical in its effect and motivation, still needed to be accomplished. The deputies would not have repeated their requests if the Cortes had acted on them. Second, the reforms remained as necessary during the restoration as before. From 1814 to 1820 Americans still clamored for reform; the king knew what they wanted, so did the government, so did the councils. The king had before him the same cogent and homogeneous set of proposed changes as the Cortes had. Third, and this was the most important fact, the reforms were simply not acted upon during the restoration because the absolutist regime, like the Cortes, understood that those Americans who wanted independence would not be satisfied by any reform short of full independence.

The real gap in Spain's response to the American rebellion was not a communications gap or a lack of information. Quite the contrary, under Ferdinand there are many memorials, representations, and letters of advice from corporations and individuals throughout the empire preserved in the archives. There was almost an information boom after the restoration, because American authorities and American subjects had a clearer sense of where authority lay after the demise of the Cortes, since the government was actually organized more rationally under the absolutist regime than under the new and essentially experimental constitutional regime. The restoration was a time of new beginnings for the weary empire, and individuals of every political persuasion wrote the king to express their ideas. In keeping with the traditions of Bourbon and Hapsburg monarchs, the king received memorials and pleas from his people—a remarkable fact, indeed, that tends to soften the image of a dour, arbitrary, tyrannical despot—for it was clearly understood in the Spanish empire that any citizen or corporation possessed the right to address the king. Naturally these letters were read by secretaries in the ministries and councils, and they were most often summarized into brief extracts for presentation to the minister involved, the council, or the king. In almost all cases, because of the great cost of paper, ink, and human labor involved, and because the court traveled with and was attendant upon the person of the king, these abstracts would be read by all three powers—minister, council, and king—with marginal notes added to explain the disposition of the matter. The documents, then, attest to the fact that Ferdinand VII read the representations and was personally aware of American affairs. It is clear from the rest of his life that Ferdinand VII desperately wanted to hold power and to use it. And, though the power to act is no doubt significant, the power not to act can have equal influence. This was the way the regime dealt with American demands or suggestions it found inconvenient.

Take, for example, the final disposition, or non-disposition, of the very cogent requests transmitted from the city council of Lima by its deputy to the Cortes in 1810, Francisco Salazar. The requests—calling for reforms in employment, mining, minting of coins, trade, suppression of monopolies, and other items—were first drawn up in 1810. Salazar presented them to the Cortes, where, as he put it, most of the items were referred to committees and "buried forever." In 1814 he responded to the king's invitation and presented Lima's demands to the Ministry of the Indies. This letter was dated 17 August 1814. It took from that date until 23 November 1818 for an extract to be drawn up and handed over to the fiscal for Peru, who on the latter date finally presented his recommendation for superior disposition. He recommended, point by point, that the demands of the Lima city council be further investigated by calling on the viceroy and other powers to render their opinions and stated that some points were matters of purely municipal jurisdiction, some were already under discussion (from which no conclusion was reached), and others were too massive in their implications to be acted on. In short, it took eight years for nothing to be done.[29]

Or take the example of one single request, repeated several times, by the deputy from Puno in Peru, Tadeo Gárate, one of the

Persas, a loyalist and subsequently royal intendant of Puno. In the Cortes he had requested that several Indian contributions be restored in his province for the support of Indian hospitals. The Council of the Indies reviewed this matter in January 1815 and in December approved it. It took a year to determine a matter relating to the reestablishment of minor Indian contributions. But when Gárate requested in the Cortes that a finance bank be established in Puno from contributions based on the output of the mines as a means of freeing the miners from their dependence on loans for supplies and for sales of unrefined silver, nothing was ever done. In 1813 the Ministry of Ultramar had advised the Cortes against the proposal, saying that it was opposed to the existing mining ordinances. The constitutional Council of State had then studied the matter, and had ended up declaring that the request presented too many difficulties for it to be acted on. Gárate then repeated the request on the king's invitation on 27 July 1814. He, at least, had the satisfaction of immediate action, perhaps because he was one of the Persas. A note added to the cover of his letters said: "Not to be acted upon, because . . . His Majesty has resolved not to concede what was asked in the Cortes and it is the same as is now asked." Apparently, having brought it forward in the Cortes was the equivalent of guaranteeing nonaction by the restored monarch.[30]

It appears, then, that the king, at least in the beginning of his restoration to power, adopted a policy of nonaction. This policy was precisely stated by Ramón de Posada, a member of the Council of the Indies, in a letter of advice to Lardizábal. When asked his opinion of what changes were needed to pacify America, Posada replied: "At the moment all reforms and general means are inopportune. Reforms might be useful, and at times necessary; but despite that they do not fail to be odious." A few troops in the right places would produce greater results. He continued: "Neither is it time to annul or to confirm the inopportune grants and declarations of the Cortes in favor of the Americans. . . . In general, the old system of royal government in America—treasury, justice, and police—is founded on solid bases . . . ; it is only necessary to put it into effect in certain regards." In a second letter a few days later he responded to Lardizábal's request for suggestions about what to do with the Cortes decree abolishing Indian tribute. His opinion: "No new taxes, no alleviation of taxes, no new grants and declarations, no revocation of those opportunely or inopportunely conceded: [keep] totally silent about everything."[31]

That, simply put, was the government's policy. Although it revoked the constitutional system in all its aspects, it made no other changes. It abolished a system it could not live with, but no alterations were contemplated. The high-sounding but empty decrees of American equality were not specifically revoked, because it would have been politically inopportune to do so, but neither were they confirmed. No one ever told Americans they were now reduced again to colonial inferiority, but no one asssured them they were not, either. Indeed, the former deputies, in their letters of advice, continued to refer to the declaration of American equality as if it were still in effect. In all regards, through a virtual conspiracy of silence, the world was supposed to return to the right and proper course it had maintained as of March 1808. America's administrative structure was to remain. How far this differs from the expressed wish of Americans can be judged by the earnest appeal of Baquíjano in his memorial: "If America is equal in rights with the provinces of Spain, make the plan of government of the Overseas provinces uniform with that of the European provinces."[32]

At the same time as this policy of nonaction was adopted in the early restoration as Spain's official view of how to keep America quiet, there arose a second powerful thesis that influenced and buttressed the other. It might be called the "love of the king" thesis. It held that the empire's love of the restored king would function as a universal panacea. In some ways it was sinister, for it constituted a sign that Spanish ultraroyalists were advocating a view of the state and of government very similar to the personalist absolutism under a divine monarch that characterized the political philosophy of the Russian emperor Alexander I and that would be enshrined in his project of a Holy Alliance of reactionary sovereigns. It was also contrary to Spain's own tradition of collegiality under the system of councils and special fueros.

Perhaps the clearest statement of the thesis came in a memorial submitted by the Conde de Puñorrostro to the Duke of San Carlos in response, again, to the invitation that Americans submit information about events in America and methods of pacifying the rebellions. His reply was that the mere name of the king would solve all the rebellions: "It would be necessary to persist in the most blind preoccupation not to recognize that those vassals, through the nature of their climate and their temperament, are docile, submissive, and gentle, and above all, lovers to the point of idolatry of the name and person of their sovereign. This is the only true restraint that can maintain the subordination of those diffuse countries, tolerating with resignation the aggravations and vexations with which they are oppressed." He assured San Carlos that only the king's absence had brought about the rebellions and that they would immediately cease upon His Majesty's restoration to the throne.[33] One of the first acts of Minister of the Indies Lardizábal in May 1814 had been to tell the royal authorities in America that the king had asked for reports from Americans about the insurrections, "and His Majesty, once he knows the truth, will place himself in the midst of his European and American children and will bring to a stop that discord that never would have happened among brothers except for the absence and captivity of the father."[34] The absolutist periodical *El Procurador General del Rey y de la Nación* phrased the sentiment bluntly in November 1814: "The name of Ferdinand is a magic or mysterious name for all good people."[35]

Throughout the summer of 1814 the king and his advisors seemed content with the happy thought expressed by these optimists. If the king's restoration was all that was needed, they would simply sit back and wait for America to restore itself to loyalty. Of course, viceregal governments were active in the military resistance against independence, and it was hoped that little further action would be necessary on Madrid's part. Throughout 1814 and 1815 the insurrections in both of the older viceroyalties, New Spain and Peru, were effectively resisted or suppressed by local royal governments. In New Spain, Viceroy Calleja succeeded in capturing and executing José María Morelos, eliminating the most serious armed insurrection. In Peru, Viceroy Abascal continued to suppress rebellions in Upper

Peru, Quito, and Chile, while he simultaneously suppressed the uprising of Cuzco that broke out in August 1814. But in Buenos Aires and New Granada revolts continued unabated. A new oidor appointed to Caracas reported by early 1814 that the situation in Caracas, Puerto Cabello, and elsewhere was so disrupted that the audiencia was no longer functioning and he had taken refuge on the island of Curaçao.[36] Even royal officials reported from Venezuela that the army of General Juan Domingo Monteverde was causing such misery in the country that it provoked continued rebellion.[37]

Meanwhile, war with foreign powers in America threatened on at least two widely separated fronts. In the Banda Oriental of the Río de la Plata (Uruguay), Portugal threatened, as it had since 1810, to stage a preemptive strike against the rebellious province in order, according to the Portuguese arguments, to remove a threat to peace and stability in the region that equally endangered Spanish and Portuguese territory, and, according to the Spanish point of view, to conquer the province, which would then become the southern border of Brazil. Spain had watched the Banda Oriental nervously since the flight of the Portuguese royal family to their American territories in 1807. The mercurial Carlota Joaquina had given the Junta Central and Regency a good deal of anxiety with her initial claim, following the captivity of her brother, that she should be recognized as his sole regent because of her position as the only free member of the dynasty. American viceregal governments, like the peninsular governments, had warily responded to her pretensions with sugar-coated but firm denials. In 1811 a Portuguese army had penetrated deeply into the Banda Oriental with the excuse of aiding Spanish royalist resistance to José Artigas but actually intent on conquest. The entry of Portugal into the fray meant there were now four powers contesting control of the province—Spain, the nationalist caudillo Artigas and his patriots, independent Buenos Aires, and Portugal. In 1811 the British had intervened diplomatically through their minister in Rio de Janeiro, Lord Strangford, who, with Lord Castlereagh's affirmation that Britain wanted "the unconditional evacuation of all Spanish American possessions," had forced the Portuguese to withdraw their army from the Banda Oriental.[38] The situation, however, remained far from settled.

At the other axis of the empire, far to the north, the Spanish remained concerned about possible Anglo-American expansion into northern Mexico. In 1814 a new fear arose with the conclusion of peace between the United States and Britain. The captain general of Cuba (and future Mexican viceroy), Juan Ruiz de Apodaca, was ordered in 1814 to take what steps were practicable to prepare for the defense of the island against possible North American aggression. Meanwhile, according to Apodaca, the fleet was almost totally unusable. Spain had ordered the outfitting of the frigates *Atocha* and *Cornelia* to strengthen the Caribbean fleet, but the minister of the navy, Luis María Salazar, reported that the order had no effect—the *Cornelia* and all the other unarmed ships at Havana were in such bad condition that unless financial assistance were made available they could be considered lost. At the end of 1814 the naval forces stationed in Cuba consisted of one corvette, four brigantines, and ten lesser vessels. The minister believed that, with money, the navy could be outfitted to the point that it could defend Cuba, but at the moment it was hopeless.[39] Meanwhile, British trade with the rebels throughout America continued to be a source of annoyance and vague foreboding. In a summary report concerning foreign relations presented to the king on his restoration, the point was clearly made that the British continued to maintain direct communication and trade with the rebellious territories in what Spain interpreted as outright violation of the mutual treaty between the two powers.[40]

This accumulation of anxieties soon broke the calm of the court of Madrid, disabusing the Spaniards of their assumption that the magic name of Ferdinand VII would restore imperial harmony. In October 1814 the ponderous machinery of empire became active again as the period of self-congratulation ended. In June 1814 Montevideo had been taken by the besieging forces of rebellious Buenos Aires, who would in turn evacuate in February 1815 and hand the Banda Oriental over to its native leaders under Artigas. A Council of the Indies consultation in October 1814 was the beginning of a more active search for a policy. The council had just heard of the capture of Montevideo by the Buenos Aires rebels. It summarized for the king the unhappy implications: the fall of Montevideo increased the power of Buenos Aires, thereby enhancing the threat to the interior of the Río de la Plata and to Upper Peru, where General Joaquín de la Pezuela (future viceroy of Peru) had thus far held the rebels at bay. It threatened Paraguay, which so far had refused to join Buenos Aires. It opened the way for rebel shipping around the Cape to Peru, as Montevideo was the last Spanish defense of the Cape. The influence of this on Peru was "supremely terrible." Most important, the fall of Montevideo denied Spain any ports in the Río de la Plata at which a future expedition of royalist forces could be landed.[41]

A number of other matters were discussed by the council and ministry of the Indies from October to December 1814. The ministry drew up a list of all the audiencias in America, noting the vacancies that existed and comparing membership to that of 1808. The audiencias of Manila, Chile, Bogotá, Buenos Aires, and Cuzco were desperately undermanned, and steps were taken to fill the vacancies. The decision was definitely made not to fulfill the order of the Cortes to erect a new audiencia in Saltillo in northern Mexico.[42] A sign of stiffening attitudes toward the American situation on the part of the council came in December with the decision to advise against making the appointment of Antonio Bergosa, acting archbishop of Mexico City, permanent. The problem was that Bergosa, who had been raised from the diocese of Oaxaca to the archdiocese of Mexico by the Cortes but whose appointment had not received Papal approval, had given every sign of being a follower of the constitution. The council thought that his being a peninsular meant "it is not believable that he could love the new institutions," and decided therefore that his support of the constitution must be a sign of weakness. The king agreed, ordering the removal of Bergosa and appointing to the premier diocese in America the conservative Pedro José de Fonte.[43]

A final matter of general importance to the empire was the council's discussion about restoring the tribute, which had been suppressed by the Cortes. In December 1814 the council agreed that in view of the shortages of revenue and the many complaints of royal administrators, particularly in Peru, the tribute should be restored to the level of 1808. One member of the council, José Navia Bolaños, offered his separate opinion that the risks of restoring the tribute were far greater than any foreseeable gains, pointing out that the tribute was a burden that divided families, disrupted community life, and oppressed youths and prevented them from marrying. The council rejected this opinion, pointing out that it derived from the denunciations of the bishop of Michoacán, Manuel Abad y Queipo, whose fears, it thought, were not proven. The desk official of the Ministry of the Indies added his comments, to the effect that the tribute was a source of tension in the empire mainly because of the varying condition of the Indians, who were described as being apathetic and stupid in cold countries, astute and hard working in the temperate, and indolent and vicious in the hot. On 10 January 1815 the king accepted the advice, ordering that the tribute be restored and that it be no higher than was paid in 1808.[44]

The decisions taken in regard to America in late 1814 demonstrated the adoption by the king's government of a hard-line point of view. They give evidence of the emergence of the party that would dominate the restoration, a party advocating a military method of pacification and opposing political solutions. At no time was this party completely dominant—in 1815 the government would reactivate the English mediation proposal—but the military party possessed enough influence over the king so that, if it was unable to stop the consideration of political solutions, it could always prevent their adoption. Prominent in this group were Francisco Eguía, captain general of New Castile and then minister of war, Tomas Moyano, minister of grace and justice after late 1814, such conservative councilors of the Indies as José Pablo Valiente, the camarilla in general, and individuals who had been active in the Comisión de Reemplazos (the military supply committee) in Cádiz such as Juan Antonio Yandiola. The last-named submitted a memorial on the pacification of America in January 1815 that set the tone for the hard line the government was then adopting. He argued that it was vain to think of pacifying America with gentle means: "force, this horrible agent, is the only thing that can suffice in the state to which things have arrived." Force was the only power that could not only pacify America but consolidate what had been pacified. Since hatred for Spain had reached such a high level in America, it was no good to try to win back the overseas subjects through concession.[45] This argument would be repeated over and over throughout 1815, until by the end of that year the Council of the Indies itself was prepared to agree with the proposition that only force would work. Delgado has suggested that this tendency to advocate military reconquest also predominated in the absolutist press, or what little of it existed after the reimposition of rigid censorship.[46] Spanish policy-makers moved rapidly toward the fateful decision to "make war on vassals," as Baquíjano had termed it.

Spain decided to prepare an expeditionary force of 10,500 men, under the command of Pablo Morillo, for dispatch to Venezuela and New Granada. The Council of the Indies, on 13 September and again on 3 October 1814, advised the king that in order to pacify Venezuela and the viceroyalty of New Granada the only method seemed to be "to send an expedition to that point and with the force that is deemed convenient." After some initial discussion of whether such an expedition should go to the Río de la Plata (which the Cádiz merchants preferred), it was decided that rebellious Venezuela should be the target. The Council of the Indies urged that the commander of the expedition be permitted to appoint a new president, intendant, and captain general of Caracas and that he issue a royal amnesty with a twenty-four–hour time limit, at the conclusion of which the Venezuelans would be attacked. He was to announce through proclamations that the king preferred gentle solutions but that if the rebels remained recalcitrant he would reduce them to order. He was to dispatch the leaders of the rebellion to Spain for trial, form cases against royal officers whose cruelty had provoked uprisings in Caracas, Quito, and elsewhere in the northern viceroyalty, and urge all royal commanders to maintain discipline among their troops in order to avoid such notorious atrocities as had already characterized the brutal war in Venezuela. While fighting in Venezuela he was to send troops to Bogotá. A junta of war was to be formed in Spain to direct the expedition, and it would consist of a number of generals and Minister of War Eguía, Minister of the Indies Lardizábal, and Councilor

Francisco de Requena, all members of the militarist party. The king would preside over this junta. On 3 October the council repeated these suggestions, making only slight changes, the chief one being to recommend the separation of the captaincy general of Caracas from the viceroyalty of New Granada. To this consultation the king on 18 October 1814 added his note of approval.[47]

The crown chose, however, to vest far greater powers in Morillo than the Council of the Indies had recommended. Morillo was appointed not only commander in chief of the expedition but also captain general of Venezuela, governor of Caracas, and president of the audiencia. He was granted, in short, the military and administrative dictatorship. In his instructions, dated 15 November and handed to him three days later, he was ordered to proceed first to Margarita, then to Cumaná, then to Cartagena. The fleet would establish a naval blockade and drive corsairs out of the Caribbean. Morillo, however, was authorized to alter these instructions as he deemed necessary. He was ordered to send troops to New Granada or, if Venezuela were quiescent, to concentrate his efforts on the viceroyalty. If he had troops to spare, he was to send them to Peru. In the realm of politics, he was to exercise a combination of military force and moderation simultaneously. "His Majesty wishes [the expedition] not to mistreat the natives who come out to it." The expedition was to publish proclamations, using moderation, and it was to treat local authorities, such as parish priests, with respect.

Morillo was first to occupy the island of Margarita, where he would then decide whether to attack Cumaná, Caracas, Puerto Cabello, or La Guaira, depending on where the rebels were. "Once having occupied the Island of Margarita, you will employ . . . all the means of softness, capturing only those persons encountered under arms." He was to issue an amnesty for rebels, offer rewards to those who had served the royal cause, issue a public forgiveness for all those not then engaged in fighting, place a price on the heads of the most influential rebel leaders, and grant liberty to slaves who were willing to join the royal army. He was empowered to suspend the audiencia of Caracas as he saw fit, to direct the judicial system, to collect taxes and decree new ones, and even to control all appointments in Venezuela. These were extraordinary powers. Throughout his instructions Morillo was admonished to remember that the war in Venezuela had reached such levels of intensity that it was critical to win public opinion to his side and to curb the excesses and atrocities committed by royalist partisans. Yet through all the instructions the captain general was given no advice as to how he was to employ force and gentleness simultaneously. The most the instructions could offer him was a final authorization that, given the distance involved and the need for hasty action, he could "alter in whole or in part these instructions."[48]

Spain had thus taken the decision to send a major European expeditionary army to the most chaotic part of America. The Venezuelan civil war was by far the most bloody—Venezuela had twice established its independence, while royal armies and royalist partisans had simultaneously continued to control much of the country—and it was the scene of the most passionate political conflict. Morillo's army of 10,500 men was the largest ever sent by Spain to the Indies (although by 1815 the decision would also be taken to dispatch an even larger expedition to the Río de la Plata), and the powers he was granted were the most extraordinary ever given to a commander in the American wars. Discontent among Morillo's troops gathered at Cádiz was so intense that the commander dared not inform his men of their true destination. After the expedition of eighteen warships and forty-two transports sailed from Cádiz on 17 February 1815, Morillo informed his men that they were headed for war-torn Venezuela and New Granada.

In the opinion of Stephen K. Stoan, Morillo's expedition was doomed to failure before it started, for "he was asked to effect an essentially unrealistic and reactionary policy in America."[49] It was unrealistic in the sense that he was to conquer a territory while applying gentle persuasion, and reactionary in the sense that the decision itself to send an expeditionary force of white Europeans to a country torn by internal racial conflict while at the same time making no provisions for major reform to solve the problems that provoked that conflict was bound to be reactionary. Morillo himself would frequently complain of the many constraints royal policy placed on his willingness to grant reforms and, indeed, would ask to be relieved of his command twelve times before 1820. In the course of his impossible mission he would become perhaps the most vilified man in the historiography of the independence era. According to Stoan, he did not deserve such a bad name, for he merely served a regime that refused to listen to the commander's frequent pleas that something more than military suppression was demanded by the complex social and political conditions of devastated Venezuela.

Shortly after establishing his military government in Venezuela, Morillo sent a personal representative to Madrid to plead for the abolition of the slave trade, for gradual manumission, for equality of rights for blacks and mestizos, for the appointment of Venezuelans to local offices, and for permission to trade with the colonies of other powers.[50] It is not surprising that Madrid ignored these suggestions of its own military commander, for in drawing up Morillo's instructions in the first place the king had largely ignored the advice of the Council of the Indies and had listened instead to the junta of war, consisting of a group of hand-picked ministers and generals drawn from the camarilla and from the military party. Morillo would shortly become engaged in a battle with the audiencia of Caracas — which he ordered to suspend operations in June 1815 — and by the middle of 1816 Morillo would be deprived of his absolute political power in Venezuela in a royal decree that brought confusion and paralysis to the royalist forces there.[51] Indeed, the conflict in Spain between militarists and civilians over Morillo's powers and authority in Venezuela would mirror the wider conflict over what general policy of pacification should be decreed. The years from 1815 to 1818 produced broad disagreement in Madrid between civilian advocates of a policy of leniency toward America and military advocates of a policy of severity.

V

In Search of a Policy

Although the military party was emerging by late 1814 as the dominant influence on the politics of the Fernandine restoration, it would be a mistake to say that the imperial regime had arrived at a single clearly-articulated policy for the pacification of rebellious America. Indeed, it occupied the years from 1814 to 1818 in an extended search for a policy. But each proposal, with the exception of those involving the use of military force, was rejected and countered by the military party, and in the end there was no coherent imperial planning.

At any rate, the period from 1814 to 1816 was a time of resurgence of royalist power in all of the American viceroyalties except Río de la Plata. Mexico was largely pacified following the capture of Morelos on 5 November 1815 and the dissolution of his rebel congress. In Venezuela, Morillo's troops occupied the country, and by late April 1815 were pressing for the submission of Cartagena; by February 1816 they were reestablishing their authority in New Granada. Viceroy Abascal of Peru had dissolved the rebel regime in Chile at the end of 1814 and had suppressed the rebellion at Cuzco and in Upper Peru. Only the Río de la Plata revolution remained, and by the end of 1815 the decision would be made to gather a new peninsular expeditionary force that, it was generally assumed, would be used to crush Buenos Aires, although no final decision as to its destination was made until 1818.

Spain also moved to enlist the support of the Pope. At the end of 1815 the Madrid government ordered its minister to the Holy See, Antonio de Vargas Laguna, to request Pope Pius VII to issue a formal encyclical calling on Americans to uphold the legitimate regime of Spain. The idea of a Papal encyclical had been under review for some years, and Pope Pius VII, who had received significant assistance from Spain and the Spanish ambassador during his own troubles with Napoleon, was more than agreeable. On 30 January 1816 the Pope issued his encyclical, entitled "Etsi longissimo," addressed to the American bishops. In it he called on the American churchmen to spare no effort in aiding the suppression of uprisings and sedition in America against the legitimate authority of Spain. The bishops were to show to their respective flocks "the terrible and grave damages of rebellion, . . . the illustrious and singular virtues of Ferdinand, your Catholic King, . . . [and] the sublime and immortal examples that the Spaniards have given Europe" of their "invincible adhesion to the faith and their loyalty to the Sovereign." The Pope followed this up by granting several other privileges to the crown during the next months. In May 1816 he confirmed the new Spanish Order of Isabel la Católica, which Ferdinand had created to supplant the Order of Charles III as a reward for loyalty and service to Americans and Spaniards serving in America. In August and September 1816 he granted the king income from certain ecclesiastical funds to aid in equipping the squadron that would be gathered in Cádiz against Buenos Aires. In January 1817 he wrote directly to the ecclesiastical cabildo of Mexico City, promising he would say pontifical masses for the restoration of loyalty to Ferdinand VII. Meanwhile, he confirmed the king's various nominees to vacant bishoprics in America.[1]

It seems to have been a false sense of security motivated by the upsurge of royal control in America that led the king in 1815 to abolish the Ministry of the Indies. He took this action without advising the Council of State or ministers. The functions of the abolished ministry were assigned instead to the ministries of war and finance; a new Junta of Pacification, composed of selected councilors and chaired by the Duke of Montemar, was established to advise on methods of settling the American rebellions; and a separate Junta Militar de Indias, under the Ministry of War, was created to advise on military policy in America, chaired by Joaquín Blake. The Junta of Pacification became the main body where pacification policy was debated. The Council of the Indies also continued to exist, under the chairmanship of the Duke of Montemar, as yet another agency for tendering advice on American questions. Thus the king, at the very moment when he should have been concentrating power over American policy in the hands of one committee, was actually widening and confusing the lines of authority (see table 2).

A number of advisors pointed out the confusion that ensued. When José Pizarro returned to the position of minister of state in 1816 he testified that he found the business of American pacification in total confusion. "There was no single center of direction for those countries, nor a political system combined with a military system."[2] Again, in 1818, in an important memorial about the pacification of America, Pizarro told the king: "The first means that I judge to be absolutely necessary for the happy conclusion of this business is that all the government of America should be in one hand." Over a year later, a special envoy of General Morillo, Juan Antonio de Roxas Queypo, told Spain that "the lack of a center is, without doubt, the primary cause of our misfortunes."[3] It says a lot that the minister of state, in both 1816 and again in 1818, and the representative of the leader of Spain's major military force in America, in 1819, effectively confessed they did not know who was in charge of American policy formulation. Even in 1816, when Spain's loyalist supporters in America were winning their greatest victories, Spanish policy at its center, in Madrid, around the person of the king and often in daily contact with him, began to drift into a period of proposals and counterproposals, debates with no resolution, and listless repetition of solutions already proposed.

At a more profound level, the basic reason for this drift in policy under the restored absolutists was suggested in a letter to the king from a former member of the Cuzco audiencia, Manuel de Vidaurre, in 1817. Vidaurre was an outspoken advocate of amelioration of the Indians' condition and reform of the American administration; he lived in Lima under a cloud of suspicion for having been compromised in the 1814 rebellion in Cuzco, the so-called Pumacahua uprising. Not until 1820 would Vidaurre be politically rehabilitated and appointed to the audiencia of Puerto Príncipe, Cuba (which position he later abandoned and returned ultimately to join the independent government of Peru). On 2 April 1817 Vidaurre wrote the king a long report on how to pacify America, advocating less military response and a softening of the oppression. But his basic point was to declare that Spain's fundamental error in contesting the rebellion was the failure of Spaniards to alter their thinking on America since the Conquest. The Americans were not what they had been three centuries earlier. "The American today is the same as a Spaniard. They have the same guns as Europeans, the same cannon, the same rifles." The best-trained Buenos Aires troops, he insisted, compared favorably with the victors at Austerlitz. Yet Spaniards continued to make policy as if they were treating of primitive peoples and wild Indians.[4] Vidaurre believed that there was thus a failure of understanding, and it can be seen repeatedly in the memorials and suggestions on pacification during the restoration.

At a more practical level there was also a failure of politics, a confusion of administration, that resulted from Ferdinand's attempt to restore absolutism in a country that had already experienced liberalism. The restoration brought back into office all the councils and agencies of the Bourbon state, but Ferdinand reserved to himself the initiative in policy-making and priorities. Though the councils and ministries filled their days with activity, the king often ignored their advice, even taking decisions he did not inform his cabinet about. In so doing, Ferdinand went beyond his Bourbon predecessors, for they had been more dependent on the advice of the ministries, councils, advisors, and bureaucrats than he was. Ferdinand created a personal autocracy that could not be made to work and that, as Suárez says, was no system of government at all.[5] Under the guise of restoring a traditionalist regime, Ferdinand actually attempted to create a personalist power that turned out to be terribly inefficient. This led to general unpredictability and uncertainty at the highest levels of power, a fatal flaw that undercut and weakened all of Spain's efforts to retain its empire.

As with many personalist regimes, the Fernandine restoration witnessed rule by camarilla while the duly constituted ministers of the government rose and fell at the whim of the king, serving an average tenure of only six months. Decisions of all kinds were made outside the proper channels of government, sometimes without the knowledge of the very minister whose job it was to administer policy. From 1816 to 1818 the camarilla can be seen at work in the memoirs of José García de León y Pizarro, the moderate minister of state in those years, and from those portions of the memoirs of José Vázquez Figueroa, minister of the navy during the same period, that are included in Pizarro's memoirs. Pizarro is not, of course, a disinterested source, since he leaned repeatedly toward moderate policies aimed at reconciliation both within Spain and in the empire at large, but his general picture of how the regime functioned in those years is often borne out by independent documentation.

The harmful effect on the camarilla lay mainly in the way in which this body of advisors functioned as a secret government within the royal palace, making for a government in which the ministers sometimes did not know what was going on and were unable to act for fear of gaining the enmity of the camarilla. The most famous example of this occurred when Ferdinand personally subscribed to the Act of the Holy Alliance formulated by Czar Alexander I without telling his own minister of state, Pizarro. For six months Pizarro continued conducting European diplomatic affairs along the lines of public Spanish policy, which was based on rejection of the Holy Alliance at the behest of the Pope. Ferdinand did not sign the Final Act of the Congress of Vienna or the Second Peace of Paris until June 1817, after the Great Powers agreed that the Duchy of Parma would return, on the death of Napoleon's widow, to the Spanish claimant, the Infante Don Luis, or to his mother, Ferdinand's sister. Again, in 1818 and 1819 the minister to Washington, Luis de Onís, negotiated a critical treaty with the United States by which Spain ceded Florida in return for a guaranteed border with New Spain. During the negotiations, however, Ferdinand personally granted a considerable portion of Western Florida—territory already formally annexed by the United States—to three of his cronies. This royal action caused a two-year delay in Spain's ratification of the treaty, led to the fall from office of Pizarro's successor as minister of state, the Marqués de Casa Irujo, and threatened an outbreak of war between Spain and the United States.[6]

In domestic affairs the camarilla's effect was equally harmful. Pizarro testified that when he and his two moderate fellow ministers, Vázquez Figueroa and Martín Garay (minister of finance) took office in 1816 their chief objective was to establish a program of national reconciliation by granting a general amnesty for liberals, *afrancesados*, and others who were the object of the king's persecution. Eguía personally wrecked this by declaring that the amnesty proposal was treason. Pizarro concluded that the revolution of 1820 would not have occurred if the amnesty had been passed. Vázquez Figueroa, meanwhile, argues that Eguía and Lozano de Torres also subverted the plan of Martín Garay to stabilize Spain's public credit through a program of austerity in pensions and salaries and confiscations of the interest on certain ecclesiastical funds.[7] Pizarro, of course, was preserving his own image in his memoirs, in which he made it sound as if he was the only disinterested minister over a span of many years, but there can be no doubt of his total loyalty to Ferdinand VII and of his ability to serve as an eyewitness in cabinet sessions and palace anterooms. Martín Garay confided to a friend of the British ambassador that, "when a measure was proposed by a Minister, it was either dismissed with a harsh negative, or else reserved for the determination of the Camarilla, against the intrigues of which no Minister was secure for a moment."[8] The image that emerges is not that of a government that was positively always misguided, but rather of a government that was paralyzed by political institutions that impeded consistency and the formulation of consensus.

It is not as if Ferdinand did not listen to liberal or moderate advice. Indeed, the choice of ministers such as Pizarro, Vázquez Figueroa, and Garay, moderate royalists but not *serviles*, suggested the king's willingness to hear dissenting opinions. One can readily agree that, as María del Carmen Pintos Vieites says, the king did consult widely when it came to critical decisions. The problem was, there was no guarantee he would take advice. The most notable example, perhaps, is his project in 1816 to grant amnesty to liberals still imprisoned or exiled for their earlier political opinions. The king on 4 May 1816 requested the opinion of every important agency in the country as to whether he should grant amnesty to the *afrancesados* and the liberals. All eight of the councils responded (the councils of State, Admiralty, Indies, Finance, Ordenes, Inquisition, the Tribunal de la Rota, and the Junta Suprema de Correos); eleven of the peninsular audiencias responded, twelve of the peninsular captains general, most of the intendants, and fifty-three archbishops and bishops. Only twenty-one of the respondents opposed amnesty; fourteen favored some indulgences; thirty-two favored amnesty with limitations; twenty-two favored amnesty with some exceptions; and thirteen favored a general amnesty. And yet, for all that, the king never issued a specific amnesty for those who had been persecuted for their politics during the Cortes era. Except for an earlier decree abolishing the special commissions empowered to investigate liberals and *afrancesados*, no amnesty, either general or limited, was issued. In October 1816, during the period of greatest relaxation in the regime— apparently largely the result of the influence of María Isabel of Braganza, Ferdinand's second wife, whom he married in 1816 and who died in 1818—a general amnesty was drafted releasing all those imprisoned for past political errors after a review by a special tribunal. But the document was never issued, partly because of opposition from within the camarilla, and partly because of the discovery of the so-called Gran Oriente conspiracy of Masons.[9] Even at its best, then, the regime only contemplated reforms, it never adopted them.

The same pattern, which might be described as much ado resulting in nothing, characterized royal policy toward America. As has already been seen, the king consulted widely. From 1815 through 1819 he continued to receive a remarkable assortment of memorials and suggestions from private persons and government figures, both in America and in Spain. It was a heyday for advice-givers, largely because, although royalist armies were nearly everywhere triumphant in America, the realization began to dawn that the victories of 1814–15 would be transitory unless Spain strengthened its hold on America with some reforms to win the hearts and minds of the disaffected population. Late in the period of the restoration the idea also began gradually to emerge that Spain lacked the military, mercantile, and even political power to hold what had been reconquered.

Even the word "reconquered" was subject to debate. In 1816, commissioners sent to Spain to represent the government of Mariano Osorio, Spanish reconqueror of Chile in 1814, requested that the medals distributed among loyalist forces in Chile with the words "Santiago reconquistada" engraved on them should be changed to "Santiago pacificada," owing to the harmful public reaction to the word "reconquered." The fiscal of the council of the Indies agreed, pointing out that one was not even supposed to use the word "conquered" for American territories restored to legitimate control. The council agreed. The king, however, resolved to the contrary: "Continue with the line it has," he ordered.[10] For general purposes, however, the words "pacified" and "pacification" were adopted.

The debate and advice within the highest power centers of the empire focused on two chief questions: that of free trade, particularly whether the British should be permitted to mediate and win the trade concessions in America they insisted on as the price for their mediation, and the method of pacification in America, particularly whether reform or military force should be used.

The matter of British mediation was reopened by Spain. On 14 May 1815 the Spanish minister of state sent a note to the English ambassador asking for reopening of the negotiations suspended in 1812, it being clear that the restoration of the king had not ended the wars in America. The English ambassador replied by saying that the offer of mediation had been made by Britain two times but that the ensuing negotiations had been suspended by Spain two times, and that the British government could not reopen the matter without knowing for certain what principles the Spanish would base their negotiations on and what conditions Spain would offer the American rebels. The Spanish responded by complaining about the anti-Spanish and pro-rebel stance of the British ambassador in Brazil, Lord Strangford, who Spain believed had given direct aid to the rebels in Buenos Aires and Montevideo. The British countered by insisting that Lord Strangford's actions constituted no grounds for suspending the greater question of mediation, and as of July 1815 the subject rested there.[11]

Since it lies in the realm of diplomatic history, and since it produced no final clear decision, the on-again, off-again negotiations with Britain need not be traced in detail here. Although the possibility of English mediation continued to be discussed until the mid-1820s, and although in 1816 the Brazilian invasion of Montevideo added yet another field for possible mediation by the British, no final agreement was ever reached. What is significant for Spanish policy is that the mediation question finally produced by 1816 a full-scale, on-going, and widespread discussion within Spanish councils of the whole principle of the trade monopoly system.

The question of British mediation received new life in May 1816 when the Council of the Indies, in the process of considering what sort of proclamation the king might make to the Americans to pacify them, declared itself of the opinion that English mediation was the most effective, fastest, and cheapest method of pacification. Arguing that the American territories could not be pacified by force and that they always returned to rebellion as soon as possible, the council told the king that a "radical cure" was necessary; palliatives would serve only to guarantee that the rebellions would be "incurable." Thus the council urged the king not to send another flowery proclamation to his American subjects, for it would be viewed as a sign of weakness. The council particularly urged the king to remember "that the rebellion in the Americas is a more terrible and disastrous event than he perhaps had thought." Hence, it was useless to offer them rewards, satisfactions, or governmental reforms "because that is the equivalent of confessing in some way that they were mistreated." Regarding the present system of trade monopoly, the council gave the first hint of the direction of its thinking: "Existing regulations [in trade] are neither just nor convenient; they only serve the monopoly and encourage contraband." The council concluded by pointing out the need for a political solution: "Even when the American territories are quieted by force alone, the fire breaks out anew; if politics does not quench it, it will continue and become more concentrated."[12]

Despite the willingness of the Council of the Indies to suggest more radical solutions, the debate on pacification might have continued at its normal lethargic pace except for the invasion of Montevideo in early 1816 by Brazilian and Portuguese forces. Since Portuguese forces drove out Buenos Aires rebels in this undertaking, they could argue that their aggression was designed merely to restore order in Montevideo and guarantee the security of Brazil's southern border. Carlota Joaquina, the sister of Ferdinand VII and queen of Portugal, at first believed the propaganda of her husband João VI. In June 1816 she wrote the Spanish cabinet assuring it that Portuguese troop activities in Río de la Plata were directed merely at the rebels there. That same month, however, the Spanish chargé in Rio de Janeiro, Andrés Villalba, told the cabinet that the official Portuguese attitude was that it was capturing Montevideo in order to guarantee its own security and that the Portuguese king did not intend to return to Europe, where he would become a puppet of the British or Spanish, but wished to stay in Brazil and strengthen his empire at the cost of Spain. Villalba reported that Carlota Joaquina, having discovered the aggressive designs of her husband, was scandalized and threatened to withdraw from residence at court "in order not be a spectator to these scenes."[13]

Combined with this new threat of foreign aggression in its American empire was the extraordinary fact that the Spanish king and his brother Don Carlos were even then in the process of completing marriage contracts with the two teenaged daughters of João VI and Carlota Joaquina. The two daughters, María Isabel, who was to marry Ferdinand VII, and María Francisca, who was to marry Don Carlos, were already at sea on their way to Spain, presenting the crown with what the Council of State called "the rare contrast of the arrival of Their Highnesses simultaneously with the invasion of our king's territories." On top of everything else, at this moment the Portuguese demanded that Spain return the town of Olivenza, which it had taken from Portugal in 1801. It was a rare dilemma indeed. After some debate it was decided that the carefully-planned double dynastic link could not be put in jeopardy and that the princesses and their mother had no blame in the duplicity of the Portuguese king. The marriages were concluded, and María Isabel of Braganza, aged only nineteen, became Ferdinand's second wife. For the two years she reigned as

queen she apparently brought a ray of brightness and moderation into
the bleak court of her husband. The perfidy of her father, João VI,
however, rankled deeply.

Unable to respond to the Portuguese invasion of the Banda
Oriental because of the total absence of Spanish power in the Río de la
Plata region, Spain turned once again to the British, requesting that
Britain, alone or in concert with other European powers, intervene in
the Río de la Plata. This request was made on 17 October 1816. In the
meeting of the Council of State on 18 October 1816, in which the
decision to call on British mediation was reaffirmed, Minister of State
Pedro Cevallos also called on the government to remember the adage,
"If you want peace, prepare for war," and urged the dispatch of a
military expedition to the Río de la Plata region.[14] The decision had
already been taken, announced on 9 May 1815, to send to America an
expeditionary force of 20,000 men, in addition to the Morillo expedition, but it would take five years to gather and finance this force, and
for the first three years no final decision was made as to its destination.

The Portuguese attack on Montevideo seems to have had a
disproportionate effect on Spanish policy-makers. Though a small and
relatively unimportant colony, it provoked many council meetings
and much discussion. The explanation is that, although much of the
rest of America was in revolt against the mother country, a foreign
invasion of a Spanish colony was perceived as being somehow more
threatening. Portuguese armies on the eastern bank also threatened
once and for all any contemplated Spanish reconquest of Buenos Aires,
for it removed the only likely staging area for such a reconquest. Then
too, a Portuguese act of aggression at the very same time as the
completion of the royal marriage contracts seemed to smack of special
duplicity. But, more than anything else, the Portuguese incursion in
Montevideo seems to have brought the cabinet and the camarilla,
perhaps even the king himself, face to face with the reality of Spanish
impotence in one large quarter of the American territories. Peru was
still safe, Mexico was quiescent, even New Granada was tenuously
restored to Spanish control, but, unless Spain did something, it would
cease to have a role in the Río de la Plata and its legal right of authority
would be utterly eclipsed by Britain and Portugal, to say nothing of

the rebels, whose claims to authority Spain did not deign to discuss.

Minister of State Pedro Cevallos effectively confessed Spain's impotence when on 13 October 1816 he wrote the Spanish ambassador in London, Conde de Fernán Núñez, urging him to do anything to interest the British in mediation in Montevideo. He was even prepared to admit that "Spain recognizes the unpardonable absurdity of having aided the insurrection of North America," fearing the British might hold that adventure against them. Cevallos ruminated that Spain was now reduced to its current discredit and disgrace because of its sacrifices in the war against Napoleon, sacrifices that made the security of the rest of Europe possible. He suggested that Fernán Núñez point out to Britain that a weak Spain, shorn of its colonies, would be more vulnerable to European aggression, but a rich Spain, in possession of its colonies, "is more dependent on Great Britain" for trade and merchandise. He concluded that Spain now "appeared in the eyes of the world as a Power incapable of reestablishing order within its own States."[15] Perhaps it was because of such negative thinking and also because he had opposed the Portuguese marriages that on 30 October 1816 Cevallos was replaced as minister of state by José Pizarro.[16]

The coming to office of Pizarro marked the beginning of the most active period of debate concerning American pacification during the entire first restoration. A devoted servant of the king, Pizarro testifies in his memoirs that one of his first acts was to gather together the correspondence and papers relating to the king's accession to the throne in 1808, the insurrection of Aranjuez, and especially the king's relations with Napoleon during his captivity at Valencay; he took them to the king and advised him that they should be destroyed. The king then burned the papers that revealed his shameful courting of Napoleon's favor. "I intended to reestablish the dignity of the throne," wrote Pizarro. "If similar papers later turned up, the fault was not mine."[17] He next set about reorganizing and rationalizing the inefficient Ministry of State, ruffling no few feathers in the process. By the end of December 1816 he had on his desk a report by an official of the Ministry of State reviewing the entire question of foreign commerce in the Spanish American colonies.[18] Clearly the Ministry was going to be shaken out of its listless and inefficient torpor. What changes might be contemplated in America? Pizarro's own thoughts provide the answer: "For me, America was lost from the time of Cádiz [1810]. . . . And in the year 1817 I had no doubt of its loss and that it was time to think of acquiring what advantages [we could] from a separation that was now inevitable."[19]

Technically the question of American commerce and of pacification as it related to commerce was vested in the Ministry of State by 1816, especially after the Ministry of the Indies was abolished (see table 2). Pizarro testified, however, that the Ministry of State possessed no power to appoint or discipline American personnel, to command the armies, or to supply them. In addition, all major changes of policy required the approval of the Council of State, the empire's highest deliberative body, composed of ministers, former ministers, and the king's appointees. It met under the chairmanship of either the king or his brother, and a vote of a "substantial majority" was required before a proposal could be enacted. Serious weaknesses existed, therefore, that militated against Pizarro's ability to affect American policy. After Francisco Eguía became minister of war on 19 June 1817, furthermore, the two ministers were engaged in a contest for superiority in policy-making. Sometimes the debate deteriorated into unseemly, if guarded, personal attacks between Pizarro and Eguía as they jockeyed for preferment in the king's eyes, and Pizarro's memoirs make it clear that the two men cordially disliked each other and totally disagreed over policy. Pizarro was the foremost moderate in the regime, Eguía the leading militarist. From late 1817 to mid-1818 Eguía complained bitterly about the order that all documents pertaining to American pacification were to be centered in the Ministry of State.[20] Courtly double talk disguised the very real conflict that raged between these two principal figures in the cabinet, but the effect was that the one often contradicted the other. The next two years would bring a flood of proposals for reform in the Indies from sources as diverse as individual American letter-writers on the one hand and the British government on the other.

The British foreign minister, Lord Castlereagh, spoke frankly to the Spanish ambassador in London, the Conde de Fernán Núñez. In response to the latest Spanish request, of 17 October 1816, for British mediation or intervention in the Portuguese occupation of Montevideo and in America in general, Castlereagh made it clear that Spain must grant liberal trade concessions and equal opportunities for state employment to the Spanish Americans. For a country to serve as mediator it had to be in agreement with the principles and ideas of the country that asked for the mediation, and without such agreement nothing could be accomplished. "Such is the case regarding England if Spain persists in wanting to continue the internal system of Government and restriction on commerce that it has always maintained in the Americas." Lord Castlereagh announced himself convinced that it was Spain's illiberal trade policy that was the one and only cause of the discontent in America, and that if Britain's own colonies such as India were so governed they would soon be lost. Spain could not reduce America by force, but, even if she could, the tranquility of America purchased by military sacrifices would forever be insecure. England herself could never consent to aid Spain by the use of force against American subjects, since the Americans were viewed by the British public as victims of oppression. There could be no basis for mediation without Spain's granting concessions to America. Such concessions would also permit a speedy intervention by the Great Powers in the Portuguese invasion of Montevideo, for it would disprove Portugal's pretense that it entered the Banda Oriental only to secure its own borders.

In response, Pizarro urged the ambassador to point out to the British that their "coldness" in regard to Montevideo would only serve to enhance the chances for survival of the weak rebel states in the Río de la Plata, potentially creating yet a third power to join the Portuguese and North Americans in their efforts to weaken British influence in the New World. In another note Pizarro reminded Fernán Núñez that the king was prepared to consider the three principle demands of the British—an armistice for American rebels, "a more open system of commerce in the colonies," and consideration of Americans for state employments.[21] The question of granting a possible amnesty and of greater opportunities for Americans to acquire state appointments had already been agreed to in principle as early as 1815, though Spain had thus far failed to specify further details and the British had remained thoroughly unconvinced.[22] It was the issue of free trade, however, that remained to be settled, and despite Pizarro's words, the king and council had made no such decision.

At long last the debate centered on its proper focus. The frankness and clarity of Castlereagh's remarks served to bring the debate down to the single issue of free trade, now recognized as the essential condition of British mediation. Perhaps just as significant a role in focusing the debate was played by a long memorandum submitted on 3 December 1816 by the Conde de Casa Flores, a Spanish diplomat whom Pizarro would soon appoint minister to the Portuguese court in Brazil. The report was submitted on the request of Pizarro, and it undoubtedly reflected some of the minister's own thoughts, since he passed it on to the Junta of Pacification in January 1817 and repeated its recommendations in his own future proposals. Mincing no words, Casa Flores declared that although most observers thought American independence was inevitable, he believed it could be prevented, but only if the system of government were changed. To support his argument that the overseas territories were on the verge of independence he made a number of assertions. The animosity of Americans toward Spain was now so strong that it was unquenchable. Only force could be depended on to restore Spanish control, but force would diminish the power and bankrupt the treasury of Spain. The government of the Cortes had seriously weakened Spanish prestige through its political errors. Finally, since this was the nineteenth century, it was no longer possible to return America to the sixteenth-, seventeenth-, or even eighteenth-century way of governing. Spain was without a navy and without funds, and thus incapable of restoring its exclusive control in America. Nor was the future of America a matter of Spanish interest alone, for all of Europe and North America awaited with lively anticipation the moment that open trade with the Spanish colonies could commence. In Britain the opposition party strongly favored American independence, and soon that objective would constitute general public opinion, against which no government could stand. The United States government was even more decided in its policy of favoring American independence. Under such circumstances, the maintenance of the Spanish trade monopoly exacerbated foreign support for independence and compromised Spain dangerously. Even the Holy Allies met periodically to change their policy in regard to certain questions. Spain's refusal to look to the future, he insisted, excluded it from its rightful place among the Allies.

These were strong words indeed, and to rectify the errors of the past Casa Flores advocated six basic reforms: (1) the word "colony" should be abolished—which meant abandonment of colonial mercantilism; (2) Americans must be totally free to plant and cultivate all species of crops; (3) viceroys and governors must be chosen from among the foremost candidates and must be men of exceptional skill; (4) Spain must find ways to guarantee that American complaints and petitions would be heard by the king quickly and without costly red tape; (5) American viceroys, as reflections of the king's majesty, must not mix in contentious or criminal legal proceedings in America; and (6) forms of government, taxes, trade, and fiscal administration must be absolutely uniform in both Spain and America. The final item was the most central. Assuming the principle of absolute equality of administration and trade would be accepted, Casa Flores proceeded to propose a list of seven bases for the creation of equal trade that, rendered to its basic element, called for full and unrestricted trade to all parts of the empire and between it and all foreign nations for all ships that flew the Spanish flag, that were owned by Spaniards or Spanish Americans, and that had a crew composed of two-thirds Spaniards or Spanish Americans. In short, Spain should make no effort to restrict American trade to the peninsula but should adopt a modernized Trade and Navigation Act granting full freedom of trade to all subjects, establishing customs duties that favored Spanish commodities, playing no favorites with any European power but treating all alike, and avoiding any private treaty of commerce with any power. The fundamental point, he insisted, was that if it were true that the independence of America could not be prevented, then at least it should be delayed as long as possible by tying American interests to Spanish interests, removing all pretext for Spanish Americans to view other nations as better friends than the mother country, and attracting Americans to Spain in such a way that they would identify their interests with those of Spain. "This must be the great object of the government," he concluded.[23]

In a separate letter to Pizarro, Casa Flores pointed out that the greatest advantage of a new Trade and Navigation Act allowing normal open trade of Spanish flag vessels to all countries would be that it would place the European nations in a position to help bind the empire together. None would have a motive to spread subversion, and, as they traded with Spanish America, so would they strengthen imperial union. All the foreign aggression in America had been motivated by the desire of others to share in America's wealth; this plan would eliminate that motive.[24]

The indications were clear that strong support for free trade existed by late 1816 among some policy advisors. It was centered in the Ministry of State and the Council of the Indies, among civilians trained in the law. On 26 October 1816 the king ordered a special Junta General, composed of representatives from the major advisory bodies, to consider the establishment of a new trade system in America. It heard standing proposals submitted earlier that year by Miguel de Lastarria and Francisco Arango for liberalization of trade. Lastarria's suggestions were for a general opening of trade contacts; those of Arango, a member of the Council of the Indies, were for raising a special contribution of twenty million pesos in Cuba through opening that island's trade to foreign vessels of all nationalities and through a vast increase in the slave trade by foreign vessels.[25] More general, but startlingly liberal in persuasion, was the formal opinion of Manuel de la Bodega, a councilor of the Indies, submitted in October 1816. The government's policy to date in dealing with the American rebellions was wrong, he insisted, resulting only in increased rancor, entire provinces ruined, and "a million men lost." He advocated a policy of "softness, persuasion, and convincing," and asked what harm there could be in change after six years of fruitless effort. Bodega pointed out that the size of the American rebellions made any non-political settlement impossible, since a majority of the Spanish nation was actually in rebellion. Strongly supporting British trade and mediation as the only means of settling the rebellions, he insisted that "free trade is the most powerful instrument not only to pacify but also to conserve the Americas."[26]

A final indication of the thinking of the Council of the Indies came in November, when it considered the suggestions for pacification rendered by a Frenchman named D'Aubignose. The suggestion under examination was rapidly dismissed, for it included the idea that Spain should dispatch to Tierra Firme an expeditionary force commanded by a foreigner who would announce in Bogotá the creation of a semi-independent or autonomous state under the immediate rule of a prince of the royal blood to be called the Príncipe de la América del Centro, who would, despite his title, function in fact as a subject of the king. The council forebore to review the entire plan on the grounds that the Frenchman's good intentions had overcome his reflection and experience. In further ruminations on the subject, however, the council told the king that the memorial did contain some important truths. The dissensions in America, it pointed out, were not mere popular tumults that could be suppressed militarily, but real civil wars designed to drive Spain out. New Spain was being converted into a desert by military destruction there; Venezuela was in even greater turmoil; Buenos Aires could only be subjected by an expedition of 10,000 to 12,000 men; Chile was so insecure that its governor could only maintain control by terror; Peru's provinces were the scene of struggles, occupations, and reoccupations. A major problem was the lack of a general plan for American pacification, even though the Council of the Indies since its reestablishment in 1814 had been proposing a political rather than a military solution. Though a Junta Militar de Indias had been created, it dealt only with fortifications and expeditions. The ministries of War and the Navy quarreled among themselves over jurisdiction. Separate juntas were appointed to consider individual matters. No one knew what the others were doing. The only solution, said the council, was British mediation, which it had urged in July 1815, again in September 1815, and yet again in May 1816. Lapsing into the exact phrases of Casa Flores, the council pointed out: "We have no treasury, we have no navy, we have no other things necessary for pacification." And again, even if America were conquered by force it would require only a spark to set the rebellions off again. It would be more difficult to consolidate peace than to conquer. The council urged opening ports to the British as the only solution.[27]

Though the Council of the Indies had frequently expressed its approval of free trade, the important Junta of Pacification had not yet come out unequivocally in favor. On 22 October 1816 it moved in that direction when, in a report signed by its chairman, the Duke of Montemar, it told the king that the consulados in Spain and America, which were the chief opponents of free trade, must understand that the aid of England was now the only hope for pacifying America because of the total lack of a Spanish fleet.[28]

The debate was finally concluded when on 8 February 1817 the Junta of Pacification reported to the king its unqualified support of free trade. In a long and frank statement the junta reviewed the arguments for and against opening trade. Focusing particularly on Cuba, where trade with foreign ships had been permitted for some time, the junta pointed out that the advantages to Cuba were so great and so palpable that to return to trade exclusion would be absurd. It rendered itself of a sweeping summary: "That the greater prosperity of those dominions consists among other things in absolute liberty of commerce with everyone, . . . and that on purely economic principles it is nonsense to pretend to convince them of the contrary, are, for the Junta, truths that require no demonstration." It proceeded to argue forthrightly that America should be granted the same trade privileges as the peninsula possessed. Reviewing the standard arguments against free trade, the junta concluded they were not convincing. The partisans of restriction and exclusion, it pointed out, repeating a point made in October, were precisely those merchants, especially in Cádiz, who benefited most from the present monopoly system. Rejecting the conservative argument that the very same nations that most wanted to penetrate Spain's colonies were those that maintained a strict mercantilist system in their own colonies, the junta pointed out that without a navy and without industry Spain could not herself adopt the same type of mercantilism as the English and French. Those empires prospered, not because of trade restrictions, but because of their advanced technology and energy and "from a combination of causes that do not exist with us."

Turning from purely economic considerations, the junta proceeded to aim at the heart of the trade monopoly in the Spanish system. "The true arguments [against free trade] are not economic, they are principally political. . . . The project [of free trade] is bound up historically with all our system of legislation, civil and political, with the system of taxation, with the fortunes of many subjects, and with our own preoccupations." The junta thus arrived at the fundamental problem: after years of repetition of the arguments for and against expanded trade, the junta pointed out that the maintenance of the monopoly was bound up with national prejudice, with dreams of imperial glory, and with centuries of law, and that even to consider changing it risked imperial control. "In effect, much thought is required to combine their [the Americans'] liberties with the metropolis's dependency. To concede them the same privileges as Spain . . . it would be necessary to be very sure of their loyalty." This was especially troublesome when the same foreign powers that most advocated open trade in America were notorious for their support of American independence. To begin to alter trade legislation now would also ruin many capitalists in Spain, for "the entire nation is accustomed to the system." More than that, the very survival of Spain was tied up with the wealth of the monopoly merchants, who provided the only ready cash contributions the government could call upon, at least in the absence of direct contributions from American subjects. All the profits that would be realized in the first years after opening America to foreign trade would accrue to foreigners and come at the cost of Spanish capitalists. This was especially true as long as Spain lacked a merchant marine. How would the pacification of America itself then be paid for? There was no doubt that free trade constituted a serious political risk to Spain.

Thus it was Spain's inability to capitalize fully on the wealth of its American territories, especially its lack of a navy, that the junta saw as a greater danger than the possible loss of future revenues. Yet opening free trade would be the only workable means of generating the wealth to build up a Spanish merchant fleet. Spain's merchants, the junta insisted, must therefore be convinced that the danger to their own interests lay in depending too much on the old trade restrictions, that change was now being forced on them, and that they must now change the basis of doing business in America. If they did that, then they would survive. At any rate, trade generated in the hands of Spanish American merchants free to travel to other nations would certainly build a new and competitive fleet flying the Spanish flag. The junta concluded: "It is necessary and urgent to change the system, ignoring the so-called fundamental law [of mercantilist exclusivism], because it is defective in its origin, and null and impracticable in present circumstances, circumstances that derive from the liking the American subjects have taken for liberty of commerce." American ships should thus be free to sail to Europe, touching on the return trip at Spain and paying taxes designed to develop a peninsular merchant fleet.[29]

A virtual consensus in favor of free trade now existed among those advisors specifically authorized to speak for American policy, since both the Council of the Indies and the Junta of Pacification were now on record supporting it and the minister of state consistently advised political solutions and supported (indeed, may have initiated) most of the Junta of Pacification's proposals of February. Pizarro first wrote his overall plan for American pacification in February 1817, following the recommendation of the Council of the Indies to revise existing trade regulations and in support of English mediation. The key to Pizarro's program, which formed the basis of internal debate for the next two years, was his belief that America should be granted free trade. In August 1817 Pizarro restated his plan of pacification to the Council of State. He urged the Council of State to adopt a multiple policy toward the American territories depending on whether Spain still controlled them or not. For Buenos Aires, which Spain did not control, he urged a strong military expedition that would carry with it promises of trade and administrative reforms. If a force of eight to ten thousand troops could not be sent to Buenos Aires, however, then foreign mediation should be adopted, the English being granted open trade in return. If English mediation was adopted, then England should have to guarantee its success by agreeing, in case mediation failed, either to join Spain in a military effort or else, at least, to cease

further trade with the rebellious territory. In territories still dominated by Spain, direct trade should be decreed under tariffs favorable
to Spain. This would have the additional advantage of guaranteeing
Spain the preferred position as a trading partner even if such territories
did go on to independence. In addition, Spain should open shipbuilding facilities in America and should give Cuba the attention and care it
now deserved as "one of the most precious jewels in the monarchy."[30]

Although Spanish diplomats readily cited these various recommendations to the British as proof that Spain was prepared to move on
free trade, the crown never gave the order to proceed further. The king
was simply not convinced. The reactionaries who surrounded him, of
course, possessed his confidence, and they opposed free trade. The
conservative or militarist point of view was best summed up in the
very influential memorial of Juan Antonio Yandiola, who in the most
extreme statement of the need to preserve America by military means
also provided three theses that were no doubt very convincing to the
king. The first was that the rebellions in America were largely the
fault of the weak and febrile policies of the Cortes and of the governments that preceeded it. Those who opposed the use of force in the
name of humanity, he said, were merely hypocritical defenders of
criminal acts. "It is time to renounce the inadequate plans of weak
politics, the multiple indulgences, the monstrous concessions; they
have only served to induce the rebels to make a sacrilegious joke of the
sacred person of Your Majesty and of the great Spanish Nation." The
second principle, which Yandiola insisted the reformers obscured in
their memorials, was the absolute necessity of preserving Spanish
control in America. "It is certain that Spain cannot now subsist
without the Americas, not only because of political considerations . . . but also because it is the only depository of Spanish
commerce." Through some very dubious mathematical calculations
Yandiola proceeded to estimate that Spain had thus far lost 247
million pesos from direct expenditures, military destruction, and war
costs in the American rebellions and that a further 270 million pesos
had been siphoned off in English exports of bullion from America and
another 170 million in English contraband. Third, Yandiola argued
that the American people lacked the energy, civic virtue, and experi-

ence to be independent and that independence would cast the American people into abject backwardness. "But such is the blindness of humans that to the ignominy and shame of our century, of our administration, and of ourselves, we have at last seen the people, the provinces, the kingdoms of America simultaneously and frantically desert the sweet repose of three hundred years and prefer ferocious anarchy to paternal authority, unbridled license to honest liberty, and primeval barbarism to relative independence."

Yandiola then outlined the most extreme measures for suppressing America, including the reintroduction of total peninsular trade monopoly, expedition of troops to America, establishment of European guard corps in the capitals of the New World, suppression of Indian communities, dissolution of creole-dominated territorial militias, prohibition of all communications with foreigners and of the right of foreigners to reside in the colonies, and creation of a central authority to administer all American affairs. The foreigners must be forced out of America, no matter what the cost.[31] Yandiola's detailed recommendations were judged by all to be unworkable, and the Junta of Pacification pointedly refused to debate the proposals as being directly contrary to its preference for open trade,[32] but the ideas expounded in his memorial were persuasive enough to cause the king to hesitate in the granting of free trade.

Nor did the negative advice derive only from the more reactionary elements. Particularly troubling to the king must have been the response of the minister of finance, Martín Garay, a moderate reformer on treasury questions, to the memorial of the Conde de Casa Flores regarding the need for free trade and British mediation. In January 1817 Garay argued firmly and persuasively against each of the reform points Casa Flores had advocated the month before, and in the process he clearly broke ranks with the other two moderate members of the cabinet, Pizarro at state and Vázquez Figueroa at the navy. All of America, Garay argued, still required the mother country to provide it with government. The king viewed the Americas as provinces or kingdoms—the term "colony" had never been applied to them. There was no plant or fruit the Americans could not now plant and harvest legally and no industry that they could not exercise "when the indolence of the country will support it." America was not as productive as it might be, he felt, because since the Constitution it was no longer possible to force the Indians and castes to labor, so he saw no need to remove prohibitions on the production of certain new commodities in America, as Casa Flores had advocated. Thus Garay proceeded to reject each of Casa Flores's reforms in turn, coming finally to the most important, the question of free trade or of making American trade regulations equal to those of the peninsula. Garay, like the up-to-date nineteenth-century economist he was, responded in a manner that might well have characterized a contemporary French or English minister: "The greatest harm that could be done to the Americans would be to make them equal with the Spaniards in the realm of Royal Treasury." Adoption of commercial equality between Spain and America would result in a "political monstrosity never before seen in either ancient or modern overseas establishments." He meant that an empire of equal parts would be no empire. "The Indies," he continued, "by their situation, state, needs, and relations, have perforce to carry out the role of colonies under the name of Spanish America, and it is not humanly possible to identify or equalize the colonies with their metropolis, because they and it have different and even contrary objects, obligations, and functions to carry by their natural constitution." He concluded by urging that the opinion of those most affected by any commercial reform in America should be solicited.[33]

Garay had thus honed down the question of free trade to its logical and unavoidable bare bones, whereupon it became a question again of politics rather than economics or fiscal policy. He was saying that either Spain controlled an empire or it did not. If America were permitted to abandon the function of colonies—which in the early nineteenth century was considered a proper role for conquered lesser peoples to play—then the empire itself would be abandoned. Many other voices repeated this refrain in varying degrees of clarity. Viceroy Abascal of Peru had stated as early as 1812 that free trade "would be tantamount to decreeing the separation of these dominions from the Mother Country."[34] An unnamed member of the Council of State, whose points sound very similar to Abascal's, stated in a separate opinion in 1817 that "I would look upon the decree of free commerce as the same as the emancipation of America and the sentence of our degradation." Free trade would not encourage Spanish merchant shipping, he insisted, but would merely open the door to the foreigners to capture Spanish America's trade. The hope of British mediation was not only impossible but dangerous, for the British were Spain's mortal enemies. What Spaniard would give them the power to decide the future of Spanish America? This councilor then recommended, among other things, that Spain proceed with its plans to send a projected expedition to the Río de la Plata, that most creole militias be suppressed, and that customs duties for national commerce with the colonies be reduced.[35]

Undoubtedly the king's thinking remained reactionary without the reinforcement of learned discussions of the political impact of trade reform. But the core consideration remained the fact that no amount of argument by the more liberal advisors who opposed a military solution and advocated a negotiated settlement could overcome the fear that gripped many policy makers that trade reform would only hasten the separation of America, enriching Spain's enemies and other powers about whom Spanish leaders felt such obvious anxiety, an anxiety born out of feelings of Spanish inadequacy in trade, commerce, and capitalist development. The chief impediment to the movement for free trade was not so much the king's intransigence, or simple reaction, as the fear of the harmful consequences of loosening the bonds that had tied America to Spain for three centuries.

It goes without saying that during this period no one in the Spanish administration was prepared to contemplate voluntarily surrendering any of the American territory. There had actually been one brief consideration of a possible voluntary cession of territory when the king of Holland had demanded payment of 30 million florins owed by Spain to various Dutch subjects and had also requested that Spain cede to Holland some minor American territory in partial compensation— citing Puerto Rico, the Philippines, or some other territory that might be convenient. The fiscal of the General Treasury, J. M. Aparici, had spoken for all the king's advisors when he pointed out that, although the debt was clear and just, Spain should be granted some leeway in payment by the European states who owed their very liberty to Spain's defeat of Napoleon. At any rate, to concede Holland's wish for American territory would encourage the neighboring Spanish territories in their struggle for independence, would show that Spain was prepared to abandon territory, and would convert some territory into a center of further contraband trade with the rebellious lands. "What cause have the inhabitants of Puerto Rico, the Philippines, Santo Domingo or any other province given to be excluded from the great family by their father?"[36] This dedication to the idea that even the weakest and least productive members of the Spanish family must be preserved would change radically in the year to come in response to the growing awareness of Spain's own weakness.

Throughout the entire debate on a possible political settlement, the military faction was by no means silent. Although officers rarely addressed the question of free trade directly, the general tone of their advice invariably opposed a negotiated settlement. The military situation took a drastic turn for the worse in 1817, in Venezuela and Chile particularly. In early 1817 the king's advisors considered the bad news from Venezuela. General Morillo's personal delegate to Spain, Juan Antonio de Roxas Queypo, informed the king in late December 1816 that Venezuela was again in danger of being lost, and painted a highly pessimistic picture of the future of royalist arms there. All the people of color, who vastly outnumbered the whites, favored independence, as did even the majority of women, who were described as "perhaps the most powerful arms . . . of the partisans of the rebellion." Morillo thus advocated that Spain adopt a policy of expelling from Venezuela persons who supported the insurgents, replacing them with colonists sent out from Spain and the Canaries. He called on the king to protest the protection provided the rebels and their supporters by English, Dutch, French, Swedish, Danish, and North American ships. He called for the reestablishment of privately-owned patrol ships operating under royal patents to protect the coastlines. And, among other things, he urged that special appointments and rewards be offered to creoles who remained loyal to the crown and that the church be mobilized in a new missionary effort to regain the obedience and to influence the consciences of the people. While these and other policies were being implemented, Morillo said, the crown should send more troops and money. Roxas Queypo, meanwhile, painted a gloomy picture of Venezuela as a country overrun with the philosophical poisons of free thought, Jansenism, Protestantism, and even Quakerism.[37] The king was so alarmed that he sent the memorial on to Minister of State Pizarro, ordering the cabinet to report back immediately. Each minister in turn replied that those requests most appropriate to their jurisdiction had either already been enacted or were impossible.

Late in the year the Conde de Casa Flores, now established in Rio de Janeiro as Spanish minister to the Portuguese king, reported that the victories of San Martín and O'Higgins in Chile that year had seriously endangered royal control throughout the continent, especially by renewing the hopes of the rebels that independence was not an impossible dream. In Buenos Aires, he reported, it was widely believed that Spain was too weak to send an expedition, and the Portuguese aggressors in the Banda Oriental similarly assumed that their hold on Montevideo was more secure. All of Spain's enemies, he reported, now believed that intervention by the Great Powers in America was out of the question and that Spain would be left alone and unable to reestablish its control. He urged the crown to take drastic actions.[38] Since the Spaniards were now thoroughly convinced that the American countries were incapable of self-government, and since they continued to view the turmoil of governments in Buenos Aires as proof of that fact, Casa Flores also reported that many porteños believed the best method of consolidating their independence was to place a prince of the Bourbon dynasty on the throne at Buenos Aires.

The suggestion that one of the Spanish infantes be sent to rule in Buenos Aires was only one example of many similar propositions that would be made in the late 1810s and early 1820s. It was such a frequent suggestion that a word needs to be said at the outset to explain why Ferdinand never gave it serious consideration. San Martín in Peru would also aspire to have an infante to establish a throne there, as would Iturbide in the Plan of Iguala in Mexico, and the Portuguese would themselves suggest in 1820 that an infante be sent to Buenos Aires. Various Cortes deputies after 1820 proposed dividing the empire into a confederation, with infantes at the head of three or four kingdoms. The British sometimes leaned toward such a solution. The idea dated back, indeed, to 1783, when the Count of Aranda, a minister of Charles III, suggested in a famous and controversial memorandum that the empire be divided in three parts, each ruled over by an infante. Some modern authors assume that such a solution would have prevented the dismemberment of the empire.[39] The idea, in short, was often proposed by many and varied sources and, if nothing else, is certainly a reflection of the prestige and general legitimacy of the idea of monarchy, and perhaps of the Spanish royal house as well.

Yet it never seems to have occurred to contemporaries that, by the time of Ferdinand VII, the idea had become utterly absurd, and even historians seem not to have noted the mathematical impossibility of the equation. Ferdinand had only two brothers. The older, Don Carlos, was his only heir until 1830, when the birth of Ferdinand's daughter Isabel by his fourth wife provided him at last with a child to succeed him. Don Carlos was thus the king's indispensable companion, and no consideration of sending him to strange foreign lands could be contemplated. Furthermore, the two men were very close during the 1810s and 1820s. Although Don Carlos in 1833 would cast Spain into civil war in a dynastic struggle motivated by his refusal to recognize a female heiress, he gave no public indication of disloyalty to Ferdinand until the late 1820s, when the Carlist faction began to rise. The younger brother, Don Francisco de Paula, was not close to Ferdinand. During his youth he was unpopular with the masses because of the widely-held but unproven belief that he was the child of Godoy and María Luisa. Would Mexico, Peru, or Buenos Aires accept a reputed son of Godoy on the throne? Furthermore, by the 1820s Don Francisco de Paula had become a noted liberal and a member of the Masonic order. Only three other infantes existed, none of them brothers of the king. One was the king's uncle Don Antonio; old and senile, he died in 1817. Another was the child Don Carlos Luis, the king's nephew, the dispossessed heir to the kingdom of Etruria, who was finally recognized by the European Powers as the heir to Parma after years of Spanish diplomatic effort on his behalf. Though he lived at Ferdinand's court, he was not technically a Spaniard. The only other male member of the royal family, in this case a lateral branch, was Don Luis de Borbón y Villabriga, cardinal archbishop of Toledo and primate of Spain, obviously unsuited for founding a dynasty in America, who because of his role as chairman of the constitutional Regency was banned from court from 1814 to 1820. None of the plans for creating American monarchies ever referred to him. The impossibility of the proposal, nonetheless, did not prevent it from being suggested by many and very disparate sources.

As the implications of the resurgence of the rebellions in Chile, Venezuela, and elsewhere settled in, the idea that Casa Flores attributed to public opinion in Buenos Aires also began to be heard among important Spanish advisors. Luis de Onís, Spanish minister to the United States, argued in 1817 that in order to prevent the nations of Latin America from falling into the hands of foreign powers it would ultimately be preferable either to grant them total equality within the empire or else establish separate kingdoms under princes of the royal family. Meanwhile, to win the support of the Great Powers, Onís suggested another radical idea: Spain should contemplate making territorial exchanges. For example, it could cede Buenos Aires to the king of Portugal in return for uniting metropolitan Portugal with Spain; the Floridas could be granted to the United States in return for a guaranteed border with New Spain (this was ultimately achieved in 1819); and Santo Domingo could be ceded to France in return for French naval and military aid to Mexico.

Onís also supported a group of suggestions of a former Cortes deputy from Santo Domingo who had fled to the United States and become an advisor to the Spanish embassy there, Juan Alvarez Toledo, who advocated that the displaced populace of Santo Domingo should be settled in the Internal Provinces of Mexico, that the Indians should be freed of all tribute, and that national militias should be founded in all parts of America. It was Toledo's idea to exchange Santo Domingo, which was in constant danger of being engulfed by the Haitians anyhow, to France in return for 6,000 soldiers who would fight in

Mexico for five years and then be rewarded with land in the Internal Provinces. In addition, France would supply the fleet Spain so desperately needed—six warships, four frigates, four corvettes, and four brigantines.[40]

Although these ideas were not discussed by any important Spanish council (Pizarro says Eguía blocked their presentation),[41] they are notable for their extremism compared with the thinking of only a year before. A serious statesman like Onís was now prepared to contemplate exchanging individual American territories for other considerations and seems not to have been troubled by the thought of creating a confederative empire. Onís and Toledo had the protection of Pizarro in their proposals. At least two of the ideas of Onís and Toledo—the concept of exchange of peripheral or unproductive territory and the willingness to do almost anything to acquire a military fleet—would appear in other guises over the next two years. José Pizarro would himself endorse an exchange of American territory with Portugal, and in 1817 the king would commit one of his greatest follies in the ill-fated purchase of a Russian fleet.

By July 1817, Minister of the Navy José Vázquez Figueroa was pleading with the minister of finance, Garay, to find resources to equip ships for America. On 18 July he informed Garay that he was negotiating with France for the acquisition of various vessels of the class of frigates and smaller. Meantime, Vázquez Figueroa said he had brought to the king's attention on several occasions that fact that "without a sufficient navy all efforts to reduce [the rebels] to duty are useless." He added that the king and cabinet seemed convinced of the truth of that fact, but no positive results were forthcoming. The only funds that had come forward to aid in the transportation of troops to America in the last months were from corporations such as the consulados. Without funds to equip and arm ships, he confessed, he could do nothing but plead that everything else would be lost. Field Marshal Pascual Enrile, returned to Spain from the war in New Granada, where he was commander of naval forces, reported that he had attended two meetings of the Junta Militar de Indias, where, after all the plans and schemes of how to undertake further operations in America had been exhausted, it was recognized, as always, that without a military fleet all efforts to restore power in America "were time and money wasted." In late July the king solemnly ordered the ministry of finance to set aside funds for naval support as a first priority, as though they were funds for the support of a land army. Little improvement seems to have resulted from this order.[42] By mid-1817 the greatest anxiety in regard to naval affairs was how to provide the large fleet necessary to transport to America the planned 20,000 troops that were beginning to gather at Cádiz to make up the major offensive force long discussed and debated. Indeed, owing to the shortage of vessels, the original sailing date for the expedition—August 1817—quietly slipped by.

Spain's financial condition was too weak to permit optimism. By 1817 the annual deficit stood at approximately 452 million reales. Although Ferdinand had promised Vázquez Figueroa that he would receive the money and ships he needed to maintain Spain's defenses and send the expedition, the condition of the fleet was deplorable. In 1808 the Spanish fleet had consisted of forty-two men-of-war and thirty frigates, but by the end of the war with France the fleet had been allowed to decline to merely twenty-nine men-of-war and seventeen frigates. Of these, however, only twenty-four ships were seaworthy, and only two or three did not require a complete overhaul. But Vázquez Figueroa estimated that to be effective the navy required, in prime condition, a minimum of twenty men-of-war, thirty frigates, and a proportional number of lesser craft, along with a budget of 120 million reales a year. For all his pleas for help, in Garay's austerity budget for 1817 the navy was allotted only 100 million reales, of which it received only 20 million in actuality. With this the Ministry of the Navy was expected not only to prepare for the expedition but also to suppress the rebel corsairs, patrol the European and American trade lanes with convoys, and suppress the flow of supplies to the American rebels.[43]

While the ministers of the Great Powers discussed the Portuguese invasion of Montevideo in a series of meetings in Paris in the summer and fall of 1817, in Madrid a most peculiar and particularly aberrant scheme to settle the Montevideo crisis was hatched. Motivated by the sort of thinking of Luis de Onís in favor of exchanging endangered American territories for political or territorial advantages elsewhere, Minister of State José Pizarro toyed with a highly dangerous and top-secret scheme that depended directly on his thesis that America was already lost. According to at least one source, an anonymous spy for Simón Bolívar who reported on the condition of the peninsula in September 1817, the Pizarro thesis was widely held. Writing from Cádiz, this unidentified source informed the Liberator: "The majority of the nation is of the opinion that the cause of America should be abandoned, that is, that they should transfer it, but the monopolists will not acquiesce to anything."[44] This thinking led Pizarro in 1817 to propose a most unrealistic scheme.

Pizarro's scheme was to turn the Portuguese occupation of the Banda Oriental and the fact that Portugal itself was left without its king and court to Spain's advantage, seizing this unique opportunity to fulfill the dream of Spanish kings since 1640—the reunification of Portugal with Spain. The plan was hatched gradually as the Buenos Aires expedition was being gathered at Cádiz. Pizarro's chief concern initially seems to have been how to plot the acquisition of Portugal without giving offense to the new Spanish queen, María Isabel de Braganza, daughter of the king of Portugal. He seems to have induced Ferdinand to mention the whole subject to María Isabel and was startled a few days later to be addressed by the queen in Ferdinand's presence. She told him to proceed with the business of the Río de la Plata without fear of offending her, for she had ceased to be a Portuguese and was now a Spaniard and only wanted what was best for Spain and her husband. With obvious relief Pizarro wrote: "Nor was this a vain ostentation on the Queen's part, because she repeated to me later, on various occasions and in the most confidential tone, 'In matters relating to Portugal, split and cut without embarrassment.'"[45] Thus, whereas Onís had proposed exchanging Buenos Aires for Portugal, Pizarro refined the idea into a plan to exchange Montevideo for Portugal.

The plan was never committed to paper and thus is impossible to set out with precision. The probable scenario would be that the expedition to Río de la Plata would invade Montevideo before it attacked Buenos Aires. Pizarro explained:

At the same time this expedition could conclude the question of Montevideo, because it would put an end to the sophism that Portugal could not give it up owing to the fact that we had no forces there and were unable to settle with Buenos Aires. There would remain no excuse, either they would give it up or they would be thrown out of it, that was evident. But it was kept a secret.[46]

Regardless of whether the Portuguese were or were not driven out of Montevideo, the direct clash of arms between Spain, the legitimate ruler of Montevideo, and Portugal, the illegal invader, would constitute just grounds for Spain to move on the peninsula against the border of Portugal. Pizarro wrote:

I manifested to the king that the scandalous Portuguese invasion against the evident rights of His Majesty also injured the delicate honor of the Monarchy, and that it not only offered just title to a vigorous war, but that the circumstances could not be more favorable for the incorporation of the peninsula. It seemed to my view a capital and perhaps unique [opportunity] for [completion] of *the true Spanish political objective*, which always, as now, justice favored. [I told him] that I believed that it was in Portugal that we should conquer the Banda Oriental.[47]

The scenario thus had a partial and a total objective. The partial objective would be that Spanish arms would lose in Montevideo, whereupon Spain would still take Portugal. The ultimate success would be if Spanish arms retook Montevideo and simultaneously took Portugal. Either way, Spain would win great advantages, and it would do so in a context of legitimacy and just response to Portuguese aggression.

What of the Great Powers? Britain, the power Spain most respected for its naval superiority, had pledged to defend Portugal's coasts during the interregnum while the king and court were living in Brazil. Here Pizarro was counting on his thesis that nothing further could be lost in America, combined with a calculation that France, in the first period of the Bourbon restoration there, was unwilling to risk national recovery on European military adventures. He explained:

> England and France would probably be the only two obstacles to
> the undertaking. England because of its true political calcula-
> tions as much as because of pledges and advantages [it has] with
> Portugal, and because it had always considered any increase in
> Spanish power as an increase in the power of France, its rival.
> France would be opposed also, because of its habitual preemi-
> nent influence over Spain and out of a cavalier lack of confidence
> in Spain's power. . . . But I thought that neither the one nor
> the other power could hinder the king's pursuit of justice. In the
> desperate situation of America, what harm could the English do
> us? And France, in the infancy of its regeneration, what could it
> do against us? Besides, neither the one nor the other power was
> fond of wars of this nature. . . . In short, the occupation of
> Portugal would be nothing but a natural result of the war and
> not a conquest of ambition. . . . His Majesty was perfectly
> convinced.[48]

Furthermore, the takeover of Portugal would be accomplished
by Spanish land forces crossing from Extremadura, thereby counter-
ing the advantage of British naval power. The Holy Allies might
acquiesce in the Spanish action in order to restore order in unstable
Portugal; besides, Spain could claim legitimacy because it was the
aggrieved party. The recent double marriage of the king and Don
Carlos to two Portuguese princesses would not hurt, either. The
Portuguese people themselves, torn between liberalism and conservatism, lacking any real enthusiasm for the regency that governed
them in Lisbon, and administered merely as an appendage of Brazil,
would not resist for long. The king, João VI, was known to prefer
Brazil, indeed, in December 1815 he had created the so-called United
Kingdom of Brazil, Portugal, and the Algarves in recognition of the
importance of the vast American territory. Brazil was many times
larger and richer than the decrepit old motherland, and João VI would
have a fair exchange if he managed to keep the Banda Oriental (though
Pizarro assumed he would not). In short, while Brazil was taking
advantage of Spain's weakness to grab a confused and divided territory

on its border in South America, Spain would take advantage of Portugal's weakness to do the same in the peninsula. At the very least, a seizure of Portugal might be used to negotiate the restoration of Montevideo.

It is not clear how far the plans to reunite Portugal with Spain proceeded, but Pizarro testified that the king agreed, at least in principle, to the proposal. Pizarro's object was to restore the tarnished honor of the nation by a bold stroke, but the timing of it would be very problematic, to say nothing, of course, of the continued delays associated with gathering the troops at Cádiz. Even so, the European Powers were suspicious. In January 1817 the ambassador to London, the Conde de Fernán Núñez, reported that there was a rumor circulating in the British court that Spain was taking no firm action against the Portuguese invasion of Montevideo because "among the various conjectures there are even some who believe that it is in accord with His Majesty's intentions to occupy Portugal with this motive, and without Europe being able to impede it, since it is the result of an exchange of territory between the two powers." In June, the chargé in London reported that there was another rumor going about that Spain had reached an accord with Russia to take over Portugal, ceding Russia the island of Minorca in return for its help.[49]

In October 1817 Spain requested the Great Powers to mediate in the Montevideo controversy, and the ministers representing the Powers began talks on that subject the same month in Paris.[50] Fernán Núñez came from London to Paris to be near the talks, where in December he was given authority to negotiate directly with Brazil and ordered to hold out for complete Brazilian recognition of Spanish sovereignty in the Río de la Plata. The Portuguese foreign minister, Pedro Souza-Holstein, Count (later Duke) of Palmella, came from London to Paris to defend his government's actions before the Allied ministers and to pursue the talks with Fernán Núñez. Immediately upon the gathering of the ministers, rumors ran through Paris of massive Spanish troop movements in Extremadura on the border with Portugal, and the Russian representative, Count Posso di Borgo, came to Spain's defense, declaring that Spain might well be forced to some aggressive act against Portugal if the Powers did not uphold

Spain's claim to Montevideo.[51] Perhaps the Spanish mobilization in Extremadura was, as the Duke of Wellington put it, "mere bully," designed to start the talks off with a show of Spain's anger against Portugal.

The question of the mediation of the Great Powers in Montevideo came to nothing. Since the Spanish expedition never finally sailed, the primary prerequisite for a voluntary handover of Montevideo back to Spain—a Spanish presence in the Río de la Plata—was not met. Neither Spain nor Portugal hastened to reach a settlement in the extended talks that ensued between them. By the middle of 1818 a draft program of agreement had been worked out, calling for Spain, on the return of Montevideo to its control, to pay compensation of 7.5 million francs to Brazil for its services in preserving the territory from the rebels. That the discussion could swing so decidedly in the direction of the Portuguese definition of what they were doing in Montevideo indicates the great skill of the Portuguese negotiator Palmella and the ineptness of Fernán Núñez, the Spanish negotiator. Several advisors to the Spanish crown urged acceptance of the program. The Duke of Infantado, however, declared that he considered the whole idea a scandalous insult, although Spain should perhaps pay half the mentioned indemnity simply in order not to delay the sailing of the expedition.[52] In the end, Ferdinand rejected the proposal. The talks dragged on intermittently to 1819 without conclusion. Clearly the Spaniards were prepared to continue talking out of the hope of some possible advantage, but without abandoning their hope or dream of a spectacular blow against perfidious Portugal.

Pizarro implied in his memoirs that the idea of absorbing Portugal was tabled after considerable discussion among the ministers because, although the minister of finance, Garay, was amenable and willing to provide the funds, the minister of war, Francisco Eguía, and his successor as minister of war, José María Alós, refused their cooperation. Pizarro never explains what happened to the idea, declaring merely: "In effect, the war in Portugal—the only means of maintaining the rights of the throne—having been made impossible, the question now was, to my thinking, one of pure national honor."[53] Yet, as shall be seen, the idea of combining an assault against the Río de la Plata with a seizure of Portugal did not die entirely, and when, in late 1819, the Buenos Aires expedition was at last nearing the time to sail, the government of the day in Madrid seemed ready to consider such a strike.

Throughout this period the fear of a possible outbreak of war with the United States also motivated the Pizarro administration. In 1815 Luis de Onís had written to say that with the arrival of the peace treaty between the United States and Britain ending the War of 1812 the United States "is going to make itself into a great Nation, full of pride, of presumption, and of ambition for conquests." Its expansionist spirit was so great that war with Spain was likely in regard to Texas or the Floridas. By late 1817, after negotiations for the cession of the Floridas had begun, José Pizarro warned members of the cabinet that if Onís were unable to get a treaty with the United States, the possibility of war was great. North American attacks would be directed against Florida, Cuba, and Mexico. Such a war would be "desolating" and would lead to immediate North American recognition of the independent rebel governments in Spanish America. By September 1818 the minister of the navy had ordered the consul in Paris to outfit corsairs to attack United States merchant shipping in the event of hostilities.[54]

In almost every other theater of activity the cause of Spain continued to deteriorate. By the end of 1817 an unnamed source reported from Cádiz that there was complete disagreement about what policy to adopt in regard to the pacification and that the condition of Spain was deplorable, "without a government, without a treasury, without a navy, and above all, without opinion, pretending to subject the New World while they cannot give their own troops their daily support."[55] Pizarro was so convinced of the uselessness of military expeditions to America that he had even lost faith in the Morillo expedition in New Granada. In a report to another minister he detailed the chaos and destruction that gripped Venezuela, the terrible and wasteful battle that raged between the captain general and the members of the audiencia, the steps Morillo had taken to create a military dictatorship there, and the effects his harsh military policies had on the Venezuelans. His conclusion was that "since the arrival of the expedition of Captain General Pablo Morillo everything has gone from bad to worse."

Spain was caught in the middle of the disagreement between the audiencia and Morillo, each of which accused the other of outrages, but Pizarro felt that the evidence indicated that the audiencia's fears about Morillo were not entirely without credit. Morillo, however, urged the use of even greater force as the only policy for pacifying Venezuela. Spanish moderates opposed Morillo's grant of the powers of dictator, militarists supported it, and Ferdinand, buffeted between opposing points of view, in December 1817 suspended for the third time Morillo's *mando absoluto*, or absolute command over both military and civilian administration in Venezuela. This was a further mark of the temporary superiority of the moderates over the militarists in late 1817. But by June 1818 the militarists, as shall be seen, were again dominant, and Ferdinand restored Morillo once again to unlimited control.[56] Both sides, nonetheless, agreed that Venezuela's public opinion was almost universally in favor of independence and that the country was devastated and on the verge of a catastrophe.[57] Meanwhile, the rebel victory in Chile, at the battle of Chacabuco, opened again the risk of the loss not only of Chile but also of Peru, a clear and constant danger from early 1817 onwards.[58]

Sources in America, or sources knowledgeable about American affairs, continued to plead for sweeping changes in policy and, more significant, in Spain's attitude toward the American crisis. In 1817, Jacobo Villaurrutia, former alcalde of the audiencia of Mexico and currently a member of the chancellery (or audiencia) of Catalonia, proposed the abolition of all the consulados in America, the appointment of a high-level tribunal to visit America and establish administrative reforms, and the creation in Mexico of a Junta of Government, composed of the viceroy, members of the audiencia, and a few other royal officials, to govern jointly with the viceroy. He also suggested abolition of the fuero militar for urban militias, the creation of economic societies, and a number of other reforms relating to public education and trade. The General Treasury sent the proposals along to the Council of the Indies, suggesting they were merely the "dreams of a man who is too diligent."[59] Villaurrutia had been transferred from the Mexican audiencia early in the war of independence period because of his dangerous creole sympathies.

A more philosophical address was presented to the king by Manuel Vidaurre, the dissident creole oidor in Peru. The king read the representation and ordered Minister of War Eguía to give his comments. In very strong language Vidaurre argued, "It is not possible for Europe to dominate in America if it wishes to use force." Reform, however, would make it easy to govern America. A key rule, he argued, was not to punish dissidents so harshly as to drive them to desperation. Citing examples from Venezuela, Upper Peru, Quito, Chile, and elsewhere, he charged Spanish military officials with cruelty and fierce exactions, which merely convinced the people that it was necessary to become guerrillas to protect their last resources. Citing Montesquieu to the king, Vidaurre argued that force merely ruined America while it stripped Spain bare of troops. The Spanish soldier died in America but left behind two newborn children by the women of the country, children who in twenty years would be guerrillas fighting against Spain. The king had only three choices: he could destroy the American people and populate the New World anew; he could surrender control of America and leave it entirely free; or he could improve the administration of government so that all would work for its preservation. Striking a note that seems to have increasingly dominated Spanish thinking about the rebellions, Vidaurre pointed out that, just as Spain could not reconquer America by force, so too the Americans could not govern themselves. Still the rebellions would continue, for, as long as a man had nothing, he would prefer to be a rebel because no other recourse remained to assure his survival.[60]

This kind of outspoken complaint, combined with the support for free trade from the Council of the Indies, the Junta of Pacification, and from Pizarro, induced the regime to turn further in the direction of the moderate program that had been proposed by Pizarro. Obviously the American situation was deteriorating rapidly by the end of 1817; the administration was now convinced of its bankruptcy of resources; it was time to consider more imaginative solutions. Pizarro's plan to permit British mediation and trade in Buenos Aires combined with open trade for those portions of America still loyal to Spain was finally presented, after months of circulation, to the Council of State in September 1817. The moderates on the council strongly supported it. These included Pizarro, Vázquez Figueroa, Garay, the Duke of Montemar (president of the Council of the Indies), the Infante Don Carlos, the Marqués de Hormazas, and Anselmo de Rivas. The opposition included Eguía, Lozano de Torres, the Dukes of Infantado, Parque, and San Fernando, Manuel López Araujo, and Guillermo Hualde, who argued that any concessions would endanger Spain's control of America. Minister of Finance Garay and Minister of the Navy Vázquez Figueroa, it should be noted, advocated only the grant of indirect trade for foreigners, requiring their ships to pay duties in Spain before sailing to America. Throughout the next several weeks the Council of State debated the issue, and by the meeting of 18 October 1817 it appeared that ten members favored either limited or unlimited free trade, four opposed it, and three urged that it be deferred to a later date. Thus the council, which according to its rule of operation required "a substantial majority" before a minister could pursue his proposed policy, was effectively deadlocked.[61]

The king, however, was prepared to allow the moderates to continue pursuing the issue. On 8 November 1817 he ordered the creation of a new junta, to be composed of three members each from the Council of the Admiralty, the Tribunal of War, and the Council of the Indies, to propose a way to reconcile supporters of the insurgents who were ready to return to loyalty to Spain. The idea, according to the minister of grace and justice, Juan Lozano de Torres, a leading member of the camarilla, was to diminish the number of rebel partisans by opening to them the path of reconciliation. Rules were to be drafted on the model of the presumably liberal treatment the king had accorded the *afrancesados* after the Napoleonic war, which only the camarilla considered a liberal path. The order was dispatched, the Council of the Indies even appointed its three representatives, and then, as with so much else in the regime, nothing further happened. In mid-1818 the minister of war wrote plaintively to ask the minister of grace and justice what had happened to the idea. Should he choose his three delegates? Would the king mind repeating the order?[62]

It turns out that the order was countermanded by yet another of the king's brain storms. On 29 November 1817 he had ordered that all matters whatsoever relating to the pacification of America were to be turned over to the minister of state, José Pizarro, so that such questions could be harmonized with Spain's foreign policy in regard especially to the North American aggression against Florida and the Portuguese aggression against Montevideo. In 1816 the king had ordered all matters relating to American commerce to be in the hands of the Ministry of State; now he ordered all matters relating to pacification in general to be there.

The order had two important direct implications. It meant that José Pizarro's star was now ascendant: the king had decided to let him try his hand at solving the American crisis. Normal logic would suggest that a single unified policy of pacification was now about to be forthcoming. It also meant, as the Council of the Indies decided in a consultation in January 1818, that the Junta of Pacification, the agency that had been set up in 1815 to supervise American policy and that had clearly failed to arrive at a policy other than recommending English mediation, was now superseded. The council therefore advised the king to disband the Junta of Pacification. On 14 August 1818 the king so ordered (see table 2).[63] With laborious effort and ponderous bureaucratic shuffling, the papers relating to American pacification were all transferred to the Ministry of State, attended, as it happened, with no little confusion and misplacement of critical documents. The indirect implication of the king's order was even more sweeping. American policy was now being placed in the hands of the man who supported the Onís-Toledo concept of exchanging Spain's nearly-lost American territories for other advantages, who opposed Morillo's absolute dictatorship in Venezuela, who was the leading opponent of the camarilla and military clique, who was the chief moderate in the cabinet, and who was the main force behind the suggestion of the Council of the Indies and the Junta of Pacification for free trade in those territories still controlled by Spain. Every indication suggested that a moderate policy of non-military pacification was about to be formulated.

VI

Rejecting a Moderate Policy

The royal order of November 1817 to turn all matters relating to American pacification over to the minister of state placed the formulation of an American policy in the hands of José Pizarro, the man who had confessed he was convinced that America was already lost. As a thoughtful and moderate statesman, Pizarro proceeded to review the vast documentation transferred to his office from both the Ministry of the Indies and the Junta of Pacification. He was already on record as having proposed a dual policy of sending a military expedition to Buenos Aires or, failing that, of accepting British mediation there, combined with direct foreign trade for the other territories where Spanish power still existed. On 28 April 1818 he once again presented the program he had been advocating since early 1817. This time he reduced his program to its three absolutely essential points: opening American trade to foreigners, granting amnesty to Spanish exiles, and determining the details of the Buenos Aires expedition.[1] These and any other proposals, of course, would have to be approved by the Council of State, where the opponents of a moderate policy could veto them.[2] Thus, not surprisingly, his recommendations of April, after heated discussions, did not pass the council. No doubt Pizarro's efforts to propose a moderate policy were doomed from the start, for he testified that during this period the anger against the Americans was so intense that "the court spoke nothing but hatred, torture, and war against them."[3] Ferdinand himself was drifting inexorably toward a purely military settlement, as indicated by the fact that on 9 June 1818 he ordered the restoration of "unlimited faculties" to Morillo in Venezuela.[4]

Despite the dangers, both to himself personally and to the nation, Pizarro spent the first months of 1818 in an intense effort to get the Council of State to adopt his proposals. He drew together the several propositions he had offered throughout 1817 into a single great all-inclusive policy recommendation for the pacification of America. Dated 9 June 1818, it was the most wide-ranging and politically-sound program ever proposed during the wars of independence. It is a moot point, of course, whether, had it ever been adopted, it would have prevented the loss of America, but it still constituted the most imaginative approach taken by this otherwise stultified and hidebound regime. Pizarro, almost unique among the major policy-makers, clearly listened to and incorporated the ideas of the American loyalists themselves as they had been expressed in so many memorials over the years. Pizarro began his statement with a short preamble in which he reminded the king that American pacification was the ultimate important topic, beside which all other questions paled into insignificance. He thus implied that the king's priorities had been confused.

The minister proceeded to explain to Ferdinand that he could save all of America, he could save part of it, or he could lose all of it. The outcome of the struggle would determine the glory not only of the king's reign but of generations to come. Pizarro urged Ferdinand to pay attention to America and to adopt a unified overall policy. Yet, striking a note not previously brought forward by Spanish advisors, Pizarro pointed out that if the dominions should be lost in whole or in part it would simultaneously open channels for political development, trade, commerce, and industry that could save the rest of the monarchy. To explain, he cited the example of the British, who, having failed militarily to prevent the separation of the United States, had moved immediately to acquire new and extraordinary advantages in trade with the former colonies. Thus Pizarro hinted at a course Spain might follow to its very great advantage even if, as he assumed, the worst came to pass. There is no question that he was one of those few Spaniards who believed the nation would be better off trading with independent Spanish American states than paying the crushing burden of trying to suppress them indefinitely.[5] The loss of America might spark the regeneration of Spain.

But since his job was to propose how to save America, Pizarro charted a number of sweeping proposals, many of which he had already suggested. The first necessity was to consolidate control of all American questions in a single authority. The current situation, in which the Ministry of State proposed policy in conjunction with all the other councils and ministries but in which it lacked the power to give orders to armies and viceroys, had, in his view, to be changed "or Your Majesty will lose America." "It is officially said, and Your Majesty believes, that everything is unified in the hands of the Ministry of State. That is an illusion, Sir, an abuse of the word. The Ministry of State does not appoint, it does not pardon, it does not punish, it does not arm, it does not control any aspect of the Indies." He added, "This is the truth of the matter, and it is not possible to hide it from Your Majesty." Secondly, he recommended "a single, quick, and strong expedition, directed precisely at Río de la Plata." This region he judged the one where military efforts would have the greatest effect, for the reconquest of Buenos Aires would cause the fall of the independent regime now forming in Chile and would save Peru and Upper Peru from the rebel pincers now threatening them. Thirdly, it was essential to open the commerce of the American countries not yet in rebel hands to foreigners, under tariffs designed to encourage Spanish development. To do so would correct the single greatest complaint of Americans while tying foreign interests to the preservation of Spanish rule and denying the rebels foreign assistance. The point seemed so obvious to Pizarro, who had repeated it many times over, that he did not expand further, except to add: "All of Europe, more or less, supports the emancipation because all of Europe is of the idea that Spain will never depart from its exclusive system."

Pizarro's fourth suggestion was the granting of a general amnesty to all Spanish dissidents. He referred chiefly to peninsular Spaniards tainted by association with French liberalism and currently being persecuted by the internal spy network formulated by Francisco Eguía. Most of the dissidents he had in mind were in exile in France and England. Pizarro firmly believed that if Eguía spent as much effort on the military resistance to American independence as he spent on searching out dissident liberals within Spain the rebellions would not have progressed so far. He continued: "I have had the honor to say to Your Majesty in writing that [an amnesty] is a moral and political necessity for Spain; but now I consider it only in regard to the Pacification. The exiles . . . , Sir, are those who have created in France and England ideas particularly in favor of those [Spanish American] countries and of their independence." Those persecuted by the Spanish government were the main movers of the rebellions. Pizarro's fifth point was a short but eloquent plea against military force: "It is very important in America not to use force except insofar as means of persuasion and possible concessions do not overcome. War, by itself, has to be considered as secondary in this business." Pizarro's next point was closely related. It was necessary to choose governmental officials from among the most talented portion of the population, even including former or amnestied dissidents and liberals. "Those subjects who have displayed political talent in the command of provinces in Spain, those statesmen who have distinguished themselves, they are the ones who should go to America." The military—particularly, he implied, the minister, Eguía—should not have the power to veto appointments of candidates with backgrounds judged to be suspicious. In general he felt that magistrates and government officials in America consisted of the overflow of the universities and ministerial anterooms of Spain, men who could find no other appointment. In addition, he urged a strict division in America between administrative officials and members of the judiciary, referring especially to the harmful effect of the institution of the real acuerdo in America, the statement of royal accord by which both governors or viceroys and audiencia judges set political policy. He believed this gave too great an opportunity for judicial officers to dabble in politics.

After making a general point in favor of granting concessions to America, Pizarro proceeded to make a startling point in favor of open immigration to America. Depopulation of such regions as Cuba, Santo Domingo, and the Mexican Internal Provinces was, he felt, the greatest invitation to foreign incursion and settlement. These frontier and peripheral areas had to be populated to order to be governed. He urged the king to open such lands to immigration by the people of all nations, giving preference, of course, to Spaniards. In this he was directly following a point frequently made by Luis de Onís, who foresaw that the depopulation of lands bordering on the United States was an open invitation to Anglo-Saxon absorption.

As his tenth point, Pizarro suggested that Spain permit the arming of private corsairs against the insurgents. Spain had thus far done little to promote this frequently suggested idea, largely, Pizarro thought, out of timidity. "Timidity serves nothing in great crises," he solemnly preached. The need was undeniably clear, for Chile and Buenos Aires had corsairs in both the Atlantic and the Pacific preying on Spanish commercial shipping, and soon the naval balance of power would swing in favor of the independent governments. As early as June 1817, rebel corsairs were capturing Spanish ships off the Canary Islands, depriving the islands of commodities and of the cash transfers sent from America by Canarian immigrants there. Furthermore, only ten days after Pizarro submitted his pacification plan, rebel corsairs from Buenos Aires attempted to capture a Spanish merchantman in Bilbao, and it was reported that insurgent ships were cruising Spain's coasts and attacking smaller ports. For the first time the American wars were reaching out and directly touching the peninsula itself.[6] The Admiralty decided in August to create special shore batteries, shore patrols, and port launches in Spanish ports receiving American shipping, such as Santander and La Coruña. Cádiz, the major recipient of American trade, had not yet been attacked, perhaps because it already had an extensive network of watchtowers on shore to defend against foreign incursion. But it had suffered grievous damage, since in 1816 and 1817 alone sixty ships from Cádiz were captured by Spanish American corsairs.[7]

Continuing with naval matters, Pizarro urged the king to encourage naval development by permitting the construction and outfitting of military and commercial ships in America. If naval construction were to continue to be restricted to European shipyards, he argued, "we will have no ships either here or over there." In addition, Spain must establish effective blockades in rebellious American territories, and merchant shipping should be dispatched in convoys for mutual protection. Finally, "the formation of wise customs levies is the key to all the protection of our commerce and industry." If the same effort expended in protecting Spanish shipping from foreign competition were spent on modernizing the tariff structure, the root problem of deteriorating trade would be addressed.

Turning to social and political policy, Pizarro's fourteenth point was a call for Spain to attract the American nobility to come settle near the court in Madrid, a useful means of political consolidation that the Catholic Kings had once employed to draw the Spanish grandees under royal supervision. Similarly, in America the Spanish governors should take whatever opportunity might exist to attract back to the Spanish side the leaders of the rebellions. In other words, concessions, particularly relating to employment, must be granted. Some would say this constituted an insult to national honor, but Pizarro said such arguments arose from ignorance and partisanship rather than from national interest. Here, as in many other points, Pizarro was remarkably conciliatory and advocated concepts suggested by moderate loyalists in America.

Turning to matters of public opinion, Pizarro advocated that Spain send its own secret agents throughout Europe to counteract the secret agents of the rebels who were active in France and England. All the diplomatic agents in Europe clamored for this too. Pizarro added: "All this will cost, but it costs little and is worth much. This is the century of charlatanism, and one gazette can save the cost of an army many times over." Indeed, Pizarro was correct in pointing out that Spain was one of the few European nations that did not maintain support for foreign journalists and opinion-makers in foreign capitals, and Spain continued to have a bad reputation and image, worse even than Portugal's, among the cabinets in northern Europe. There is evidence that the Spanish regime employed Spaniards to produce replies to rebel propaganda circulating in Europe—a friar named Manuel Martínez produced a reply to a manifesto of the Chilean Supreme Director, Bernardo O'Higgins; the reply was then ordered to be translated and circulated by Spanish embassies. The Ministry of State, meanwhile, carefully collected and preserved editorial comment from various British newspapers that was favorable to Spain or derogatory of the rebels.[8] The Marqués de Casa Irujo, however, once noted that to translate and print pro-Spanish propaganda in the United States "was money lost."[9] After 1819 the crown, acting on Pizarro's recommendation, attempted to establish in London a propaganda newspaper called *El Observador Español en Londres*, but only a few copies of it ever appeared and they were in Spanish, which nullified their effect on British public opinion.[10] The established view of the king and his advisors that the press was ultimately linked with the liberal excesses of the constitutional period made them determined to maintain rigid censorship in the peninsula after 1814 and made them hesitant to pursue Pizarro's suggestion for foreign propaganda sponsorship further, out of fear it would encourage new publishing activity in Spain.

In a similar vein, Pizarro advocated that Spain should receive and use foreign mercenaries who offered their services. Such offers had been refused in the past because of the dedication to keeping foreigners out of the Indies, with the result that mercenaries took their skills and experience to the rebel side. The creation of an English battalion among royalist forces fighting in America "would cause a prodigious moral effect on the forces of the insurrection." The presence of Britons in battle on the royalist side would attract and hold the favorable interest of the British press, creating vast interest in the royal cause among the British public. This idea, which might appear to be peripheral, was really quite insightful. The adventures of Lord Cochrane in Chile, General Miller in Peru, and General O'Leary in New Granada, among many others, had a great influence in swaying both contemporary opinion and subsequent historiography in favor of the independence cause. Nor did all the foreign mercenaries join the rebel side in America out of advocacy of the principles of independence; many were merely in search of employment as military officers following general European demobilization in the wake of Napoleon's defeat.

To encourage a resurgence of loyalty to the idea of the monarchy,

Pizarro advocated using missionaries, since "ideas and not arms are what has separated [the rebels] from the throne." The church would have to be reformed, though, for it was now lethargic and tainted with rebel clerics. Some attention had been paid to sending missionaries to America as a means of pacification, but in 1818 it was reported that the expenses of transport for those missionaries willing to go could not be met because funds were being diverted to military priorities. Nonetheless, Minister of War Eguía proposed in early 1819 that prelates and monasteries in the peninsula should be invited to ask their religious if any of them wished to go to America for this purpose.[11]

Pizarro's nineteenth and final suggestion was a sweeping plea for Spain to end its rivalry with its own overseas provinces, which he believed was especially responsible for the discontent of the American upper classes. "The elements of this disgraceful rivalry are a badly understood national pride, an exaggerated and misdirected provincialism, the exclusive and pernicious mercantile spirit, especially of haughty Cádiz, the ignorance that there is in the court about those countries, and dark and sordid passions and interests." In this, Pizarro was virtually repeating a major point made in his 1814 memorial by José Baquíjano, who accused Spain of outraging the loyalty of the creole upper classes by petty acts of spite as much as anything else. Pizarro felt particularly strongly about the misrepresentation and petty partisanship he saw in Spanish attitudes toward America, since he himself, though born in Spain, had grown up in Quito, where his father served as president of the audiencia.

The response to Pizarro's comprehensive and thoughtful plan of pacification provides the clearest example of the institutional impediments that existed in the Fernandine regime to deflect or defeat imaginative proposals. Pizarro himself testified that it was received by the other ministers and advisors around the king with shock and suspicion. In Pizarro's view the main point of his plan was his plea to legitimize foreign commerce, but, he testified, "the party of Eguía, Lozano, and company, to whom neither America nor Spain mattered, . . . gave out a heated cry at the mere mention of the term commercial franchise." The camarilla and several ministers resisted

Pizarro's proposals strongly. Anselmo de Rivas, a member of the Council of State, was commissioned by the king to render a studied opinion of the Pizarro plan and largely approved most of its provisions. Most notably, Rivas supported the proposal for foreign trade, pointing out that the only persons who would resist it were those "who thought they lived in another time and under other circumstances." Pizarro noted in his memoirs that Rivas "with notable facility and eloquence declared that my plan was natural and simple; that the Americas were truly lost; that on the east and west coasts of our Americas the only flag that did not fly was our own; and that therefore we should not consider ceding, but rather converting to some advantage, that which we had lost."[12] Yet Rivas's opinion, dated 14 July 1818, actually failed to focus on the proposal for foreign trade franchises, and, though it endorsed all of Pizarro's suggestions with greater or lesser enthusiasm, it singled out the proposal to send the expedition to Buenos Aires as the most direct method of pacification. And, since ships to transport the expedition to Buenos Aires were still lacking, Rivas ended up converting his opinion into a long harangue on the necessity of reopening negotiations for British mediation—a proposal that, it should be noted, Pizarro had carefully avoided bringing up and that he supported only as a last resort and only for Buenos Aires.[13] Rivas advocated that Spain open negotiations immediately with Britain, "offering them in recompense whatever conditions and sacrifices may be necessary." Equally important, Rivas urged the king to try to get direct representation at the forthcoming meeting of the Holy Allies at Aix-la-Chapelle, or, failing that, to at least send special envoys to speak privately with the gathered European sovereigns.

Thus Pizarro's program, which had proposed genuinely new and imaginative formulas for possible pacification of America, ended up being interpreted as a plea for Spain to depend on foreigners in the diplomatic realm and to return to the old and still impossible proposal of British mediation. And it was this path of least resistance that Spain followed. During the next two years the regime's attention was focused almost exclusively on Britain and on the Holy Allies. Pizarro's proposals for reform within the empire, for a profound change of perception regarding the American crisis, was heard from no more. This is the classic example of Spain's assumption of its own weakness; after years had been spent in search of a policy, Pizarro's program was ignored because it would undeniably require some effort to implement and because its proposals for immediate open trade and for amnesty to dissident Spaniards were totally unacceptable to the camarilla. Instead, Spain began to cast its eyes longingly again toward its British ally, which, it was hoped, would come and take the burdens of solving Spanish imperial problems off the regime's weary shoulders.

Far more important, indeed, to the determination of future policy than Pizarro's proposals was a letter addressed on 27 June 1818 to the king by the Duke of San Carlos, one of Ferdinand's close friends and now ambassador to London. San Carlos told the king, as a friend, a confidant, and an ambassador, that he should understand that the spirit of rebellion in America was now nearly unquenchable. Spain possessed insufficient force to oppose it. In Europe, the Great Powers "more favored than opposed" the movement toward American independence. Circumstances were such, he said, that "Your Majesty will deduce, as I have sadly done, that the greatest sacrifices have been made indispensable for the conservation of America."[14] Anselmo Rivas was ordered to comment on this letter simultaneously with the Pizarro report. He declared that San Carlos's letter reaffirmed the necessity of depending on foreign powers for pacification. "There is no measure, no effort, no attempt that should not be used to preserve Your Majesty's kingdom from the intolerable misfortune of losing for yourself and for your successors the richest and vastest possessions ever held by the greatest sovereign on earth."

What is perhaps most ironic about the abandonment, or lack of hearing, of the Pizarro plan is that the Duke of San Carlos had himself proposed several of the same measures in a long memorial written in London in December 1817. Following a long conversation with that famous student and traveler of Latin America, the Baron Alexander von Humboldt (then serving as Prussian ambassador to London), San Carlos had submitted a number of ideas suggested by Humboldt. Since Britain wished only to have open trade with Spanish America,

Humboldt argued, and since the rest of Europe would also wish for the right to trade with those lands, Spain should open trade with all the European powers. This trade should go to the loyal American provinces, since the king should not deny to the loyal what he was already prepared to grant to the rebel territories. If foreign nations could trade with Mexico, for example, they would have a stake in stopping the corsairs preying in the Caribbean off Veracruz. Second, Baron Humboldt strongly recommended the granting of a general amnesty and the concession to the Americans of all civil liberties and economic privileges compatible with their security. Privileges not granted now would simply be taken by force later. These were all great sacrifices for Spain, but indispensable if she was to avoid losing America.[15]

The letter of the Duke of San Carlos and the cogent suggestions offered by Baron Humboldt, a man whose opinion of American affairs was taken seriously in Spain, seem to have turned Spanish attention back to negotiating a British mediation. By March 1818 Lord Castlereagh had been informed that Spain was willing to grant free trade in return for British mediation. Castlereagh, however, was far less enthusiastic than he had been in 1816, and merely informed San Carlos that if Spain had expressed the same tolerant views a few years ago there would not now be a revolution in America.[16]

In July the Junta of Pacification, only two weeks before its disbandment, again endorsed the mediation. The British were very reluctant to get involved again in so fruitless a negotiation, and the Junta of Pacification showed signs of panic at the realization. "The Junta was uniform in its opinion of the gravity of the danger and about the single remedy it could have. . . . All its members agreed that the revolution in the Americas announced its imminent emancipation, and that this fatal blow for the state could not be contained except by the mediation of England, resting on free foreign commerce in those countries." The junta assured the king "that there was no other recourse humanly possible." In 1816 the junta had called for the opening of trade in the ports of Cuba, Santo Domingo, Puerto Rico, Venezuela, Cartagena, Buenos Aires, and Chile, but now the rebellion was much more advanced and, as a result, free trade already effectively existed in most of America, even in areas still loyal to Spain. "Thus there is no motive whatsoever to limit the liberty that is proposed, nor to defer it until the time of the pacification." Thus the junta recommended that formal negotiations be opened with the British government, offering England trade with America, and soliciting its mediation. In the meantime, the junta urged an expedition of from 16,000 to 20,000 troops be sent to America as quickly as possible so that Spain could speak from a position of strength rather than weakness.[17] With this final admission of helplessness, the Junta of Pacification passed out of existence.

Faced with the reluctance of Britain to undertake the mediation proposal again, Spain was now prepared to offer inducements. On 8 August Pizarro told the Duke of San Carlos that he could tell Castlereagh that Spain was prepared to offer four major concessions to get British or Allied mediation: general amnesty, free trade, American equality in offices, and Spanish predisposition to adopt the suggestions of the Allies in the course of the mediation. If all that was not enough, San Carlos was authorized to drop the hint that Spain would consider the cession to Britain of some territory in America, specifically Santo Domingo.[18] Thus the administration had come fully around to the basic demands of Britain before 1816—at least, so it said: there is some question, had the mediation actually begun, if Spain would have granted all four of the concessions. And, in addition, Spain was now prepared to offer some small territory to Britain. Unfortunately for Spain, however, by mid-1818 the British were no longer prepared to make any special efforts in behalf of opening America to their trading vessels, since by that point the American rebellions were so far advanced that British ships faced little resistance when they entered a new Spanish American port to trade. Even in Peru, by 1818, a desperate viceroy, hard pressed for customs revenues to finance his forthcoming military confrontation with Chile, began to grant individual permissions to British and other foreign ships to trade at Callao. There was no reason for Castlereagh to lift a finger now.

The rapidly escalating sense of crisis in Madrid also forced a final decision concerning the destination of the giant expedition being gathered in Cádiz, which by 1818 was known as the Great Expedition. Since 1816 everyone had more or less assumed Buenos Aires was the target, but the loss of Chile in 1817 and 1818 forced a reconsideration. Should all or part of the expedition be sent to Chile and Peru? Pizarro called the Junta Militar de Indias to discuss the problem in May 1818. When the junta met, its members, most of whom were military commanders with broad experience in the Americas, including several former viceroys, could not reach a decision. Pizarro, whose opinion of the military caste was low, wrote that their advice was so confused that he had not understood a word of it. He testified that one member had actually proposed that the expedition should sail first to Lima and then to Buenos Aires, which of course was an absurdity. Finally he ordered the chairman of the junta to write a report for the king, and when the chairman said he could not understand their advice either, Pizarro sent the king each of the member's opinions.[19] Pizarro himself strongly supported Buenos Aires as the target because, as he had written in April, it was such a focus of British trade and settlement that it would soon become a virtual British colony. It was the hydra of the revolution; its tariff revenues paid for the extension of the insurrection to Chile and it was now planning to strike at Peru.[20]

Pizarro's scornful allegation that the members of the Junta Militar were too confused in their thinking to be able even to understand the import of their own advice is largely borne out by the individual opinions he sent on to the king. The dictamen of the Marqués de Concordia, José de Abascal, former viceroy of Peru, rambled on at some length about how the Argentine gauchos were so fierce and warlike that they could probably not be defeated, but the expedition should go to Buenos Aires even so. This from a man whose chief object from 1806 to 1816 had been the defense of Peru. The Conde de Guaqui, José Manuel de Goyeneche, the former commander in Upper Peru, made equally little sense when he urged that Buenos Aires be the target because it would permit the royalists to take advantage of the resources of Paraguay. The former captain general and governor of Río de la Plata, Gaspar Vigodet, argued that entering the Río de la Plata estuary would be very risky. Unable to land at Montevideo, which was in Portuguese hands, where would the troops disembark? Where would 12,000 to 14,000 men and 60 or 70 transports, convoy vessels, and disembarking craft anchor? If Buenos Aires were taken, how would the troops be supplied when the interior was hostile to them? When in 1813 some 2,000 expeditionary troops were sent to Montevideo, over 900 arrived sick and the rest scarcely able to walk. Would the problems not be even greater now that Buenos Aires had its own corsairs? What would happen if the army were besieged in Buenos Aires? With all these questions unanswered, Vigodet, a man who would have been expected to advocate Buenos Aires as a target, recommended that the expedition go south to the Pacific. The only problem, he recognized, was the practical impossibility of transporting a huge army around the Cape. Anyhow, once they arrived on the Pacific coast, then, he said—in a flight of extraordinary fancy—the troops could perhaps travel overland across the continent to Buenos Aires and intermediary points. Then there was Pedro de la Cuesta, who argued that Buenos Aires should be the target because the porteños, he was convinced, would not be prepared to defend their city. But, if in the off-chance they did drive the Spanish forces back for lack of supplies and force them to reembark, then the expedition could go wherever else it liked. Two former Mexican viceroys gave equally contradictory advice. Félix María Calleja (who in less than a year became commander in chief of the expedition) suggested that the troops go to Chile because it was not possible to send a large enough force to Río de la Plata to assure the neutrality of the Portuguese. He ignored the much greater difficulty of sending a large enough force around the Cape to assure victory over O'Higgins and San Martín. Francisco Javier Venegas said that, if there was a large enough force, then Río de la Plata was the target, if not, then Chile. The other members each voted with equal solemnity, and in the end seven preferred Río de la Plata, six preferred the Pacific.[21]

The crucial question was carried over into a cabinet meeting on 1 August 1818. By this time news had reached Madrid of the catastrophic defeat of the royalist army of Mariano Osorio at Maypu in Chile.[22] The four ministers who met to discuss the planned expedition to America fell to squabbling among themselves. Pizarro pursued an "I-told-you-so" attitude, pointing out that only a few million reales and a liberal use of indulgences could have avoided the present miserable state of affairs if a liberal policy had been adopted eight years ago. Spain could have stopped Artigas and divided the Buenos Aires leaders among themselves. In Mexico, he insisted, only the mobs were revolutionary and the insurrection there should have been suppressed long ago. Garay lamented that even the Great Expedition would not be enough to pacify America, and how could Spain pay for it? He favored sending it to Lima. Eguía wanted Buenos Aires, though he warned that the failure of Morillo's expedition showed the kind of troubles Spain was in for. Pizarro argued that if Morillo had been sent to Buenos Aires in the first place the result would have been different. Garay thought only British help could now make a difference. "The expedition, I repeat, . . . besides being ineffective, is not possible to outfit because of a lack of resources. There are no means, there are no tax revenues, there is no credit, the ecclesiastical estate cannot give more, nor can the civil. We cannot look for foreign loans; the most enormous sacrifices would be necessary, and we could not pay the creditors." Spain should give Britain whatever it wanted, he thought, in return for transports and mediation. Pizarro admitted he had already informed the Council of State and the king that the expedition alone would not be enough to pacify America, but he did not wish to give the English exclusive powers in America, no matter how much their influence might be appreciated. Vázquez Figueroa concluded the gloomy discussion by reminding everyone that it was not even clear if Spain might not soon be at war with the United States over Anglo-American incursions in Florida.[23]

Pizarro carried the deadlocked decision of the Junta Militar de Indias to the Council of State, reporting that the military junta, despite its disagreements, strongly supported the idea of sending an expedition and that the Pacific destination had been discussed only as an alternative. The Council of State then voted to send the expedition directly to the Río de la Plata. Principally, the risks of sailing around the Cape closed the possibility of sending any really large reinforcements to Peru (though smaller reinforcements were attempted in 1818). It was not clear at any point in the discussion what Portugal's response to the Spanish expedition would be, and Vázquez Figueroa estimated the fleet, which would consist of six men-of-war, eight frigates, ten brigantines, and twenty gunboats, would cost between 28 million and 38 million reales, depending on whether Portugal chose to be friendly or hostile. Pizarro estimated the cost of the expedition in all would be 100 million pesos. It ended up costing four times that. [24] Both Francisco Zea Bermúdez at Aix-la-Chapelle and the Conde de Casa Flores in Rio de Janeiro were informed that Buenos Aires was the expedition's target but were ordered to spread the rumor that it was headed for Peru. [25] Peru would have to be left without as many reinforcements as its viceroy pleaded for to face the liberating expediton of General San Martín that Chile was preparing. A note from the naval ministry complained, "What good would it do to be the masters of Buenos Aires and its pampas if we lose all of Peru?" [26]

While these desperate discussions were going on in mid-1818, Ferdinand VII, motivated by the pathetic inadequacy of Spain's navy, committed a grievous folly that for some months was unknown to his own ministers. Members of the camarilla—to judge from the memoirs of Vázquez Figueroa and Pizarro—notably Eguía, Lozano de Torres, the Russian ambassador, Dimitri Tatishchev, the Spanish ambassador to Russia, Francisco Zea Bermúdez, and the king's confidant Antonio Ugarte, had induced the king in 1817 to agree to purchase a fleet of five ships of the line and three frigates from the imperial Russian navy. These vessels were desperately needed to help transport the Great Expedition to America, and Ferdinand trusted his dear friend Czar Alexander I to help him in his time of need. The total purchase price of the fleet (which was never paid) was 13.6 million rubles, but Ferdinand made an initial deposit of the entire 400,000 pounds sterling that Spain had received from Great Britain in 1817 for agreeing to suppress the slave trade. [27] The three ministers who should have been in charge of negotiating the deal—Pizarro at State, Vázquez Figueroa at Navy, and Garay at Finance—were totally unaware of the deal and learned of it only after it was completed. Indeed, no one knew anything about the condition of the ships until they arrived at harbor in Cádiz. Fernán Núñez in Paris informed the Great Powers of the purchase of the fleet and assured them that in the matter of a possible mediation in Montevideo only their obstinance or Portugal's bad faith could now delay the "healthful effects of these forces."[28]

When the ships were at last inspected in Cádiz, however, it was discovered, to the shock of all concerned, that they were utterly unseaworthy, technologically outdated, waterlogged, and worm-eaten. Only two of them ever saw any active duty, and both of them unsuccessfully. The *Alejandro* and the *María Isabel* were considered sufficiently usable to be sent to America. The *Alejandro* turned back at sea, too rotten to cross the Atlantic. The *María Isabel*, bound for Lima as the flagship of a major reinforcement effort, managed to cross the ocean, only to be captured by the newly-formed Chilean navy as it entered the Pacific, nearly crippled by the effort of rounding the Cape and with its position having been given away by mutineers. All the other ships were stored in the naval arsenal at Cádiz, where they were gradually broken up for scrap. Perhaps equally damaging to the regime was the fact that a Spanish newspaper published the story that the acquisition of the fleet was a direct act of the king. It was a serious blow to plans for departure of the expedition and to the king's prestige. To a certain extent, of course, one can sympathize with the efforts of the king to strengthen his hopelessly inadequate navy and, perhaps, even with his well-meant if ill-handled intervention in a matter that should have been entrusted to his government. Yet the king's tendency to make uninformed and ill-prepared personal decisions in questions of importance to the empire provided yet another indication of the dangers of absolutism and resulted in this case in scandal and failure.

For Pizarro and his allies the scandal of the Russian fleet fell like a blow from the skies, the more devastating because it came from such an unexpected source. Although he and his cabinet allies were entirely blameless in the debacle, it revealed to them and to their enemies their isolation and vulnerability—the king had not consulted them in a most important matter directly involving their three ministries. By any logic of ministerial administration the event informed them that they did not possess the king's confidence. The entire Pizarro program for American pacification was threatened. But what option could he pursue? His only option was to try to convince the king of the error of the camarilla's advice. It was thus the unpleasant duty of Pizarro and Vázquez Figueroa to confront the king with the evidence of the extent to which Ugarte, Tatishchev, Lozano de Torres, and Eguía had misled him in the purchase of the useless fleet. Pizarro told the king that the monarchy was in great danger from stupid intrigues. According to Vázquez Figueroa, the king said not a word. The game was already up. Nonetheless, for two months the court buzzed with intrigue as the camarilla plotted to be rid of Pizarro and his allies, while they in turn struggled to maintain some credibility. Pizarro, feeling his influence slipping, lashed out against his court enemies in scathing denunciations in his memoirs. Of the camarilla he wrote: "And a country where such vermin live and thrive wants to prosper? No, it is not possible, it will not be."[29] The camarilla, of course, had suffered a serious misstep in the fleet affair, but in an absolute monarchy power depends on possessing the king's confidence, and the camarilla still did. At any rate, the Pizarro policy for American pacification received its coup de grâce as the king lost confidence in his chief minister.

By August 1818 Pizarro's position was untenable. A final plea for the formulation of a conciliatory pacification policy was made in the form of an unsigned memorial sent to Minister of Justice Lozano de Torres. Although unsigned, it reflected Pizarro's concepts and style of writing. The memorial declared that circumstances in America had changed so greatly that the government must also change. Conciliation alone remained. America must be conceded its demands. Following the thesis that America was already lost, the report declared:

> From everything said in this memorial and in earlier ones it seems that in fact we have lost the two Floridas; that we are on the verge of losing the island of Puerto Rico, the Internal Provinces of Mexico, and the Spanish part of the island of Santo Domingo. We have introduced discontent in the island of Cuba with the ruin that threatens from the inevitable decadence of its agriculture and commerce, the infallible consequence of the abolition of the slave trade. The rest of northerly America is in revolt and violent. Southerly America no longer exists for us.

The recent events in Chile have determined the future of Buenos Aires and Peru. How shall we attend to so many needs? How shall we avoid so many evils? How shall we impede the dissolution of the monarchy?

To answer those questions, the report stated:

It is necessary to understand and to confess in good faith that only a new order of things, a new system contrary to that which we have followed up to now but in accord with the general progress of modern thought, can save us. This change also requires a change in the major part of the ministers and councilors of State. Neither they nor the persons who surround His Majesty and who are able to council him are capable of doing so with judgment. . . . I granted them all the good wishes imaginable, but they lacked the knowledge and the strength of soul necessary to propose the needed reforms and attack the abuses and disorders where they could encounter them.

Making a final plea for the seizure of Portugal as part of an exchange for Montevideo, the report continued:

From this violent condition of Portugal, combined with the danger in which the provinces of Río de la Plata currently are, the Court of Madrid can acquire very great advantages if our government would only convince itself of the very great utility that would result from reuniting Portugal with Spain. Although it be at the cost of sacrificing the provinces of the Río de la Plata to the ambition of the Portuguese government, I believe the advantages even then would weigh in Spain's favor.

The report, finally, cited the example of the Portuguese king himself, who, in a moment of defeat and disaster had fled to Brazil and there recovered his power. In short, with the loss of all of the American empire pending, Spain was facing its darkest hour. But imagination, good will, and reform could turn the disaster into the beginning of national renovation.[30]

But it was already too late: in the wake of the affair of the Russian fleet the moderates had lost the king's confidence entirely. On 15 September 1818, Minister of State Pizarro, Minister of the Navy Vázquez Figueroa, and Minister of Finance Garay were all deposed from office and summarily ordered to withdraw from the capital. Pizarro and Vázquez Figueroa both believed that although their removal from office was the king's order, their forced withdrawal from Madrid in disgrace and without any prior warning was the act of the camarilla.[31] The camarilla was ascendant, and throughout the next year and a half it would make policy in Spain. The more conciliatory policy of Pizarro was completely abandoned. The new interim minister of state, the Marqués de Casa Irujo, was totally absorbed in planning for the forthcoming meeting of the European sovereigns at Aix-la-Chapelle, the new minister of the navy would depart for Cádiz to supervise preparation of the Great Expedition, and Eguía and Lozano de Torres remained in charge of policy since they possessed the strongest influence over the king. Eguía's Ministry of War spent most of its time in internal surveillance, arresting and purging suspected Masons and liberals; disorder was widespread, and rumors of an impending revolution swept the country.

The major policy change affecting American affairs after Pizarro's overthrow was the abandonment of Spain's decision to seek European mediation at any cost. Spain executed a total about-face on the issue. Within less than a week of taking office, the new interim minister of state, the Marqués de Casa Irujo, wrote the king to say that in the matter of pacification, mediation, and Montevideo he totally disagreed with the actions of his predecessor. He was convinced that the effort to get England to mediate in return for free trade would not succeed because the British government would be unwilling to take coercive measures against the rebels. Indeed, it could not, for British public opinion now viewed the American rebels as fighters for liberty—"the magical divinity of that island." They forgot the difference between liberty and license, the impossibility of representative government existing in the American countries, where civic virtue was so thinly spread. Thus Spain could not expect success in the matter and should let it drop. The British intervention in Montevideo, he believed, would threaten royal authority in New Spain,

New Granada, Venezuela, Central America, and Peru. "This is a conjecture, of course, but a conjecture based on calculation of probabilities and on experience." Foreign trade was always the vehicle of revolution. Only in Cuba did widespread foreign trade appear to have no adverse affect, and that was only because of the Cubans' fear that revolution would unleash the fury of the slaves as it had done in Haiti. Consequently, Casa Irujo urged that the ambassador to London, San Carlos, be ordered to stop pursuing the mediation question with Castlereagh and that other ambassadors be informed that English intransigence had spoiled Spain's hopes in this matter. The king wrote on the margin of this document: "I approve these ideas, you can proceed with regard to them."[32]

In American affairs the ascendancy of the military clique and the fact that the moderate opposition was put to flight had a major effect. The king, who for four years had toyed with possible reforms and legalistic policies to effect pacification of the rebellions, now opted for an exclusively military settlement. From the time of Pizarro's fall until the revolution of 1820 no serious consideration was given to political solutions. When the Council of the Indies in September 1818 asked the king whether he had considered its earlier strong statements in opposition to Morillo's possessing the powers of military dictator in Venezuela, the king responded in October that Morillo was to continue with absolute command "in all branches of public administration in the provinces of Venezuela."[33] All of the moderates' advice and warnings of the dangers involved in this were simply ignored. For the first time in Ferdinand's restoration there was a consensus on what policy to adopt for America. The problem was, it was a false consensus, arrived at by virtue of the moderate opposition's having been driven from the field.

The Great Expedition for Buenos Aires was the primary focus of military attention, and here the ascendancy of the military clique was not only notable, it was absolute. The king vested total control and authority over gathering the Great Expedition and planning for its eventual departure in the hands of the camarilla. The entire undertaking was now under the control of Antonio Ugarte, Lozano de Torres, and Francisco Eguía and his successor as minister of war, José María

Alós. Lozano de Torres himself once wrote the king referring to "Don Antonio de Ugarte, the only one of the three (himself, Alós and Ugarte) who has exact knowledge about the expedition."[34] On 1 July 1819, when Ferdinand was preparing to depart Madrid to spend some time taking the baths at his favorite resort, Sacedón, he wrote Ugarte:

> Ugarte: with the object that there should not appear to be the slightest delay in the outfitting and departure of the great expedition, I authorize you, during my absence in Sacedón, to dispatch without delay . . . all correspondence relative to this expedition, and all eventualities no matter what they may be, giving me advice of everything you have done, and working in accord with Alós, who must sign [the military orders].[35]

With Eguía spearheading a national purge of suspected dissidents, it is not surprising that in early 1819 the commander-in-chief of the Great Expedition, Enrique O'Donnell, Conde de la Bisbal, was removed from command after becoming compromised with the dissident liberals. He was replaced by Félix María Calleja, Conde de Calderón, the former Mexican viceroy. One setback after another delayed the army's departure, and the troops who waited listlessly in Cádiz and southern Andalusia provided a prime environment for the spread of rumors and conspiracies. With supreme power emanating from the camarilla in Madrid, the expedition's commanders had little real control over their troops. Insurrectionary and liberal conspiracies grew and multiplied among them. In 1819 an epidemic in Cádiz further delayed the expedition's departure.[36]

Delays in the expedition and the about-face on permitting foreigners into Spanish America largely accounted for Spain's poor showing in the meeting of the sovereigns of the Holy Allies at Aix-la-Chapelle in October and November 1818. Although Ferdinand was not invited to the meeting, several topics of importance to Spain were considered. The European Powers were startled by Spain's reversal of policy on the foreign trade issue. Spain's chief observer at the conference, Francisco Zea Bermúdez, normally ambassador to Russia, was instructed to play on the reactionary sympathies of the Russians,[37] but, other than that, Spain had no plans or proposals to offer, even as the Holy Allies discussed the question of a possible joint mediation in Montevideo. Zea Bermúdez fired off a note to Madrid declaring that the regime's silence on the Montevideo question and the American pacification question had been noted by the sovereigns, "and it has embarrassed the different cabinets no little bit." Spain's friends, notably Russia, could do nothing to help, and "those who wish us ill . . . attribute [our silence] to irresolution, apathy, and obstinate pride on our part." The Powers had previously worked out in Paris a treaty on a joint Montevideo mediation, but now Spain, determined to permit no foreign presence in Spanish America, preserved a maddening silence.[38] By the end of November 1818 the meeting was over, and Zea Bermúdez transmitted to Spain the Russian minister Capodistria's report that Castlereagh and Metternich had proposed that the Great Powers write Ferdinand inviting him to accept definitely the mediation of all the Powers in America. Russia, taking Spain's part, had opposed this as an unwarranted intervention in Spanish affairs. Capodistria told Zea Bermúdez that in Russia's view the most important thing now was for Spain to send the expedition at any cost, since it was the only initiative it could employ in regard to Montevideo.[39] Thus Spain's change of policy subverted another possible mediation.

The Spaniards were determined, however, to resist any flood of foreigners to America. In November 1818 Spain announced that any foreigner caught with arms in hand in the service of the rebels in America would be subject to the same penalties as Spanish nationals. The king in his royal order declared that the uprisings "are indisputably the work of the intrigues of foreigners."[40] In early 1819 the king ordered notes sent to Britain and the United States informing them that "no foreigner can nor should communicate with the inhabitants of America; and if by individual pact or agreement this is permitted in some provinces and some ports [Cuba still had foreign trade], there is no similar liberty in any of the Pacific ports or provinces."[41] Thus the Casa Irujo policy was implemented in its entirety: no mediation, no expansion of foreign trade in America, and maintenance of Cuba's special privileges in foreign trade on the correct assessment that its fear of slave disorders would keep it loyal.

Shortly after the conclusion of the conference at Aix-la-Chapelle, the king's and the court's attention was diverted by a series of royal deaths that left a pall of gloom over all the court and virtually guaranteed that no action would be taken in regard to America other than to continue outfitting the expedition. After the fall of Pizarro the only moderate voice left in the court was that of the young queen, María Isabel, Pizarro's great ally and the object of his particular enthusiasm. Pizarro spoke of his group as "the queen's party" and obviously placed great trust in her moderating role. Ramón de Mesonero Romanos, although writing from the vantage-point of fifty years later, agreed: "The marriage of Ferdinand with Isabel de Braganza served to modify somewhat the situation at court, and created hopes for some moderation in the system of government." The birth of an heir was widely expected. In August 1817 the queen gave birth to a daughter who died in a few months. She was pregnant again in late 1818 and the whole nation waited anxiously. In November 1818 Ferdinand wrote his uncle the king of Naples: "My very beloved wife continues very well in her pregnancy and everything promises that I shall soon be a father again, if Heaven concedes me the succession that my family and my people need and for which they pray and which I desire for their good."[42] But on 26 December 1818 the queen, aged only twenty-one, died in childbirth. Pizarro quoted a palace source who reported that she died from lack of medical skill on the part of her attendants: "The blood flowed by the quart, the operation without any order, the body indecently flung over a table." Mesonero Romanos vividly recalled that night when the alcalde of Madrid interrupted a gala Christmas party with the announcement: "The Queen has just died giving birth to an Infanta, who also is dead."[43] The nation was deeply saddened, since even the king's adversaries wanted a guaranteed succession to the throne.

Before the court had quite absorbed the shock of the queen's death there came news of the deaths, in Italy and only a few days apart, of the Reyes Padres, Charles IV and María Luisa. Though he had not been close to his parents, Ferdinand was deeply affected. The court remained in uninterrupted mourning for all of 1819, and court practice prohibited most normal political or social activity during this period. Since the king received few visitors and made few appearances, he depended on the in-house camarilla more than ever, and 1819 was the high point of their influence. The Ministry of State changed hands three times that year. Casa Irujo fell in June 1819 over delays in the Florida treaty; his interim successor, Manuel González Salmón, lasted three months, being replaced by the Duke of San Fernando in September.

By late 1819 the Great Expedition, after countless delays, appeared to be nearing completion. On 8 September 1819 the commander in chief, General Calleja, issued a statement to the troops proclaiming that they were going to America "not to punish but to correct, not to fight against enemies but to liberate our brothers. . . . The Americans will recognize their interests once we have driven from their midst those miserable ones who have seduced them, and in both hemispheres happy cries of 'Long live the King' will resound simultaneously." Somewhat contradictorily, however, Calleja also told his troops that history would hail them as superior to Pizarro and Cortés in the annals of South American conquest.[44] That same day, the acting minister of state sent Calleja an order to the effect that the expeditionary army was to protect English subjects and property in Buenos Aires but that movable property of English nationals was to be shipped out of the region. Amnesty was to be conceded to any English subject who had given active service to the insurrection, after which any further trade was to be absolutely prohibited. Calleja responded to the minister of state, explaining that although he understood the intent of the order he had to point out that "in my view the absolute prohibition of foreign commerce before the army is militarily established [in Río de la Plata] . . . will be little favorable to the happy outcome of the undertaking." This was owing to the possibility that the expedition, after seizing Montevideo, would then be operating in a region devastated by previous rebel activity and unable even under normal conditions to support a European army. Since the army would not be able to depend on supply by convoy because of the danger of insurgent corsairs, foreign trade should continue for some weeks. Calleja also said he doubted that after the seizure of Montevideo the conquest of Buenos Aires would take only four or five months, as the Ministry of State believed.[45]

On 12 September 1819 the Duke of San Fernando assumed the Ministry of State amid the last-minute rush of plans and stratagems for the expedition. In a secret letter in December to his old friend and ambassador to London, the Duke of San Carlos, San Fernando made it clear that plans for the possible reacquisition of European Portugal were again afoot. San Fernando had many things on his mind, and in the letter he informed the ambassador confidentially that his position as minister of state was not secure because there were courtiers who wished to see him thrown out of office. He said that he expected the expedition to sail soon and that everything depended on it. Revolutionary ideas were spreading rapidly throughout the army, and the sailing was therefore essential. Suspecting that his days in office were numbered, San Fernando added this revealing thought: "Anything that contributes to preparing the reunion of Portugal to our monarchy enters fully in my thinking, and I assure you that it is the object that always guides me, and thus you can understand with what pleasure I see that in our days such a very useful enterprise advances toward its completion. I also know the great dangers of doing it."[46] At the last moment, therefore, the Pizarro plan for the seizure of Portugal after the expeditionary army attacked Montevideo was again alive. The minister of state knew about it and the ambassador to London knew about it. Finally, even the king knew about it. On 4 January 1820, Minister of War José María Alós had an audience with the king to see to it that the monarch was fully apprised of the terrible dangers the enterprise entailed. Alós reported to San Fernando that the Great Expedition was about to sail, and, since it was clear that its first object would be to attack Montevideo, and since a movement against Montevideo would provoke war with Portugal, the king was informed "of the necessity of being prepared for whatever event of this nature might occur, placing our frontiers in good defensive order, filling the ranks of the army, and taking the means and precautions dictated by politics." Brigadier Ramón Losada Bernardo de Quiroz had been chosen to enter Portugal to act as a spy and to bring back an exact report of the state of Portugal's defenses.[47]

The king of Portugal, from his residence in Brazil, was hardly unaware of the danger to his policy of the departure of the Great Expedition. Though he was perhaps unaware of the secret Spanish plan for seizing Portugal, it was clear that a large Spanish force in the Río de la Plata estuary would probably drive Portugal out of the Banda Oriental. Rio de Janeiro never expected the Spanish expedition to sail (no one in Europe seems to have, either), but, as the time for its departure drew near, the Portuguese court made a desperate offer to forestall the danger. On 6 January 1820 San Fernando informed Spain's ambassadors in Europe that the Portuguese had offered to restore Montevideo immediately to Spain without any compensation if Ferdinand "will decide to send with the expedition destined [to the Río de la Plata] one of the Infantes, . . . in which case the Court of Brazil will renounce any pecuniary indemnification that it has claimed heretofore."[48] In return for the guarantee of a monarchy in Buenos Aires to defend against the spread of South American republicanism the Portuguese king would surrender Montevideo. The Spaniards, for dynastic reasons already mentioned, gave no serious consideration to the proposal.

Spain, at any rate, had made the decision to risk its entire American policy on the single military venture of the Great Expedition. Not only did the regime expect the expedition to save America, freeing even Peru from rebel attack, but it also anticipated it would fulfill the ancient dream of peninsular reunification. Meanwhile, the dispatch of the army was expected to eliminate the risk of liberalism and Masonic intrigue among the armed forces that had been Eguía's chief concern for two years. Originally budgeted to cost no more than 38 million reales, by October 1819 the giant and as yet unused expeditionary force, which ultimately consisted of 14,000 men, had cost 400 million, and that does not include the treasure wasted on the purchase of the Russian fleet. Yet, for all the money, Vázquez Figueroa says the naval officers were reduced to begging alms in the streets of Cádiz and "were dying of hunger."[49]

While the king and his friends plotted and schemed, the expeditionary forces gathered at Cádiz, in the eleventh hour before their departure, rose against the crown in a revolt. Angered by military demobilizations since 1814 that were designed by the king

and Eguía to disband the huge army of 150,000 left standing at the
end of the war with Napoleon and to reduce Spain's forces to 64,000
men, the army was composed of officers who thought their careers
endangered and by enlisted conscripts who were poorly paid and
poorly supplied. Liberal dissent had grown up among them, and the
prospect of being sent to fight in the distant American lands, where
most Spaniards assumed independence was already a reality, only
added the final straw to the army's anger. Limited by the constraint of
resources, Ferdinand had been extraordinarily stingy in rewarding the
officers and men whose sacrifices during the Napoleonic war had saved
his throne for him, and had actually demoted or demobilized many
war heroes. The officers and soldiers at the beginning of 1820 had no
consensus on what they wanted, but all agreed that change was
necessary.[50] A portion of the troops stationed in Cádiz and commanded by Major Rafael Riego determined to rise up in the name of
restoring the Constitution of 1812.

The Riego revolt began on 1 January 1820. For several weeks in
January it seemed that the revolt might come to nothing, and final
plans for the sailing of the expedition were continued. The call to
restore the Constitution did not attract support; rather, it was the
general discontent that prevailed throughout the army in the peninsula that finally had the effect of spreading the revolt. In February the
uprising spread to other regiments of the royal army in La Coruña,
Zaragoza, and Barcelona, units not affected by the threat of being sent
to America.[51] There was a last desperate attempt to save the expeditionary army when it was suggested that the soldiers be given the
right to import goods for sale in the Río de la Plata and that they be
granted unclaimed land there, but it was to no avail. It was taken for
granted that some of the expedition's officers had been infected with
the American disease of insurrection, transmitted by American rebel
agents agitating among the bored troops at Cádiz.[52]

The Madrid government took no effective steps to stop the
revolution. Throughout February, as the revolt was spreading to the
disaffected north, the Council of the Admiralty lethargically obeyed
the king's order to discuss what to do with the naval force drawn up to
conduct the expedition to the Río de la Plata should it happen that the

expedition's departure was delayed. Should Buenos Aires be block-aded without the land forces? All the members opposed the idea of attempting a blockade of the Río de la Plata; most agreed to keep at least one-third of the assembled fleet in Spanish waters to be used if the rebellion in Spain spread, as it shortly did, to the northern maritime regions, such as Galicia, Asturias, and Catalonia; but the members could not agree on how many ships, if any, should be sent to Mexico, Peru, Cuba, or other American territories. Although Peru in only one year would be begging for the dispatch of only a few ships to help defend against the spread of San Martín's revolution from Chile, one member of the council actually argued that no ships need be sent as yet to Peru because the squadron there was large enough. In the end the council recommended sending one ship apiece to New Granada, Mexico, and Peru.[53]

By March the Madrid government was at last aware of the extent of the danger and began to make ineffectual gestures of reform. As city after city proclaimed the Constitution, the king created a special Royal Council, presided over by his brother Don Carlos, that on 3 March announced a pledge of future reforms and called on all the other councils to advise the king immediately on what reforms were neces-sary. On 6 March the council debated whether to call the Cortes, as the king had promised in 1814. Composed chiefly of conservatives, this body generally advised the king to call the Cortes, but said that it should not be modeled on the Cortes of Cádiz and should instead conform to traditional law, being composed of the estates and formu-lated by the king rather than by the Constitution of 1812.[54] Don Carlos warned the king that restoring the Constitution of 1812 and its Cortes would stagger both the throne and the altar. After a full day of debate, the king issued a decree on 6 March stating that he would call the Cortes but not specifying its makeup.

How hasty and ill prepared the government's response to the crisis was is indicated by the order Ferdinand dispatched at 11 p.m. on the night of 4 March to the president of the Council of Finance, the Duke of Veragua: "Veragua: I want you within twenty-four hours to send me that council's consultation of what it judges most useful to the wellbeing of my people." Facing the impossible task of advising the king within twenty-four hours how to reform the treasury so as to counteract the uprising, the council members ended up confessing their inability. One day was not enough time to shake off the cobwebs of six years. Only one councilor was so bold as to advise "that something should be said to His Majesty about the uselessness of these decrees [promising reform] as long as he fails to reanimate the confidence of the nation."[55] Faced with the need to say something, the council advised the king to cut expenses, lower salaries, grant no new favors, and create an agency to discuss improving agriculture, industry, and commerce.

The revolution could not be stopped. Unable to stem the tide, Ferdinand was forced to give in. He appeared on the palace balcony on 7 March 1820 and declared his consent to the restoration of the Constitution of 1812. The camarilla members fled into exile. In rapid order the abolition of the Inquisition was decreed, the constitutional city council of Madrid was reestablished, political prisoners were freed, and a Provisional Junta was created to supervise the government until the Cortes met. It was presided over by Cardinal Luis de Borbón, who had been the president of the last Regency Council in 1814. The king then assented to the formation of a new ministry composed of men Ferdinand called the "jailbirds," since many of them had been imprisoned in the restoration of 1814. The head of the government was Agustín Argüelles. For the next three years, the so-called constitutional triennium, the king was forced to function as constitutional monarch with a succession of increasingly more radical liberal regimes composed of men he had persecuted, imprisoned, or exiled in 1814.

The uprising of the expeditionary army ended forever the hope of sending a single large force to South America and effectively guaranteed the independence of Buenos Aires and perhaps of the entire continent. The new constitutional government debated the possibility of reorganizing an expedition, but a consulta of the Council of State—the supreme council that superseded all the others in the constitutional regime—determined on 1 August 1821 not to send an expedition, and on 7 November the decision was reaffirmed.[56] Despite the length of the debates over sending troops to America and despite all the anger and hostility such troops provoked from creole spokesmen, since the restoration of the king in 1814 really very few troops had been transported from Spain to America—only 27,342 in the estimation given by Minister of War the Marqués de las Amarillas to the Cortes in July 1820. As Fernández Almagro points out, over half of them had gone in small groups and in improvised expeditions to a large variety of destinations and had thus failed to have the effect they would have had in a single force.[57]

Amid the general wreckage of royalist pretensions and dreams, the fundamental lesson of the catastrophe was lost on the king and his friends. They never understood that their policies had created the revolution in Spain. Regardless of whether the expeditionary army could ever have been salvaged in the first place, and regardless of whether it would actually have reconquered Buenos Aires and led to the seizure of Portugal, the essential point is that the crown had allowed itself for the last six years to pursue a disastrously mistaken policy. Instead of dealing with the genuine demands for reform from America and from patriotic Spaniards, Ferdinand and his advisors concentrated on a strictly military solution, creating a large expedition that only ended up by turning on the king. No reforms, no policy had been worked out for addressing the revolts in America, revolts that in the next year, 1821, would become universal throughout the American empire and would lead to the independence of all the colonies except Cuba, Puerto Rico, and the Philippines. Casa Flores, the ambassador to Brazil, had stated the failures of the Spanish response most succinctly when he wrote in May 1818 to warn that the Buenos Aires rebels would soon have a very respectable navy in both the Atlantic and Pacific: "They are not sleeping like us."[58]

There are many points in the period 1814 to 1820 when Spain failed to come to grips with the reality of the American crisis. But if there is any single period when it can be said that Spain lost America, it was in the last months of 1818 and the first months of 1819. The defeat of Pizarro's initiatives for reform within the empire; the overthrow of Pizarro and his group; the death of Queen María Isabel and consequent elimination of the voice of moderation at court; the reversal of policy on foreign trade and mediation; the ascendancy of the camarilla; the decision to place all Spain's eggs in the one basket of the Great Expedition; and the failure to respond to the dissent spreading within the armed forces — all these occurrences drove Spain away from the path of reality toward which it had been groping since 1814 and toward the attempted implementation of reconquest by force as the preferred policy. The political impediments inherent in the structure of the absolutist regime made a more pluralistic response to the rebellions impossible. The domestic revolution of 1820 was the peninsula's response, and in America the response was a renewed vigor on the part of those rebellions already afoot and the outbreak of new ones in other regions.

(

VII

Once Again, with Feeling

As it happened, the performance of the restored constitutional regime from 1820 to 1823 in regard to the American crisis was a case of "once again, with feeling." In 1820, at least, the constitutional government consisted of many of the same men—the *doceañistas* or moderates—who composed the first constitutional regime in 1812. Before the government began to shift to a more extreme radical position with the rising influence of the so-called *exaltados*, or radical liberals, its policy toward the American rebellions was not much different from what it had been in 1812. The same sort of reforms were implemented or passed newly, but the second opportunity added greater precision and clarity to the liberal objectives, and the reforms as well as the pronouncements of the government were marked by a deeper commitment and a tinge of greater radicalism. Spain was no longer fighting for its survival against Napoleon; the king was himself at the head of the constitutional government and shared power with the Cortes in a mode of "cogobierno," as it was sometimes called. Of course, the chances of restoring American loyalty by 1820 were much dimmer than before, but there is little indication that the restored liberals, with a few exceptions, were prepared to write America off as a lost cause. American policy would be less erratic than under the absolutists, franker, more open, and there would be a final and long-overdue recognition of the necessity of political settlement; but the liberals, dependent as before on the support of the merchant bourgeoisie of southern Andalusia, would not move toward granting free trade and would not contemplate a grant of outright independence. Bankrupt and tired policies were polished up and given the shine of newness, but nothing essentially changed.

The mind-cast that caused Spaniards to look at America as a mere reflection of the peninsula, an appendage that performed some vague function but the absence of which could not be contemplated, remained to color the views of liberals as it had of absolutists. Like the French revolution before it, the Spanish revolution would drift toward greater radicalism, until after July 1822 the *exaltados* controlled both the Cortes and the cabinet, but there remained, as had been the case with revolutionary France's view of Haiti, a barrier of perception, a gap in consciousness, that made American independence unthinkable. Policy-makers could not quite formulate any longer what value America had for Spain, but total separation remained out of the question. The reasons were essentially the same as before: the liberals wished Spain to continue to control American trade — even as Spanish shipping disappeared and was totally replaced by foreigners plying American waters — and the glory of Spain required America. Besides, the king was still on his throne, and, though he was required to accept governments he would never have called on himself and though he was required to sign legislation he despised, he still shared power and symbolized the state. He was king of Spain and the Indies; the Cortes was the supreme legislative power of Spain and the Indies.

With the restoration of the constitution came the reestablishment of the governmental agencies and councils prescribed by that document. By a royal decree of 12 March all matters relating to litigation were referred to the Supreme Tribunal of Justice and all existing councils — including the councils of Castile, of the Indies, and of the treasury — were suppressed.[1] On 18 March the restoration of the Council of State, in charge of political and administrative matters including American affairs, was announced. Its members were principally those men who had composed it in 1812, with Joaquín Blake as chairman and including former regents Pedro Agar and Gabriel Císcar, Cardinal Borbón, the Americans José Aycinena and the Marqués de Piedrablanca, and former ministers Martín Garay and Pedro Cevallos.[2] Officially viewed as the intermediary between the executive and the legislative powers and between the king and the nation, the Council of State during the triennium was active and important. According to the Constitution it was to consist of forty members, of whom twelve were to be Americans, but the revolutions in America were deemed to constitute an impediment to immediate fulfillment of this requirement. In October 1820 it was decided to have thirty councilors on an interim basis, of whom nine were to be Americans. Not until May 1821 was the council completed with its full roster of forty members.[3] In addition, the return of the Constitution brought about the reestablishment of the Ministry of Ultramar, with Antonio Porcel appointed in April as first minister.

The Provisional Junta, created in March to supervise the government, remained in existence until the Cortes opened on 9 July 1820, at which time it automatically dissolved. This means that during the first three months of the new regime the Provisional Junta effectively shared power with the new ministry, functioning as the major advisory body for both the king and the government. It was the Provisional Junta that issued the first important orders of the new regime: declaring that all office holders must accept the Constitution by oath or be removed from office; calling for the reappearance of the National Militia required by the Constitution, to become the armed defense of the liberal regime; decreeing the return of exiled *afrancesados*; and raising to the rank of general the officers, such as Rafael Riego, who had initiated the troop uprising in January. In March the Provisional Junta, indicating no less vindictiveness than the absolutist regime, ordered the arrest and detention of all the Persas—those Cortes members who in 1814 had requested that the king restore absolutism. It was eventually decided that the Persas would not be tried for treason as originally planned, partly in response to the warnings of Viceroy Juan Ruiz de Apodaca of Mexico, who wrote to announce that the imprisonment and planned trial of one of the Persas, the bishop of Puebla, Antonio Joaquín Pérez, had provoked two days of riots in that city and had united the other Mexican bishops in his support.[4]

The first major pronouncement of the new regime on the American crisis contained in a nutshell everything that Spain was prepared to offer. At first glance it is highly conciliatory, but on inspection its poverty of thought becomes clear. On 11 April 1820 the Provisional Junta and Council of State jointly addressed the American viceroys and captains general in a secret order sent to

Caracas, Bogotá, Lima, and Mexico City. The heads of government in America were to publish the king's decree reestablishing the Constitution. They were to invite by whatever means they found opportune the leaders and inhabitants of the dissident countries to adopt and swear to the Constitution, sending deputies to the Cortes. "You are to insist on this point, making them see the advantages that will result to them as coparticipants in a system that will elevate the nation to the highest level of prosperity and glory." Those rebel leaders who rejected the Constitution were to be offered permanent tenure and command if they would submit themselves to the royal regime. "You are to propose to the chiefs of the dissidents that, in case they show repugnance to swearing to the Constitution, they are to be preserved for an unlimited time in the command of their provinces [if they will] subordinate themselves to you or to the metropolitan government directly." This was potentially the most extreme concession Spain had ever offered, since it authorized recognition of Bolívar, O'Higgins, and other rebel leaders as rulers of the areas they controlled if they would submit themselves to royal authority. In fact, of course, it was a dead letter, since Bolívar and O'Higgins considered themselves heads of sovereign states. It did, nonetheless, open a door for future negotiation and communication. Buenos Aires, where no Spanish royal presence existed, was not included. A separate note was added for the viceroy of Mexico that effectively invalidated this offer for Mexico as well. Spain told Viceroy Apodaca that, there being no rebel government in Mexico, he was to apply the order in light of prevailing conditions.

For all the territories the government announced a cease fire to open negotiations with the rebels about accepting the Constitution. The royal commanders were to request cease fires from the rebel commanders and an exchange of prisoners, after which negotiations would begin. To undertake such negotiations, Spain announced that it was going to send commissioners to hear the rebels' complaints against Spanish rule and to arrive at provisional settlements on the foundation of acceptance of the Constitution. If the dissidents accepted the Constitution, Spain would consider the rebellion terminated and would publish a total amnesty. The rebels were invited to send their own commissioners to Spain, with assurances that they would be received by Madrid. But, if the rebels refused these negotiations, the war was to continue, the only provision being that it was not to be as "cruel as heretofore but more in conformity with the principles of humanity and the law of nations." The royal commanders were ordered to pursue this conciliatory policy energetically, giving evidence to the rebels of Spain's "good faith and cordiality." And if the rebels should reject all offers of conciliation, the royalists could rest assured that they had given Europe and the world irrevocable proof of their moderation. Any further bloodshed would not be the fault of Spain. A final note declared that commissioners were not being sent to Mexico because, again, it was not the scene of a standing rebel government. The minister to Rio de Janeiro, Spain's only source of communication with Buenos Aires, was to write directly to Buenos Aires with news of this revolution in Spain, coordinating his actions with the Peruvian viceroy.[5]

This concept of sending commissioners to America to listen to dissident complaints and bargain for acceptance of the Constitution in rebel-held countries was the first important policy breakthrough since 1814. Yet at its core was an idea that was not only not revolutionary but not even original. As the constitutionalists had done in 1812, the moderates who made up the Provisional Junta and Council of State assumed as a matter of faith that restoration of the Constitution would be perceived by American dissidents as the solution to their complaints about imperial governance. They would repeat the myth of 1812 that the Constitution automatically made Americans fully equal to peninsular Spaniards. The periodical press of Spain, which came alive once again and enjoyed a period of great activity following the new proclamation of freedom of the press, helped to foster and spread the myth. *El Universal*, which in the opinion of Jaime Delgado was the prototype of the liberal journals of the triennium, ascribed the American rebellions to the ambitions of the creole upper class and repeatedly announced that the Constitution would solve the insurrections. "The insurrection in America will probably be calmed if the Constitution is made general," it solemnly pronounced. It even reported that Bolívar, on hearing that Ferdinand had sworn to the

Constitution, proposed a two-month truce to see if he had sworn to it freely, "because should it be so he thought to desist in his undertaking and unite with the mother country."[6]

Yet, as before, the Constitution did nothing to answer American complaints. Overseas representation remained disproportionate; no sign of full commercial equality was contemplated; royalist viceroys and captains general remained autocrats even if their titles were changed to "political chief." Although the new government was aware of the possible danger that American conservatives would reject the liberal enactments of the forthcoming Cortes, it does not seem to have been fully conscious of the gap American dissidents perceived between the Constitution's promise and Spain's past failures of performance. In 1812 a Spanish government assumed that establishment of the Constitution would settle American demands; in 1814 a Spanish government assumed that restoration of Ferdinand VII would do it; in 1820 the same bankrupt assumption was made that a change of government in Spain would solve the crisis. Of all the leading journals, only the *Miscelánea* recognized the absurdity of the assumption, pointing out that American independence might be postponed, but it could not be avoided. It advocated compromise and tolerance as the solutions.[7]

Just over a week after its announcement of the new American policy, the Provisional Junta on 19 April 1820 advised the king and the minister of ultramar of some of the dangers and some of the opportunities it foresaw in reestablishing the Constitution in America. The chief danger was that abolition of the absolute system would encourage the creation of regional juntas and simultaneously encourage local functionaries to disobey the orders of the viceroys, thereby weakening the constitutional regimen. In the course of discussing this point the junta made an extraordinary admission. "In the year 1810 . . . the peninsula was surrounded by the greatest dangers and very nearly exposed to the total loss of its independence, and it seemed natural that the overseas provinces should provide for their own security by whatever means and that they should follow the example of the peninsula in the formation of provincial juntas." This was the first time the central government had admitted the naturalness and possible legality of the response of America in 1810. But, the junta continued, what possible necessity or authority could the creation of juntas of government now have? The king had satisfied the demands of Spaniards in both hemispheres, accepting the solemn compact that guaranteed the throne and formed the happiness of his people, and "equalizing in every way the rights of Spanish Americans with peninsulars." Even so, in Chile, Montevideo, Buenos Aires, Caracas, and New Granada juntas of government now existed, "and all those territories are today effectively separate from the Monarchy." This was a second extraordinary admission, the first hint that the central government viewed independence in some countries as de facto. Even so, the Provisional Junta made it clear that Spain, though it might see the reasoning of the Americans in 1810, could not see the justice of their actions in 1820.

A second major problem was the opportunity afforded by the Constitution for the seizure of self-mandated power by royal functionaries in America. The junta felt that the answer to this danger was the choice of skilled and loyal governors for America. "It is not possible to deny that in the six years of general disorder [during the restoration] merit and aptitude have not been the qualities that were always consulted in granting offices in America." And, striking a point that would begin to loom ever larger in government planning, the junta urged that special care be taken in selecting officials for Cuba and Puerto Rico, "which form the bulwark of the New World and the precious key to New Spain." As the rebels whittled away at the Spanish control of America, the Caribbean islands took on an importance they had not previously possessed. Soon Spaniards would console themselves that rule over Cuba and Puerto Rico somehow made up for the loss of the other lands.

The Provisional Junta concluded its advice by urging that the most important step was for the Constitution to be firmly planted in America. Striking what would be the prevailing view of the constitutional era, it declared: "The Junta is firmly convinced that the pacification of America is now more the work of politics than of force, and that only the Constitution can reestablish the fraternal bonds of union with the mother country." In a final extraordinary admission, the junta advised that in order to guarantee American acceptance of the Constitution it was important "to repeat to the common people [of America] that the Peninsula does not ever want to make them equal to their native people, nor to continue to treat them as colonies."[8] Thus treatment as colonials and internal racial equality were both recognized as devastating losses of status for American creoles. Even so, the most extreme forms of abuse of the Indians were clearly illegal under the Constitution, and on 25 April the government issued a decree reaffirming the Cortes decree of 1812 abolishing the mita and repartimiento and all other forms of personal servitude of the Indians.[9]

The Provisional Junta had set the tone for the constitutional government's pacification policy by decreeing the preference for political solutions over military and by announcing a plan to send constitutional commissioners. In the second constitutional period Spain was thus prepared to take a more precise view of American pacification and, even though the lamentable tendency to expect the Constitution to have a magic effect remained, the government had some concern for the reaction of American creoles. Yet the same gap between promise and performance that paralyzed the first constitutional government in its American policy continued to exist in the second era, and military steps were not ignored. In the first month after the revolution, Spain ordered the dispatch of a division of four ships to Costa Firme under command of Captain Angel Laborde, who would also assume command of the naval station of Puerto Cabello.[10] At the same time, a frigate was ordered to Cartagena to pursue corsairs and protect commerce.[11] These naval reinforcements were in response to the rapidly deteriorating position of royalist forces throughout New Granada and Venezuela, where General Morillo's expedition was on the verge of total defeat.

These orders provoked an immediate response from liberal Americans resident in the Cádiz area. One was a petition signed by eleven Americans living in Cádiz pointing out that the preparations of naval reinforcements against America were contrary to the king's statement "that the complaints of members of a single family cannot be determined and settled with arms in hand." The petition asked that Spain suspend all manner of hostilities until the Cortes could meet and determine purely pacific means of dealing with America.[12] In the same month, eighty individuals in San Fernando (the former Isla de León) petitioned the king to suspend hostilities, which they said produced nothing and merely destroyed the American territories. They also asked that the commissioners sent to inform America of the political changes in Spain should be men who had not engaged in the fighting overseas and that commanders in America known for their outrages against citizens should be removed.[13] The government's only response was to note that it had already ordered the suspension of hostilities.

In March the new government showed its interest in military pacification by continuing the Junta Militar de Indias and appointing as one of its members General Félix María Calleja, former viceroy of Mexico and commander of the ill-fated expeditionary army at Cádiz, who had been arrested by his own troops in the revolution. Perhaps it was to him the petitioners referred when they asked that no individual notoriously connected with suppression of revolt overseas should be appointed to a position where he would come in direct contact with American rebels. At any rate, it was certainly contradictory to its declared preference for political settlement for the new government to maintain the Junta Militar de Indias. Although the junta had little apparent influence in the next year, its continuation in office was one of many signs of the confusion of the new regime regarding American policy.

Of all the early indications of the direction of the new regime, perhaps the most ominous was a decision made in early April to withhold the permission requested by Viceroy Joaquín de la Pezuela of Peru for Lima's most prominent merchant, José Arizmendi, to outfit an armed ship in England for service as a corsair in Peruvian waters and, of course, to carry British merchandise to Peru. The defeat of Peruvian viceregal arms at Maypu in Chile in April 1818 had left Peru itself exposed to rebel attack and, more immediately, to gradual strangulation of vital trade links as Chilean naval forces took to the Pacific in a successful drive to force Spanish merchant shipping out of the waters. Acting on his own initiative, therefore, Viceroy Pezuela in early 1818 had begun to grant licenses to foreign vessels to sell their cargoes in Peruvian ports. Convinced that free trade provided the only salvation for Peru, Pezuela bombarded Spain with requests for approval and continued granting licenses without direct approval, all accompanied by the loud opposition of the Lima consulado. In November 1818 he signed a contract with the commander of the English naval squadron for the free entry of English goods into Callao for two years. In response to the protests of the consulado and the Spanish ambassador in Brazil, the Conde de Casa Flores, Spain in 1819 had appointed a committee to study the matter. By that time the Chilean fleet of Lord Cochrane was already periodically blockading and bombarding Callao, which merely confirmed the viceroy in his opinion that free neutral trade was essential for survival. Lima had become entirely dependent on foreign vessels to supply its needs, and before the peninsular revolution the Spanish government seems to have winked an eye at this necessary countermanding of ancient laws. José Arizmendi was granted viceregal permission to import four shiploads of foreign goods in early 1820, each shipment paying special government loans or contributions in place of standard import duties.

News of the viceroy's open door policy spread through London, where merchants began to outfit expeditions to break into Peruvian markets. By 1820 the British merchants were openly advertising for investors in expeditions to Peru, and insurance underwriters spread the word that Viceroy Pezuela permitted any foreign ship to land. Former Viceroy Abascal, now retired to Spain and a major advisor on Peruvian affairs, strongly opposed Pezuela's actions, as did many merchants interested in the Peruvian monopoly.[14] Yet it was not until the rise of the new liberal government that Spain spoke out against Pezuela's policy. Given the fact that prices in Peru had quadrupled owing to the cutoff of trade and that the viceregal government's ability to respond to the expected rebel attack of San Martín was seriously undermined by lack of resources, it is surely incredible that in April 1820 the Ministry of Finance informed the Council of State in Spain "that the viceroy of Peru at the moment does not need ships nor stores because of those [Peru] has received from Spain and North

America" and that José Arizmendi was in league with English contra-
bandists and "a man of ominous influence" on the viceroy. Another
advisor warned that, because of his influence over the viceroy, Arizmendi was able to get the viceregal government to favor his trade
projects. As a result, the Ministry of State in April 1820 refused
permission to Arizmendi to outfit a corsair in England. [15]

This rebuke from the liberal regime was not interpreted by
Pezuela as an order to cease and desist in his other individual contracts
for introducing foreign ships and merchandise in Peru, and, pleading
"the iron law of necessity," he continued to permit foreign trade until
the officers of his army overthrew him in January 1821, replacing him
with Viceroy José de la Serna. Lima and Cádiz merchants, whose
influence over the liberal regime in 1820 was apparently as great as it
had been in 1812, continued to demand prohibition of foreign trade.
After the Cortes began meeting in July it undertook to discuss the
matter of Peruvian and Cuban foreign trade in closed sessions. A
spokesman for the monopolists, in a long representation, brought the
Cortes up to date on the Peruvian trade, referring to the opposition of
the Conde de Casa Flores and Abascal to free trade, the Lima Consulado's offer to cover deficits in the viceregal treasury in return for
prohibition of outside trade, and the activity of London merchant
houses. The gradual spread of free trade would destroy both parts of
the empire. Bitter complaint against the trade that was continuing
between Cuba and the United States expanded the issue. The contract
granted by the intendant of Havana to a North American merchant
house for the import of wheat was, like Pezuela's contracts in Peru,
condemned as "monstrous and anti-mercantile." [16]

The foreign trade did not stop in either Peru or Cuba. The
Cortes never absolutely prohibited it, but neither did it permit it. The
trade continued on the authority of local royal officials. In Peru it was a
matter of survival. Spanish commercial shipping simply disappeared
from Peruvian waters. At the end of May 1820 it was reported that in
the previous twenty-eight months only two Spanish merchant ships
had arrived in Lima from the peninsula, and in all of 1820 only two
ships landed at Cádiz from Lima. There was no Spanish shipping left

on the Pacific. The Cuban trade was a different matter—in 1820 fifty-nine Spanish ships landed at Cádiz from Havana. Yet the political impossibility of denying Cuba a foreign contact it had come to depend on was just as pressing. By the end of 1820 the Ministry of Finance, at least, recognized the effective bankruptcy of Peru, pointing out that the lack of national trade and the heavy taxes had destroyed industry and commerce and that Peru "was not even able to supply the troops with what is necessary for their daily subsistence." The fiscal of the Ministry of Finance actually recommended that Pezuela's free trade arrangements be approved, but no decision was ever made.[17] Even in the face of the most pressing need, the revolutionary regime in Spain did not favor free trade.

The Cortes opened its sessions on 9 July 1820 with the king formally renewing his oath to the Constitution. In a short discourse that constituted Spain's first speech from the throne, Ferdinand promised to devote his authority to the preservation of the Constitution. For the first time in its history the constitutional system was now fully implanted, with the king as the executive and the Cortes as the legislative branch. The Cortes, however, would soon begin to abrogate to itself ultimate responsibility for political affairs, thereby invading the royal terrain. Within the Cortes two factions immediately appeared—the moderates or *doceañistas* on the one hand, and the more radical branch of liberals, the *exaltados* on the other. The work of the Cortes got under way with the presentation of reports from the ministers. Minister of Ultramar Antonio Porcel reported on the situation of the American colonies, promising happy consequences from the reestablishment of the Constitution.[18] The new Cortes proceeded quickly to pass legislation completing the unfinished work of Cádiz, especially as it related to internal ecclesiastical reform. The most important legislation of the first session included renewed suppression of the Jesuits, reduction of tithes, suppression of ecclesiastical entails, and, most important, suppression of monastic orders and reduction in the numbers of monasteries of the regular orders.

By October 1820 the king, who at first refused to sign the act limiting the regular orders but was forced to give in by the pressure of public opinion, had begun to abandon his short-lived experiment of cooperating with the Cortes. He withdrew to the Escorial and refused to participate in the closing of the regular Cortes session. He began a secret policy of anticonstitutional resistance, hoping to disrupt the smooth operation of government by interposing his authority against that of the Cortes whenever possible (mainly in regard to appointments), while simultaneously searching abroad for foreign assistance to reestablish his personal authority by coup d'etat or by foreign military intervention. At first he even contemplated an alliance with the *exaltados* to bring down the moderate ministry, but the plan was soon abandoned. In the first series of showdowns the king lost, and was forced in November 1820 to return from the Escorial to Madrid and to fire certain members of his household staff on the demand of the provincial deputation of New Castile. Ferdinand got his revenge when in February 1821 he added a paragraph of his own to the end of the speech from the throne that the ministry had written for him to deliver at the opening of the new Cortes session. In this famous postscript he made public the differences that had existed between the cabinet and himself, thereby publicly announcing his lack of confidence in the ministers. The following day he exercised his constitutional powers and accepted the resignation of the cabinet, replacing it with the second constitutional ministry headed by Eusebio Bardají, a weak government with no substantial support.[19]

The gradual escalation of tension during 1820 between the king and the government, featuring the king trying to disgrace and paralyze his ministers and his ministers trying to humiliate and control him, is no doubt the fundamental explanation of the failure of the new liberal regime to implement a genuinely renewed policy of American pacification. Ferdinand himself remained opposed to substantive reform in America, as he would be opposed to any move to recognize American independence. The Cortes and government, as in 1812, were simply too preoccupied by domestic struggles in Spain to give American questions the attention they deserved. So it was that, after the initial decision of the Provisional Junta and Council of State to send commissioners to America to collect the dissidents' oaths of loyalty to the Constitution, the question of pacification was for some time overlooked. It never attracted the proportionate amount of

government attention or sustained Cortes debate that it deserved or
that the ecclesiastical reforms, for example, received.

The decision to send constitutional commissioners to the rebellious countries seems to have satisfied the liberal regime that everything possible was being done already. On 15 April 1820 the
commissioners' instructions were drawn up. The commissioners were
to announce a cease fire and to urge the dissidents to adopt the
Constitution, providing them with direction in the choice of deputies
to the Cortes. If the colonists accepted these terms, a general amnesty
was to be promised. If they did not accept the Constitution, the
commissioners were to await further instructions from Spain. There
was no instruction for the commissioners to assess or report on local
conditions or American demands. Instead, they were to try to persuade dissident leaders "that direct commerce in foreign ships is
ruinous for those countries and for the metropolis." If they did not
succeed in convincing the colonists that trade in Spanish ships was
inevitably more advantageous, then they were permitted to negotiate
gradually, and "with much resistance," some form of more open
trade, but at no time could they abandon the principle that foreign
goods were to pay double customs duties if brought in on foreign
ships. In essence, the commissioners were being authorized to negotiate provisional conventions of commerce between Spain and the
colonies.[20]

In their discussions with rebel leaders the commissioners were to
urge them to remember how natural it was for the Americans to defer
to Spain because of the ancient ties of a common language, religion,
and customs. They were to be told "that the political interest of
America is to maintain intimate connections of union and fraternity
with its metropolis in order to protect themselves from the insidious
politics of some Powers who only await the moment of separation in
order to begin the conquest . . . of some military and mercantile
position in America." Striking a chord that would increasingly be
repeated, the commissioners were to point out to Americans that their
independent governments were weak and troubled by factionalism
and constant change of leaders, conditions that made it impossible to

defend themselves against foreign aggression. Along with these reflections, they were to offer that Spain would recognize the chiefs currently in control, and their titles, incomes, hereditary positions, and whatever other perquisites, if they would recognize the Constitution. To the common people they were to point out how heavy the burden of taxation and military service was under the independent governments, a burden that made them worse off than they had been under Spain. They were to gain the support of American ecclesiastics "by whatever means possible," because of their influence over the common people. And they were not to admit the mediation of foreigners that dissident chiefs might propose, "because nothing could be more antipolitic than to call on a stranger to intervene in a domestic altercation, and history teaches us that the third party always appropriates to himself that which is under litigation."[21]

Simultaneously with these instructions, the government drew up a royal decree entitled "Proclamation of the King to Overseas Inhabitants," which was a royal statement by Ferdinand VII of his personal culpability and political error in abolishing the Constitution in 1814. He appealed to the rebels all over America to return to the Spanish fold, for the new order of constitutional guarantees would provide them all the things for which they had been fighting. The king excused himself for abolishing the Constitution by saying that he had been caught up in the general enthusiasm of his return to Spain in 1814 and that mere habit had led him to believe the old institutions were preferable to the new ones. He prayed his subjects to remember "that errors in judgment are not crimes," and he urged them "quickly to forget all past evils." The king, with what humiliation might be imagined, personally signed one copy of this extraordinary statement, which was then dispatched throughout the empire in the hope that it would maintain the crown's dignity.[22] The statement was published in Mexico, for example, even though commissioners did not go there.

On 25 April the ministers of state, war, and marine were asked to nominate commissioners, and on 8 June the names were announced. Two men each were chosen to go to Venezuela, New Granada, Peru, and Chile, and three men were named for Buenos

Aires. These countries, in Spain's view, were those in which organized rebel governments existed, or, as the circular letter put it, those "which have the misfortune of suffering all the horrors of civil war."[23] The commissioners chosen for Peru immediately declined appointment, and the government ended up ordering the viceroy of Peru to select his own commissioners to negotiate with the rebels in Upper Peru.[24]

Precisely what luck befell the commissioners on their appointed rounds differed only in detail from country to country. In general, all of them failed, as might well have been expected. The three commissioners to the Río de la Plata reached Montevideo on 19 November 1820. They launched their appeal by announcing their arrival to the legislature of Buenos Aires and requesting a safe conduct to enter that territory and begin the assigned task, informing the legislature of their instructions and reasons for coming. The Buenos Aires government simply turned a cold shoulder to their appeal, doing nothing to encourage them in their mission, and they soon returned to Spain.[25]

Meanwhile, in Venezuela, General Morillo, commander of the royal forces there, obeyed the government's orders by sending his own commissioners to General Simón Bolívar and the Colombian congress then meeting at Angostura, announcing the publication of the Constitution and the king's manifestoes and requesting a cease fire. The patriots responded enthusiastically, since a cessation of hostilities suited their plans admirably. General Bolívar, "who is entitled the Liberator and President of Colombia," said Morillo, replied that he would gladly receive Morillo's representatives if they were coming to discuss peace and to recognize Colombia as a free and sovereign state. "But if their mission had some other object, it was his intention neither to receive them nor to hear their propositions." Morillo then abandoned the mission, recognizing that the object of the rebels "was not to improve their system but to put in effect the emancipation and absolute independence." Morillo contented himself with instituting the cease fire and informed Spain "that the situation of his army was never more critical owing to the superiority of the enemy in both public opinion and in power."[26]

In fact, the offer of Morillo's various commissioners, according to their own report, was rebuked rather more sharply than the Spaniards at home liked to hear, and with rather clearer logic than the metropolis might like to admit. Rafael Urdaneta and Pedro Briseño Méndez, respectively commander in chief and minister of war of Colombia, told Morillo's commissioners that Colombia's ten years of sacrifice and struggle "gives us the right to expect that you will spare us the pain of hearing propositions of dependency on Spain, whatever its name and form." Colombia had achieved her own power and no one else could give her anything. The commissioners who went to General José Antonio Páez, commander of the independent forces in Venezuela, received much the same answer. Liberty and independence, he said, were all he would take from Spain. The congress at Angostura replied that it would only negotiate with Spain if recognition of Colombia's independence was the basis. And General Bolívar, as president of the congress, replied to Morillo that recognition of independence was the only basis for negotiation.[27]

Despite this inability to discuss the fundamental question, both sides desired an armistice, and thus, in November 1820, they agreed to a six-month armistice and regularization of the rules of war. Morillo, convinced that defeat of the royalist army was inevitable, having lost over two-thirds of the European troops who originally made up his expedition, turned command over to Miguel de La Torre in December and left Venezuela. Thus, by the time the commissioners sent out from the peninsula reached Caracas in December 1820, the matter had already been concluded. They learned that Bolívar intended to send his own commissioners to Spain to negotiate for peace and decided to send one member from the missions to New Granada and Venezuela to Spain to accompany his agents. The remaining Spanish commissioners drifted to the West Indies. Shortly after the conclusion of the six-month armistice, Bolívar won independence in the battle of Carabobo in June 1821.

Only in Peru did the constitutional commission provoke any sort of sustained negotiations, and there it was because of a peculiar confluence of circumstances that prevailed. José Rodríguez de Arias and Manuel Abreu were appointed as the commissioners to Chile. They reached Panama in January 1821, where Arias gave up the journey because of illness. Abreu proceeded to the viceroyalty of Peru, where he discovered that the Chilean forces of General José de San Martín had already landed. Hence he decided to remain in Peru rather than proceed to Chile. As usual, Peru, because of its geographical isolation, heard of the revolution in Spain late. Viceroy Pezuela was informed of the change via Panama in July 1820, but chose to withhold formal proclamation of the Constitution until he received specific royal orders to do so. The reestablishment of the Constitution was thus public knowledge several months before Pezuela finally received a direct order to proclaim it on 4 September. Only six days later, on 10 September, the long-awaited rebel expedition under San Martín landed on the Peruvian coast at Pisco. Having previously received the royal instructions to negotiate a cease fire with the rebels, Pezuela proceeded to agree to negotiations in the last week of September, long before Abreu's ultimate arrival in April 1821. San Martín, for his part, agreed to a cease fire because his small expeditionary army was thought to be inadequate to face the entrenched royal army immediately, and he hoped for time in order to win over Peruvian public opinion without force of arms. During the last week of September the two sides negotiated at the suburb of Miraflores outside Lima, but the talks came to nothing and were broken off on 30 September.

In the following months the situation changed drastically in Lima. Viceroy Pezuela, refusing to risk the loss of Lima by challenging the Chilean expeditionary force directly, incurred the enmity of his chief officers. On 29 January 1821 he was overthrown by the commanders and replaced by an old opponent, General José de la Serna. Continued control of the city of Lima was judged by the royal commanders as a fatal weakness in the royalist defenses against San Martín, and La Serna made up his mind to abandon Lima. It was at this critical juncture, in April 1821, that Commissioner Abreu arrived in Peru. Abreu was immediately impressed by San Martín's earnestness and tendency to conciliation, as well as with the rebel leader's monarchist proclivities. In many ways he was won over by San Martín, with whom he visited for four days before coming on to Lima to be received by the very reluctant Viceroy La Serna.

Despite his immediate distaste for the Spanish commissioner, who was a naval officer and in the viceroy's view too sympathetic to San Martín, La Serna obeyed royal orders and agreed to peace talks. They were held at the hacienda of Punchauca north of Lima. On 23 May a twenty-day armistice was agreed to, and on 2 June Viceroy La Serna and General San Martín met personally at the hacienda. Later the negotiations moved to Miraflores and from there to the frigate *Cleopatra* in Callao harbor. However, because the royalist commanders had already determined on taking the offensive against the rebels, no settlement was reached. In July the royalists set in action their plan to abandon Lima, while Abreu continued on his own the essentially fruitless negotiations with San Martín. The rebels' final proposal was for an armistice of eighteen months, during which time the viceroy would name two deputies, the government of Chile one, and San Martín a fourth, to go to Spain to negotiate directly with the Cortes. San Martín apparently hoped that Spain would send one of the infantes to Peru to head the independent regime. Nothing further came of this prospect, however, because La Serna abandoned Lima on 4 July and hostilities soon commenced in earnest. In addition, La Serna hated Abreu and informed Spain that he was acting "more like an agent of the dissidents than a deputy of His Majesty." Abreu responded in kind, accusing the viceroy of being uncooperative, abusive, and disrespectful.[28] Abreu remained in Lima with San Martín for some six months, providing the unique example of one of the commissioners having the support of the local rebel government but not of the local royalist government.

In each instance, the commissioners sent out in 1820 failed to achieve a settlement. In Peru the problem was that the commissioner did not receive the support of the local royalist commanders, who were only just beginning their struggle against rebel forces in the viceroyalty and thus felt no need to contemplate settlement. In New Granada and Venezuela, where Morillo's army was on the verge of total elimination and where the royalist commander was fully prepared to negotiate, the rebels felt themselves too close to victory. In the Río de la Plata there was not even any royal force to threaten the independent state and absolutely no motivation for the leaders of

Buenos Aires to negotiate. Commissioners never got to Chile, where, at any rate, the independent regime felt itself sufficiently secure to reject any compromise. Nor did they get to Upper Peru, where the royalists were still firmly in control. About the only outcome of Spain's new policy was that both Bolívar and San Martín would feel encouraged to dispatch their own representatives to try to open talks in Spain, where they invariably foundered over the single impediment of Spain's refusal to contemplate negotiating outright independence. At any rate, by late 1820 the Spanish empire was gradually disintegrating. The only really secure royal regimes, besides those in Cuba and Puerto Rico, were those in Mexico, Central America, Quito, and Upper Peru, but even they would soon face destruction. General Morillo had summed up the attitude of Venezuelans in terms that would soon apply to the rest of the empire:

> It is nonsense, in my view, to believe that this part of America wants to reunite with [Spain] and adopt the Constitution. . . . The American dissidents, as I have said, have not been fighting to improve the system of government, and it is an error to believe they are ever capable of agreeing to unite with the metropolis. They do not want to be Spaniards, . . . and whatever our conduct or our government may be, absolute independence or war is the only choice that they leave us.[29]

It is worth noting that in regard to other issues besides the implementation of the Constitution, the new regime's policy did not change significantly from that of the previous absolutist regime. This was especially true in regard to American trade and Spain's attitude toward Britain. The liberal government exhibited considerable suspicion of British trade incursions. When this was combined with the natural antipathy that existed between Spain as Europe's leading radical state and Britain as its leading exponent of free trade, it made for an atmosphere of coldness in relations. Particularly troublesome were the English trade incursion in Peru and the indications of illegal exports of silver bullion on British merchant and naval vessels. In early 1820 Viceroy Pezuela had admitted that several leading Peruvian merchants in league with British interests had illegally exported millions of pesos of silver. Two million pesos had been exported on the British warship *Blossom*. In Spain, the Contaduría General, or general accounting agency, discussed the matter and reaffirmed that under no circumstances could precious metals be exported from any American port by foreign ships or the nationals of other nations, or even by Spanish ships if their destination was a foreign country.[30]

By June 1820 a distinct chill in relations with Britain and all the other Great Powers had set in. Spain had to accede to a demand from British merchants in Spain that they be exempted from special duties designed to raise money for the American war effort on the grounds of their most favored nation status and the British declaration of neutrality in the American wars. But an official of the Ministry of State, Diego Colón, reported that in the official view Britain's neutrality was a type of recognition of South American independence since one could only be neutral in a contest between states. Extreme anger over the British trade incursions was expressed. In Spain's view the insurrection in America "has opened to the speculators of Bristol, Liverpool, Cork, Glasgow, etc., a new and secure screen for the sale of their merchandise where previously they could only be introduced . . . as contraband." The American wars merely delayed the moment, he said, in which Spanish America would be converted into "an immense factory of Great Britain."[31] Even so, in order to guarantee against possible incidents that might force the intervention of a foreign power, Spain in April 1820 declared a pardon for all North Americans caught under arms in aid of the rebels or imprisoned for spying or in other ways helping the rebellion, and in August it extended the decree to include British and all other foreign nationals.[32] Like it or not, foreign neutrality was infinitely preferable to direct foreign involvement.

Spanish perception that Britain was strongly inclined to support Latin American independence was intensified by the notices that the Spanish ambassador to London, the Duke of Frías, sent along from the British press. In September 1820 the *Morning Post* of London, which, Frías reported, normally voiced the government's views, editorialized that the sharp turn of Spain toward a radical, even a potentially republican, government further inclined Britain toward supporting the Latin American rebellions, in hopes of seeing new governments established there to act as a counterweight to Spain. "To this consideration are now to be added the probability that Old Spain will gradually become more republican than she is, and the certainty that the less power she has the less is the peace of Europe likely to be disturbed. New rulers are always fond of foreign adventures." This, Frías said, confirmed what he had already reported—that the refusal of the rebellious provinces to accept the Spanish Constitution, the continued instability of Portugal, and British fears that Spain had aggressive designs against Portugal "will be motive enough to incline the politics of England to help the insurgents in America and perhaps to recognize their independence, neutralizing in this way the increase in power that Spain might attain, more or less immediately, from its union, either absolute or federative, with Portugal."[33] The British, at any rate, still believed that Spain was plotting aggressive acts against Portugal and that the new government, in order to win domestic support, was inclined to some sort of dramatic adventure.

In fact, Spain's ambitions, even in regard to American pacification, were decidedly low. In June 1820, Minister of State Evaristo Pérez de Castro reported to the Cortes that the mediation of the Great Powers in the Portuguese occupation of Montevideo, frequently disrupted and pursued unenthusiastically by all parties, had come to nothing. The minister believed it was because of Spain's preoccupation with the Cortes reforms and, more important, because Spain had been unable to send the expeditionary force that was the necessary first step in the mediation. In essence, he admitted that Spain was too weak and too preoccupied internally to exert the necessary effort to regain control of a territory the valid title to which all the Powers recognized. In addition, he frankly admitted that European dislike of the constitutional revolution in Spain embarrassed attempts to work in unison with the Great Powers.[34]

The remainder of 1820 and much of 1821—the critical months for the resolution of the independence question in most of America—was a time when little direct attention was paid in the councils of the Spanish government to American questions. The flourishing liberal press continued to debate possible means of pacification while trying to keep up, often inadequately, with the ever-changing developments in America. The press remained predominantly convinced that the constitutional system would attract America and that the political immaturity of the Americans would force them to reestablish loyalty. These assumptions were combined with an often facile and incorrect assertion of the thesis that support for independence among Americans was still very limited. They did not want separation, *El Universal* insisted, and those who did want it were merely rascals. When the press found its optimistic prognostications refuted by events in America—such as the fall of Lima or the success of Iturbide—it tended to report these events without comment.[35]

Meanwhile, the first warnings of a possible movement toward recognition of an American country by one of the Great Powers was sounded when, in November 1820, the ambassador to France, the Marqués de Santa Cruz, wrote to say that the French government was secretly contemplating recognizing Venezuela. Based on indirect and unclear evidence, the report could not be verified, but the ambassador was ordered to keep watch on the situation.[36] By January 1821 it was known that President Monroe of the United States had urged Congress to recognize the independence of the Latin American republics. The Duke of Frías, ambassador to London, held several conversations with the American ambassador there about the topic and wrote to warn Spain that the United States clearly preferred Latin American independence. Frías had pointed out many times the favors Spain had accorded the United States, especially in the cession of the Floridas, and had argued that the United States had no motives for recognizing the separation of Spanish America. To this the North American ambassador had made no reply.[37]

While the Cortes, ministry, and king largely ignored American questions, awaiting no doubt the expected positive outcome of the commissions sent to negotiate with the rebels, America moved inexorably toward the final break. Chile had joined Buenos Aires in 1818 as the second more-or-less secure independent state. In 1819 Bolívar's forces in Venezuela defeated and routed the remaining Spanish defenders. By 1821 Bolívar would be victorious in New Granada. Meanwhile, in the last month of 1820 Agustín de Iturbide, a royalist officer, proclaimed a revolt against Spain in Mexico. In February 1821 he announced the program of independence in the Plan of Iguala, calling for the creation of a constitutional monarchy in Mexico based on the Constitution of Cádiz and headed by an infante or by Ferdinand VII himself, guaranteeing the privileges and interests of the clerical and military elite and promising reform and progress of a vague sort for the masses. Spain took no action in response to these drastic shifts in loyalty.

The failure to respond was largely owing to the total absorption of the Cortes and government in late 1820 in debating and passing their legislative program for fundamental domestic reform. The decrees of September 1820—suppression of the monastic orders, reform of the regular orders, abolition of the Jesuits, disentailment of the clergy, and abolition of the ecclesiastical fuero and of the military fuero for militiamen in America—constituted a controversial body of reforms. It should be quickly added that they were not implemented directly or fully in the colonies because of the disrupted conditions in those that remained under royal control, such as Mexico and Peru, but knowledge of them weakened support for the royalist cause among those Mexicans, notably the clergy and creole officers, who were threatened by the laws and who had the option by February 1821 of supporting the Iturbide rebellion.[38] The laws were not implemented in Peru, where the news of their passage was received at about the same time Viceroy La Serna was evacuating Lima and the country was being divided between the royalists and the patriots. But there too they served to drive the royalist commander of Upper Peru, Pedro Antonio Olañeta, to mutiny against the viceroy in 1823 in the name of supporting a return to absolutism.

The Cortes, meanwhile, moved on from the consideration of these basic social reforms to legislation of economic reforms. The first major item was discussion and adoption in September 1820 of a new customs code, which had the effect of establishing a new set of trade regulations. The new code established protective tariffs, equality of tariffs throughout the empire, and freedom of trade for Spanish vessels. It did not, however, permit free foreign trade, since Articles

19 and 20 permitted the entry of foreign vessels in Spanish ports only to repair damages or supply their crews on humanitarian grounds, and it had to be reciprocal at that. Thus the new 1820 customs code was designed to encourage the Spanish merchant marine by excluding foreigners.[39] From October to the end of 1820 the Cortes proceeded to turn most of its attention to discussion of the reorganization, rationalization, and payment of Spain's national debt, an undertaking of such massive proportions that American pacification was, again, lost in the shuffle. For America, the most important consequence of the peninsula's absorption in financial matters was a decree of October 1820 that, in order to restore the treasuries in America, the intendants should lose their command over the military in those regions where civil and military command had been joined so that they could concentrate exclusively on financial restoration.[40]

The first months of 1821, at any rate, mark a subtle but important turning-point in the history of Spain's relations with, and control over, its overseas empire. Although Madrid was not at first aware of it, and although the peninsular government still had important moves in store for American pacification policy, it was at this point that the system of government from the center, government by remote control in Madrid, definitively broke down. The American countries that had already established de facto independence, of course, ceased to receive Madrid's orders. More important, those countries such as Mexico and Peru where royal regimes still existed were by now so disrupted that royal orders were not received or, if received, not acted on. In Mexico the royal government disintegrated in only seven months after publication of the Plan of Iguala in February 1821. In Peru, withdrawal of the royal government from Lima to the highlands in July 1821 meant that, although royal power remained very much alive for another four years, normal channels of policy decision and implementation were broken. Viceroy La Serna, isolated from contact with the metropolis in his highland enclave, went a whole year without receiving communications from Madrid. Spain continued to speak, but America either did not listen or was prevented from hearing.

Three minor incidents at the end of 1820 illustrate the way in which channels of communication and decision were becoming obstructed either by American separation or by peninsular confusion. An order of 31 December 1820, for example, creating poor houses, or casas de amparo, in America in the buildings now supposedly vacated by suppressed regular orders constituted a progressive social policy for the vagrants and beggars who roamed the major cities. Yet the only notes of receipt of the order came from Havana and Santo Domingo.[41] Other orders could be obstructed by the internal bureaucratic confusion inherent in the conversion back to a previously suppressed constitutional system. A royal order of November 1820, for example, that no set term of office should be established for viceroys, captains general, and governors in America was countermanded when it was discovered in the Ministry of Ultramar that the Cortes in 1811 had decreed specific terms of office. A consultation was then necessary to resolve the confusion, and the matter had to return to the Cortes.[42] And then there are instances of what can only be called simple incompetence. In November 1820 the Junta Militar de Indias, recognizing it possessed no adequate maps of America because the finances for its office had not yet been released, attempted to secure a set of maps that had been purchased at a cost of 5,000 reales each by the commander of the ill-fated expeditionary army in Cádiz. But the Cádiz Comisión de Reemplazos reported that the maps had never been delivered and that they must have been filed with the general staff or some other office.[43] So the committee charged with recommending military action in America had to set about its duties without even the basic advantage of maps. Not surprisingly, the Junta Militar de Indias was rarely heard from again.

Thus an air of unreality begins to sweep over the observer who watches the Spanish government legislating and decreeing for an empire that effectively no longer existed. While American deputies to the Cortes withdrew one by one as their home countries became independent, peninsular lawmakers were free to pass acts that sounded desirable in principle and that no one had to worry about implementing. For example, in June 1821 the Cortes adopted a grandiose program for the establishment of primary and secondary

schools and universities in America. Secondary schools, to be called
"provincial universities," were to exist in nearly every overseas province. Proper universities, for professional training, were to exist in
twenty-two cities (not counting Venezuela and Río de la Plata, of
which there was no mention). Medical schools were decreed for fifteen
cities, veterinary schools for six, experimental agricultural schools for
ten, fine arts schools for eight, schools of commerce for fourteen,
schools of astronomy and navigation for five, and academies of mining
for six. The decree was never even circulated.[44] But it is also important to remember that this air of unreality was not as great as it would
become after September 1821 and the accomplishment of Mexican
independence. Until that time, deputies in the Cortes could content
themselves with the knowledge that Spain still controlled most of the
old empire and that the outcome of independence in the two major
viceroyalties, Mexico and Peru, was still open to question.

Arrival of the news of the Iturbide uprising in Mexico jolted the
Cortes, or at least some of its members, out of their lethargy regarding
the American crisis. Mexicans now composed the largest block of
overseas deputies in the Cortes, forty-four of the fifty-nine deputies
elected in Mexico having taken their seats in the 1820–21 session of
the Cortes. With seven alternates, the total Mexican representation
was thus fifty-one members. They had many new proposals for the
pacification of America to present but were obstructed by the lack of
interest of the peninsular deputies. Two Mexicans, Mariano
Michelena and Miguel Ramos Arizpe, petitioned that more time be
spent in the Cortes on resolving the problems of the overseas provinces. Their appeal was not acted on until May 1821, when the
Spanish deputy the Conde de Toreno recommended that a committee
present to the Cortes a proposal for bringing peace to America. The
Cortes approved, and a committee of pacification was chosen with four
Spaniards and five Americans as members. The Americans were Felipe
Fermín Paúl of Venezuela and four Mexicans, Lucas Alamán, Francisco Fagoaga, Bernardino Amati, and Lorenzo Zavala. According to
Alamán, this committee met frequently but fruitlessly. Shortly before
the scheduled conclusion of the regular session of the Cortes in June
1821, the committee rendered an innocuous and meaningless report

that totally failed to mention a fundamental proposal the American members had made during committee deliberations. Instead, the pacification committee ended up urging the government to present proposals for the solution of America's problems.

Angered at the failure to mention their proposal, the American members of the committee made their own report to the Cortes on 25 June. In a long preamble they repeated the often-heard motives for unrest that the Mexicans had pointed to in both the earlier Cortes era and the second era. They added a new twist, however, in arguing that the meeting of the Cortes in Spain exercised a disadvantage on American delegates, who were unable to reflect the wishes of their constituents because at such a distance they were cut off from their homelands. What was needed was the creation of branches of the Cortes in America. The plan, first conceived by the deputy Mariano Michelena and later worked on by Ramos Arizpe, called for the creation of three divisions of the Cortes in America: one for New Spain and Central America, one for New Granada and Tierra Firme, and one for Peru, Buenos Aires, and Chile. Each of these Cortes would preside over a vast region, together with an executive, appointed by the king, that might include members of the royal family. Each would have its own ministry, supreme tribunal of justice, and council of state. In short, they proposed the creation of a federative empire. Commerce between the peninsula and the Americas would be considered as that between one province and another in a monarchy. If it were established, the Mexican deputies guaranteed that New Spain would make massive payments to the peninsula for application against the foreign debt and for upkeep of the navy that would be required to knit this commonwealth together.[45] The periodical *La Miscelánea* was alone among the liberal journals in strongly endorsing this recommendation. *El Telégrafo Mejicano*, a journal edited by Juan López Cancelada that reappeared on 20 August 1821, insisted that the proposal proved the American deputies to be partisans of the rebellions, an assertion that was pretty close to the truth.[46] The government, however, responded to this proposal with a secret report rejecting the concept of a federative commonwealth on four grounds. It was contrary to the Constitution; the deputies to the Cortes did not have the power to adopt such a scheme; public opinion was not prepared for it; and there was no reason to assume that the Americans themselves would favor it.[47]

Thus, the first regular Cortes came to an end on 30 June 1821 with no action being taken on pacification. In the closing days of the session the Cortes decided to ask the king to grant an extraordinary session to take care of pending legislation on peninsular affairs. Four American deputies urged that the petition to the king also include the business of America. After some discussion, this was agreed to. It was in this context that the king, in his address closing the regular session on 30 June, assured the members that the government would propose measures for the welfare of America and avowed that he desired nothing so much as the happiness of Spaniards in both hemispheres. The king granted permission for the extraordinary session, which opened in Madrid in September. Ferdinand's personal motives for referring to the American crisis, however, were decidedly mixed. In conversations with the French ambassador to Madrid he gave, as early as June 1821, the first intimations of the extent to which the American question was becoming mingled in his mind with his own personal degradation at the hands of the liberal regime. The French ambassador wrote to his home government: "This prince hopes that the policy of the Allies will cause them to interfere in the affairs of Spanish America and he desires that this intervention will lead to explanations about the duress of his position."[48]

Several months before the closing of the regular session, the Ministry of Ultramar had sent letters to the American Cortes delegates asking them, as had been done after the king's restoration in 1814, to answer what were the causes of the dissent in America, whether the main complaints were derived from the 1808–14 period or the 1814–20 period, and what they would recommend to restore peace and union.[49] This time, however, few answers were received from the Americans, mainly because most overseas members had withdrawn from the Cortes. The Mexican deputation, for example, had rapidly fallen to twenty-three members. The joint reply of the Mexican deputies pointed to the chief cause as "the despotism and constant arbitrariness of the government." In a philosophical vein, the deputies pointed out how natural it was that America had outgrown its infancy and as a result had outgrown its dependence. The Enlightenment and the ideas of the new age had changed the nature and the character of the people. In any political system, they averred, those who commanded would tyrannize their subjects, and Mexicans had grown aware of that fact. The individual liberties guaranteed by the Constitution were not being protected or enhanced in Mexico, and never could be under the current system of government. The Mexicans concluded by urging that the upcoming special session of the Cortes pay particular attention to the affairs of New Spain.[50]

The Cuban deputies, meanwhile, jointly urged the conservation, protection, and increase of free trade as the absolute necessity for preserving Cuba. A Guatemalan delegate replied at great length, but his recommendations chiefly dealt with the need for improved trade, navigation, and education in Central America.[51] The reply of José María Murguía y Galardi for Oaxaca was particularly complete, since it included the report of twenty-five subdelegates in the intendancy on conditions in their localities and four notebooks of detailed reports and recommendations on Indian affairs, agriculture, education, commerce, and politics.[52] The theme that appeared in the answers of the few American deputies still in Spain was very different from that of the answers to the same question in 1814. Americans were no longer content to wait in expectation of improvement. As Morillo had said, they no longer wanted an improvement in the system, they wanted to get out of it. The Mexican deputies put an end to the thesis of the "ties that bind," the belief that the culture and traditions and ethos of Spain knit its American subjects to the motherland in a mystical union, when they told the minister of ultramar: "A chain of events, whose first link is in the tomb of Cortés and whose last shackles our hands, has undermined and entirely ruined the confidence of [the New] World." Those Mexicans who remained to await the opening of the special Cortes session did so in order to attempt to introduce discussion of the recognition of American independence.

The extraordinary session of the Cortes opened in Madrid on 22 September 1821. Most of its attention was occupied with peninsular questions, such as a penal code, national militias, commerce, and the division of Spanish territory. The American question had been included for discussion, but it took a month for American deputies to get the matter before the house. When they did, they could only urge that the government itself should bring forward proposals for the pacification of America, it being impossible to induce the Cortes to take the initiative. This proposal led to a five-month consideration of pacification policy within the executive branch.

Thus it was that on 7 November 1821 the Council of State, with thirty-three members in attendance, sat down to a broad discussion of the apparent hopelessness of the military situation in Peru, Quito, Popayán, Tierra Firme, and Mexico—those territories that, according to their latest information, were on the brink of independence. (Independence had already been completed in Mexico by mid-September but word had not yet arrived). The situation was hopeless. Not only was it not possible to make any new military effort in the rebellious countries, but the danger of mutiny among the troops made it risky to send fresh forces even to Cuba. The council recommended that only volunteers be sent to Havana. In the absence of a military option, the council declared it a "general principle" that only moral force and public opinion remained to make the insurgents submit and to make the dissident countries reunite again with the metropolis, if that was even possible.

Thus it was that with reluctance and over the protest of several individual members, the Council of State—whose members included one cardinal, one prince, four former regents, at least four former ministers or chief ministers; in short, the most influential men of the day—proposed several recommendations to the government: (1) Spain should not consent to the dismemberment of any part of the empire. (2) This determination should be solemnly published. (3) A naval force should be sent immediately to the Pacific to reinforce Callao, and a smaller squadron should be sent to Veracruz. (4) For now, no land forces should be sent to America, especially since this would delay the collection and dispatch of a naval force. (5) If the government could not get together the resources to dispatch such a naval force, it should call upon England to help in the pacification and preservation of America, offering commercial advantages in return.

(6) Spain's exclusive trade system must stop, being incompatible with the enlightened ideas of the age and being the chief and most just complaint of the Americans: "Free commerce is so much in the natural order of things that only by tyrannical violence can it be withdrawn." (7) Special efforts should be made to try to assure that America would send Cortes delegates for the 1822–23 session. Finally, (8) The rejection by Mexicans of the clerical reforms was such an obstacle to restoration of order that the suspension in America of the decrees reforming the regular orders was imperative, and the government should request the Cortes to do so. The unhappiness of the army, meanwhile, should be corrected by counting the years of service overseas by all members of the permanent army as double. And complete equality of appointment to office, based entirely on merit with no special preference for Europeans, should be decreed.[53] This was undoubtedly the most important statement on American questions ever made by the Council of State. It was no longer a case of too little too late, just too late.

The consultation of the council of State went forward to the king and government with a long and important separate opinion by four councilors, the Prince of Anglona, José Aycinena, José Luyando, and Luis Antonio Flores. It was perhaps as literate and intelligent a postscript to empire as any ever written. Ranging over all the topics considered in the council's statement, the four councilors explained how Spain had lost, or nearly lost, its vast empire. If America had been controlled by a large and strong navy and if its land forces had been restricted, it would not now be near loss. If America had not been saddled with the cost of the land forces, and if distribution of offices had been on merit only, and if aspirants for employment had not had to have representatives at court, and if Spain had known its true interests and had opened some American ports to foreign commerce and had abandoned trade exclusivism, the New World would not have fallen. Why had Spain sent troops (they estimated 40,000 in all) instead of naval forces? Because it was the policy forced on the nation by the blind petitions of the merchants of Cádiz and Mexico City. And if Mexico was now lost because of lack of ships, what of Peru, where the loyalists had clamored for two years to be given only two ships of the line. Spain had not been able to respond, because it lacked a navy. Spain should therefore have attempted to gain England's aid for American pacification. Only England of the Great Powers wished Spain well after 1814. "England does not want nor has it wanted to conquer America." What England wanted was to participate in American affairs. Yet Spain had repulsed all British advances, forcing England to remain a passive spectator in American affairs. The denial of free trade was America's chief rationalization for independence. "The desire [for free trade] burst forth into a clamor, the clamor was elevated to a grievance, and the grievance was converted into a pretext that for some made independence not only plausible but necessary." The new Cortes customs regulations did not answer the cry because it still prohibited open foreign trade and antagonized England. Two or three ships of the line must be sent, at the cost of any sacrifice, to Peru. Those territories not yet engulfed in flames—Cuba, Puerto Rico, and the Philippines—must be granted open trade and a simple and economical government administration. The four councilors concluded by pointing out that America lacked the necessary elements with which to create governments that could preserve domestic order, and Spain would default on its most sacred duty if it allowed the wellbeing of fifteen million Americans to fall into the hands of the untrained and unskilled leaders of rebel governments. No American province possessed the power or ability to resist the physical and moral attacks being planned against them by the aggressive Powers who wanted to dominate them. Hence it was essential for Spain to renew its pact with America, in order to save America itself. "This is a new America that we must discover and conquer."[54]

It would take the government two months before it acted on the Council of State's recommendation by sending the Cortes a series of proposals that followed from the council's. Meanwhile, evidence of the collapse of the empire continued to be received in Madrid. The greatest blow was receipt of the news that the captain general newly dispatched from Spain to Mexico, the liberal former minister of war in the earlier constitutional era, Juan O'Donojú, had signed the Treaty of Córdoba with Agustín de Iturbide on 24 August 1821, in which

O'Donojú, unilaterally and without permission from Spain, recognized the fait accompli of Mexican independence. By late September the royalist expeditionary forces remaining in Mexico City had surrendered to O'Donojú, and Iturbide made his triumphal entry in the capital of the new Mexican Empire. The formula for independence in Mexico, the Plan of Iguala, was accepted in Central America as well, and all the kingdom of Guatemala became independent in September 1821.

O'Donojú wrote to the Spanish government of his reasons for signing the treaty without authorization. Resistance to independence was useless, he said, for Iturbide not only had an army of 30,000 well-armed troops, he had the substantive support of all Mexico. The overthrow of Viceroy Apodaca in July, by the Spanish forces who thought he had not made enough of an effort to suppress the Iturbide rebellion, had merely provoked the withdrawal of any further support for the royal regime by civil authorities. The last-ditch stand to resist independence was a hopeless effort, and under those circumstances, O'Donojú declared, he had thought it preferable to work out an accommodation permitting the honorable withdrawal of remaining royalist troops, the protection of Spaniards in Mexico, and the erection of a monarchy modeled on the Constitution of Cádiz and, according to the Plan of Iguala, governed by a member of the royal dynasty.[55]

In Spain, the Council of State recommended that an announcement be made that O'Donojú had no authorization to alienate national territory. On 7 December 1821 the minister of ultramar, Ramón Pelegrín, sent such a note to American royalist authorities and Spanish diplomatic personnel, stating that the king had not authorized anyone to negotiate a treaty acknowledging the independence of any territory and that Spain was even then considering how to pacify the rebellious colonies. Thus Spain turned its back on the political accommodation that O'Donojú had hoped would permit the creation of a monarchy in Mexico presided over by a member of the Bourbon dynasty and the maintaining of close fraternal and commercial relations with the motherland. Spain's refusal to accept the treaty, of course, meant that the hope of placing a Spanish prince on the

Mexican throne was also dashed, and Iturbide would proceed in 1822 to engineer his own election as emperor.

Meantime, news began to arrive indicating the serious deterioration of the situation in Peru and other parts of South America. The first direct letters from the overthrown viceroy of Peru, Joaquín de la Pezuela, began to arrive from Rio de Janeiro, where he had at last landed following a six-month effort to find passage by ship from Peru through waters entirely controlled by rebels.[56] By December 1821 the new Peruvian viceroy, José de la Serna, chosen by the officers to supplant Pezuela, had settled in Cuzco as his headquarters and there began the two-and-a-half-year stalemate between royalist and independence forces, who divided the country between them.

Furthermore, King João VI returned from Brazil to Portugal, leaving his son Pedro behind to become, only a few months later, emperor of an independent Brazil. Shortly before the king's departure, the court of Rio de Janeiro recognized the independence of Buenos Aires, the first European state to extend formal recognition of a Spanish American state, and dispatched an agent to Buenos Aires, promising to receive in Lisbon the agent sent by that country. With that, the Conde de Casa Flores, uncertain whether his mandate to represent Spain in the Portuguese court resident in Brazil was the same thing as in a separate Brazilian court, and the issue having become academic after Portuguese recognition of Buenos Aires, departed Rio de Janeiro.[57]

A last blow in that fateful year of 1821, though it was more symbolic than real, perhaps, was the declaration of independence of Spain's first colony, Santo Domingo, on 1 December 1821. In strongly-worded prose, the declaration mourned the "ignominious pupilage of 328 years" that the Dominican people had undergone. They had remained loyal and dependent—"enduring with a stupid patience the neglect of Spain, not living, not moving, not being for ourselves but only for Spain." But the failure of Spain to aid them in their struggle to survive the attacks of the Haitians, the adoption by the Cortes of the new customs regulations, which did nothing to rescue them from their deprivation, the internecine turmoil of Spain's political factions, and the lack of a Spanish navy had convinced them it was the height of absurdity to await help from Spain. "No more dependence, no more humiliation, no more submission to the caprice and fickleness of the Madrid Cabinet."[58]

The shock of the loss of Mexico and its absorption of Central America was so great that it convinced some policy advisors to go the further step from urging conciliation to urging recognition of independence. One of the most important of these was Gabriel Císcar, a councilor of state and former regent, who in a statement to the king on 12 December 1821 urged that Spain take the lead in recognizing the new reality that prevailed in the world. In his view, all efforts taken by Spain to conciliate America were insufficient and the time for simple conciliation itself was past. It was essential to adopt the generous path of cooperating with Spanish Americans in the establishment and consolidation of their independence, cementing the bonds with the creation of a federation of states presided over by Spain. This harked back to the proposal of the Mexican deputies, but, in this case, the argument was based on what was best for Spain. Such a federation of states would permit a new flourishing of trade between Spain and America, more advantageous for Spain than the trade that had existed in the time of Spanish domination. America no longer produced revenues for the motherland but instead was a drain on her resources. The establishment of a new, lucrative trade between equals was the path England had adopted toward the newly-independent United States, and the most liberal Spaniards continued to insist that it was just as suitable to Spanish policy. If Spain did not provide America the assistance necessary for its prosperity, Císcar warned, other European nations would, and Spain would lose through arrogance advantages that were rightfully hers.[59]

By the end of 1821, therefore, Spanish policy-makers once again appeared to be on the brink of a major breakthrough in their attitude toward policy for America. Many elements accepted independence as a fact and hoped to accommodate policy to a group of states where once there had been one empire. Some elements advised going beyond mere conciliation. Some even suggested that Spain assist Americans to consolidate their independence. Would the extraordinary session of the Cortes follow these extreme suggestions, would it settle for simple conciliation, or would it persist in its refusal to contemplate a change in its relations with America, to recognize that there was virtually no empire left? The power to alter the direction of America, to stop the flood of independence, was irretrievably gone, but could Spain accommodate itself in time to a new reality in the world and even help formulate and shape that reality? Could Spain, as the four councilors urged, discover and conquer the "new America" being born before its very eyes?

VIII

One Last Chance

Spain now stood on the brink of the total loss of its overseas empire. This was the time to adopt a policy that would at last take genuine account of the demands of Americans, although it was a moot question whether even the most liberal policy would alter the fact that independence was already established by late 1821 in every territory except Quito, Peru, Upper Peru, Cuba, Puerto Rico, and the Philippines. Still, Peru itself was the second most important colony, and meeting the demands of its creoles might effect an alteration in that country, where the victory of the independence forces was still some years away. Even Mexico, which had now declared itself independent but had not yet consolidated the form or selected the head of its new regime, might be positively influenced by a dramatic change of policy in the peninsula. With these hopes in mind, and using the recommendations for a new policy that the Council of State had issued on 7 November 1821, the government prepared its suggestions for the reestablishment of order in America.

Presented to the Cortes on 17 January 1822, the government report declared it did not believe it was yet time to recognize the independence of those American colonies in which there was an insurrection. On the contrary, it was its duty to try to end America's misfortunes. To that end it proposed eight recommendations: (1) There should be a two-year suspension of hostilities signed by armistice with the overseas provinces. (2) During that time all the American provinces, through their provincial deputations, would send to Spain their complaints and suggestions. (3) Meanwhile, the deputies from America in the Cortes would be allowed to propose the suspension of those parts of the Constitution that they thought an obstacle to America's prosperity or the reestablishment of order. (4) The decrees involving loss of the ecclesiastical fuero, suppression of monastic orders, and reform of regular orders should be suspended in America. (5) Only moderate duties should be imposed by one province of Spanish America on the products of any other province, and all obstacles to commerce between those provinces and the peninsula should be removed. (6) Free trade in America for friendly foreign powers should be granted for six years. (7) The distribution of public lands in America to the Indians and castes should be undertaken, removing any obstacles that previously prevented this action; once land was divided, the government pointed out, the proprietors would have something to lose and would thus work to keep public order, "since no one doubts that almost always revolutions are made and sustained by those who, having nothing, aspire to have something." (8) Active cooperation with and protection of the pacification process should be negotiated with one of the Great Powers in return for trade and other advantages (the word "England" was crossed out in the original draft).[1]

This program was the farthest Spain ever went in attempting to accommodate the demands of Americans as expressed over so many years and as narrowed down and focused in the last year. The extent to which the Iturbide rebellion in Mexico influenced it is seen in the two suggestions to allow overseas deputies (of whom Mexicans were still the most numerous even if their numbers had fallen considerably) to propose suspension of some parts of the Constitution and to suspend the desafuero and other decrees relating to the clergy to which Mexicans had so much objected. The proposal to distribute public lands had been discussed and adopted in principle by the Cortes in 1813 and 1820, and had recently been brought back to the government's attention in July 1821 by a proposal by Juan López Cancelada, the editor of *El Telégrafo Mejicano*, who had argued "that he who has something to lose never becomes a revolutionary."[2] Viceroy Abascal of Peru had even gone so far as to order plans drawn up for the distribution of lands to Indians in 1814, but nothing had come of it. Free trade for foreigners in America, open and equal trade within the empire, and foreign mediation had, of course, been paramount issues since the beginning of the wars of independence. And the suggestions for a cease fire and consultation over American demands had been briefly attempted with the constitutional commissioners in 1820. There was certainly nothing new here, it was only that this was the first time these proposals had gotten so far as to become the government's recommended policy. But government recommendations had to be accepted by the Cortes before they could be implemented. And once again there was an unavoidable institutional impediment to the implementation of a cohesive American policy, for the Cortes did not accept these recommendations.

The Cortes discussion of the government's recommendations was perhaps the most significant debate ever held with regard to American pacification. The government, to reinforce its proposals, submitted to the Cortes a memoir prepared at the request of Minister of Ultramar Pelegrín by Miguel Cabrera de Nevares, a liberal military officer who had lived for ten years in the viceroyalty of the Río de la Plata. Cabrera de Nevares said that there was no need to find out what the Americans wanted, since it was clear they wanted independence. The Americans would not delay their rush to independence for a year or more in order to submit their demands once again to Spain. During the period of consultation other nations would continue to rush to the aid of the independent regimes, and Spain would lose its natural advantage in American trade and commerce. "Spanish America is a colossus that moves steadily toward its independence, and there is not on the globe a human power that is capable of arresting its impetuous march." The only recourse available by which Spain might still maintain its influence in America would be to recognize the independence of those countries that had achieved it. And it must be done promptly. "One of the chief motives that ought to impel our government to a prompt recognition is the consideration that, if Spain does not so act, there are other nations that are ready to do so." He even suggested that the American nations might be willing to grant Spain special trade privileges and a pecuniary subsidy, and might even allow

Spain to retain some ports or even an entire province in America in repayment for prompt recognition. In a second memoir submitted three days later by the Spanish deputy Francisco Golfín, Cabrera de Nevares suggested a confederation of the different states with Ferdinand as its ruler and with a federal congress.[3] These suggestions by Cabrera de Nevares were not, of course, original ideas.

The overseas committee of the Cortes, however, was not prepared to consider the more extreme proposals of the government. In a report presented on 24 January the committee expressed the opinion that it was not necessary to occupy the Cortes's time with the government proposals because some suggestions related to matters over which the Cortes had no authority, others had already been agreed on, and still others were not amenable to discussion nor would the Americans respond favorably to them. Instead, the committee suggested another old idea—that commissioners be chosen to go to America to confer with the dissident governments, receiving in writing the proposals of the Americans. These proposals would be sent to the Cortes, which would remain in session until they had been acted on.

Lively debate followed the report of the overseas committee. The trend of opinion seemed clearly against the government's suggestions, which would imply refusal to recognize independence, and in favor of the committee's, which left something of an open door in that regard. At any rate, two Mexican deputies—Lucas Alamán and José María Puchet—favored the committee's proposal precisely because, in their interpretation, it opened communication, which was a necessary first step to Spain's formal recognition of American independence. A spokesman for the Ministry of Ultramar was forced to rise and say that the feeling that the committee report was a move toward recognition of independence was a misinterpretation, and suggested the addition of a clause to the committee report saying in so many words that the sending of commissioners would be purely a means of conciliation. Without this waiver, he said, the government would not accept Cortes action in regard to commissioners. Minister Pelegrín, on 13 February, announced that this plan, and the waiver clause amended to it, were acceptable to the government. Juan Gómez de Navarrete, deputy from Michoacán, accused the government of trying to nullify the committee's action by adding this clause.

Thus the Cortes concluded debate on the issue in the ensuing days by concentrating on the waiver clause and the plan to send commissioners. The Mexican deputies now opposed the plan, since the addition of the clause closed the door on whatever real conciliation the commissioners might be able to work out with the American governments. Meanwhile, two Spanish deputies, the Conde de Toreno and José María Moscoso, proposed four further additions to the overseas committee suggestion. The first was that the Cortes declare the Treaty of Córdoba celebrated between Iturbide and O'Donojú, and any other act acknowledging Mexican independence, to be illegitimate and void. Second, that Spain would consider it a treaty violation for any friendly nation to recognize the independence of Spanish American territories. Third, that the government propose further methods of strengthening America's ties to the mother country. And fourth, that those overseas provinces that had declared independence and that did not recognize Spanish supremacy should not be represented in the Cortes. The final point was withdrawn, being needlessly provocative to those American deputies still sitting, but the other points were quickly adopted. The decree of the Cortes was adopted on 13 February. It declared Spain would again send commissioners to America, this time to the rebellious governments, to hear the propositions of those governments. The Treaty of Córdoba and any other act signed between O'Donojú and Iturbide were declared null and illegitimate in Spain's view. Spain would send declarations to other powers that recognition of the partial or absolute independence of the overseas territories would be viewed as a violation of existing treaties, since Spain had not renounced any of its rights over its colonies. And finally, the government would do whatever was possible to preserve whatever loyal provinces existed overseas.[4] On that same day, the extraordinary session having completed its more important domestic business, the Conde de Toreno observed that the overseas committee felt that remaining American business should be carried over to the next Cortes. There being no opposition, the Cortes closed its special session. The remaining American deputies, except for a handful from the Caribbean, had entirely withdrawn by that day.[5]

Thus the Cortes pulled back once again from a grant of genuine new concessions to America or a possible consideration of the recognition of American independence, and instead ended up deciding to send commissioners to "hear" the dissident governments. This lame proposal was tied down with a waiver declaring Spain's only intention was to open the door to conciliation, not to consider settlement on American terms, and the strong rejection of the Treaty of Córdoba indicated that Spain would not accept treaties worked out in its name by any of its own officials. The statement warning the foreign powers against recognition would be perceived by American dissidents and rebel governments as closing further consideration of negotiation. Finally, the withdrawal of the few remaining American deputies meant that when the Cortes reopened in its new regular session shortly thereafter, none of the rebellious countries would be directly heard.

One element in Spain's continued unwillingness to deal with the genuinely changed world of America was the continued nostalgia of its policy planners for the days when American bullion and trade had enriched the motherland and enhanced its self-image. In 1821 the king had appointed a high-level committee of nine men with records of distinguished service in America to propose new policies in American trade regulations. This committee had presented a long but totally inept report on 16 June 1821. In it they attempted to measure the trade that had existed between Spain and each of the overseas territories. Most of their statistics, however, were drawn from the 1790s or else from Humboldt's studies in 1803 and 1804, and were thus hopelessly out of date. Still, on the basis of statistics from 1790 for Buenos Aires, 1792 for Mexico, Guatemala, and New Granada, 1793 for Venezuela, and 1811 for Peru, they deduced that Spain's total trade with America in both directions had been 108 million pesos a year. Only in the case of Cuba did they have more recent statistics, showing the annual trade in 1816 was 21 million pesos. Recognizing that foreign powers had almost entirely supplanted Spain in the trade with the New World, they urged the king to remember that Spain's future independence rested on modernizing its commercial system and its merchant marine. With this motivation, the committee, flying directly in the face of the trends that were developing in 1821, recommended that Spain restrict all trade and navigation in America and the peninsula to national ships and crews. Since Spain lacked both ships and sailors, the committee recommended that permission be granted for five years for the purchase of foreign ships by Spaniards and that for five years half of the crews could be composed of foreign mariners. In order to attract capital for the construction of a new merchant marine, investors were to be allowed tax incentives for building ships, and various free ports should be established in America and Spain.

The committee report on trade was finally considered by the Council of State in December 1821, and it reported itself disinclined to undertake a revision of American trade regulations at a time when America was in such turmoil. It advocated doing nothing until America's political loyalties were determined. The king accepted this advice, and on 27 March 1822 suspended further consideration of the question as long as the overseas provinces remained in their present condition.[6] It is, nonetheless, startling to realize that as late as 1821 a special committee should have urged the reestablishment of Spanish trade exclusivity for an America that had long ago rejected it and for a Spain that no longer possessed adequate shipping to undertake it.

It was now the government's task to decide precisely what the powers and instructions of the new commissioners to America should be, and how many of them should be appointed. A committee of the Ministry of Ultramar pointed out that the commissioners would be useless unless they were empowered to enter into negotiations with the insurgent governments. But the Council of State urged that the commissioners should "listen to the insurgents and negotiate with them without deciding anything." Shortly after the regular session of the Cortes opened in March, the deputy Juan José Sánchez urged that the commissioners be empowered to negotiate six-year truces in the various countries, during which time the Spanish government would refrain from interference in the affairs of those countries, and that they be authorized to negotiate provisional trade treaties. The Ministry of Ultramar rejected the first proposal as being in danger of tying the hands of the government in those countries where royal armies were still in the field, but it found no objection to allowing the commissioners to "initiate negotiations and frame treaties of commerce with the de facto governments that were established where Spain no longer had any military influence," so long as the ministry and Cortes had the final approval. On 4 May the Council of State approved this point of view, with the exception of three members who in separate opinions suggested radically different policies. Gabriel Císcar, the former regent, continued his ultra-liberal line by urging full recognition of the independence of the American states, pointing out that the commissioners' jobs would be impossible if they lacked such authority. As long as Spain did not recognize independence the American countries would be unable to negotiate and unwilling to reach agreements. The Marqués de Piedrablanca urged that the commissioners be sent immediately, no matter what their powers, owing to the danger of foreign incursions in America. And the Conde de Taboada urged that the commissioners be empowered to recognize American independence if the countries would become constitutional monarchies under princes of the Spanish royal house.[7]

The arrival of the unsettling news that President James Monroe had announced in his message to Congress of 8 March 1822 that the United States would recognize the independence of some of the new Spanish-American nations appears to have given the liberal regime in Spain renewed interest in sending the commissioners, as it would be possible to cite it as evidence that Spain had not withdrawn from its colonies but was even then formulating a new policy. Joaquín de Anduaga, Spanish minister to Washington, dispatched a strongly-worded note of protest to the United States government, complaining of Spain's ill treatment by a government to which it had given such recent and notable favors as the cession of the Floridas. Protesting that there were no solid and dependable governments to recognize in Spanish America, he asked: "Where is the proof that these provinces will not reunite with Spain when enough of their inhabitants desire it, and where is the right of the United States to sanction and declare legitimate a rebellion that has been without cause and whose success is still not decided? I solemnly protest against the recognition of the so-called governments of the insurgent Spanish provinces of America by the United States; declaring that this in no way can, now or ever, diminish nor invalidate in the slightest the right of Spain to those provinces and to employ whatever measures are at its disposal to reunite them to the rest of its dominions." But privately Anduaga wrote the minister of state, Martínez de la Rosa, that the mistreatment of which he had complained "is and will always be the price of weakness." He said he would withdraw to Philadelphia in order to avoid meeting the new ministers of Colombia, Mexico, and other countries who would soon be arriving in Washington.[8]

Spain acted quickly to counteract what damage the United States move toward recognition might have on the European Powers. Instructions were sent to the Spanish diplomats in London, Paris, Vienna, St. Petersburg, and Berlin telling them to say that Spain did not recognize the de facto governments in the dissident American provinces directly or indirectly. The diplomats were to remind the European governments that the United States was predisposed to American independence and that its policy was governed by self-interest. The representatives in Vienna and Berlin were to remind those governments of the need to assure the stability of legitimate governments and to prevent America from becoming "an open theater of revolution." The Russian government was to be reminded that Spain expected it to be one of its principal supporters, that the United States opposed the existence of Russian colonies in North America, and that Russia's interests were therefore in accord with Spain's.[9]

Shortly thereafter, Martínez de la Rosa sent a longer manifesto to the ambassadors at the European courts, in which he denounced the recognition by the United States as a violation of Spain's rights and set forth Spain's official view on independence. His Majesty could console himself, the manifesto said, with the knowledge that the American desire for separation was not the product of abuses of power or the weight of oppression but rather the crisis of the Napoleonic invasion. This was an internal Spanish matter, not amenable to intervention. The king was even now appointing commissioners to go to the various parts of America, hear their propositions, and transmit them to Spain. "There has never been initiated a more important transaction. Nor is it possible that any government has ever prepared to initiate such a negotiation with greater loyalty and good faith." It was also a question of importance to Europe in general, he said, because the spread of revolution could not but influence political relations in Europe. The "mere fact" that a province had separated from the state of which it had been a part did not give it the right of recognition by other powers. To believe it did was merely to recognize the right of insurrection and its implications for Europe were thus obvious. The manifesto went on to point out that Spain's attitude toward trade exclusivity had entirely altered, that Spain had abandoned its exclusive monopoly, that the prosperity of the overseas provinces depended now on a "frank and liberal system." All the laws and actions of the liberal regime since the restoration of the Constitution tended toward an attitude favorable to foreign colonization and trade in America, he insisted. The civil war and the political instability of the American dissident states, however, were hardly conducive to the commercial interests of the European Powers. The manifesto concluded with the standard reference to the weakness and instability of the rebel governments.[10]

It is fascinating to watch Spain working out and beginning to state its official rationale in the face of the awareness of its defeat and the loss of its empire. It was not mere posturing, however, for when official Spain referred to the "rebellious overseas provinces" it was adopting a term that would be employed well into the 1830s. United States recognition was clearly the symbol that the end of the empire was at hand, but, like the Portuguese recognition of Buenos Aires before it, official Spain interpreted it as an aberration based on the self interest and even the wishful thinking of the power involved. The official rationale, then, in all its contradiction, was: that the dissident American provinces had been driven to rebellion by the imperial crisis of 1808–14 and not by Spanish oppression or abuse; that the countries that had merely separated from Spain were not independent sovereign states; that the turmoil and confusion of government in those de facto independent countries was so extreme that they might at any time reunite themselves with the mother country; and that recognition of them by another nation encouraged the dark menace of general revolution that postwar Europe so much feared.

This rationale, it should be emphasized, was the point of view of an increasingly radical constitutional government, for by 1822 the more extreme liberals were beginning to exercise increased influence in the constitutional regime. In the elections for the 1822–23 regular Cortes, the *exaltado* radicals showed major gains, winning a majority. To counter the *exaltado* majority the king had named Francisco Martínez de la Rosa, another "jailbird" and moderate, as chief minister of a third cabinet in March 1822. For several months the new cabinet tried to function but found the task impossible in the face of the hostility of the Cortes, which elected Rafael Riego, the ultimate symbol of the radicals, as its president and declared his "Hymn" the national anthem. The crisis intensified until 1 July 1822, when four of the six battalions of the royal guards marched out of Madrid and led liberals to the assumption that a royal coup to overthrow the Constitution was at hand. The Martínez ministry tried to resign, but the ministers were forcibly confined to their offices by order of the king. On 6 July the royal guards tried to overpower Madrid, but were defeated and disarmed by radical militia, regular regiments, and volunteers led by Riego and Evaristo San Miguel. This compelled the king to name a radical government headed by San Miguel, the fourth ministry since the restoration of the Constitution, which took office on 10 July 1822.

In this context, the attitude of the king toward the American independence also began to define the official Spanish view. In many subtle ways the king's attitude had to be considered, for he possessed the counterbalancing power to the government, not only because he could exercise his extensive constitutional powers, but also because he remained the symbol of legitimacy, of authority, and of the state itself. The king's attitude toward America was totally wrapped up in his attitude toward the constitutional system and the governments that he viewed as his oppressors. By early 1821 Ferdinand had established highly secret communications with the Holy Allies, chiefly with Russia and France, through which he plotted with them the overthrow of the constitutional regime. His chief confidants were the Count Bulgari, Russian chargé in Madrid, the Viscount Montmorency Laval, French secretary of foreign relations, and the Count La Garde, French ambassador to Madrid. The Spaniards who were his chief co-conspirators included several members of the former camaril-la and several leading militarists returned from the American wars. The Marqués de Casa Irujo, Spanish ambassador in Paris, served as a major co-conspirator. Francisco Eguía, living in exile in Bayonne, was designated as the king's spokesman in southern France. And Pablo Morillo, former captain general of New Granada, was designated as an absolutely trustworthy friend. By June 1821 Count Bulgari presented to Ferdinand, and Ferdinand approved by certifying with his rubric, a tentative plan for the king to overthrow the ministry by a coup and impose a new government that would include such trustworthy people as Morillo. "Two important considerations should oblige the king to make a quick decision within a very few days," Bulgari wrote for the king's approval. One was the return of the king of Portugal to Lisbon, which it was expected would unleash a planned counter-revolution against the liberal regime there. "The other circumstance militating for the prompt execution of this plan is the imminent danger that threatens Spain of the loss of its vast and rich colonies. His Majesty should persuade himself that they will be irremediably lost if important steps are not taken in Spain." These were, in essence, the thoughts of the Russian emperor, transmitted by Bulgari to Ferdinand.[11]

Ferdinand replied to Bulgari, for transmission to the emperor, in a long letter in his own hand. He said he could not take the emperor's advice to stage a simple coup because he lacked the support of the army; he needed outside financial or military aid. France and England, he said, were the two powers that wished him most harm, and they were motivated in this by their desire to see America independent:

> France and especially England are the two Powers who together are the secret promoters of the disturbances in Spain because they alone are those who will most immediately seize the fruit. England has for many years secretly worked for the indepen-dence of the Spanish Americas from the metropolis (which is the

hobgoblin in all this) in order to be master of the seas and to acquire, among other advantages, that of having free direct commerce, which will produce many millions and will also lead to the dismemberment from Spain of such rich and powerful possessions with nearly 20 million souls, from which dismemberment it will have nothing to fear from Spain in the future. France has the same interests, by and large, because with the emancipation of the Americas it will also have direct commerce with them and Spain will be reduced to the 10 million souls who compose the Peninsula, freeing it from the powerful influence that Spain had when united with America to oppose France in whatever political event, and thus all their effort leads to gaining time for the emancipation of the Americas, which is not far off.[12]

So Ferdinand, speaking for himself and unobstructed by the formality of courtly language, interpreted American independence as the hobgoblin that was the prime cause of the political troubles he faced in Spain. The revolution at home and the revolution in America were one and the same thing, two faces of a single coin.

Despite his reservations about the long-term objectives of French policy, Ferdinand soon opened direct correspondence with the Bourbon king of France, Louis XVIII, who seemed in the most advantageous position for assisting the overthrow of the revolution with military aid. By January 1822 Ferdinand corresponded with Louis through Francisco Eguía in Bayonne. Transfers of money began to occur, letters in cipher and secret codes were transmitted, Ferdinand kept in his personal file letters from France he had copied out in his own hand. An agent to France carried the king's signature for corroboration.[13] In a personal letter to Louis in February Ferdinand spoke of his moral captivity, the great dangers surrounding him and the royal family, and the request for armed intervention "sufficient to organize and pacify my kingdom, making in it the reforms and improvements compatible with the dignity and security of my throne." Ferdinand's appeal to Louis was pointed—that the Spanish liberals planned the spread of their extreme Jacobinism to the rest of

Europe and that France would be the first victim. The new Cortes was about to sit, and the need for intervention was urgent. Ferdinand was convinced that the royal family was in personal danger, as the specter of the French revolution's regicide was never far from his thoughts. He promised to recompense France in any way he could for its aid in rescuing him. He designated as his trusted agents in France the Marqués de Casa Irujo, the Duke of Fernán Núñez, Pedro Labrador, and Francisco Eguía.[14]

By July 1822, as the government was discussing what precise instructions the commissioners to America should have, the king was discussing what precise form of government he would establish in Spain with French armed intervention. He asked the French representative Count La Garde to come to his room to discuss whether it was absolutism he wished to restore. "I have said to you and I repeat it now that it has never been my intention that things should return to the regimen that is incorrectly called absolutism."[15] The French made the establishment of a moderate form of government their chief condition for aiding Ferdinand. By this point they had even worked out a code for written communication within the palace, certain persons being designated by numbers, and Ferdinand had invented a special sign to begin his letters with which to authenticate them. A few days later he wrote the French king directly, assuring him he would not restore the old absolutism but not committing himself on the French desire that he retain the Cortes or reestablish it in the more traditional form of a Cortes of the estates. The government had prohibited him from going to the Escorial, and he repeated that he and the royal family were prisoners.[16] By this time he was receiving huge sums of money from the French. On 26 July he signed a receipt for one-and-a-half million reales he had received from La Garde.[17] And again the colonial question was linked. The Russian representative, Bulgari, urged Ferdinand to sweeten the pot for French intervention not only by offering full indemnification but also by promising France some American territory in return for its expenses and effort. Bulgari suggested that Ferdinand offer France not only Santo Domingo but whatever other colony the French might wish.[18]

Apparently Ferdinand never went so far as to offer France

American territory, because he was himself convinced by mid-1822 that the empire was lost. In an extraordinary letter to Alexander I he repeated all of his complaints against the Constitution of Cádiz and the anarchists now in power, urging the emperor to realize that they threatened all the thrones of Europe. "Until the edifice raised by revolution is destroyed there is no sovereign secure on his throne, because we will all perish, some earlier and some later." In an extraordinary extension of his logic, the king drew together in one sentence all the dangers threatening Spain and its empire and made it clear in this highly confidential note that he knew the American territories were gone: "The Constitution formed in Cádiz, and the revolution made in Spain, were the work of the machinations of those who desired to separate the Americas from the metropolis. Thus it has happened. Now they are lost, and only with difficulty can they be recovered."[19] Thus the king again asserted his belief that the loss of America and the liberal revolution at home shared primary links. Though he recognized that American separation was now a fact, he also felt that the recovery of the colonies was a possibility. He did not abandon that illusion throughout the rest of his life.

That this vain illusion was shared by most members of the Cortes and the Spanish government is indicated by the discussion about framing precise instructions for the American commissioners and by the instructions themselves. Preliminary instructions for the commissioners were approved on 16 May 1822. In June a Cortes committee suggested that additional instructions be drawn up to determine measures to protect loyalists in the Indies and to encourage the establishment of commerce between America and Spain. In the ensuing discussion, several Cortes members strongly urged that the commissioners also be granted the power to recognize, acknowledge, or at least imply future recognition of American independence. Alcalá Galiano, for one, asked rhetorically if it were possible for Spain to restore its control. Since the answer was no, he urged that the commissioners be empowered to negotiate independence in return for trade advantages, that Spain in effect say to America, "Here is your independence. Give us, in return, some advantages."[20] The Cortes, however, rejected this, making it clear that no serious negotiations with the American governments could occur. The minister of the United States, interpreting these discussions for his government, wrote home that "there exists a perverse determination not to adopt the only measure which promises to be advantageous to Spain."[21] In the end, the Cortes did agree to expand the commissioners' instructions somewhat to allow them to negotiate provisional treaties of commerce with the revolted provinces. This decision, taken on 28 June 1822, also allowed supporters of Spain to come to the peninsula or other loyal parts of the empire, and allowed Spanish Americans or Spaniards living in America to move to the peninsula with their property. Thus, although Spain was prepared to act as if the game were up in America, it was not prepared to recognize independence, which would naturally be the basic condition for the dissident governments.[22] This obviously guaranteed the failure of the commissioners while signaling the British that they would have to proceed to recognition, if they were ever going to do so, without waiting on their Spanish ally.

The reason for Spain's obstinate dedication to the proposition that it would not recognize independence was Madrid's view, long simmering and now fully formed, that the political instability of the Spanish American states, the rise of party factionalism and of military caudillism, guaranteed the emergence of some movement to reunite with Spain. In the instructions drawn up in May for the commissioners, the government set forth a number of assertions—several unsubstantiated but no less firmly held—about the political condition of the American states. Among other things, the commissioners were informed that "Opinion in America is not fixed decisively either for independence or for the continuation of union with the metropolis; that is to say, there is a numerous party inclined to the first, in the major part seduced by the charms of a liberty that they themselves do not know how to explain and that will never be greater than that conceded by the Spanish Constitution; and there is another much larger party for the second [point of view] to which is united the general mass of the people and almost all the Indians generally, who, guided by the principles they were taught in their youth, are worshippers of their King, and conserve a purity of religion that makes them believe that everything that opposes submission and obedience offends." The commissioners were told to try to make use of this habit of submission. The government also asserted that there was a large party of support for the Spanish constitutional system in America and that its major opponents came chiefly from the regular clergy.

In each of the independent countries, according to the instructions, there existed different opinions about the form of government to be established there. Where the revolution was oldest these parties had already clashed, and it was greatly to be expected that they would also do so in the new countries. "And in one and the other this difference of opinion, or rather this thirst for power, which is what the overseas insurrection constitutes thus far, has to produce frightful evils." Though the commissioners should not take part in these struggles they should adapt their operations in light of them. If a government was about to fall, they should wait for its replacement before beginning serious negotiations. Furthermore, it was asserted that, in those countries that had suffered long wars of independence, "the people do not aspire to anything more than peace and a return to belonging to Spain," and that in the countries where independence resulted from a coup the people had not yet got over their surprise and were still in suspense. Thus the commissioners should expect to be greeted with joy, wherein they risked offending the new governments and should take care not to do so. They would find that in most places the upper classes and principal persons of fortune had not taken part in the revolutions or had done so only after being forced into it. They would also find such extreme provincialism that each province refused to be subject to another. Probably the commissioners would hear many complaints about the government officials Spain had sent out, especially those in the 1814–20 period. Although there was some justification in this complaint, it was not generally valid, especially since the restoration of the Constitution. The presence of foreign soldiers of fortune was a potential problem. Since their livelihood depended on the wars, they might oppose efforts to end them. Their presence would be very dangerous once peace was concluded. Other foreign powers should be kept uninvolved.

Several of the new governments, the commissioners were told, had decreed the end of slavery. The commissioners should generally oppose this, though it was a very delicate question and one they could not press too hard. The commissioners should try to limit the amount of scurrilous or insulting remarks appearing in the American press about Spain, and they should inform the American governments that the insulting statements carried in the Spanish military press (especially from Cuba) about the new leaders were not ordered by the Spanish government. The commissioners were informed that some of the American countries had written their own constitutions, usually copied largely from the Spanish Constitution. They should remind the Americans that the Spanish Constitution offered what they were seeking, and in a far more perfect form than their own. Finally, the commissioners were not to let it be thought that their mission was the same as that of the peace commissioners who came in 1820.[23]

These extraordinary instructions fittingly summarize Spain's official attitude toward the accomplished fact of Spanish American independence. They insisted, in essence, that it was a temporary separation only. In May the commissioners were named by a panel consisting of several of the chief former royalist officials in America. The commissioners were Juan Ramón Osés and Santiago Irisarri for Mexico, the Marqués de Casa Ramos and Brigadier Francisco del Pino for Guatemala (this commission lapsed because Guatemala was part of Mexico), Brigadier José Sartorio and naval Captain Juan Barry for Colombia, and Antonio Luis Pereyra and Colonel Luis de la Robla for Buenos Aires. Commissioners for Peru and Chile were to be chosen later, but they never were. The commissioners for Mexico left Cádiz on 7 October 1822; Robla left for Buenos Aires to join Pereyra, who was living in Rio de Janeiro; and the instructions for Sartorio and Barry in Costa Firme were dispatched.[24] Before sailing they were given "additional instructions" dated 4 August 1822, largely dealing with the provisional commercial agreements that they could negotiate.

The commissioners, when they were finally appointed and duly instructed, met with as little success as the 1820 peace commissioners had. Osés and Irisarri, the commissioners to Mexico, reached the castle of San Juan de Ulloa in Veracruz harbor, where a handful of royalists occupied the fort, in January 1823. They entered into negotiations with the agents of the emperor, Iturbide, who had been instructed to demand recognition of independence as a first step before further negotiation could take place. After Iturbide was overthrown in April 1823, the new government of Guadalupe Victoria made the same demand. Since Spain's agents were unable to meet this demand, no further discussions took place and the Mexican government ordered the Spanish commissioners to depart. The agents to Gran Colombia, meanwhile, failed to receive the funds for traveling from Havana to Bogotá and thus never got to their destination. The commissioners to Río de la Plata achieved the most success. Luis de la Robla and Antonio Pereyra went to Montevideo, where they entered into communication with the government of Bernardino Rivadavia of the United Provinces of La Plata. The legislature of Buenos Aires decreed that no treaty could be adopted with Spain until Spain terminated hostilities with all the American states and recognized their independence. Thus the Buenos Aires government worked out a preliminary treaty of peace calling for cessation of hostilities between Spain and the United Provinces and dispatched notes to Chile, Peru, and Upper Peru urging them to send agents to Spain or to open negotiations. A provisional treaty of commerce was also projected. In August 1823 the Cortes was urged by the overseas committee to open negotiations with Spanish agents on the bases that the Americans "should consider most suitable, without, in case of necessity, excluding independence." Before these negotiations could proceed, the French invasion ended the radical government in Spain.

After the restoration of Ferdinand VII to full authority, the king decreed that all acts of the constitutional government were null and void, for he had sanctioned them under duress. In December 1823 the Council of the Indies proposed that all proceedings of the Cortes with regard to the pacification of America should be annulled. And on 26 January 1824 the king issued such a decree, declaring null and of no value the powers granted to the commissioners by the "so-called constitutional government" and decreeing as illegitimate any negotiations they had undertaken, ordering them to return immediately to Spain.[25]

The number of Spaniards fleeing independent America was now great, and it would intensify in the next few years when to the Spaniards fleeing from Mexico and Central America were added those from Peru. To take account of this the Cortes decreed in November 1822 that Spanish emigrants from America returning to Spain might introduce their belongings in gold, silver, or other goods duty free, or paying only nominal duties if the ship they sailed on had happened to touch at a foreign port, regardless of whether they sailed in a Spanish or foreign vessel.[26]

At the same time, the Spanish government received and duly noted a series of long memorials by Luis Galabert, a French-born officer who had long been in service to Spain, for which he was awarded a colonel's salary. Galabert presented a three-part series of ideas on how to defend the Indies, how to reconquer Mexico, and how to keep the United States and other foreign powers out of Texas and other parts of Spanish America. In October 1822 he presented a report on how to defend Cuba from the triple threat of Haitian invasion, United States aggression, and Mexican attack. It was particularly feared that the Mexican emperor, Iturbide, who had placed orders in the United States for the construction of four steamships, was contemplating the seizure of Cuba. To counter the threat, he urged the creation of local militias of all the inhabitants in Cuba, along with the creation of a Spanish fleet of steamships. These steamships would then be used to disembark an attack party in Tampico that could march inland and seize Mexico's major mining centers at San Luis Potosí, Guanajuato, and Zacatecas. From there, the Spanish could make rapid marches on Guadalajara and Mexico City, paralyzing the empire and destroying Iturbide. In December, in a second report, Galabert recommended the appointment of a viceroy for Mexico, who, accompanied by 3,000 soldiers, would land in Mexico, where he would, Galabert assumed, be recognized as the legitimate ruler by the Mexican people, who would still respond to the prestige of a royal viceroy. While the new viceroy marched overland to Mexico City he would somehow create an army in the north to defend against United States encroachments. This was an interesting foreshadowing of the assault plan of simultaneous attack against the northern states and against the heartland via Veracruz that would be adopted twenty-five years later by the United States in its successful war with Mexico. It was also essentially the plan Spain employed in an unsuccessful attempt to reconquer Mexico in 1829. Finally, Galabert drew together his many contradictory ideas in a memorial entitled *La América, los Ingleses, los Estados Unidos y la España.*[27]

The painful reality of Spain's military situation in America was illustrated by the attempt throughout 1822 to respond to the desperate pleas of the captain general of Puerto Rico that the naval forces in the Caribbean be strengthened in order to protect normal mail delivery and communication between Puerto Rico, Cuba, and the remaining royalist enclaves on Venezuela's coast. In December 1821 the minister of the navy reported there was no money to outfit new ships or even to pay the sailors. Though the Cortes ordered the ministry to equip and prepare ships, this was no solution. In January 1822 the king ordered five ships to Callao on the Pacific, with others for Puerto Cabello and Havana. Not until March 1822 was an offer forthcoming by a naval contractor to equip the necessary ships—and those were only for Havana and Puerto Cabello, not for Callao. In July 1822 the Cortes decreed a special loan of fifty million reales for the exclusive purpose of arming and equipping the ships.[28] In the end, no ships were sent to Peru, and rebel control of the coast was so secure that after Cochrane's fleet left Peruvian rebel service in October 1821 the independent government of San Martín in Lima could proceed to the creation of a Peruvian fleet without fear of royalist attack on the coast. The absence of a Spanish fleet on the Pacific went a long way toward guaranteeing the eventual victory of the rebels in Peru. The royalist forces under the command of Miguel de La Torre, clinging to Puerto Cabello on the coast of Venezuela, were never relieved by royal ships either. They held out under siege and amid great privation until 1823. Galabert's plan to reconquer Mexico with a fleet of brand-new steam-powered warships takes on a certain absurdity in the light of Spain's inability to refloat or equip its own decrepit fleet.

Any further consideration of possible means of American pacification was put aside in late 1822 by the internal political crisis that gripped Spain. After the defeat of the royal guards in July, Ferdinand consented to the appointment of the fourth ministry of the constitutional period, a ministry composed of *exaltado* radicals, all of whom were Masons, under Evaristo San Miguel. It is assumed that Ferdinand's motive in accepting such an extremist government was to create an internal situation that would provoke foreign intervention, the negotiations for which were already well advanced. The Holy Alliance, which had already authorized a successful armed intervention by Austria against the constitutional governments in Naples and Piedmont, met in the Congress of Verona in October 1822 and there gave France the mandate to suppress the constitutional regime in Spain. Of the Great Powers, only the British opposed the intervention. On 6 January 1823 the French, Russian, Austrian, and Prussian ambassadors presented identical notes to the Spanish foreign minister demanding that the king be restored to his rights. Ten days later the envoys demanded their passports. At the same time, the Papal Nuncio withdrew from Madrid in opposition to the government's proposals for radical clerical reform. On 25 January, King Louis XVIII told the French Chamber of Deputies that an army of 100,000 men —"sons of Saint Louis," he called them—under command of the Duke of Angoulême, was about to march to save the throne of Spain. In Madrid, the impending foreign invasion led the Cortes to authorize the government to move to Seville.

Ferdinand's own testimony describes the crisis that followed. The king, informed by the government of the decision to transfer to Seville, refused for several weeks to agree to accompany it as the government demanded. On 18 February 1823 the seven ministers presented him a representation, signed by all of them, firmly calling on him to go with them. As a result, on the next day Ferdinand deposed the cabinet and replaced it with the chief officials of each ministry. This provoked a mob assault against the palace, where for the first time the crowd cried, "Death to the King," shouting insults against the royal family and, according to Ferdinand, "treating the queen [his third wife, María Amalia of Saxony] and the infantas like public women." This provoked Ferdinand to restore the cabinet, but over the ensuing days most of the ministers resigned on their own. By the end of the month the king had selected a new compromise ministry.

When the Cortes reopened on 1 March it gave the king a twenty-four-hour deadline to name the location in the south to which he would retreat, and promised to send him against his will if necessary. Ferdinand spent several days stalling, insisting his health did not permit travel. Although he was only thirty-eight years old, he suffered from gout. On 11 March he called together a panel of doctors chosen by himself, and they testified that he was not well enough to travel. In retaliation, the Cortes chose a commission to interview the king's doctors, and they reported that he was fit to travel. Thus on 20 March the king gave in to the pressure and departed Madrid with the entire royal family. After fifteen years on the throne, this was the king's first visit ever to his southern provinces of Andalusia. This novelty, combined with his intense consciousness of lese majesty, provoked the king to dictate to his private secretary in 1824 a day-by-day account known as the Real Itinerario.[29] The crisis of July 1822 had also provoked the creation in the north of an army of royalists who seized the town of La Seo de Urgel near the French border and proclaimed a regency in the name of the king, who they said was a prisoner of the radicals.

Ferdinand's trip to Seville lasted from 20 March to 11 April 1823, as he proceeded in easy stages via Valdepeñas, Bailén, Córdoba, Ecija, and Carmona. In Seville he and his brothers performed the familiar rites of the tourist, visiting the cathedral, the port district of Triana, the tobacco factory, the Giralda, and other sights. Two things most impressed him. One was the leather factory of Nathan Wetherell, which was equipped with the first steam engine Ferdinand had seen. The other was the Lonja, or board of exchange building, which now housed the Archivo de Indias. In the king's words, it was "composed of two grand and magnificent salons, with its marble floors and grandiose staircase, all in mahogany; but what is most interesting and recommendable are the precious documents that are kept there, relative to the Indies and their discovery."[30] The marble floors, the great staircase, the mahogany shelves, are all still there.

The documents preserve the record of the empire Ferdinand was even then losing. Meanwhile, as Ferdinand contemplated the documentary evidence of Spain's former power, the Cortes, meeting in Seville, debated a massive project, introduced in February 1823, to reorganize and rationalize local representation, cabildos, and provincial deputations in America. The speedy collapse of the liberal regime prevented the taking of any action.[31] Both king and Cortes thus paused for a moment to reflect on the vastness of their losses before plunging into the final crisis.

On 8 June 1823, a month after Ferdinand visited the Archive of the Indies, the government informed him that they must move to Cádiz because of the speed with which the French army of the Duke of Angoulême was marching toward the south. When Ferdinand refused this further indignity—because of his fear, he said, that the arrival of so many people in the port city would cause an outbreak of epidemic—the Cortes named a regency of three men (Cayetano Valdés, Gabriel Císcar, and Gaspar Vigodet) to replace him, determining that Ferdinand's refusal indicated his temporary incapacity to rule. The next day Ferdinand agreed to go to Cádiz as a virtual prisoner.

On 12 June the king and royal family fled hastily and amid confusion from Seville and proceeded down the road past mutinying members of the national militia of Madrid, who lined the king's route and shouted, "Death to all the Bourbons." For four days they journeyed in haste, according to the king's testimony, without stopping longer than a few hours and without the usual state residences to spend the nights in, in the stifling heat of June, "suffering without cease the greatest insults, entering the towns between two files of soldiers like prisoners of State."[32] The royal family was lodged in the customs house in Cádiz. On 18 June the interim Minister of War Estanislao Sánchez Salvador, convinced of the impossibility of defending the liberal regime, committed suicide in his residence. (There were no less than eight ministers of war during 1823). On 24 June the French army arrived at Puerto de Santo María, across the bay from Cádiz. The regency that had been created in order to overcome the deadlock when the king refused to go to Cádiz was disbanded on his arrival in the port and the king's royal powers were returned to him, but he never forgot or forgave the ultimate indignity of having been declared incapacitated to rule. The three temporary regents were the first targets of his anger when he was finally liberated.

The sole object of the Duke of Angoulême's forces was to achieve the liberation of the king. The French army thus established a siege of Cádiz that lasted for two months. In the last weeks of August the French attacked the Trocadero, the defense outwork on the bay side. The city, blockaded by land and sea, again underwent French bombardment as it had during the Napoleonic war. By 16 September the government was prepared to negotiate surrender, for clearly it lacked popular support and military defense. José Luyando, current head of the government, asked the king if he would promise a general amnesty for the defeated liberals. He said yes. Luyando asked him if he would offer a representative government. "I responded that I would give the government that the nation most desired." When Luyando asked him to name a government in Cádiz just in order to get out of there and said that the king could change things when he got to Madrid because "in the end Spain would be what [he] wanted it to be," the king answered that he would do nothing until he got to Madrid. When Luyando asked him again if he would appoint another representative government, he again replied, "I would give [the government] that the nation most desired," and stated that in order to name a government he no longer had to consult with deputies or ministers but only with the true will of the people.[33]

On 30 September Ferdinand signed decrees exonerating his ministers. On 1 October he was set free. "A happy day for me, for the royal family, and for all the nation; for we recovered at that moment our desired and just liberty, after three years, six months, and twenty days of the most ignominious slavery imposed upon us by a handful of conspirators and obscure and ambitious officers who, not even knowing how to write their names well, had raised themselves up as the regenerators of Spain, imposing on it the laws that suited them to obtain their sinister ends and make their fortunes, destroying the nation."[34] He crossed the bay with the royal family to Puerto de Santa María, where he was received by Angoulême. That same day he issued decrees annulling all the acts of the constitutional regime.

The constitutional regime fell as much from its own weaknesses as from the French invasion. The French troops, indeed, were greeted as liberators throughout most of the country and were met with little resistance even among the revolutionary officers. The Martínez de la Rosa ministry from March to August 1822 had tried to create fiscal responsibility, but in general the constitutional governments of the triennium had been characterized by fiscal mismanagement, economic greed, and inability to provide good government. The four constitutional governments had floated more than three billion reales in foreign loans. The liberals had engaged in a frenzy of patronage for themselves and their friends. Meanwhile, political factionalism had closed the door to the absorption into the government of talented individuals. As a result of the factionalism between *moderados* and *exaltados* the constitutional government was discredited.[35]

The day of the king's liberation, 1 October 1823, was the beginning of a vast wave of terror and reprisal, greater than the one that occurred in 1814, as Ferdinand and his supporters struck out in fury against the liberals who, in his view, had debased the throne, ignored his sovereignty, and conducted him to the very threshold of regicide. The king immediately broke his promise of amnesty by calling for the deaths of the men who had made up the temporary regency that deposed him in Seville. The day after his liberation he signed in Jérez an order forbidding constitutionalist officials and generals from coming within five miles of the route of his return journey to Madrid. In Madrid, meanwhile, the crowds seized a number of liberals and conducted them to jail. Before the month of October was over, the French king, Louis XVIII, alarmed at Ferdinand's breaking his promise not to reestablish absolutism, wrote the king warning that "blind despotism, far from increasing the power of kings, weakens it."[36] The Duke of Angoulême, shocked at the reprisals, warned Ferdinand: "All the efforts of France will be useless if Your Majesty continues loyal to the pernicious system of government that provoked the misfortunes of 1820. It is fourteen days since Your Majesty recovered your authority and still nothing is known from Your Majesty but detentions and arbitrary decrees; disquiet, fear, and discontent are beginning to spread. I ask Your Majesty to concede an amnesty and to give your people some guarantee for the future." The king did neither.[37] Huge crowds greeted Ferdinand at every stop on his return to Madrid, and he wrote happily at the conclusion of his personal account of his captivity, "These are the real people."[38] Before the king's arrival in Madrid a number of executions took place, the most prominent being that of Rafael Riego, who was hanged and quartered.

Finally, in December, and as a result of pressure from France and Russia, the king appointed a new ministry whose chief figure would be Minister of Justice Francisco Tadeo Calomarde, the man who was in charge of the "purification" of the civil service and military that went on for several years. All public employees lost their posts until juntas of purification investigated their past political action and found them untouched by the taint of liberalism. In May 1824 Calomarde issued an amnesty law that was largely the result of French pressure on the king to moderate the repression, but that seems to have had little effect. At any rate, in October 1824 a new decree established the death penalty for all "enemies of the legitimate rights of the throne . . . or partisans of the Constitution," as well as for authors of dissident pasquinades, Masons, persons advocating a change in the form of government, or persons shouting "Death to the king," "Long live Riego," "Long live the Constitution," "Death to the *serviles*," "Death to tyrants," and "Long live liberty."[39] This provoked a second and greater reign of terror, which lasted until the summer of 1825. One author estimates that in the general purge of Ferdinand's second restoration "44,000 people suffered imprisonment, 20,000 exile, and 100,000 loss of their posts."[40]

Ferdinand's purpose in the second restoration was not merely the extirpation of liberal elements, it was also, as Artola sketches it, the reestablishment of the entire texture and content of absolutism. From the time of his captivity in Cádiz the king's chief object was the creation not only of the Old Regime but of the "absolute absolutism" of his ally and friend Czar Alexander I. In pursuing this path, of course, he broke his frequent pledge to the French that he would not reestablish absolutism. He declared repeatedly that there would never be the slightest alteration in the fundamental laws of the monarchy or in the location of sovereignty in his royal person. In 1824 he publicly declared himself resolved "to conserve intact in all its plenitude the legitimate rights of my sovereignty, without ceding now nor at any time the smallest part of them, and without permitting the establishment of chambers or other institutions, whatever their title." There was no repetition of his promise of 1814 to create a proper Cortes. When Portugal received a new constitution in 1826, Ferdinand publicly circulated a statement that "whatever may be the circumstances in other countries, we will be governed by ours."[41] The object was to return Spain to a society of estates, returning privileges and properties to those institutions and individuals affected by the revolution.

This preoccupation with restoration led the king to decree the suppression of a free press, the restoration of mayorazgos (which required returning an estimated one billion reales worth of property that had been disentailed during the triennium), a review of all judicial decisions taken during the triennium, and a review of all titles of lawyers, public scribes, and procurators, and even of academic degrees granted during the triennium.[42] A renewed Council of State became the supreme organ in the administration, with its membership composed largely of extreme absolutists, called *apostólicos*, including Francisco Eguía, Antonio Ugarte, the former ambassador to the Vatican Antonio de Vargas Laguna, and the Infante Don Carlos. In 1825 the Council of State was even granted jurisdiction over American questions and over domestic peninsular questions. The ministers were required to meet weekly with the council and render detailed reports to it, thereby losing their previous status as a governing cabinet.

Historians still disagree on the precise nature of Ferdinand VII's government in the second restoration. Carr argues: "Nowhere have the preconceptions of liberals so distorted the history of Spain as in the description and judgment of what they term 'the ominous decade,'" and proceeds to point out that Ferdinand's major opposition during the decade came from those extreme royalists called *apostólicos* who advocated a virtual theocracy and who would later break away in support of the reactionary Don Carlos.[43] At best, however, there seems to be agreement that the regime was divided between royalists and super-royalists, who would come to be classified as moderates and Carlists. This being the case, the Spanish refusal to acknowledge American independence was beyond debate. The nullification of the powers of the commissioners dispatched by the Cortes ended all attempts at accommodation and even communication. The emphasis of the restoration was on the king's royal powers and authority, and this was reenforced as a first priority. In such an environment no thought could be or was given to possible recognition.

Meanwhile, British foreign secretary George Canning had engaged throughout the summer of 1823 in efforts to arrive at an agreement with the United States on a joint Anglo-American declaration designed to forestall possible intervention by the Holy Alliance in Spanish America, but this had come to nothing because of the insistence of the United States that England recognize the American republics. Canning had then turned to France, and on 9 and 12 October, during the very days following the liberation of Ferdinand VII, negotiated with Prince Polignac, representative of Louis XVIII in London, the Canning-Polignac memorandum, in which both sides affirmed their opposition to the use of force. This had the effect of satisfying the British cabinet in its fears of a possible French intervention in Spanish America while keeping open the possibility of collective mediation by the European Powers. Meanwhile, after his restoration, Ferdinand VII invited the members of the European alliance to a conference in Paris to discuss aid to Spain in suppressing the rebellions. Events moved too rapidly, however, for, in his message to Congress on 2 December 1823, President Monroe formulated the official view of the United States, to the effect that intervention by the Holy Allies to suppress the independence of Spanish America would constitute an unfriendly act toward the United States. This famous Monroe Doctrine did not impress the Europeans, but it did have the effect of forcing Canning to speed up his move toward accommodation with Spanish America in order to deny the United States the advantage of being the only major power to have recognized Latin American independence.

Thus Canning quickly replied to Spain's offer to meet in Paris to discuss European action to suppress the dissident colonies with a note of his own, dated 30 January 1824, in which he declared Britain's dedication to the proposition that force could not be used in the New World to restore a lost hegemony. He announced Britain's intention to recognize the independence of the established South American countries but expressed the wish that Spain do so first.[44] Spain was unmoved by this, but did agree, after both British and French pressure was applied, to issue on 9 February 1824 a decree throwing open the commerce of the New World to all friendly foreign nations.[45] This event, which might have saved an empire if the step had been taken years earlier, made hardly a ripple in the courts of Europe because, on the one hand, Spain never implemented the decree with specific regulations and, on the other, it was too late for Spain to exercise control over American commercial affairs. There is no indication it was even known in Spanish America. France and Austria had also come to realize the necessity of recognition, and the European Powers were merely jockeying with each other in an attempt to gain the greatest credit and the most advantageous trade agreements from the Latin Americans without simultaneously breaking their various alliances with Spain. France was in a particularly difficult position because its role as the upholder of Bourbon legitimacy limited its freedom of action. Forty thousand French troops still remained in Spain in 1824 to guarantee Ferdinand's security. The diplomatic maneuvering that accompanied this game was intense and complex and need not detain us here. The fact is, Europe, like the United States, moved inexorably toward recognition throughout 1824. Peru and Bolivia were still one year away from de facto independence, but Buenos Aires had enjoyed it for fourteen years, Colombia for five, Mexico for three. It was high time for recognition.

The inevitable was accomplished when in a note of 31 December 1824 Canning announced to Spain the British intention of negotiating treaties of commerce with the three Spanish American nations that had the most established governments and that possessed no direct threat of Spanish arms within or near their national territories—Mexico, Colombia, and the United Provinces of Río de la Plata. Canning sent a special representative to Madrid with this message, indicating the most scrupulous desire to break the news to Spain as gently as possible. He announced that his government was convinced that it was impossible to rejoin Mexico and Colombia to Spain, and pointed out that Buenos Aires had been established in its separation for many years longer. "In Peru a struggle is still maintained in behalf of the mother country. With regard to Peru therefore a just consideration of the rights of Spain, and for the chance, whatever it may be, of the practical assertion of them, forbids any interference on the part of His Majesty's Government." Since the condition of Chile was not clearly known, Britain would forbear to recognize it as well. The effect of treaties of commerce would be a diplomatic recognition of the governments of the three major countries. Canning concluded by offering the good offices of the British government "for the establishment of a friendly understanding with countries which [Spain] can no longer hope to reduce under her control."[46] Pressed with the need to make some rejoinder, Spain replied that such treaties would not invalidate its just claims to America.[47] Canning, pleased at having beaten the rest of Europe to a position of influence in Spanish America, wrote Lord Granville in Paris: "The deed is done, the nail is driven, Spanish America is free; and if we do not mismanage our affairs sadly, she is *English*."[48]

Not all the ripe fruit had yet fallen, however, for even as late as the end of 1824, as the British were informing Spain of their intention to recognize the three major Latin American states that together accounted for over two-thirds of the population of Spanish America, Peru and its reabsorbed appendage, Upper Peru, remained in Spanish control. Indeed, the Spanish under Viceroy José de la Serna had managed not only to hold out in Peru but in 1824 came very close to recapturing it. Although the Liberator, Simón Bolívar, had entered Peru in September 1823, he was forced to watch helplessly as the erstwhile independent government centered in Lima under its first president, José de la Riva Agüero, and its second president, the Marqués de Torre Tagle, rapidly disintegrated. Patriot armies deserted or collapsed in late 1823, and Torre Tagle opened negotiations with the royalists in an attempt to forestall the political dictatorship of Bolívar, whom he viewed as an interloper. In February 1824 a mutiny in the fort of Callao, Lima's port, returned the capital to royalist control. The royalist commander offered amnesty to any inhabitant of Lima who would support the royal cause, and almost the entire leadership of the republican forces, including the president, Torre Tagle, went over to the Spanish cause. Spanish general José Ramón Rodil held Lima, while the viceroy, La Serna, remained in Cuzco. Former president Torre Tagle called on the people of Peru to reject Bolívar, "the greatest monster that has existed in this land."[49]

The royalists held Lima from February to November 1824, while all the rest of the country except the province of Trujillo in the north—Bolívar's center of operations—returned to royalist hands. In response to the overthrow of the Constitution in Spain, Viceroy La Serna in March 1824 issued a formal decree in Cuzco abolishing all the acts of the constitutional government. Tadeo Gárate, royal intendant of Puno and one of the Persas of 1814, reported that in abolishing the Constitution Peru had undergone a "happy transition from democracy or anarchy to a legitimate Government recognized by all the world."[50] This news reached Spain by the end of 1824 and must have given considerable comfort in the face of the British recognition of Mexico, Colombia, and Buenos Aires.

Bolívar, however, did not give up, and spent most of 1824 in Trujillo rebuilding and reequipping his army, preparing it to march into the highland stronghold where Viceroy La Serna's army held sway. Meanwhile, the overthrow of the Constitution led to the disastrous mutiny of General Pedro Antonio Olañeta, royalist commander of Upper Peru. In January 1824, having been informed via Buenos Aires of the fall of the liberal regime in Spain before La Serna himself knew of it, Olañeta mutinied against the viceroy, seizing control of Upper Peru and implanting an absolutist regime composed of his own followers. Olañeta proclaimed absolute monarchy in the name of Ferdinand VII and declared himself commander of the "Provinces of the Río de la Plata." This action, which was incorrectly interpreted in Spain as the opening of a campaign against Buenos Aires, actually had the effect of crippling the viceroy in Cuzco, for it denied him the security of a friendly Upper Peru while it absorbed the attention of the royalists at the very moment Bolívar was at his weakest and most vulnerable to a combined royalist attack that could not take place.

La Serna's representatives in Spain submitted a bitter memorial to the peninsular government, accusing Olañeta of threatening the entire royal campaign in Peru. They urged that he be ordered to court for risking the reconquest of all Peru. The king, however, illustrated the danger of absolutism by ignoring the pleas of his own loyal officers and appointing Olañeta viceroy of Buenos Aires, on Olañeta's claim that he could reconquer the region. The appointment was suspended in May 1825 when the cabinet received word of the royalist defeat at Ayacucho, but, in an incredible Council of the Indies consultation in July, the councilors voted to overrule the strong objections of La Serna and allow Olañeta's appointment to stand.[51] This was "government by remote control" run completely amok because, besides the fact that Olañeta had personally sabotaged the royalist army in Peru, he was already dead by the time of the king's appointment.

The denial of the support of royalists in Upper Peru for the legitimate royal commander, Viceroy La Serna, meant that Bolívar could direct his attention wholly against the La Serna army. Bolívar's forces ascended into the Andes and on 6 August 1824 defeated a portion of the royalists at the battle of Junín. Both sides regrouped and prepared for what was recognized as the final showdown for the control of South America. La Serna's army was now the only loyal Spanish force left on the continent. As the royalist defense of Lima fell apart, Bolívar gained control of the coast of Peru by November 1824, leaving his highland army under the command of Antonio José de Sucre. The two armies met in the battle of Ayacucho on 9 December 1824. The royalists, exhausted by four years of resistance to independence, were defeated. Viceroy La Serna and his officers were taken prisoner and were permitted to leave Peru. The battle of Ayacucho ended Spanish power on the entire continent. Sucre, now bearing the title Marshal of Ayacucho, swept on to final victory over the dissident Olañeta (who was killed in battle) in Upper Peru in April 1825. Upper Peru was rechristened Bolivia. These last events were unfolding even as British diplomats arrived to open negotiations in Mexico City, Buenos Aires, and Bogotá.

The era of heroics was over; the time for vain martyrdom had come. There were four widely-separated instances of dramatic last-ditch stands by vestiges of the royal forces in America. The first was the attempt of Miguel de La Torre and a few troops to hold out at Puerto Cabello on the Venezuelan coast; it lasted until 1823. Meanwhile, following the surrender and withdrawal of the royal troops in Mexico in 1821, a vestige of the royal army seized the fort of San Juan de Ulloa in Veracruz harbor and held out there until November 1825. In the isolated archipelago of Chiloé, off the lower coast of Chile, royal naval forces under the command of Antonio Quintanilla held out against independent Chile until January 1826.

But by far the most dramatic of these gestures, and the only one to involve not only large numbers of troops but of royalist civilian collaborators as well, occurred at the forts of the port city of Lima, Callao. When Lima returned to patriot hands in November 1824, its intendant, José Ramón Rodil, withdrew to the forts at Callao and refused to surrender after the capitulation at Ayacucho. Rodil commanded a total of more than 2,500 royalist soldiers, who were joined by at least 3,000 civilians who sought refuge in the forts when Lima fell to Bolívar. The civilian refugees included former president Torre Tagle and his family, the former vice-president and his family, the former minister of war, nobles, merchants, members of the patriot congress, and many of the other former rebels who had collaborated with the royalists in the last year. Rodil thus made a final attempt to restore the honor of the royal flag, holding on to the strongest fortification on the entire Pacific coast in the vain hope that reinforcements might arrive by sea from Spain. The patriots imposed a siege by land and sea, and for over a year were able to deny the forts any further supplies.

Rodil—who by many accounts was a fanatic megalomaniac—imposed a regime of terror on the occupants, executing as many as 200 of them for conspiracy, spying on them, forcing those who had not brought their own provisions to leave. Little by little, 2,380 civilians were forced out of the forts to face the often hostile reception of the patriots. Many persons starved to death in the mile of land separating the two sides. After May 1825 Rodil ordered rations only for civil employees, soldiers, and collaborators. Chickens sold among the refugees for 25 to 30 pesos each. When stores were gone the refugees ate horses, mules, cats, dogs, and even rats, as scurvy and typhus swept the forts. When the forts were finally surrendered only 444 soldiers remained alive; 2,095 of them had died. Among the civilians the death toll was anywhere from 2,700 to 4,000, including the former president, vice-president, minister of war, governor of Lima, and director of the first Peruvian national bank. It was all a ghastly mistake, for there had never been any chance that Spanish ships might arrive to reinforce the defenders. It is not even clear if Spain even considered trying to send aid. On 11 January 1826 Rodil finally agreed to receive patriot negotiators, and an agreement for the surrender of the forts was signed on 22 January. Of the 444 surviving soldiers, 94 chose to go to Spain.[52] Rodil got passage on an English frigate then in port at Callao.

In Spain, Rodil's vain attempt at preserving a foothold in South America made him a hero. Before he could even disembark in Spain in August 1826 he was granted a commander's cross in the Order of Isabel la Católica.[53] Many Spaniards had at first refused to believe the news of the defeat at Ayacucho, placing their hope in an unsubstantiated report from Havana that the news was a hoax of the Colombians, or preferring to believe that Olañeta in Upper Peru would withstand the patriots. The *Gaceta de Madrid* referred to Ayacucho as "a momentary reverse" in royalist fortunes.[54] It would take some time for the realization to settle in that the empire was truly lost.

Spain was left the unhappy task of receiving and absorbing the hundreds of civilian officials and clerics who returned to the motherland from Peru between 1821 and 1825. Many fled in the months following San Martín's takeover of Lima in 1821; others remained as late as 1825 under guarantees offered in the capitulations of Ayacucho but were then ordered out by Bolívar.[55] All of them lost their homes, property, income, and inheritances. Spanish officials were occupied for several years in granting temporary salaries or pensions to the emigrés and searching for positions for them in church or state. In March 1824 the king decreed that royal employees who fled the rebels and emigrated back to Spain should receive preferment in appointment over those royal officials who remained in America, with the exception of those appointed by the constitutional regime.[56] This was essentially meaningless, but it did have the general effect of stating the king's favor for the emigrants. A few months later, however, the king decreed that all emigrant officials from America were required to undergo the purification process before receiving pensions or appointments to prove they had not been addicted to the constitutional system.[57] No definite statistics have been found, but the impression left in the documents is that most of the emigrants from Peru received special government pensions rather than being appointed to equivalent offices in the peninsula.

The loss of America was a stunning economic blow to Spain, leading to continued national penury in the nineteenth century. The total value of gold and silver imported into Cádiz from 1797 to 1821 was 183 million pesos. The permanent conclusion of this trade was a disaster. In 1809 the remission of wealth from America in Cádiz had been 43 million pesos; it fell gradually over the ensuing war years until by 1821 the trade had dried up entirely.[58] Cádiz never recovered its position as the premier Spanish port, even though in 1829 it was declared a free port in an attempt to rescue it from total destruction. The liberal merchants of Cádiz who had supported the Cortes and resisted any extension of open trade to America were finally ruined. A vindictive Ferdinand VII put the final touch to the story of the collapse of Spain's trade with America by decreeing in 1824 the cutoff of all legal trade to the former dominions. In 1828 he lifted the decree but required that all trade to and from America had to pass through Cuba and Puerto Rico.[59]

Throughout the remainder of his reign Ferdinand VII never admitted the possibility of recognizing American independence. The Council of State met many times during the decade to discuss "the pacification of the revolted provinces of America." Members of the council that debated and discussed possible expeditions of reconquest included former viceroys and generals, like Venegas and Apodaca of Mexico, as well as the king's two brothers and Cardinal Borbón. The king was often present himself.[60] Plans such as those presented in 1823 by Galabert for the reconquest of Mexico seem always to have predominated. Given the political turmoil and discontent in America, many Spaniards considered reconquest of the colonies to be virtually a humanitarian undertaking, in which Spain would restore the kindly yoke of empire on deluded and unhappy junior brothers. This philosophy had emerged in the constitutional triennium and continued to be the main opinion expressed until about 1833. After years of discussion, the regime in 1829 launched its major attempt to retake America with the dispatch of an expedition of three thousand troops to Mexico under the command of Brigadier Isidro Barradas. They were decisively defeated on the Mexican coast. The king believed their failure was owing to poor organization and lack of troops, and the next year continued plans for another expedition, which never sailed.[61]

Final recognition of American independence had to await the king's death in 1833 and the accession to the throne of his daughter Isabel II. In February 1834 Spain announced its intention to negotiate with the dissident states of America. Negotiations opened in 1835 and thereafter with those American countries that chose to apply for recognition. In December 1836 Spain signed a treaty of diplomatic recognition with Mexico, which thus became the first former colony to reestablish relations with the mother country. Other recognitions came very slowly, with Ecuador reaching agreement in 1840, Chile in 1844, Venezuela in 1845, Bolivia in 1847. Spain reopened commercial relations with most of the Latin American republics and exchanged consuls before the formal diplomatic settlement.[62] The last former colony to be recognized was Honduras in 1895. That was just in time for the second and final great shock—the loss in 1898 of Cuba, Puerto Rico, and the Philippines, the last vestiges of empire.

Notes

Preface

1. Juan Friede, *La otra verdad, la independencia americana vista por los españoles*, p. 9.

2. Such as Melchor Fernández Almagro, *La emancipación de América y su reflejo en la conciencia española*; Jaime Delgado, *La independencia de América en la prensa española* and *La independencia hispanoamericana*; Margaret L. Woodward, "Spanish Apathy and American Independence (1810–1843)," Ph.D. dissertation, University of Chicago, 1964; and Luis Miguel Enciso Recio, *La opinión pública española y la independencia hispanoamericana, 1819–1820*. An exception to this is Enoch F. Resnick, "The Council of State and Spanish America, 1814–1820," Ph.D. dissertation, American University, 1970, which details the council's debates during the first restoration.

3. Claudio Véliz, *The Centralist Tradition of Latin America*; Jorge I. Domínguez, *Insurrection or Loyalty: The Breakdown of the Spanish American Empire*.

Chapter 1

1. Frank Jay Moreno, "The Spanish Colonial System: A Functional Approach," *Western Political Quarterly* 20 (June 1967):308–20; Richard M. Morse, "The Heritage of Latin America," in *Politics and Social Change in Latin America: The Distinct Tradition*, ed. Howard J. Wiarda, pp. 25–69; John L. Phelan, "Authority and Flexibility in the Spanish Imperial Bureaucracy," *Administrative Science Quarterly* 1 (June 1960): 47–65; John L. Phelan, *The Kingdom of Quito in the Seventeenth Century: Bureaucratic Politics in the Spanish Empire*, especially pp. 320–37; and Magali Sarfatti, *Spanish Bureaucratic-Patrimonialism in America*.

2. "Letter from Jamaica," in Simón Bolívar, *Selected Writings of Bolívar*, comp. Vicente Lecuna, ed. Harold A. Bierck, Jr., tr. Lewis Bertrand. 2 vols. (New York: Colonial Press, 1951), 1:103–22.

3. Junta Central to Ayuntamiento of Bogotá, Seville, 14 January 1809, Archivo Histórico Nacional, Madrid (hereafter cited as AHN), Estado 60.

4. Delgado, *La independencia . . . en la prensa española*, p. 84.

5. Richard Graham, *Independence in Latin America*, pp. 6–7.

6. Marvin Goldwert, "The Search for the Lost Father-Figure in Spanish American History: A Freudian View," *The Americas* 34:4 (April 1978): 532–36.

7. Morse, "The Heritage of Latin America," pp. 25–69; O. Carlos Stoetzer, *The Scholastic Roots of the Spanish American Revolution*.

8. Moreno, "The Spanish Colonial System: A Functional Approach," pp. 308–20.

9. Ibid., p. 319.

10. John Lynch, *The Spanish American Revolutions, 1808–1826*, pp. 1–24.

11. Ibid., p. 2.

12. Quoted in J. R. Fisher, *Government and Society in Colonial Peru: The Intendant System, 1784–1814*, p. 154.

13. Jacques A. Barbier, "Peninsular Finance and Colonial Trade: The Dilemma of Charles IV's Spain," *Journal of Latin American Studies* 12:1 (May 1980): 21–37. On Cuban trade, which continued open, see Domínguez, *Insurrection or Loyalty*, p. 105.

14. Timothy E. Anna, *The Fall of the Royal Government in Peru*, p. 22.

15. Mark A. Burkholder and D. S. Chandler, *From Impotence to Authority: The Spanish Crown and the American Audiencias, 1687–1808*, pp. 88–90, 95–96, 99, 104, and appendix VI.

16. Magnus Mörner, ed., *The Expulsion of the Jesuits from Latin America* (New York: Knopf, 1965).

17. N. M. Farriss, *Crown and Clergy in Colonial Mexico, 1759–1821: The Crisis of Ecclesiastical Privilege*.

18. Lyle N. McAlister, *The "Fuero Militar" in New Spain, 1764–1800*.

19. Leon G. Campbell, "The Army of Peru and the Túpac Amaru Revolt," *Hispanic American Historical Review* 56:1 (February 1976): 31–57; Leon G. Campbell, *The Military and Society in Colonial Peru, 1750–1810*; María del Carmen Velázquez, *El estado de guerra en Nueva España, 1760–1808* (Mexico City: Colegio de México, 1950); Christon I. Archer, *The Army in*

Bourbon Mexico, 1760–1810; and Allan J. Kuethe, *Military Reform and Society in New Granada, 1776–1808*.

20. D. A. Brading, *Miners and Merchants in Bourbon Mexico, 1763–1810*, pp. 30, 95–128, 208–19, 251–54.

21. Alexander von Humboldt, *Ensayo político sobre Nueva España*, pp. 129–32; Romeo Flores Caballero, *La contrarevolución en la independencia*, pp. 15–24. Note that Humboldt's estimates for New Spain are considerably inflated, so that, by extrapolation, they may be inflated for the whole empire as well.

22. Jacques A. Barbier, "Tradition and Reform in Bourbon Chile: Ambrosio O'Higgins and Public Finances," *The Americas* 34:3 (January 1978): 381–99; see also Jacques A. Barbier, *Reform and Politics in Bourbon Chile, 1755–1796*.

23. Brian R. Hamnett, "Mexico's Royalist Coalition: The Response to Revolution, 1808–1821," *Journal of Latin American Studies* 12:1 (May 1980): 55–86; see also Brian R. Hamnett, *Politics and Trade in Southern Mexico, 1750–1821*, pp. 72–94.

24. Carlos Marichal, *Spain (1834–1844): A New Society*, pp. 18–27.

25. Gabriel H. Lovett, *Napoleon and the Birth of Modern Spain*, 1:8–16; Jacques Chastenet, *Godoy, Master of Spain, 1792–1808*; Richard Herr, *The Eighteenth Century Revolution in Spain*; Hans Roger Madol, *Godoy*; John D. Bergamini, *The Spanish Bourbons: The History of a Tenacious Dynasty*, pp. 102–10, 121–31.

26. Juan de Escoiquiz, *Memorias*, p. 5.

27. Bergamini, *Spanish Bourbons*, p. 124.

28. José García de León y Pizarro, *Memorias*, 1:87–89. Despite his long last name, he preferred to be known as Pizarro.

29. Ibid., 1:99.

30. For a rapid review of the Olivenza question see Shirley J. Black, "Olivenza: An Iberian 'Alsace/Lorraine'," *The Americas* 35:4 (April 1979): 527–37.

31. Lovett, *Napoleon and the Birth of Modern Spain*, 1:21.

32. Ibid., 1:26–27.

33. Juan de Escoiquiz, *Idea sencilla de las razones que motivaron el viaje del Rey Don Fernando VII a Bayona en el mes de abril de 1808*, p. 191.

34. Antonio Alcalá Galiano, *Recuerdos de un anciano*, p. 53.

35. Lovett, *Napoleon and the Birth of Modern Spain*, 1:88–91.

36. Ibid., 1:98.

37. Escoiquiz, *Idea sencilla*, pp. 193–97.

38. Lovett, *Napoleon and the Birth of Modern Spain*, 1:112.

39. Ibid., 1:116.

40. Escoiquiz, *Memorias*, p. 132.

41. William Spence Robertson detailed some of the French commissioners and documents dispatched to various Spanish American territories in Napoleon's unsuccessful attempt to win colonial loyalty: *France and Latin American Independence*, pp. 40–71.

42. Quoted in Lovett, *Napoleon and the Birth of Modern Spain*, 1:168.

Chapter 2

1. Anna, *Fall of Government in Mexico City*, pp. 37–54.

2. Anna, *Fall of Government in Peru*, pp. 39–43.

3. Juan José de Sanllorente to Supreme Junta of Government, Cartagena de Indias, 10 October 1808, and Antonio Amar to Supreme Junta, Bogotá, 23 September 1808, both in AHN, Estado 60.

4. Juan José Odeniz to Supreme Junta of Seville, Cartagena de Indias, 14 September 1808, AHN, Estado 58.

5. Marqués del Real Tesoro to Junta Central, Mexico City, 1 November 1808, AHN, Estado 58; Juan Antonio de la Mata to Junta Central, Panama, 1 September 1808, AHN, Estado 58.

6. Proclamation of Fernando Miyares, Maracaibo, 31 August 1808, AHN, Estado 57.

7. Extract of report of Juan Jurado, Caracas, 29 November 1808, AHN, Estado 60.

8. Lynch, *Spanish American Revolutions*, pp. 39–44.

9. Joaquín de Molina to Supreme Junta of Seville, Buenos Aires, 10 January 1809, and two letters of 27 January 1809, all in AHN, Estado 55.

10. José Manuel de Goyeneche to Viceroy Abascal, Buenos Aires, 27 August 1808, and Goyeneche to Junta of Seville, Buenos Aires, 14 and 15 September 1808, all in AHN, Estado 55; Goyeneche to Junta of Seville, Córdoba del Tucumán, 2 October 1808, AHN, Estado 57.

11. Goyeneche to Conde de Floridablanca, Lima, 22 April 1809, Archivo General de Indias, Seville (hereafter cited as AGI), Lima 1442.

12. Reports of Juan Jabat, Seville, 27 December 1808, AHN, Estado 58E and Seville, 10 and 17 January 1809, both in AHN, Estado 58; "Plan de oposición a las impresas que pueda intentar la República de los Estados Unidos contra las Provincias del Norte de este Reyno," Félix Calleja, no date

but with accompanying note of 29 October 1808, AHN, Estado 58.

13. Report of León de Altolaguirre, Nicolás de Herrera, and Manuel Rodrigo, Madrid, 30 September 1808, AHN, Estado 56.

14. "Instrucción de la Junta Suprema de Sevilla a sus diputados a la Junta Central," Seville, 24 August 1808, and accompanying documents, AHN, Estado 82.

15. *Gaceta Extraordinaria de Guatemala*, 20 January 1809, publishing a letter of Antonio Porcel, Madrid, 20 October 1808, AHN, Estado 57.

16. A comprehensive list of ministers of the Spanish government is provided in the *Enciclopedia Universal Ilustrada Europeo-Americana* (Madrid: Espasa-Calpe, 1908) under the entry "ministro," which lists ministers from 1754.

17. Pizarro, *Memorias*, 1:114–31.

18. *El Concejo de Estado (1792–1834)*, pp. 20–26.

19. Pizarro, *Memorias*, 1:132.

20. Many of the letters of recognition are preserved in AHN, Estado 54.

21. Mexico City Mining Tribunal to Junta Central, Mexico City, 12 December 1808, AHN, Estado 54.

22. Vicente Palacio Atard, *Fin de la sociedad española del antiguo régimen*. See also Doris M. Ladd, *The Mexican Nobility at Independence, 1780–1826*, and Marichal, *Spain*, pp. 7–40.

23. Robert Rouiere Pearce, *Memoirs and Correspondence of the most noble Richard Marquess Wellesley*, 3:80–82.

24. Junta Central circulars to America, Seville, 10 May, 31 July, and 1 December 1809, AHN, Estado 54; Juan de Aguilar to Martín de Garay, Havana, 24 August 1809, AHN, Estado 54.

25. Junta Central to Inquisition of Mexico, Seville, 2 February 1809, AHN, Estado 58.

26. Letter of Lorenzo Calba, Seville, 15 February 1809, AHN, Estado 54.

27. Opinion of Antonio Valdes in Junta Central, Seville, 3 February 1809, AHN, Estado 58; draft letter of Junta Central and replies, Seville, 8 and 9 February 1809, AHN, Estado 54.

28. Instructions of Junta Central to Cisneros, Seville, 24 March 1809; Additional Instructions, Seville, 9 April 1809; Letter of Cisneros, Seville, 9 May 1809; Letter to Cisneros, Seville, 22 May 1809, all in AHN, Estado 55.

29. The handwritten original of the decree is in AHN, Estado 54.

30. Archivo del Ex-Ayuntamiento, Mexico City, Actas del Cabildo,

vol. 128, 17 April 1809; ibid., Elecciones de diputados a Cortes, vol. 870, exps. 1 and 2.

31. Ibid., Elecciones de diputados a Cortes, vol. 870, exp. 2, poem of Bruno Larrañaga.

32. Junta Central to Decano del Consejo de España e Indias, Seville, 12 January 1810, AHN, Estado 60.

33. Barbier, "Peninsular Finance and Colonial Trade," pp. 21–37.

34. John Lynch, "British Policy and Spanish America, 1783–1808," *Journal of Latin American Studies* 1:1 (May 1969): 1–30; D. B. Goebel, "British Trade to the Spanish Colonies, 1796–1823," *American Historical Review* 43:2 (January 1938): 288–320; Frances Armytage, *The Free Port System in the British West Indies: A Study in Commercial Policy, 1766–1822*, pp. 69–70, 91–125.

35. Ladd, *Mexican Nobility*, pp. 96–102; Michael P. Costeloe, *Church Wealth in Mexico, 1800–1856* (Cambridge: At the University Press, 1967); Flores Caballero, *La contrarevolución*, pp. 28–65; Asunción Lavrin, "The Execution of the Law of *Consolidación* in New Spain: Economic Aims and Results," *Hispanic American Historical Review* 53:1 (February 1973): 27–49; Brian R. Hamnett, "The Appropriation of Mexican Church Wealth by the Spanish Bourbon Government: 'The Consolidación de Vales Reales,' 1805–1809," *Journal of Latin American Studies* 1:2 (November 1969): 85–113. On the disamortization in Spain itself see Richard Herr, "Hacia el derrumbe del antiguo régimen: crisis fiscal y desamortización bajo Carlos IV," *Moneda y Crédito* 118 (September 1971): 37–100.

36. Anna, *Fall of Government in Mexico City*, p. 39; Anna, *Fall of Government in Peru*, p. 40.

37. Ibid., Mexico City, p. 153; ibid., Peru, p. 11.

38. Antonio García-Baquero González, *Comercio colonial y guerras revolucionarias*, p. 199; Barbier, "Peninsular Finance and Colonial Trade," pp. 21–37.

39. The towns comprising the Cortes of 1789 were Burgos, León, Zaragoza, Granada, Valencia, Palma de Mallorca, Sevilla, Córdoba, Murcia, Jaén, Barcelona, Avila, Zamora, Toro, Guadalajara, Fraga, Calatayud, Cervera, Madrid, Extremadura, Soria, Tortosa, Peñíscola, Tarazona, Palencia, Salamanca, Lérida, Segovia, Galicia, Valladolid, Gerona, Jaca, Teruel, Tarragona, Borja, Cuenca, and Toledo.

40. Lovett, *Napoleon and the Birth of Modern Spain*, 1:343–45.

41. Ibid., 1:367.

42. Council of Regency to Spanish America, León, 14 February 1810,

AGI, Ultramar 795; "Junta Superior de Cádiz da cuenta a la América . . . " in Juan E. Hernández y Dávalos, ed., *Colección de documentos para la historia de la Guerra de Independencia de México*, 2:22–27.

Chapter 3

1. William Walton, *The Revolutions of Spain, from 1808 to the end of 1836*, 1:181. Walton was the son of the honorary Spanish consul in Liverpool. Educated in Spain, a Catholic, he had owned property in Santo Domingo, where in 1808–11 he assisted the Spanish leader Juan Sánchez Ramírez and the British expedition of Gen. Hugh Lyle Carmichael to drive out the French. In London in 1811–13 he served the interests of the Spanish liberals, and in 1820 he professed to be a great advocate of the Cortes and asked for a suitable reward as its agent in Britain. William Walton to Diego Correa, London, 24 May 1820, AGI, Ultramar 811. Obviously he later turned against the liberals, for in 1837 he published perhaps the most violent attack on the Cortes to appear in English. He was equally critical of Ferdinand VII, however.

2. Lovett, *Napoleon and the Birth of Modern Spain*, 1:371.

3. Miguel Artola, *Los orígenes de la España contemporánea*, 1:404.

4. Mario Rodríguez, *The Cádiz Experiment in Central America, 1808 to 1826*, p. 54.

5. Cortes decree, León, 15 October 1810, Archivo del Ex-Ayuntamiento, Cédulas y reales órdenes, 2979, exp. 255; James F. King, "The Colored Castes and American Representation in the Cortes of Cádiz," *Hispanic American Historical Review* 33:1 (February 1953): 33–64.

6. King, "The Colored Castes," pp. 33–64.

7. "La población compuesta de los naturales que por ambas líneas sean originarios de los dominios españoles."

8. King, "The Colored Castes," pp. 33–64; David T. Garza, "Mexican Constitutional Expression in the Cortes of Cádiz," pp. 43–58 in Nettie Lee Benson, ed., *Mexico and the Spanish Cortes, 1810–1822*.

9. King, "The Colored Castes," pp. 33–64.

10. Memoria of Baquíjano, Conde de Vistaflorida, Madrid, 31 August 1814, AGI, Estado 87.

11. "Informe del Real Tribunal del Consulado de México . . . ," 27 May 1811, Hernández y Dávalos, *Colección de documentos*, 2:450–66.

12. Memoria of Baquíjano, AGI, Estado 87.

13. Lovett, *Napoleon and the Birth of Modern Spain*, 2:470–81.

14. Hamnett, "Mexico's Royalist Coalition," pp. 55—86.

15. Lovett, *Napoleon and the Birth of Modern Spain*, 2:465—67.

16. John H. Hann, "The Role of the Mexican Deputies in the Proposal and Enactment of Measures of Economic Reform Applicable to Mexico," in Benson, *Mexico and the Spanish Cortes*, pp. 153—77.

17. Conde de Toreno, *Historia del levantamiento, guerra y revolución de España*, p. 393.

18. John Preston Moore, *The Cabildo in Peru under the Bourbons* (Durham: Duke University Press, 1966), pp. 208—9; *Cortes, 1810—1813, Proposiciones que hacen al Congreso Nacional los diputados de América y Asia* (Madrid: Imprenta de Francisco de Paula Periu, 1811); W. Woodrow Anderson, "Reform as a Means to Quell Revolution," in Benson, *Mexico and the Spanish Cortes*, pp. 185—207.

19. Yermo to Supreme Junta, Mexico, 9 November 1808, AHN, Estado 57 E.

20. J. R. Fisher, *Silver Mines and Silver Miners in Colonial Peru, 1776—1824*, Centre for Latin American Studies, Monograph Series no. 7 (Liverpool: University of Liverpool, 1977), p. 84.

21. Memoria of Baquíjano, AGI, Estado 87. On this and the entire issue see Michael P. Costeloe, "Spain and the Latin American Wars of Independence: The Free Trade Controversy, 1810—1820," *Hispanic American Historical Review*, 61:2 (May 1981): 209—34.

22. Toreno, *Historia*, p. 299.

23. Royal order of Hacienda de Indias, Cádiz, 20 September 1811, and Esteban Varea to Secretariat of Cortes, Cádiz, 15 May 1811, both in AGI, Indiferente 668.

24. Decree of Regency, Cádiz, 27 June 1810, AGI, Estado 82.

25. Toreno, *Historia*, pp. 306, 398. These sums do not include the large British grants.

26. Toreno, *Historia*, p. 396.

27. Ibid., pp. 452, 484.

28. Memoria of Baquíjano, AGI, Estado 87; Anderson, "Reform," pp. 185—207; "Informe que hizo el Dr. D. José Beye de Cisneros a las Cortes . . . ," 1811, Archivo del Ex-Ayuntamiento, Elecciones de diputados a Cortes, vol. 870, no. 9.

29. "Representación de la diputación americana en las Cortes," 1 August 1811, Archivo General de la Nación, Mexico (hereafter cited as AGN), Impresos oficiales, vol. 60, no. 44.

30. Anderson, "Reform," pp. 185—207.

31. Unsigned note of Minister of Ultramar to King, Madrid, no date, AGI, Indiferente 1354.

32. "Nota de los diputados de las Americas a quienes se les ha comunicado la circular de 17 de junio de 1814," AGI, Indiferente 1354. The replies are scattered throughout Indiferente 1354 and 1355. Two deputies merely referred to their successors.

33. Memoria of Baquíjano, AGI, Estado 87.

34. Abascal to Secretary of Grace and Justice, Lima, 30 November 1813, AGI, Lima 744; Abascal to Secretary of Ultramar, Lima, 31 July 1814, AGI, Lima 747.

35. Juan José de Leuro to Secretary of Hacienda, Lima, 7 December 1811, AGI, Lima 1014 A.

36. Venegas to Minister of Hacienda, Mexico, 6 March 1811, AGI, Mexico 1635.

37. Rodríguez, *Cádiz Experiment*, p. 85.

38. Anna, *Fall of Government in Mexico City*, pp. 103–17.

39. Anna, *Fall of Government in Peru*, pp. 53–93 passim.

40. Toreno, *Historia*, p. 299.

41. Ibid., p. 300.

42. Ministry of Ultramar to Regency, Madrid, 2 February 1814; Report of Minister of Ultramar to Cortes, Madrid, 1 March 1814; Royal decree, Madrid, 28 June 1814, all in AGI, Indiferente 1355; Royal decree, Madrid, 26 June 1814, AGI, Indiferente 669.

43. Lovett, *Napoleon and the Birth of Modern Spain*, 1:337–38; 374.

44. *Consejo de Estado*, pp. 20–35, 114–86.

45. Delgado, *La independencia . . . en la prensa española*, pp. 97–109, 187–93.

46. Michael P. Costeloe, "Spain and the Spanish American Wars of Independence: The *Comisión de Reemplazos*, 1811–1820," *Journal of Latin American Studies* 13:2 (November 1981): pp. 223–37; Costeloe, "The Free Trade Controversy," pp. 209–34; Resnick, "Council of State," pp. 183–84.

47. Memoria of Baquíjano, AGI, Estado 87.

48. Germán Leguía y Martínez, *Historia de la emancipación del Perú: El Protectorado*, 7 vols. (Lima: Comisión Nacional del Sesquicentenario de la Independencia del Perú, 1972), 1:226–27, 420.

49. Minister of War to Vigodet, Cádiz, 19 December 1812, and José Vázquez Figueroa to Vigodet, Cádiz, 11 April 1813, both in AGI, Estado 82.

50. Extract, Ministry of Grace and Justice, Cádiz, 16 April 1813;

Report, Cádiz, 21 June 1813, both in AGI, Indiferente 1353.

51. Pizarro, *Memorias*, 1:148–50.

52. "Extracto histórico y razonada de la negociación seguida entre el Gobierno Inglés y la España acerca de la mediación . . . ," 1826, AGI, Indiferente 1571.

53. See John Rydjord, "British Mediation between Spain and her Colonies: 1811–1813," *Hispanic American Historical Review* 21:1 (February 1941): 29–50; William W. Kaufmann, *British Policy and the Independence of Latin America, 1804–1828*, pp. 64–75.

54. "Extracto histórico," AGI, Indiferente 1571.

55. Toreno, *Historia*, p. 358.

56. Pizarro, *Memorias*, 1:151–52.

57. Quoted in Rydjord, "British Mediation," pp. 29–50.

58. This is the wording of the Spanish summary, in "Extracto histórico," AGI, Indiferente 1571.

59. Toreno, *Historia*, p. 439.

60. Ibid., p. 440; "Extracto histórico," AGI, Indiferente 1571.

61. Rydjord, "British Mediation," pp. 29–50.

62. Consulta of Council of State, Cádiz, 19 May 1813, AGI, Estado 88.

63. Toreno, *Historia*, p. 440.

64. Report of Minister of Ultramar to Cortes, Madrid, 1 March 1814, AGI, Indiferente 1355.

65. Order of Regency, Madrid, 15 March 1814, AGI, Indiferente 669.

66. Cortes decree, Madrid, 19 March 1814, AGI, Indiferente 669.

Chapter 4

1. Federico Suárez Verdeguer, *La crisis política del antiguo régimen en España (1800–1840)*, p. 29.

2. Ibid., pp. 53–60.

3. Toreno, *Historia*, pp. 486–87.

4. Ibid., pp. 488, 489.

5. María Cristina Diz-Lois, *El Manifiesto de 1814*, pp. 28–34.

6. Lovett, *Napoleon and the Birth of Modern Spain*, 2:546–50.

7. Ibid., 2:813–14.

8. Toreno, *Historia*, p. 519.

9. Ibid., p. 520.

10. Diz-Lois, *Manifiesto de 1814*, p. 106.

11. Lovett, *Napoleon and the Birth of Modern Spain*, 2:818; Federico Suárez Verdeguer, *Conservadores, innovadores y renovadores en las postrimerías del Antiguo Régimen*, p. 101; for a complete copy of the Manifesto of the Persas see Diz-Lois, *Manifiesto de 1814*, pp. 192–277.

12. Toreno, *Historia*, p. 520.

13. Ibid., pp. 521–24.

14. The complete decree is printed in ibid., pp. 522–23.

15. Ibid., p. 524.

16. María del Carmen Pintos Vieites, *La política de Fernando VII entre 1814 y 1820*, pp. 156–62.

17. See also Resnick, "Council of State," pp. 19–24.

18. Pintos Vieites, *Política de Fernando VII*, pp. 167–80.

19. Pizarro, *Memorias*, 1:188, 258–62.

20. Ibid., 1:194. Pizarro was a special envoy to Berlin at the time.

21. Quoted in Lovett, *Napoleon and the Birth of Modern Spain*, 2:840.

22. Calleja to Minister of Grace and Justice, Mexico City, 27 August 1814, AGI, Mexico 1482; Abascal to Minister of Ultramar, Lima, 25 October 1814, AGI, Lima 748; Rodríguez, *Cádiz Experiment*, pp. 122–23.

23. Secretariat of Ultramar to Regency, Madrid, 2 February 1814, AGI, Indiferente 1355; Reglamento, Secretaria Universal de Indias, Madrid, 15 August 1814, AGI, Indiferente 1355.

24. Royal decree, Madrid, 2 July 1812, AGI, Indiferente 669.

25. Miguel Maticorena Estrada, "Nuevos noticias y documentos de don José Baquíjano y Carrillo, Conde de Vistaflorida," in *La causa de la emancipación del Perú* (Lima: Instituto Riva Agüero, 1960), pp. 145–207.

26. Council of Indies consulta, Madrid, 5 September 1814, AGI, Indiferente 803.

27. Royal cédula, Cádiz, 21 September 1810, AGI, Indiferente 667.

28. Expediente about José Antonio Molina, Madrid, 1814, AHN, Consejo 51692; Antonio Ignacio de Cortabarria to Secretary of Indies, Madrid, 19 September 1814, AGI, Indiferente 1354.

29. Francisco Salazar to Secretariat of Indies, Madrid, 17 August 1814, and accompanying documents, AGI, Lima 1018 B; Minutes of Cortes, Cádiz, 8 March 1813, AGI, Lima 1015; Informe de D. Francisco de Salazar, Lima, 15 September 1817, AGI, Lima 613.

30. Tadeo Gárate to Ministry of Indies, Madrid, 27 July 1814, extracts, accompanying notes, AGI, Indiferente 1354.

31. Ramón de Posada to Lardizábal, Toledo, 6 and 10 August 1814, AGI, Estado 87.

32. Memoria of Baquíjano, AGI, Estado 87.

33. Conde de Puñorrostro to San Carlos, Madrid, 22 May 1814, AGI, Estado 87.

34. Melchor Fernández Almagro, *La emancipación de América y su reflejo en la conciencia española*, p. 76.

35. Delgado, *La independencia . . . en la prensa española*, p. 214.

36. Thomás Gutiérrez Sanz to King, reporting for Ildefonso José de Medina, Madrid, 2 October 1814, AGI, Ultramar 815.

37. Pedro Rodríguez de Argumedo, contador of Puerto Cabello, to Secretary of Hacienda, Madrid, 23 April 1814, AGI, Ultramar 815.

38. Lynch, *Spanish American Revolutions*, pp. 94–95.

39. Luis M. Salazar to Secretary of the Indies, Madrid, 5 December 1814, AGI, Indiferente 1603.

40. "Memoria sobre nuestras relaciones políticas con las demás naciones de Europa," 1814, AHN, Estado 3024.

41. Council of Indies to King, Madrid, 4 October 1814, AGI, Ultramar 780.

42. "Estado del número de ministros señalado a cada una de las audiencias de América," Madrid, 5 October 1814, AGI, Indiferente 1355.

43. Consulta, Cámara de Indias, Madrid, 19 December 1814, AGI, Ultramar 780.

44. Council of Indies consulta, Madrid, 22 December 1814, AGI, Indiferente 803; on Abad y Queipo see Lillian Estelle Fisher, *Champion of Reform, Manuel Abad y Queipo* (New York: Library Publishers, 1955).

45. Memoria on pacification by Juan Antonio Yandiola, Madrid, 29 January 1815, AGI, Estado 87.

46. Delgado, *La independencia . . . en la prensa española*, pp. 201–26.

47. Council of Indies consulta, Madrid, 3 October 1814, AGI, Indiferente 1568, and Madrid, 13 September 1814, AGI, Ultramar 780.

48. Francisco de Eguía to Secretary of State, enclosing Morillo's instructions, Madrid, 31 July 1817, AGI, Estado 64.

49. Stephen K. Stoan, *Pablo Morillo and Venezuela, 1815–1820*, p. 65.

50. Ibid., p. 75.

51. Ibid., pp. 95–115.

Chapter 5

1. Pedro de Leturia, "La encíclica de Pío VII sobre la revolución hispanoamericana," *Anuario de Estudios Americanos* 4 (1947): 423–518. Also

J. Lloyd Mecham, *Church and State in Latin America*, rev. ed. (Chapel Hill, University of North Carolina Press, 1966), p. 64.

2. Pizarro, *Memorias*, 1:263.

3. Exposition of Pizarro, Madrid, 9 June 1818, AGI, Estado 89; Juan Antonio de Roxas Queypo and Matías d' Escute to Duke of San Fernando, Madrid, 18 November 1819, AGI, Estado 90.

4. Vidaurre to King, Lima, 2 April 1817, AGI, Indiferente 1568.

5. Suárez, *La crisis política*, pp. 58–60.

6. Miguel Artola Gallego, *La España de Fernando VII*, pp. 578–93.

7. Pizarro, *Memorias*, 1:259–60, 2:295–96.

8. Resnick, "Council of State," p. 21.

9. Pintos Vieites, *Política de Fernando VII*, pp. 196–211.

10. Council of Indies consulta, Madrid, 26 August 1816, AGI, Ultramar 781.

11. "Extracto histórico," AGI, Indiferente 1571.

12. Council of Indies consulta, Madrid, 17 May 1816, AGI, Estado 88.

13. Carlota Joaquina to Pedro Cevallos, Rio de Janeiro, 15 June 1816, AGI, Estado 98; Andrés Villalba to Cevallos, Rio de Janeiro, 28 June 1816, AGI, Estado 98.

14. Minutes, Council of State, Madrid, 18 October 1816, AGI, Estado 83.

15. Minister of State to Conde de Fernán Núñez, Madrid, 3 October 1816, AGI, Estado 98.

16. Resnick, "Council of State," p. 21.

17. Pizarro, *Memorias*, 1:216.

18. Report to Pizarro by Rafael Morant, Madrid, 31 December 1816, AGI, Estado 86 A.

19. Pizarro, *Memorias*, 1:263.

20. Francisco Eguía to Ministry of State, Madrid, 14 August 1818, AGI, Estado 89.

21. Conde de Fernán Núñez to Pizarro, London, 10 January 1817, AGI, Estado 100.

22. Lardizábal to Pedro Cevallos, Madrid, 4 September 1815, AGI, Estado 88.

23. Memoria of Conde de Casa Flores, Madrid, 3 December 1816, AGI, Estado 87. On the trade issue in general see Costeloe, "The Free Trade Controversy," pp. 209–34.

24. Casa Flores to Pizarro, Madrid, 3 December 1816, AGI, Estado 87.

25. Secretariat of the Council of State, Madrid, 22 February 1817, general summary, AGI, Indiferente 1568.

26. Separate opinion of Manuel de la Bodega on pacification, Madrid, 24 October 1816, AGI, Estado 87.

27. Council of Indies consulta, Madrid, 9 November 1816, AGI, Estado 88.

28. Report of Duke of Montemar, Madrid, 22 October 1816, AGI, Estado 86 A.

29. Junta of Pacification consulta, Madrid, 8 February 1817, AGI, Estado 86 A.

30. Fernández Almagro, *Emancipación*, pp. 86–89; Resnick, "Council of State," pp. 33–45.

31. Memoria of Juan Antonio Yandiola, Madrid, 29 January 1815, AGI, Estado 87.

32. Secretariat of the Council of State, Extract of the consulta made on 8 February, Madrid, 22 February 1817, AGI, Indiferente 1568.

33. "Apuntes del Sr. Garay sobre el papel de Casaflores para pacificación de America," no date, probably January 1817, AGI, Estado 87; and extract in Secretariat of the Council of State, pacification of the Americas, Madrid, 22 February 1817, AGI, Indiferente 1568.

34. Quoted in Fisher, *Government and Society*, p. 154.

35. Separate opinion, unnamed member of Council of State, Madrid, July 1817, AGI, Estado 88.

36. Report of J. M. de Aparici, Madrid, 25 May 1816, AGI, Indiferente 846.

37. Juan Antonio de Roxas Queypo to King, Madrid, 21 December 1816, AGI, Estado 71.

38. Conde de Casa Flores to Pizarro, Rio de Janeiro, 3 October 1817, AGI, Estado 100.

39. Fernández Almagro, *Emancipación*, pp. 22–23, 63.

40. "Ideas sobre pacificación de D. Luis de Onís y D. Juan Alvarez Toledo," 1817, AGI, Estado 88.

41. Pizarro, *Memorias*, 2:181.

42. José Vázquez Figueroa to Secretary of Hacienda, Madrid, 18 July, and two letters of 26 July 1817, all in AGI, Indiferente 1356.

43. Resnick, "Council of State," pp. 177, 192–97.

44. Anonymous to Simón Bolívar, Cádiz, 13 September 1817, AGI, Estado 71.

45. Pizarro, *Memorias*, 1:220.

46. Ibid., 1:263.

47. Ibid., 1:221.

48. Ibid., 1:221–22. "S. M. estaba perfectamente penetrado."

49. Fernán Núñez to Pizarro, London, 7 January 1817, AGI, Estado 100; Joaquín Francisco Campusano to Pizarro, London, 17 June 1817, AGI, Estado 100.

50. Fernán Núñez to Pizarro, Paris, 6 October 1817, AGI, Estado 100.

51. Fernán Núñez to Pizarro, Paris, 15 October 1817, AGI, Estado 100; Enoch F. Resnick, "Spain's Reaction to Portugal's Invasion of the Banda Oriental in 1816," *Revista de Historia de América* 73–74 (1972): 131–43.

52. Duke of Parque to Secretary of State, Madrid, 6 June 1819; Duke of San Fernando's opinion on Montevideo negotiations, Madrid, 6 June 1819; Duke of Infantado's opinion, Madrid, 10 July 1819, all in AGI, Estado 83.

53. Pizarro, *Memorias*, 1:223.

54. Luis de Onís to Duke of San Carlos, Philadelphia, 13 February 1815, AGI, Indiferente 1603; José Pizarro to Secretary of Grace and Justice, Madrid, 3 November 1817, AGI, Estado 88; and José Vázquez Figueroa to Pizarro, Madrid, 9 September 1818, AGI, Estado 88.

55. Anonymous to unnamed recipient, Cádiz, 12 September 1817, AGI, Estado 71, part of a group of letters eventually addressed to Bolívar but captured by royalists.

56. Stoan, *Morillo*, pp. 134–39.

57. Pizarro to Secretary of Grace and Justice, Madrid, 28 September 1817, AGI, Indiferente 1357; Audiencia of Caracas to Secretary of Grace and Justice, Caracas, 3 February 1817, AGI, Estado 64.

58. Andrés Villalba to Pizarro, Rio de Janeiro, 23 March 1817, AGI, Estado 99; Antonio Garcias to Secretary of Grace and Justice, Rio de Janeiro, 8 June 1817, AGI, Estado 100.

59. Extract of recommendations of Jacobo Villaurrutia, Madrid, 2 October 1817, AGI, Indiferente 1568.

60. Vidaurre to King, Lima, 2 April 1817, AGI, Indiferente 1568.

61. Resnick, "Council of State," pp. 102–12; Costeloe, "The Free Trade Controversy," pp. 209–34.

62. Juan Lozano de Torres to Council of Indies, Madrid, 31 December 1817, AGI, Indiferente 1357; Francisco Eguía to Secretary of Grace and Justice, Madrid, 14 August 1818, AGI, Indiferente 1358.

63. Council of Indies consulta, 26 January 1818, Madrid, AGI, Indiferente 1358.

Chapter 6

1. Resnick, "Council of State," p. 169; Costeloe, "The Free Trade Controversy," pp. 209–34.

2. Pizarro, *Memorias*, 1:240–50.

3. Ibid., 1:263.

4. Stoan, *Morillo*, p. 139.

5. Exposition of José Pizarro about America, Madrid, 9 June 1818, AGI, Estado 89; also printed in Pizarro, *Memorias*, 2:264–72.

6. Pedro Rodríguez de la Buria, Captain General of the Canaries, to Minister of State, Santa Cruz de Tenerife, 12 July 1817, AGI, Estado 105; José Vázquez Figueroa to Minister of State, Madrid, 24 August 1818, AGI, Estado 89.

7. García-Baquero, *Comercio colonial*, pp. 199–250.

8. Scattered examples are preserved in AGI, Estado 86 A, 101, 102, and 103.

9. Luis de Onís to Casa Irujo, Washington, 19 January 1819, AGI, Estado 103.

10. Luis Miguel Enciso Recio, *La opinión pública española y la independencia hispanoamericana, 1819–1820*, pp. 70–80, 160–71.

11. Extract, Los comisarios colectadores de Indias to King, Madrid, 2 October 1818, AGI, Indiferente 1358; Eguía to Minister of Grace and Justice, Madrid, 21 January 1819, AGI, Indiferente 1359.

12. Pizarro *Memorias*, 1:264.

13. Anselmo de Rivas and Domingo Dutari to King, Madrid, 14 July 1818, AGI, Estado 89.

14. San Carlos to King, London, 27 June 1818, AGI, Estado 102.

15. "Observaciones sobre el estado actual de las relaciones de la Inglaterra con la España con respecto a los asuntos de América," London, 17 December 1817, AGI, Estado 88.

16. Castlereagh to San Carlos, London, 24 March 1818, AGI, Estado 88.

17. Junta of Pacification consulta, Madrid, 31 July 1818, AGI, Estado 90.

18. Pizarro to San Carlos, Madrid, 8 August 1818, AGI, Estado 88.

19. Pizarro, *Memorias*, 1:265.

20. Pizarro to Secretary of Navy, Madrid, 13 April 1818, AGI, Estado 102.

21. Junta Militar de Indias, session of 8 May 1818, AGI, Estado 102.

22. Duke of San Carlos to Pizarro, London, 12 July 1818, AGI, Estado 101.

23. Cabinet meeting minutes, 1 August 1818, AGI, Estado 90.

24. Resnick, "Council of State," pp. 226–29. In addition to forty-three or forty-four warships, there were to be ninety-four transports. On the herculean efforts of the Comisión de Reemplazos to finance the expedition (it eventually raised 123 million reales), see Costeloe, "The Comisión de Reemplazos," pp. 223–37.

25. Order to Casa Flores, Madrid, 16 December 1818, AGI, Estado 102; Resnick, "Council of State," p. 232.

26. Note from Ministry of Navy, 1818, AGI, Estado 101.

27. Artola, La España de Fernando VII, p. 586; Vázquez Figueroa's memoirs, in Pizarro, Memorias, 2:285; Russell H. Bartley, Imperial Russia and the Struggle for Latin American Independence, 1808–1828, pp. 121–27; the decree suppressing the trade is dated Madrid 19 December 1817, in AGI, Indiferente 670, and the agreement with Britain is dated 23 September 1817. Bartley says that the Russians made partial amends for this embarrassing incident by selling Spain three further frigates in 1818.

28. Fernán Núñez to Pizarro, Paris, 10 March 1818, AGI, Estado 102.

29. Pizarro, Memorias, 1:281.

30. Report to Lozano de Torres by unnamed source, Madrid, 13 August 1818, AGI, Estado 89.

31. Pizarro, Memorias, 1:278.

32. Casa Irujo to King, Madrid, 21 September 1818, AGI, Estado 89.

33. Stoan, Morillo, p. 139.

34. Quoted in Artola, La España de Fernando VII, p. 634.

35. Quoted in ibid., p. 668.

36. Ministry of Navy to Ministry of Grace and Justice, Madrid, 25 September 1819, AGI, Indiferente 1359.

37. Letter to Francisco Zea Bermúdez, Madrid, 17 October 1818, AGI, Estado 101.

38. Zea Bermúdez to Casa Irujo, Aix-la-Chapelle, 29 October 1818, AGI, Estado 101.

39. Zea Bermúdez to Casa Irujo, Aix-la-Chapelle, 25 November 1818, AGI, Estado 101.

40. Royal order, Madrid, 23 November 1818, AGI, Estado 89.

41. Eguía to Secretary of State, Madrid, 12 February 1819, AGI, Estado 103.

42. Ramón de Mesonero Romanos, Memorias de un setentón, p. 90;

Ferdinand to King of Naples, Madrid, 17 November 1818, AHN, Estado 2645.

43. Pizarro, *Memorias*, 1:284; Mesonero Romanos, *Memorias*, p. 93.

44. Proclamation of General Calleja to Expeditionary Army, Cádiz, 8 September 1819, AGI, Estado 103.

45. Manuel González Salmón to Conde de Calderón, Madrid, 8 September 1819, and Calleja to Minister of State, cuartel general de Arcos, 29 September 1819, both in AGI, Estado 103.

46. San Fernando to San Carlos, Madrid, 19 December 1819, AGI, Estado 104.

47. José María Alós to Minister of State, Madrid, 4 January 1820, AGI, Estado 104.

48. San Fernando to Zea Bermúdez, Madrid, 6 January 1820, AGI, Estado 104.

49. Pizarro, *Memorias*, 1:274; 2:297.

50. E. Christiansen, *The Origins of Military Power in Spain, 1800–1854*, pp. 18–22.

51. On the Riego revolt see José Luis Comellas, *Los primeros pronunciamientos en España, 1814–1820*, pp. 303–53, and Margaret L. Woodward, "The Spanish Army and the Loss of America, 1810–1824," *Hispanic American Historical Review* 48:4 (November 1968): 586–607.

52. Miguel de Lastarria to San Fernando, Madrid, 23 February 1820, AGI, Estado 104.

53. Council of Admiralty, Madrid, 4–25 February 1820, AGI, Estado 102.

54. Artola, *La España de Fernando VII*, pp. 659–61.

55. Minutes of Council of Hacienda, Madrid, 5 March 1820, AGI, Ultramar 781.

56. Council of State consulta, Madrid, 7 November 1821, AGI, Estado 89.

57. Fernández Almagro, *Emancipación*, p. 92.

58. Note from Casa Flores, Rio de Janeiro, 29 May 1818, AGI, Estado 101.

Chapter 7

1. Royal decree, Madrid, 12 March 1820, AGI, Indiferente 1359.

2. *Concejo de Estado*, p. 201.

3. Ibid., pp. 42–48.

4. Cortes order, Madrid, 26 October 1820, AGI, Indiferente 672.

5. Royal orders, Gobernación de Ultramar, Madrid, 11 April 1820, AGI, Indiferente 1568.

6. Delgado, *La independencia . . . en la prensa española*, p. 265.

7. Ibid., pp. 247–50. On the general question of American aspirations and the Cortes's failure to fulfill them see Mario Rodríguez, "The 'American Question' at the *Cortes* of Madrid," *The Americas* 38:3 (January 1982): pp. 293–314.

8. Cardinal Borbón to Secretary of Ultramar, Madrid, 19 April 1820, AGI, Indiferente 1568.

9. Antonio Porcel to Ministry of Justice, Madrid, 25 April 1820, AGI, Indiferente 671.

10. Minister of Marine to Minister of Ultramar, Madrid, 23 March 1820, AGI, Indiferente 1359 and Estado 64.

11. Minister of Marine to Minister of Ultramar, Madrid, 23 March 1820, AGI, Indiferente 1359.

12. Eleven Americans resident in Cádiz to the king, Cádiz, 23 April 1820, AGI, Indiferente 1359.

13. Extract of a petition, San Fernando, April 1820, AGI, Indiferente 1568.

14. Anna, *Fall of Government in Peru*, pp. 138–49.

15. Ministry of State rough draft and extract, April 1820, AGI, Estado 101.

16. Juan Manuel Subric to Ministry of Ultramar, Madrid, 27 July 1820, AGI, Indiferente 1359; Representation of Agustín de Blas, Madrid, 27 July 1820, AGI, Ultramar 811.

17. Estados, ships entering Cádiz, year of 1820, Cádiz, 4 May 1821, AGI, Indiferente 2293; Vicente Romero to Secretary of Hacienda, Madrid, 16 November 1820, AGI, Indiferente 2440.

18. Artola, *La España de Fernando VII*, pp. 677–79.

19. Ibid., pp. 695–96.

20. This is the interpretation William Spence Robertson derived from the instructions, "The Policy of Spain toward Its Revolted Colonies, 1820–1823," *Hispanic American Historical Review* 6:1–3 (February-August 1926): 21–46.

21. "Instrucciones reservadas para los comisionados que van de Orden del Rey a procurar la pacificación de las Provincias disidentes de Ultramar,"

April 1820, AGI, Indiferente 1568.

22. "Proclama del Rey a los habitantes de Ultramar," April 1820, AGI, Indiferente 1568.

23. Circular letter, Madrid, 8 June 1820, AGI, Indiferente 1568.

24. Ministry of Ultramar to Viceroy of Peru, Madrid, 3 July 1820, AGI, Indiferente 1568.

25. Robertson, "Policy of Spain," pp. 21–46.

26. Pablo Morillo to Secretary of Ultramar, Cuartel general de Valencia, 23 June 1820; Extracts of letters of Morillo, Madrid, 1820, both in AGI, Indiferente 1568.

27. "Oficio de los Comisionados cerca del Gobierno de Colombia," Pueblo de Bayladores, 24 August 1820, AGI, Indiferente 1568.

28. Anna, *Fall of Government in Peru*, pp. 160–61, 175–76.

29. Morillo to Secretary of Ultramar, Cuartel general de Valencia, 26 July 1820, AGI, Indiferente 1568.

30. Contaduría General to Council of Indies, Madrid, 19 February 1820, AGI, Indiferente 994.

31. Statement by Diego Colón, Madrid, 30 June 1820, AGI, Estado 3024.

32. Royal cédula, Madrid, 15 April 1820, AGI, Indiferente 670; Evaristo Pérez de Castro to Secretary of Grace and Justice, Madrid, 20 August 1820, AGI, Indiferente 671.

33. Duke of Frías to Pérez de Castro, London, 19 September 1820, AGI, Estado 89.

34. Memoria of Secretary of State to Cortes, 11 June 1820, AHN, Estado 3024.

35. Delgado, *La independencia . . . en la prensa española*, pp. 261–63, 275–82.

36. Marqués de Santa Cruz to Pérez de Castro, Paris, 13 November 1820, AGI, Indiferente 1568.

37. Duke of Frías to Pérez de Castro, London, 6 January 1821, AGI, Indiferente 1569.

38. James M. Breedlove, "Effect of the Cortes, 1810–1822, on Church Reform in Spain and Mexico," in Benson, ed., *Mexico and Spanish Cortes*, pp. 113–33; N. M. Farriss, *Crown and Clergy in Colonial Mexico, 1759–1821*, pp. 248–53; Lynch, *Spanish American Revolutions*, pp. 318–21.

39. "Sistema general de las Aduanas de la Monarquía Española en ambos Emisferios," Madrid, 1820, AGI, Indiferente 673. The author is

grateful to Michael P. Costeloe, who in correspondence pointed out the meaning of the complex wording of Articles 19 and 20.

40. Royal order, Madrid, 22 October 1820, AGI, Indiferente 1360.

41. Royal order, Madrid, 31 December 1820, AGI, Indiferente 671.

42. Antonio Zarco del Valle to Ministry of Ultramar, Madrid, 17 November 1820, AGI, Indiferente 671.

43. Zarco del Valle to Secretary of Hacienda, Madrid, 19 November 1820, AGI, Ultramar 812.

44. Cortes decree, Madrid, 29 June 1821, AGI, Indiferente 672.

45. Anderson, "Reform as a Means to Quell Revolution," in Benson, ed., *Mexico and Spanish Cortes*, pp. 185–207; Rodríguez, "The 'American Question'," pp. 293–314.

46. Delgado, *La independencia . . . en la prensa española*, pp. 256–57, 298–314.

47. Robertson, "Policy of Spain," pp. 21–46; Anderson, "Reform as a Means to Quell Revolution," in Benson, ed., *Mexico and Spanish Cortes*, pp. 185–207.

48. Robertson, "Policy of Spain," pp. 21–46.

49. Ministry of Ultramar to Cortes Deputies from America, Madrid, 23 March 1821, AGI, Indiferente 1569.

50. Cortes Deputies of New Spain to Ministry of Ultramar, Madrid, 8 August 1821, AGI, Indiferente 1569.

51. Cortes Deputies of Cuba to Secretary of Ultramar, Madrid, 25 May 1821; Julián de Urruela (Guatemala) to Secretary of Ultramar, Madrid, 16 June 1821, both in AGI, Indiferente 1569.

52. José María Murguía y Galardi to Secretary of Ultramar, Madrid, 8 November 1821, AGI, Indiferente 1569.

53. Council of State consulta, Madrid, 7 November 1821, AGI, Indiferente 1569 and Estado 89.

54. "Voto particular de los Consejeros Aycinena, Luyando, Flores y Príncipe de Anglona," Madrid, 7 November 1821, AGI, Indiferente 1570.

55. O'Donojú to Minister of Ultramar, Córdoba, 21 August 1821, AGI, Mexico 1680.

56. Pezuela to Conde de Casa Flores, Rio de Janeiro, 20 August 1821, AGI, Estado 104.

57. Conde de Casa Flores to Eusebio de Bardají, Rio de Janeiro, 4 September 1821, AGI, Estado 104; Memoria of Secretary of State to Cortes, 3 March 1822, AHN, Estado 3024.

58. Declaratoria de independencia del Pueblo Dominicana, Santo Domingo, 1 December 1821, AGI, Indiferente 1569.

59. Gabriel Císcar to King, Madrid, 12 December 1821, AGI, Estado 90.

Chapter 8

1. "Informe del Gobierno a las Cortes sobre medidas de pacificación de Ultramar," Madrid, 17 January 1822, AGI, Indiferente 1571.

2. Juan López Cancelada to Minister of Ultramar, Madrid, 19 July 1821, AGI, Indiferente 1569.

3. Anderson, "Reform as a Means to Quell Revolution," in Benson, ed., *Mexico and Spanish Cortes*, pp. 185–207; Robertson, "Policy of Spain," pp. 21–46.

4. Cortes decree, Madrid, 13 February 1822, AGI, Indiferente 1570. Rodríguez calls the plan to send new commissioners "an unreal scheme, a flight of fancy" ("The 'American Question,'" pp. 293–314).

5. Anderson, "Reform as a Means to Quell Revolution," in Benson, ed., *Mexico and Spanish Cortes*, pp. 185–207.

6. Royal order, Madrid, 27 March 1822, AGI, Ultramar 812, including committee report and Council of State report.

7. Extract, Ultramar, Madrid, 18 May 1822, AGI, Indiferente 1571; Robertson, "Policy of Spain," pp. 21–46.

8. Joaquín de Anduaga to Minister of State, Washington, 12 March 1822, AGI, Estado 90.

9. "Instrucciones reservadas a los Representantes de S. M.," Madrid, 6 May 1822, AGI, Estado 90.

10. Manifesto to Spanish diplomatic personnel, Madrid, 1822, AHN, Estado 3024.

11. Plan reservado, copy certified by Ferdinand's rubric, included in letter of Conde de Bulgari to King, Madrid, 6 June 1821, AHN, Estado 2579.

12. Ferdinand to Alexander via Conde de Bulgari, Madrid, 21 June 1821, AHN, Estado 2579.

13. "Copia del papel remitido en 28 de enero (1822) al Sr. Vizconde de Montmorency," AHN, Estado 2579.

14. Ferdinand to Louis, Madrid, 16 February 1822, AHN, Estado 2579.

15. Ferdinand to La Garde, Madrid, 18 July 1822, AHN, Estado 2579.

16. Ferdinand to Louis, Madrid, 24 July 1822, AHN, Estado 2579.

17. Receipt, Madrid, 26 July 1822, AHN, Estado 2579.

18. "Traducción literal de unas observaciones hechas por el Conde de Bulgari sobre el auxilia de tropas franceses," no date, AHN, Estado 2579.

19. Ferdinand to Alexander, Madrid, 10 August 1822, AHN Estado 2579.

20. Fernández Almagro, *La emancipación*, pp. 119–21.

21. Quoted in Robertson, "Policy of Spain," pp. 21–46.

22. Extract, Gobernación de Ultramar, 1822, AGI, Indiferente 1570.

23. "Prevenciones muy reservadas que S. M. hace a los comisionados nombrados para las provincias disidentes de Ultramar," 1822, AGI, Indiferente 1570.

24. Extract, Gobernación de Ultramar, 1822, AGI, Indiferente 1570.

25. Robertson, "Policy of Spain," pp. 21–46; Royal order, Madrid, 26 January 1824, AGI, Indiferente 1571.

26. Cortes decree, Madrid, 25 November 1822, AGI, Indiferente 1360.

27. Apuntes sobre la isla de Cuba, 31 October 1822; Apuntes sobre la situación de la América, 27 December 1822; *La América, los Ingleses, los Estados Unidos y la España*, by Luis Galabert, all in AGI, Indiferente 1360.

28. Francisco de Paula Escudero to Secretary of Hacienda, Madrid, 28 December 1821; 9 January 1822; Francisco Osorio to Hacienda, Aranjuez, 10 March 1822, all in AGI, Ultramar 812; and Cortes decree, Madrid, 12 July 1822, AGI, Indiferente 1360.

29. "Itinerario de la retirada que el govierno constitucional obligó a hacer a Sus Majestades y toda su Real Familia a la ciudad de Cádiz . . . ," in *Memorias de Tiempos de Fernando VII*, ed. Miguel Artola, pp. 441–73.

30. "Itinerario," p. 451.

31. Proyecto de instrucción por el govierno económico-político de las provincias de Ultramar, 1823, AGI, Indiferente 1565.

32. "Itinerario," p. 455.

33. Ibid., pp. 463–64.

34. Ibid., p. 471.

35. Charles Wentz Fehrenbach, "Moderados and Exaltados: The Liberal Opposition to Ferdinand VII, 1814–1820," *Hispanic American Historical Review* 50:1 (February 1970): 52–69.

36. Artola, *La España de Fernando VII*, 846

37. Quoted in ibid., pp. 846–47

38. "Itinerario," p. 472.

39. Artola, *La España de Fernando VII*, p. 862.

40. Bergamini, *The Spanish Bourbons*, p. 180.

41. Artola, *La España de Fernando VII*, p. 868.

42. Ibid., p. 869.

43. Carr, *Spain*, pp. 146–50. See also Marichal, *Spain*, pp. 41–56.

44. Canning to William A'Court, London, 30 January 1824, AGI, Estado 90.

45. Charles K. Webster, ed., *Britain and the Independence of Latin America, 1812–1830*, 1:22; William Spence Robertson, *France and Latin-American Independence*, pp. 306–7.

46. Canning to George Bosanquet, London, 31 December 1824, AGI, Estado 90.

47. Council of State, résumé, Madrid, 29 May 1828, AGI, Indiferente 1564.

48. Kaufmann, *British Policy*, p. 178.

49. "El marqués de Torre Tagle a sus compatriotas," Lima, March 1824, AGI, Estado 75.

50. La Serna to Minister of Grace and Justice, Cuzco, 15 March 1824, AGI, Lima 762; Gárate to King, Puno, 18 April 1824, AGI, Indiferente 1325.

51. Council of Indies consulta, Madrid, 6 July 1825, AGI, Lima 604; Fernández Almagro, *La emancipación*, pp. 161–62.

52. Anna, *Fall of Government in Peru*, pp. 234–37.

53. Marqués de Zambrano to Secretary of Hacienda, Madrid, 12 August 1826, AGI, Lima 1480.

54. Fernández Almagro, *La emancipación*, pp. 132–40.

55. Such was the case with Tadeo Gárate, Gárate to Secretary of Grace and Justice, Rio de Janeiro, 21 September 1825, AGI, Indiferente 1352.

56. Royal order, Madrid, 10 March 1824, AGI, Indiferente 1360.

57. Royal order, Madrid, 27 July 1824, AGI, Indiferente 674 A.

58. García-Baquero, *Comercio colonial*, pp. 199–250.

59. Mark J. Van Aken, *Pan-Hispanism: Its Origin and Development to 1866*, p. 17.

60. Council of State, Madrid, 29 May 1828, AGI, Indiferente 1564.

61. Delgado, *La independencia hispanoamericana*, p. 74.

62. Van Aken, *Pan-Hispanism*, pp. 30–36.

Selected Bibliography

For the sake of brevity, this bibliography is mainly limited to sources used in the text. Additional items not listed here receive full citation in the notes. A particular effort has been made to include the most recent titles.

In addition, this work is largely dependent on archival sources, cited fully in the notes. The primary archives are the Archivo General de Indias (AGI) in Seville and the Archivo Histórico Nacional (AHN) in Madrid. From the AGI most information came from the section of Estado; considerable use was also made of the sections of Indiferente, Ultramar, Mexico, and Lima. From the AHN most documents came from the section of Estado, with further material from the section of Consejo. Additional documents derived from two archives in Mexico City, the Archivo General de la Nación (AGN) and the little-used but rich Archivo del Ex-Ayuntamiento, which contains duplicates of many state papers of the period.

Alcalá Galiano, Antonio. *Obras escogidas de D. Antonio Alcalá Galiano.* Edited by Jorge Campos. 2 vols. Madrid: Biblioteca de Autores Españoles, nos. 83–84, 1955.

————. *Recuerdos de un anciano.* Madrid, 1878. Reprint. Buenos Aires: Espasa-Calpe Argentina, 1951.

Anna, Timothy E. "The Buenos Aires Expedition and Spain's Secret Plan to Conquer Portugal." *The Americas*, 34:3 (January 1978): 356–80.

————. *The Fall of the Royal Government in Mexico City.* Lincoln: University of Nebraska Press, 1978.

————. *The Fall of the Royal Government in Peru.* Lincoln: University of Nebraska Press, 1979.

————. "Institutional and Political Impediments to Spain's Settlement of the American Rebellions." *The Americas* 38:4 (April 1982): 481–95.

———. "The Last Viceroys of New Spain and Peru: An Appraisal."
American Historical Review, 81:1 (February 1976): 38–65.

———. "Spain and the Breakdown of the Imperial Ethos: The Problem
of Equality." *Hispanic American Historical Review* 62:2 (May 1982):
254–72.

Archer, Christon I. *The Army in Bourbon Mexico, 1760–1810.* Albuquer-
que: University of New Mexico Press, 1977.

Armytage, Frances. *The Free Port System in the British West Indies: A Study
in Commercial Policy, 1766–1822.* London: Longmans, Green and
Co., 1953.

Artola Gallego, Miguel. *La España de Fernando VII.* Vol. 26 in Ramón
Menéndez Pidal, ed., *Historia de España.* Madrid: Espasa-Calpe,
1968.

———. *Memorias de Tiempos de Fernando VII.* 2 vols. Madrid: Biblioteca
de Autores Españoles, nos. 97–98, 1957.

———. *Los orígenes de la España contemporánea.* 2 vols. Madrid: Instituto
de Estudios Políticos, 1959.

Ayerbe, Marqués de. *Memorias sobre la estancia de Fernando VII en Valencay, en el principio de la guerra de la independencia.* In *Memorias de
Tiempos de Fernando VII,* 1. Madrid: Biblioteca de Autores Españoles, no. 97, 1957.

Azanza, Miguel José, and Gonzalo O'Farril. *Memoria sobre los hechos que
justifican su conducta política, desde marzo de 1808 hasta abril de 1814.*
In *Memorias de Tiempos de Fernando VII,* 1. Madrid: Biblioteca de
Autores Españoles, no. 97, 1957.

Barbier, Jacques A. "Peninsular Finance and Colonial Trade: The Dilemma of Charles IV's Spain." *Journal of Latin American Studies* 12:1
(May 1980): 21–37.

———. *Reform and Politics in Bourbon Chile, 1755–1796.* Ottawa:
University of Ottawa Press, 1980.

———. "Tradition and Reform in Bourbon Chile: Ambrosio O'Higgins
and Public Finances." *The Americas* 34:3 (January 1978): 381–99.

Bartley, Russell H. *Imperial Russia and the Struggle for Latin American
Independence, 1808–1828.* Latin American Monographs, no. 43.
Austin: Institute of Latin American Studies, 1978.

Bécker, Jerónimo. *Historia de las relaciones exteriores de España durante el
siglo XIX,* vol. 1 (1800–1839). Madrid: Jaime Ratés, 1924.

Benson, Nettie Lee. ed. *Mexico and the Spanish Cortes, 1810–1822: Eight*

Essays. Latin American Monographs, no. 5. Austin: University of Texas Press, 1966.

Bergamini, John D. *The Spanish Bourbons: The History of a Tenacious Dynasty.* New York: G. P. Putnam's Sons, 1974.

Black, Shirley J. "Olivenza: An Iberian 'Alsace/Lorraine.' " *The Americas* 35:4 (April 1979): 527–37.

Brading, D. A. *Miners and Merchants in Bourbon Mexico, 1763–1810.* Cambridge: At the University Press, 1971.

Burkholder, Mark A., and D. S. Chandler. *From Impotence to Authority: The Spanish Crown and the American Audiencias, 1687–1808.* Columbia: University of Missouri Press, 1977.

Campbell, Leon G. *The Military and Society in Colonial Peru, 1750–1810.* Philadelphia: American Philosophical Society, 1978.

Canga Argüelles, José. *Diccionario de hacienda.* 5 vols. London, 1826–27. Reprint. Madrid: Ediciones Atlas, 1968–.

Carr, Raymond. *Spain, 1808–1939.* Oxford: Oxford University Press, 1966.

Chastenet, Jacques. *Godoy, Master of Spain, 1792–1808.* London: Batchwork Press, 1953.

Christiansen, E. *The Origins of Military Power in Spain, 1800–1854.* London: Oxford University Press, 1967.

Coatsworth, John H. "Obstacles to Economic Growth in Nineteenth-Century Mexico." *American Historical Review* 83:1 (February 1978): 80–100.

Comellas García-Llera, José Luis. "Las Cortes de Cádiz y la Constitución de 1812." *Revista de Estudios Políticos* 126 (November-December 1962): 69–110.

———. *Historia de España moderna y contemporánea (1474–1965).* 2nd edition. Madrid: Rialp, 1968.

———. *Los primeros pronunciamientos en España, 1814–1820.* Madrid: Consejo Superior de Investigaciones Científicas, 1958.

———. *Los realistas en el trienio constitucional (1820–1823).* Pamplona: Publicaciones del Estudio General de Navarra, 1958.

———. *El Trienio Constitucional.* Madrid: Rialp, 1963.

El Consejo de Estado (1792–1834), vol. 7 in *Documentos del Reinado de Fernando VII.* Edited by Seminario de Historia Moderna, Instituto de Estudios Administrativos. Pamplona: Ediciones Universidad de Navarra, 1971.

322   Selected Bibliography

Costeloe, Michael P. "Spain and the Latin American Wars of Independence: The Free Trade Controversy, 1810–1820." *Hispanic American Historical Review* 61:2 (May 1981): 209–34.

———. "Spain and the Spanish American Wars of Independence: the *Comisión de Reemplazos*, 1811–1820." *Journal of Latin American Studies* 13:2 (November 1981): 223–37.

Delgado, Jaime. *La independencia de América en la prensa española*. Madrid: Seminario de Problemas Hispanoamericanos, 1949.

———. *La independencia hispanoamericana*. Madrid: Instituto de Cultura Hispánica, Colección Nuevo Mundo, 1960.

———. "La 'pacificación de América' en 1818." *Revista de Indias* 11 (1950): 17–67, 263–310.

Diz-Lois, María Cristina. *El Manifiesto de 1814*. Pamplona: Ediciones Universidad de Navarra, 1967.

Domínguez, Jorge I. *Insurrection or Loyalty: The Breakdown of the Spanish American Empire*. Cambridge: Harvard University Press, 1980.

Enciseo Recio, Luis Miguel. *La opinión española y la independencia hispanoamericana, 1819–20*. Valladolid: Universidad de Valladolid, 1967.

Escoiquiz, Juan de. *Idea sencilla de las razones que motivaron el viaje del Rey Don Fernando VII a Bayona en el mes de abril de 1808*. In *Memorias de Tiempos de Fernando VII*, 1. Madrid: Biblioteca de Autores Españoles, no. 97, 1957.

———. *Memorias*. In *Memorias de Tiempos de Fernando VII*, 1. Madrid: Biblioteca de Autores Españoles, no. 97, 1957.

Farriss, N. M. *Crown and Clergy in Colonial Mexico, 1759–1821: The Crisis of Ecclesiastical Privilege*. London: Athlone Press, 1968.

Ferdinand VII. *Itinerario de la retirado que el govierno constitucional obligó a hacer a Sus Majestades y toda su Real Familia a la ciudad de Cádiz*. In *Memorias de Tiempos de Fernando VII*, 2. Madrid: Biblioteca de Autores Españoles, no. 98, 1957.

Fernández Almagro, Melchor. "Del Antiguo Régimen a las Cortes de Cádiz." *Revista de Estudios Políticos* 116 (November-December 1962): 9–28.

———. *La emancipación de América y su reflejo en la conciencia española*. 2nd ed. Madrid: Instituto de Estudios Políticos, 1957.

———. *Orígenes del régimen constitucional en España*. Barcelona: Editorial Labor, 1928.

Fisher, J. R. *Government and Society in Colonial Peru: The Intendant System,*

1784–1814. London: Athlone Press, 1970.

Flores Caballero, Romeo. *La contrarevolución en la independencia: Los españoles en la vida política, social, y económica de México (1804–1838)*. Mexico City: Colegio de México, 1969.

Friede, Juan. *La otra verdad, la independencia americana vista por los españoles*. 2nd ed. Bogotá: Ediciones Tercer Mundo, 1972.

García-Baquero González, Antonio. *Comercio colonial y guerras revolucionarias: La decadencia económica de Cádiz a raíz de la emancipación americana*. Seville: Escuela de Estudios Hispanoamericanos, 1972.

García de León y Pizarro, José. SEE Pizarro, José García de León y

Goebel, D. B. "British Trade to the Spanish Colonies, 1796–1823." *American Historical Review* 43:2 (January 1938): 288–320.

Goldwert, Marvin. "The Search for the Lost Father-Figure in Spanish American History: A Freudian View." *The Americas* 34:4 (April 1978): 532–36.

Graham, Gerald S., and R. A. Humphreys, eds. *The Navy and South America, 1807–1823, Correspondence of the Commanders-in-Chief on the South American Station*. London: Navy Records Society, 1962.

Graham, Richard. *Independence in Latin America*. New York: Alfred A. Knopf, 1972.

Griffin, Charles C. *The United States and the Disruption of the Spanish Empire, 1810–1822*. New York: Columbia University Press, 1937.

Hamnett, Brian R. "Mexico's Royalist Coalition: The Response to Revolution, 1808–1821." *Journal of Latin American Studies* 12:1 (May 1980): 55–86.

———. *Politics and Trade in Southern Mexico, 1750–1821*. Cambridge: At the University Press, 1971.

———. *Revolución y contrarrevolución en México y el Perú: Liberalismo, realeza y separatismo (1800–1824)*. Mexico City: Fondo de Cultura Económica, 1978.

Hernández y Dávalos, Juan E., ed. *Colección de documentos para la historia de la Guerra de Independencia de México*. 6 vols. Mexico City: José María Sandoval, 1877–82.

Herr, Richard. *The Eighteenth Century Revolution in Spain*. Princeton: Princeton University Press, 1958.

Humboldt, Alexander von. *Ensayo político sobre Nueva España*. Introduction, selection, and notes by Luis Alberto Sánchez. Santiago: Ediciones Ercilla, 1942.

Izquierdo Hernández, Manuel. *Antecedentes y comienzos del reinado de Fer-*

nando VII. Madrid: Ediciones de Cultura Hispánica, 1963.

Kaufmann, William W. *British Policy and the Independence of Latin America, 1804–1828.* New Haven: Yale University Press, 1951.

King, James F. "The Colored Castes and American Representation in the Cortes of Cádiz." *Hispanic American Historical Review* 33:1 (February 1953): 33–64.

Kuethe, Allan J. *Military Reform and Society in New Granada, 1773–1808.* Gainesville: University Presses of Florida, 1978.

Ladd, Doris M. *The Mexican Nobility at Independence, 1780–1826.* Latin American Monographs, no. 40. Austin: Institute of Latin American Studies, 1976.

Lanning, John Tate. "Great Britain and Spanish Recognition of the Hispanic American States." *Hispanic American Historical Review* 10 (November 1930): 429–56.

Leturia, Pedro de. "La encíclica de Pío VII sobre la revolución hispanoamericana." *Anuario de Estudios Americanos* 4 (1947): 423–518.

Livermore, Harold. *A History of Spain.* London: Allen and Unwin, 1958.

Lynch, John. "British Policy in Spanish America, 1783–1808." *Journal of Latin American Studies* 1:1 (May 1969): 1–30.

———. *The Spanish American Revolutions, 1808–1826.* New York: Norton, 1973.

Lovett, Gabriel H. *Napoleon and the Birth of Modern Spain.* 2 vols. New York: New York University Press, 1965.

McAlister, Lyle N. *The "Fuero Militar" in New Spain, 1764–1800.* Gainesville: University of Florida Press, 1957.

Madol, Hans Roger. *Godoy.* Translated by G. Sans Huelin and M. Sandmann. Madrid: Alianza Editorial, 1966.

Manning, William R., ed. *Diplomatic Correspondence Concerning the Independence of the Latin American Nations.* 3 vols. New York: Oxford University Press, 1925.

Marichal, Carlos. *Spain (1834–1844): A New Society.* London: Tamesis Books, 1977.

Mesonero Romanos, Ramón de. *Memorias de un setentón.* Edited by Carlos Seco Serrano. Madrid: Biblioteca de Autores Españoles, no. 203, 1967.

Moreno, Frank Jay. "The Spanish Colonial System: A Functional Approach." *Western Political Quarterly* 20 (June 1967): 308–20.

Morse, Richard M. "The Heritage of Latin America." In *Politics and Social Change in Latin America: The Distinct Tradition,* edited by Howard J. Wiarda, pp. 25–69. Amherst: University of Massachussetts Press, 1974.

Palacio Atard, Vicente. *La España del siglo XIX, 1808–1898.* Madrid: Espasa, 1978.

———. *Fin de la sociedad española del antiguo régimen.* 2nd ed. Madrid: Rialp, 1961.

Payne, Stanley G. *A History of Spain and Portugal.* 2 vols. Madison: University of Wisconsin Press, 1973.

Pearce, Robert Rouiere. *Memoirs and Correspondence of the most noble Richard Marquess Wellesley.* 3 vols. London: Richard Bentley, 1846.

Phelan, John L. "Authority and Flexibility in the Spanish Imperial Bureaucracy." *Administrative Science Quarterly* 1 (June 1960): 47–65.

———. *The Kingdom of Quito in the Seventeenth Century: Bureaucratic Politics in the Spanish Empire.* Madison: University of Wisconsin Press, 1967.

Pintos Vieites, María del Carmen. *La política de Fernando VII entre 1814 y 1820.* Pamplona: Estudio General de Navarra, 1958.

Pizarro, José García de León y. *Memorias.* Introduction and notes by Alvaro Alonso-Castrillo. 2 vols. Madrid: Revista de Occidente, 1953.

Resnick, Enoch F. "The Council of State and Spanish America, 1814–1820." Ph. D. dissertation, American University, 1970.

———. "Spain's Reaction to Portugal's Invasion of the Banda Oriental in 1816." *Revista de Historia de América* 73–74 (1972): 131–43.

Rippy, James Fred. *Rivalry of the United States and Great Britain over Latin America (1810–1830).* New York: Octagon Books, 1964.

Robertson, William Spence. "An Early Threat of Intervention by Force in South America." *Hispanic American Historical Review* 23:4 (November 1943): 611–31.

———. *France and Latin-American Independence.* Baltimore: Johns Hopkins Press, 1939.

———. "Metternich's Attitude toward Revolutions in Latin America." *Hispanic American Historical Review* 21:4 (November 1941): 538–58.

———. "The Policy of Spain towards Its Revolted Colonies, 1820–1823." *Hispanic American Historical Review* 6 (February-August 1926): 21–46.

———. "The Recognition of the Hispanic American Nations by the

United States." *Hispanic American Historical Review* 1:3 (August 1918): 239–69.

———. "Russia and the Emancipation of Spanish America, 1816–1826." *Hispanic American Historical Review* 21:2 (May 1941): 196–221.

Rodríguez, Mario. "The 'American Question' at the *Cortes* of Madrid." *The Americas* 38:3 (January 1982): 293–314.

———. *The Cádiz Experiment in Central America, 1808 to 1826.* Berkeley: University of California Press, 1978.

Rydjord, John. "British Mediation between Spain and Her Colonies: 1811–1813." *Hispanic American Historical Review* 21:1 (February 1941): 29–50.

———. "Napoleon and Mexican Silver." *Southwestern Social Sciences Quarterly* 19 (1938): 171–82.

Santillán, Ramón de. *Memorias (1815–1856).* Edited by Ana María Berazaluce. 2 vols. Colección Histórica del Estudio General de Navarra. Pamplona: Editorial Gómez, 1960.

Sarfatti, Magali. *Spanish Bureaucratic-Patrimonialism in America.* Institute of International Studies. Berkeley: University of California Press, 1966.

Stoan, Stephen K. *Pablo Morillo and Venezuela, 1815–1820.* Columbus: Ohio State University Press, 1974.

Stoetzer, O. Carlos. *The Scholastic Roots of the Spanish American Revolution.* New York: Fordham University Press, 1979.

Street, John. "Lord Strangford and the Río de la Plata, 1808–1815." *Hispanic American Historical Review* 33:4 (November 1953): 477–510.

Suárez Verdeguer, Federico. *Conservadores, innovadores y renovadores en las postrimerías del Antiguo Régimen.* Pamplona: Universidad de Navarra, 1955.

———. *La crisis política del antiguo régimen en España (1800–1840).* 2nd ed. Madrid: Rialp, 1958.

———. "Sobre las raíces de las reformas de las Cortes de Cádiz." *Revista de Estudios Políticos* 126 (November-December 1962): 31–64.

Toreno, Conde de (José María Queipo de Llano Ruiz de Saravia). *Historia del levantamiento, guerra y revolución de España.* Madrid: Biblioteca de Autores Españoles, no. 64, 1953.

Van Aken, Mark J. *Pan-Hispanism: Its Origin and Development to 1866.* Berkeley: University of California Press, 1959.

Véliz, Claudio. *The Centralist Tradition of Latin America*. Princeton: Princeton University Press, 1980.

Villanueva, Joaquín Lorenzo. *Mi viaje a las Cortes*. In *Memorias de Tiempos de Fernando VII, 2*. Madrid: Biblioteca de Autores Españoles, no. 98, 1957.

Villa-Urrutia, Wenceslao Ramírez, Marqués de. *España en el Congreso de Viena*. 2nd ed. Madrid: Francisco de Beltrán, 1928.

Walton, William. *The Revolutions of Spain, from 1808 to the end of 1836*. 2 vols. London: Richard Bentley, 1836.

Webster, Charles K., ed. *Britain and the Independence of Latin America, 1812–1830: Select Documents from the Foreign Office Archives*. 2 vols. London: Oxford University Press, 1938.

———. "Castlereagh and the Spanish Colonies, I, 1815–1818." *English Historical Review* 27 (1912): 78–95.

———. "Castlereagh and the Spanish Colonies, II, 1818–1822." *English Historical Review* 30 (1915): 631–45.

Woodward, Margaret L. "Spanish Apathy and American Independence (1810–1843)." Ph. D. dissertation, University of Chicago, 1964.

———. "The Spanish Army and the Loss of America, 1810–1824," *Hispanic American Historical Review* 48:4 (November 1968): 586–607.

Zabala y Lera, Pío. *España bajo los Borbones*. 5th ed. Barcelona: Editorial Labor, 1955.

Index

trip to south, 279–82; weaknesses of, 23, 24; mentioned, 62. *See also* King, as symbol; Asturias, Prince of

Fernán Núñez, Conde de, 23, 159, 160, 182, 183, 204, 271

Flores, Luis Antonio, 252

Florida (the Floridas): cession to United States, 152, 176, 184, 243; United States incursions into, 203; mentioned, 8

Floridablanca, Count, 30, 42, 53

Foncerrada, José Cayetano de, 121, 128

Foncerrada, Melchor de, 99

Fonte, Pedro José de, 142

Force, debate over use of, 102, 143, 144, 146, 169, 192, 209, 253

France: alliance with Spain, 18–19; attitude toward Spain, 180, 181; invades Spain, 21, 25, 270–71, 279, 287; possible recognition of American independence, 243

Freedom of the press, 75, 95, 96, 121, 125; restored, 225; suppressed, 129, 195, 285

Free trade: and British mediation, 105–7; and commissioners, 234; debate over, 155, 162–69, 170–72; decreed, 287; granted on limited basis, 53, 54, 82, 250; mistakenly granted, 81–82; opposed, 101, 209, 211, 222, 263–64; in Peru, 230–32; supported, 66, 79, 80, 191, 196, 199, 200, 252, 253, 259, 260; mentioned, 9

Frere, John H., 31

Frías, Duke of, 23, 119, 126, 241, 242, 243

Gaceta de Madrid, 292

Galabert, Luis, 277–78, 294

Gamiz, Antonio de, 134

Gárate, Tadeo, 89, 136–37, 289; as Persa, 121, 128

Garay, Martín: on Council of State, 222; on Expedition to Río de la Plata, 203; fall of, 204–6, 208; and Junta Central, 30, 41; as minister of finance, 153, 170–71, 183, 187; mentioned, 127, 177, 178

García, Andrés, 110

García Herreros, Manuel, 124, 128

Godoy, Manuel de: American views toward, 29; fall of, 22; and policy with France, 18–19; mentioned, 15–16, 122, 175

Golfín, Francisco Fernández, 124, 128, 261

Gómez Labrador, Pedro, 23, 108, 120, 123, 126, 271

González, Pablo, 90

González Salmón, Manuel, 213

"Government by remote control," 10, 36–37, 245, 290

Goyeneche, José Manuel de, 36, 37, 201

Great Expedition. *See* Expedition to Río de la Plata

Gremios, 45, 76

Guatemala, kingdom of: abolition of tribute, 94–95; and Constitution, 95–96; independent de facto, 254; mentioned, 7, 63. *See*

Medinaceli, Duke of, 23, 42
Mejía Lequerica, José, 67, 68, 117
Meléndez, Joseph, 34
Mendiola, Mariano, 73
Mercantilism, 7
Mercenaries, 195, 274
Mercury, 80, 81
Mesonero Romanos, Ramón de, 212
Mexico: abolition of tribute in, 94;
    and British mediation, 106, 107,
    108, 109, 110; and the Constitu-
    tion, 95–96; Cortes reforms in,
    244; independent de facto, 251,
    254, 288, 294; north of, 8, 38–
    39, 140–41; pacified, 139, 148;
    reconquest attempt, 277–78,
    294; revenue to Spain from, 56,
    57; revolts in, 63, 244, 245;
    mentioned, 14, 31, 48, 49. *See
    also* Internal Provinces
Mexico City Mining Tribunal, 43
Michelena, Mariano, 247, 248
Micheo, Manuel de, 90
Mier, Servando Teresa de, 84
Military clique, ascendancy of, 143,
    147, 148, 208, 209, 210; men-
    tioned, xii–xiii, 173
Military fuero, 12, 244
Militias, in America, 11–12
Miller, General, 195
Mining, 111
Mining College in Mexico City, 12
Ministerial despotism, 16, 76, 115,
    122
Ministry of finance, 232
Ministry of state, 160, 164, 191
Ministry of the Indies (or Ultramar):
    abolished, 98, 149; in restora-
    tion, 132–33; restored, 223;
    mentioned, 137, 249

Miranda, Francisco de, 1
Miscelánea, La, 226, 248
Missionaries, 12, 103, 173, 195–
    96
Moderados, 283
Molina, Joaquín de, 35, 36, 50
Monasteries: restored, 129; suppres-
    sed, 75, 232, 244, 259
Monroe, James, 243, 265, 286
Monroe Doctrine, 286
Montemar, Duke of, 133, 134,
    149, 150, 166, 187
Monteverde, Juan Domingo, 140
Montevideo: and Expedition to Río
    de la Plata, 202; mediation in,
    211, 242; Portuguese invasion of,
    156, 157, 158, 178, 180, 181,
    182, 183, 214. *See also* Banda
    Oriental
Montijo, Conde de, 119, 126, 128
Montmorency Laval, Viscount,
    268–69
Morales Duárez, Vicente, 70, 72
Morelos, José María, 1, 85, 139,
    148
Morillo, Pablo: ceasefire with rebels,
    236, 237; defeat of, 173–74,
    228, 237; expedition of, 144–
    47, 148, 184–85, 203; powers
    of, 189, 209; view of conflict,
    240; mentioned, 250, 269
Morning Post, 241
Moscoso, José María, 262
Mosquera, Joaquín, 134
Moyano, Tomás, 143
Muñoz Torrero, Diego, 73, 124,
    128
Murat, Joachim (Grand Duke of
    Berg), 22
Murguía y Galardi, José María, 250